Praise for
I Used to Live Here Once

"The best biographies marry the talents of a perceptive biographer and a complicated subject. In Miranda Seymour's new biography of British writer Jean Rhys, readers will find a perfect match."
—Mary Ann Gwinn, *Minneapolis Star Tribune*

"Seymour meticulously stitches Rhys's stories to events in her life, while scrupulously maintaining the distinction Rhys herself insisted on: the women who people her fiction are not self-portraits."
—Madison Smartt Bell, *American Scholar*

"A first-class life and a rollicking read. Seymour skilfully interweaves the autobiographical stories and novels with the people and fortunes in Rhys's crazily adventurous life. . . . The result is close to a masterpiece."
—John Walsh, *Sunday Times* (UK)

"Seymour's investigations into Rhys are inseparable from her sensitive close readings of the novels. She is shrewd and careful. . . . [A] compelling biography."
—Amber Medland, *Times Literary Supplement*

"Intimate and insightful. . . . [*I Used to Live Here Once*] is full of magics."
—Laura Freeman, *Times* (UK)

"An eloquent defence of the biographer's art in a clear-eyed yet sympathetic portrait of the extraordinary life of a complicated, not always likeable, woman. . . . Seymour is clearly a Rhys aficionada, albeit a subtle one, fully cognisant of the failings of the woman. [The] greatest service a literary biographer can perform is to send the reader back to her subject's work with fresh insight, renewed pleasure and enhanced admiration. This, Seymour achieves magnificently."
—Annalena McAfee, *Financial Times*

"Since Jean Rhys's death 42 years ago our obsession with her life and work . . . has only grown. . . . Now it is Miranda Seymour's turn to re-tell the story, with informative new material on her early life in the Caribbean, and a more generous tone than some of her predecessors. . . . Perhaps it's that ghostly opacity that makes her such an intriguing subject—a writer on whom we can project our own fears and desires."

—Sameer Rahim, *Telegraph*

"An exhaustive, definitive ride around both the idea and the reality of Jean Rhys. . . . Authoritatively woven together, Seymour addresses a writer and woman who is at once self-absorbed and thoughtful, sardonic and sensitive, harnessing an independence that was created and sustained by circumstance, and deftly draws out the wildness of Rhys that threatened to break as well as make her. This is also a love letter to the different ways that writers work, and how they are not always disciples of discipline, how sometimes great work comes piecemeal and from the messy brutality of living. While Rhys herself wrote that she 'would never really belong anywhere,' somehow, Seymour has brought her home."   —Siobhán Kane, *Irish Times*

"Seymour makes a convincing case for Rhys's intelligence and agency as an artist. The writer who emerges from these pages is not the sluttish savant of Alvarez' fevered imagination, but a woman who fought heroically to realize her own prodigious talent and to salvage something lasting from the wreckage of her life."

—Zoë Heller, *Book Post*

"One of the many strengths of this biography is that Seymour is aware of the danger of the too-easy read-across from fiction to life, while being alive to the hidden truths of literary archaeology. . . . A gem of literary biography."   —Alan Judd, *The Oldie*

"Miranda Seymour has written a compelling and stylish new biography of Jean Rhys, whose life and work have often been cast in melancholic shadow. Seymour adds color and complexity to Rhys's story, and suggests the haunting influence of her early years on the Caribbean island of Dominica. This is a fresh, empathetic portrait of an iconic and unconventional woman writer whose searing novels of trauma, race, gender, and exile were ahead of their time."

—Heather Clark, author of *Red Comet:*
The Short Life and Blazing Art of Sylvia Plath

"The multiple guises and conflicting personae of Jean Rhys—reckless and reclusive, captivating and appalling—demand a particularly agile biographer. Miranda Seymour is ideally suited to the task. An empathetic but unsparing critic, a tenacious and resourceful researcher, and a historian of literary cultures with a novelist's sense of the evocative detail, she has produced an enthralling biography of a haunting—and maddening—modern writer."

—Elaine Showalter,
professor emerita of English, Princeton University,
and author of *A Literature of Their Own:*
British Women Novelists from Brontë to Lessing

"It's a high-wire act to hold so witty and eloquent a balance between this writer's recklessness and diligence. The honesty too is appealing, the acknowledgement of dark places no one can fully visit."

—Lyndall Gordon, author of *The Hyacinth Girl:*
T. S. Eliot's Hidden Muse

"Brilliantly written, compulsively readable and insightful, Miranda Seymour's biography does full justice to a remarkable and complex life."

—Pat Barker, author of *The Silence of the Girls*

"One of Miranda Seymour's finest biographies, this is an utterly riveting voyage into a writer's mind. You can almost feel Jean Rhys breathing in the room, and what a ferociously complicated woman she was! I was spellbound from start to finish."

—Deborah Moggach, author of *The Carer* and *The Black Dress*

"Absolute gold. A beautiful and fascinating in-depth study of how a writer works, how books emerge from a life, from messy emotions, a Caribbean island, and a uniquely sensitive imagination."

—Ruth Padel, author of *Daughters of the Labyrinth*

"Miranda Seymour's illuminating and brilliant book shows how Jean's life—and especially the island of Dominica—informed her genius. It goes a long way toward making the reader understand, forgive, and even applaud her rage—more, it explains why so many of us loved Jean, and her books."

—Diana Melly, author of *Take a Girl Like Me*

I used to live here once

I used to live here once

The haunted life of
JEAN RHYS

Miranda Seymour

W. W. NORTON & COMPANY
Independent Publishers Since 1923

First American Edition 2022
First published as a Norton paperback 2024

For information about permission to reproduce selections from
this book, write to Permissions, W. W. Norton & Company, Inc.
500 Fifth Avenue, New York, NY 10110

For information about special discounts for bulk purchases,
please contact W. W. Norton Special Sales at
specialsales@wwnorton.com or 800-233-4830

Manufacturing by Lakeside Book Company
Book design by Chris Welch
Production manager: Devon Zahn

ISBN 978-1-324-07459-5 pbk.

W. W. Norton & Company, Inc.
500 Fifth Avenue, New York, N.Y. 10110
www.wwnorton.com

W. W. Norton & Company Ltd.
15 Carlisle Street, London W1D 3BS

1 2 3 4 5 6 7 8 9 0

TO LENNOX HONYCHURCH AND POLLY PATTULO,

KEEPING THE SPIRIT OF JEAN RHYS ALIVE IN DOMINICA,

THE ISLAND OF HER BIRTH; AND TO SAMANTHA MOSS,

DOING THE SAME AT RHYS'S LAST HOME IN DEVON

I would never be part of anything. I would never really belong anywhere, and I knew it, and all my life would be the same, trying to belong, and failing. Always something would go wrong. I am a stranger and I always will be, and after all I didn't really care.

—JEAN RHYS, *Smile Please: An Unfinished Autobiography* (1979)

Contents

Dominica, c.1900

Capuchin

Blenheim
Cabrits
Hampstead 'Bertrand' Bay
Hampstead
Calibishie
Pointe Baptiste

Portsmouth
Prince Rupert's Bay

Atlantic Ocean

Sargasso Sea

Douglas-Charles Airport

Hatton Garden

Morne Diablotin

MAROONS

Neg Mawon

Pagua Valley

CARIB QUARTER

Grand Chemin

18th century French dirt track followed by Rhys, 1936

Castle Bruce

Proposed new road

Bells

Layou

Warner

Imperial Road

Rosalie

Caribbean Sea

Massacre
Amelia
Bona Vista

18th century dirt track Roseau to Rosalie

Canefield

Laudat
Chemin Letang

Goodwill

Boiling Lake

ROSEAU (Fort Young)
Morne Bruce

Pointe Mulatre

Puerto Rico
Virgin Islands
Atlantic Ocean
Anguilla
Barbuda
St Kitts & Nevis
Antigua
Guadeloupe
Dominica
Martinique
Caribbean Sea
St Lucia
St Vincent & Grenadines
Barbados
Grenada
Trinidad

Geneva
Stowe
Grand Bay

Soufrière
Scott's Head

0   2 miles
0   2 km

Foreword

The reason that I always think of Jean Rhys as a hurt and angry child trapped in the body of a sensual woman is that I came to her work, not through her novels or stories, but through *Smile Please*. Written at the end of her long life, in a voice as clear as though she were recalling yesterday's events, Rhys's evocative, tender and painfully truthful memoir describes the first years of her life in Dominica, the wild and still untamed Caribbean island where she grew up—and where she said that she wanted her bones one day to lie. *Smile Please* ends in 1924, five years after Rhys had unregretfully exchanged a hand-to-mouth existence in London for a vagabond's life in Paris, the city which would provide the setting for her first novel, *Quartet*.

Later, as I read the short stories and the five novels on which Rhys's enduring reputation as one of the best women writers of the twentieth century justly stands, I began to understand the tremendous importance of those early years in Dominica. Memories of the island haunt Rhys's work; they inhabited her mind until her death in 1979.

Seeing Dominica with my own eyes while visiting the places that Rhys knew and loved best—all her family's former residences are now destroyed or buried under a verdant island's lush, fast-growing vegetation—helped me to understand Rhys's passion for her Caribbean birthplace, and why the hostility that she first sensed there bred her enduring feeling of alienation. She poured both the passion and the alienation into the characters of the women about whom she wrote. Self-knowledge meant everything to Rhys. Each of those fictional women was granted elements of their author's pitilessly scrutinised personality. As painfully self-aware as their creator, they, too, can be by turns watchful; shocking; angry; witty, and ruthless. Like Rhys herself, they learn to rely on drink for courage and consolation. Unlike her, they neither read much—Rhys was an avid and discerning reader, especially of French poetry and modern French fiction—nor do they write.

"I must write," Rhys once wrote in a private diary, before adding that it was only by her writing that she could "earn" death. ("A reward?" she asked herself in the same entry, and answered, simply: "*Yes*.") Deprived of their author's crucial sense of purpose, the women who belong to the world of Rhys's bleak and often savagely comic fictions are more helpless than their strong-willed—and often downright wilful—maker ever was.

Rhys needed to be strong in order to keep faith with her vocation. I can't think of another woman writer of her time who overcame such dismaying and ongoing setbacks with such determination. Nor can I think of one who created so many problems for herself by her transgressive behaviour: a persistent and audaciously perverse refusal ever to comply with what was expected from her. Heartbreak, poverty, notoriety, breakdowns and even imprisonment: all became grist to Rhys's fiction-making mill. What she never wrote about were the challenging years of literary oblivion from which "Jean Rhys" emerged at last into a blaze of international celebrity that the reclusive writer had neither sought nor desired.

Today, Rhys's work is widely taught. Young graduates who know nothing about her life find it easy to relate to her proud and vulnerable loners. Teachers like to suggest an exercise in which comparisons are made between Virginia Woolf's celebrated "room of one's own" and one of the coffin-like hotel rooms in which Rhys's victimised characters hide away from a world they dread and despise. Students like the concept of Woolf's idealised private study. They *believe* in Rhys's imagined haunts.

Imagined? Rhys did experience times of forlorn desperation when she lived in just such rooms. But not always. In the same way that she bestowed only specific traits from her personality on her characters, she allowed them to experience some—but never all—of her own adventures. Rhys was a novelist, not a journalist. Much was added;

much more was withheld. Researching this book and talking to the people who knew Rhys have helped me to appreciate the depth of the chasm that separates the composite creature whom many critics still knowingly categorise as "the Rhys woman" from the writer who created that vulnerable entity.

Rhys often said that she wrote about herself because that was all she knew. Today, her readers still intuitively relate to a voice that whispers terrible truths into the ears of each and every one of us. I hope that I've succeeded in showing what courage and faith it took to create that unique voice, and to persist when hope seemed dead. I know already how much I shall miss the daily company of a demanding, volatile, self-absorbed and often darkly funny writer, a woman whom the hypercritical Francis Wyndham once fondly praised as the most bewitching companion that he had ever known.

I used to live here once

I

A WORLD APART
Gwen

ELIZÉ MALEWÉ

Tout mama ki ti ni jen fi
Pa lésé yo allé en plési yo,
Pa lésé yo allé en jewté yo.
Si diab la vini yi kai anni mé yo.
Elizé malewé
Elizé malewé
Elizé malewé.
On pon innocen la ou van ba de demon la.

All mothers with young daughters!
Don't let them go follow their own pleasures,
Don't let them go follow their joy.
If the devil comes, he will just take them away.
Poor Elizé
Poor Elizé
Poor Elizé.
You took an innocent child and sold her to the two devils.

(Translation by Sonia Magloire-Akba, with thanks.[*])

[*] The largest single holding of Jean Rhys's personal papers is at the handsomely Gothic-styled McFarlin Library, which forms part of the University of Tulsa, Oklahoma. The library contains a digitalised recording of Jean Rhys singing this old island song in July 1963, when she was almost seventy-three years old. I'm grateful to Sonia Magloire-Akba, an authority on the Kwéyòl (Creole) language still in use today on Dominica, for her informal translation.

1

Wellspring (1890–1907)

"You turn to the left and the sea is at your back, and the road
goes zigzag upwards...Everything is green, everywhere
things are growing...That's how the road to Constance is—
green, and the smell of green, and then the smell of water and
dark earth and rotting leaves and damp."

—Jean Rhys, *Voyage in the Dark, Part Three* (1934)

NEAR TO THE end of her long life—she was almost ninety when she
died in May 1979—Jean Rhys wrote what her Devonshire neighbour
William Trevor praised as one of the finest short ghost stories he'd
ever read. She called it "I Used to Live Here Once." The dreaming
narrator—evidently Rhys herself—follows the trail of stepping stones
that guide her across a shallow, familiar river and onto a rough forest
path that leads to her own childhood home. She feels "extraordinarily
happy." But when she walks across the parched grass to where a boy and
girl seem to await her, they register her presence and timid greeting
only as a sudden chill in the afternoon air. The children turn away. The
story ends abruptly: "It was then that I knew."

Rhys lived in a secluded village in the south-west of England for the
last nineteen years of an extraordinary and often reckless life, one that
took her from poverty, imprisonment and obscurity to eventual recognition as perhaps the finest English woman novelist of the twentieth
century. The island which haunted her mind and almost everything

that she wrote lay on the far side of the world. There—not in Devon, or London, nor even in Paris—lay the wellspring of Rhys's art.

JEAN RHYS WAS born on 24 August 1890 in Dominica, a small and sternly beautiful Caribbean island of green mountains (*mornes*), tangled forests, rushing rivers, forest pools and impenetrable ravines. Dominica's larger neighbours—Martinique and the archipelago that forms Guadeloupe—were French, as Dominica itself had been until the island was ceded to the British in 1763, at the end of the Seven Years' War. By the close of the nineteenth century, when Dominica had almost 29,000 inhabitants, the island's white population had shrunk to fewer than a hundred. Living in an impoverished outpost of the British Empire, white Dominicans clung to a romanticised vision of England as the centre of their own diminished world, marooned on an island that still spoke in the French-based creole language known today as Kwéyòl.

Jean Rhys's father, William Rees Williams, was a Welshman with an Irish mother. A ship's doctor, he came to Dominica in 1881 in search of better pay as a twenty-seven-year-old British-funded medical officer. He went ashore at the tiny coastal village of Stowe in the area known as Grand Bay, lying below the once prosperous plantation of Geneva in the south-east of the island. In January 1882, the Welshman married Minna Lockhart, a white Creole, a term which, despite its pejorative sound, meant only that Minna, whose family still inhabited Mitcham, the old Geneva estate house, had been born on Dominica. The newlywed couple spent their honeymoon year at Stowe. Dr. Rees Williams brightened the sitting-room walls of their little shoreside home with the four prints of Betws-y-Coed in Snowdonia that had adorned his shipboard cabin. In 1885, Williams was promoted from a relatively humble job in the island's Southern Medical District to a more lucrative position in the capital town of Roseau, where private patient care usefully augmented his income. Here, after renting a house near to the Roseau river on Hillsborough Street (where Jean Rhys was born), the doctor purchased a more substantial property closer to the centre of town.

The Lockhart twins. Rhys's proud mother Minna (*left*) and (*right*) her unmarried, more cultured twin sister, Brenda ("Auntie B") grew up at Geneva, formerly a slave-owning sugar estate, on the Caribbean island of Dominica. (*McFarlin*)

It was burly, hazel-eyed Willie Rees Williams who named the couple's fourth child Ella Gwendoline. Gwen, as she was always known to her relatives, followed two older brothers, Edward and Owen, and a sister named Minna, like their mother. A fifth child, a girl, died as an infant, three years before the birth in 1895 of Brenda Clarice, named both for Minna Lockhart's adored twin (Brenda) and the doctor's devoted sister (Clarice Rees Williams).[*]

Pale-skinned, sapphire-eyed and exceptionally sensitive in spirit,

---

[*] There is dispute about whether it was a slightly older or younger sister who died. Rhys herself had no doubt: "My mother had . . . two sons first, whom she really liked, then a daughter, then me, and after me, a little daughter who died . . . " (Jean Rhys to David Plante, nd, McFarlin, Plante Papers, 1987–007.15.f3). In "Heat," an unashamedly autobiographical story set in 1902 (see Jean Rhys, *The Collected Short Stories*, Penguin, 1987. p. 283), the narrator mentions regular visits to the grave "of my little sister." It seems best to trust Rhys herself on this unresolved issue.

Gwen resembled neither of her parents, nor her more heavily built and dark-haired siblings. Almost from birth, as Rhys remembered it in *Smile Please* (a memoir which still remained unfinished when she died), she had felt like an outsider; a changeling; a ghostly revenant in the hard light of day. True or not, that was the role which would come to fit both the writer and her work as closely as a handstitched glove.

———————

NO FAMILY PAPERS survive against which to test the accuracy of *Smile Please*, Jean Rhys's published account of the seventeen years she spent in the West Indies. An unpublished novel by her brother Owen related the story of a white Creole girl who breaks her family's unspoken social code by falling in love with an island boy. But it was Owen—not his sister—who was sent away from Dominica for forming intimate relationships with local girls (one was an employee in his parents' home), an infringement that embarrassed his strait-laced mother. Nothing in Rhys's own recollections suggests that any such romance took place in her early life, although Antoinette Cosway in *Wide Sargasso Sea* recalls having exchanged a final "life and death kiss" with her handsome illegitimate cousin Alexander ("Sandi") before she travels to England as Rochester's wife.[1] Hearsay in the family of Rhys's father's medical colleague Sir Henry Nicholls suggested that Gwen had been labelled "fast" as a young girl. Nicholls and his wife were probably recalling Gwen's childish crush on their son Willie, a youth whose wild ways would eventually lead to his discreet banishment to Scotland, to study medicine.[2]

Travel writers and historians (among them the lushly romantic Lafcadio Hearn and earnest James Froude) have provided magnificent descriptions of Dominica's invincible appearance: a small island rearing up from a range of submerged volcanic peaks like an emerald cathedral of soaring rock. A voracious reader throughout her life, Rhys became familiar with the books written by Froude and Hearn. (Froude toured the island with one of Gwen's Lockhart uncles in the 1880s, as an unofficial representative of Britain's Colonial Office; Hearn, visiting the

West Indies for two years just before Rhys was born, first wrote about Dominica with a lyricism that artfully concealed the fact that he was describing its forested heights from aboard a passenger ship.)

But Jean would remember Dominica best from her own early experiences. She had seen the gigantic wheel and iron mangles at Geneva's disused sugar mill (one of sixty mills on the island from which a cluster of white planters had once prospered); she had listened to the family stories told about her own mother's Lockhart forebears, once the wealthiest of a small plantocracy. The island held a more powerful grasp on her imagination through the enduring presence in her mind of an unforgettable landscape: the green and densely mantled mountains that Rhys knew from childhood as Morne Micotrin, Morne Anglais, Morne Trois Pitons and—towering above them all—Morne Diablotin. They offered a majestic presence, along with a rich stew of gossip, island stories and family scandals that would nourish Jean Rhys's fiction.

Questions abound. How much of the material on which Rhys seems to draw for her novels was based on historical fact? Should a reader believe in the actual existence of Maillotte Boyd, simply because Anna Morgan, the dream-laden protagonist of Rhys's third novel (*Voyage in the Dark*), remembers having seen Maillotte's name on an old list of house-slaves? Does a real Maillotte gain credibility because Rhys also made use of her unusual name in *Wide Sargasso Sea*? (There, in Rhys's extraordinary prequel to *Jane Eyre*, Maillotte's daughter appears both as the twin spirit and the nemesis of unhappy Antoinette Cosway, Mr. Rochester's young Creole wife.) More likely, Rhys was playing with a name that chimes with the word "*mulatto*," a term still in use on Dominica today. Mixed race was not uncommon in families like hers. James Potter Lockhart, Minna's grandfather, had taken two of his slaves as mistresses. Gwen, from an early age, was discouraged from making friends with any of the darker-skinned Lockhart cousins on the island, cousins whose fortunes began slowly ascending as those of her poorer white relatives fell.

RHYS'S FIRST MEMORIES were of the freehold house in Dominica's capital, Roseau, that her father, a proud Welshman, named Bod Gwilym ("William's Home"). A large timber-framed corner house, standing between Cork Street and Grandby Street, Bod Gwilym was painted white, with green-shuttered windows. Gwen's bedroom gave onto a high platform, hidden from public view. From here, as a secret observer, she watched the village women striding down to the marketplace near the bay, dark heads crowned by their bright baskets of mangoes, yellow passionfruit and small, green oranges. Dominica was a Catholic island: there was uproar when an outspoken newspaper editor—described in Rhys's early story "Against the Antilles" as "a stout little man of a beautiful shade of coffee colour" who lived close to the Rees Williams's house—criticised the money being spent on a new palace for the town's Catholic bishop. When a band of angry women marched into town ("Against the Antilles" described the crowd as "throwing stones and howling for the editor's blood"), the shutters of Bod Gwilym were closed and barred. Peeping over the edge of her hidden observation platform, Gwen saw the exhilaration in the women's faces and understood it. As with the mob on the street, so it was indoors between Minna Lockhart and her timid, fiery daughter. Rage might hurt others; never oneself. Rage brought relief.

Standing with her family at an open window and dressed in her best clothes, little Gwen watched the town's annual carnival with longing, waiting for the moment when she was allowed outside, just long enough to present a sixpence to the tall stilt-walker who always stopped to perform a stiff-legged dance beside Dr. Rees Williams's house. Passionately, Gwen had wanted to join the whirling dancers, but she distrusted the brightly daubed wire masks that screened their watchful eyes from view. Once, not perhaps intending to frighten a nervous child, a kitchen visitor spoke in a strange falsetto voice and thrust a thick pink tongue through the white wire mesh that concealed darker skin. Gwen ran away crying. She was inconsolable. Later, Rhys would place that scene among Anna Morgan's Caribbean recollections in *Voyage in the Dark*.

Grandest of all Roseau's public spectacles were the religious processions led by the Catholic bishop and a retinue of stately priests in splendid robes. Watching from the broad wooden gallery that separated the doctor's house from the street, young Gwen gazed out at a dazzle of colourful headdresses, banners and effigies. Listen hard enough, and she could hear the froufrou crackle of paper-hemmed petticoats worn under the ladies' sweeping trains.

Catholicism played no active part in Gwen's home life, but her father, the product of an Anglican upbringing in South Wales, often lunched with a friendly priest and he offered free medical advice at the Catholic Presbytery and the town's convent school. Dr. Rees Williams was not considered a prejudiced man. He saw his white patients privately in the afternoons, but his mornings at the surgery which formed an extension wing to his house were reserved for the black islanders. All patients, black or white, were treated with equal courtesy and only Minna Lockhart raised objections when the doctor despatched his socially sensitive daughter to walk along the surgery queue with small offerings of bread or money.

The doctor's wife cared more than her husband for how she, a proud Lockhart (one sister had married John Spencer Churchill, a former Governor of the Virgin Islands), would be perceived by those whom she regarded as her peers. Gwen's father seems to have quietly favoured Catholicism although he was never a churchgoer, but on Sunday mornings, Minna Rees Williams and her children processed slowly up the hill from Bod Gwilym to St. George's, the town's Anglican church, built for the benefit of the island's leading white families. A pause was always made beside the tiny grave of Gwen's dead baby sister before the doctor's wife swept on to take her position in a pew near the head of the nave, the preserve of the town's white worshippers. Sometimes, bored of watching her mother fan her broad, expressionless face with a fronded palm leaf, Gwen tried to translate an impressive Latin wall tablet that honoured her great-grandfather, James Potter Lockhart. She learned a few of the punning words by heart, well enough to make later use of them, over and again, in her work: *Locked Hearts I open. I have the heavy key.*[3]

Rhys could always summon up Bod Gwilym in vivid detail. A framed dark print of Mary Queen of Scots being led to her execution hinted at the doctor's Catholic sympathies. Recent copies of *The Lancet* and *Cornhill* magazine lay beside the armchair in which he relaxed on the long wooden gallery facing towards the street. Ripe mangoes dropped from the glossy-leaved garden tree that shaded both the smoky kitchen quarters and the cool, windowless room in which a vast stone trough of dark green water served as the family's bath. Gwen preferred to wade—she disliked swimming—deep into one of the island's innumerable forest pools.

The exactness and ease with which Jean Rhys could always evoke her family's home in Roseau suggests that the town was where she had spent most of her early life. The memories were not always happy ones. Evening expeditions with her sea-loving father, rowing her across a wide bay spangled with tiny lights from the Roseau fishing boats, filled a nervous child with a dread that she failed to conceal. "You're not my daughter if you're afraid of being seasick," a father chides the narrator of one of Rhys's most troubling stories, "The Sound of the River." "You're not my daughter if you're afraid of the shape of a hill, or the moon when it is growing old. In fact you're not my daughter."[4]

Less frightening was the annual summer journey in the hollowed-out trunk of a tree up the island's west coast to Massacre. Gwen wouldn't register until later that the village's grim name recorded the murder in 1674 of Carib Warner, stately Sir Thomas Warner's half-white rebel son, or that the English troops confronting him were led by the renegade's white half-brother. For Gwen, Massacre simply marked the place where the Rees Williams family disembarked with their provisions, ready for the slow horseback ride up the 200-foot ascent to her personal favourite of their two summer homes.

Bona Vista was impetuously purchased by the doctor shortly after his move to Roseau, together with a smaller and almost adjoining inland estate called Amelia. Bona Vista stood high above the sea. Writing *Voyage in the Dark* in the early Thirties, Rhys gave them a combined identity with a Welsh name: "Morgan's Rest." From Bona Vista, she remembered: a hammock; a spyglass with which to spot the yellow flags of anchored, quarantined ships; a shadowy drawing room in which the children played halma and bezique on stormy afternoons; her father cradling a nervous, weeping wife in his arms while a high wind rattled the shutters and thunder rolled across the mountains. Evoking an unnamed Bona Vista in the early story she would title "Mixing Cocktails," Rhys dwelt less upon her family's "very new and very ugly house," a bungalow on stilts, than on slow, dreamy days of watching the distant sea change from "a tender blue, like the dress of the Virgin Mary," to a glitter of midday light and, finally, a rich sunset purple that she thought unique to the Caribbean ("The deepest, the loveliest in the world . . . ").*

Bona Vista was where Rhys would choose to open the late memoir she named *Smile Please*. Posed centre stage for a photograph recording a family play—it had been arranged to honour her sixth birthday—Gwen wore a new white dress and a scented wreath of frangipani flowers. So attired, an improbable Red Riding Hood sat perched between her parents, all ready to receive a well-staged visit from her brothers; but Edward, the eldest boy, refused to perform in his role as the honest woodcutter, and Owen's listless growls as he represented the wolf (in a trailing white sheet), failed to convince. Happy endings have no place in Rhys's work. She remembered only a little girl's sadness as she stared down at a picture of Miss Muffet and a hungry spider in the storybook (a birthday gift from Gwen's grandmother in faraway South Wales) hesitantly placed on her lap as a consolation.

Gwen liked her older sister, Minna. She would miss the twelve-year-old girl when she went to live on another Caribbean island with the childless John Spencer Churchill and his wife, Edith (Gwen's little-known "Aunt Mackie"), as the couple's unofficially adopted daughter.

---

* "Mixing Cocktails" and "Against the Antilles" were published in *The Left Bank: Sketches and Studies of Present-Day Bohemian Paris* by Jonathan Cape in 1927. Like *Voyage in the Dark* (Constable, 1934), these stories reflect Rhys's earliest memories of the island more precisely than her later work.

Dominica has more than 300 rivers. Rhys loved bathing in the island's forest pools, some of which are fed by waterfalls. *(Author picture)*

Little Brenda was too young to become a playmate. Left in the company of her older brothers, Gwen felt excluded: a hanger-on. At the smaller Amelia estate (retained after the improvident doctor sold Bona Vista in order to save money), their tumbledown summer home was enclosed by broad mountains and luxuriant woods. Sometimes, Gwen trailed Edward and Owen when they set off armed with an old gun, exploring trails that led deep into the tangled green jungle. Once, wandering off on a separate track, away from the crackle of gunfire, she found herself standing alone and trembling with fear in an open, sunlit glade. *Was* she alone? "The sunlight was still, desolate and arid. And you knew something large was behind you. But what? A stranger? A ghost? You ran," Rhys would later write about Julia Martin's memory of a similar childhood adventure in her second novel, *After Leaving Mr Mackenzie*. "But when you got home you cried."[5]

Gwen saw little of her hard-working father at Bona Vista, since the ride up from his Roseau surgery took over three hours. At Amelia, however, where he tried to make a little money from growing crops, the doctor paid longer visits. Sometimes, he took his daughter along with him to examine a row of young nutmeg trees: in *Voyage*, Anna Morgan's alert pair of eyes are sharp enough to help her father spot the critical difference between a male and female bud.

In Rhys's memories, her father had always been gently encouraging, unjudgemental, trying to do what was best for his favourite child, while her mother missed no opportunity to crush and humiliate a daughter of whom she was perhaps a little jealous. She remembered how Minna Lockhart put an end to Gwen's zealous attempts to teach the Amelia estate's illiterate overseer to read, warning her that John's jealous, cutlass-carrying wife might not appreciate the favour. When one of John's village friends offered Mrs. Lockhart the princely dowry of one large yam to purchase her pretty daughter as his child bride, Minna shared the news with Gwen's siblings and led the chorus of mockery. (And what would such a bride be required to do, young Gwen wondered after being puzzled and upset by the sight of her pet fox-terrier, Rex, rutting in a public place? Her mother wouldn't say. Sex was a forbidden topic.)

Gwen was only three or four when she was taken on her first visit to Geneva, connected to Roseau by a steep and treacherous bridle track that ran south and then east across the southern end of the island before winding uphill to Mitcham House, the original family home of the Lockharts. Later, in one of the coloured exercise books which recorded her private thoughts and episodes for use in her fiction, Rhys wrote that Geneva—thinly disguised as "Constance" in *Voyage in the Dark*—was where she turned four. She remembered the exact year and setting because it was on her fourth birthday, in August 1894, that a local woman, young Elisa Farsa, shot herself on the public road, where a shoreside, slave-descended community were housed below the bluff that protected the Lockharts' home from attack. Within the privacy of her notebooks, Rhys recorded Elisa's name, the date and the place of her death over and again, sometimes changing her name to "Elisa Blank," but without ever offering any explanation.[6] Why did Elisa Farsa's name carry such significance for Gwen? How had the poor young woman obtained a gun? Always discreet about a brother, Owen, who fathered two families on the island, and about her own father, a man who evidently enjoyed the company of women other than his wife, the older Rhys was never prepared to say. All she would acknowledge in *Smile Please*, a memoir written in her eighties, was that the doctor would "flirt outrageously" with any attractive visitor to their home, and that her mother might have minded more than she ever showed.

Riding from Roseau to Geneva one day with Aunt Brenda, her mother's unmarried twin sister, as her guide, Gwen admired the stoicism with which her aunt continued the difficult, three-hour journey, despite having broken several ribs along the way when she was thrown off by her skittish mare. The Lockhart twins prided themselves on their riding skills. Timid Gwen preferred her father's docile nags, Preston and March, to Aunt Brenda's wild-eyed mount. Years later, Rhys would fondly name Antoinette Cosway's obedient horse "Preston."

Brenda Lockhart had helped to nurse Willie Rees Williams back to health when he fell ill shortly after his arrival on the island back in 1881. But if Aunt Brenda had briefly shared her twin's hopes of exchanging an isolated life at Geneva for marriage and children, she bore no apparent grudge. To Gwen, it seemed that her mother, a silent, wary woman, only smiled and laughed when Brenda was with her, little though the twins appeared to have in common. Minna, despite a fondness for the lurid romances of Marie Corelli, disliked books, hated cleverness in a woman and saw no merit in giving her daughters an education. Brenda enjoyed the novels of Rhoda Broughton, a clever, progressive-minded writer who was regularly invited to dine alone with the ageing, London-based Henry James. Minna ordered two evening dresses a year from a London designer. Aunt Brenda, who dabbled in art, loved the theatre and wore dashing hats and the gowns she herself designed and stitched as skilfully as any French-trained couturier.

At Geneva, the unmarried Brenda Lockhart shared Mitcham House with the Woodcock sisters. Julia Lockhart, Gwen's long-widowed granny, was a chatty old lady from St. Kitts whose favourite companion was the green parrot that perched, squawking, on her shoulder. Gwen's granny would eventually provide Aunt Cora's salty warning to Antoinette Cosway against marrying Mr. Rochester, although Granny

Lockhart's comment ("not if his bottom was stuffed with diamonds") was toned down for the readers of *Wide Sargasso Sea*.[7] Gwen formed a closer relationship with Julia's unmarried sister, Jane Woodcock—a sprightly Victorian figure who once created, just for Gwen, an exquisite cardboard doll's house: "Cardboard dolls with painted faces, cardboard tables and chairs, little tin plates for the dolls' meals."[8] The house and its tiny inhabitants were Miss Woodcock's consolation gift after a weeping Gwen confessed to having smashed a coveted doll that had been bestowed upon her little sister.

Gwen first heard the family history of the Lockharts from Jane Woodcock. The old lady didn't always get the details right, but the version she provided took firm root in the mind of an impressionable child. Describing the fiery end of a decaying plantation house in *Wide Sargasso Sea*, Rhys modelled her account on Miss Woodcock's descriptions of a marooned and besieged Geneva.

Long ago—as Aunt Jane explained—back in the 1760s, a family of French Protestants called Bertrand had given Geneva its name when they settled there during the island's French occupation. (Calvinist Geneva had previously provided the Bertrands with a Swiss haven in Europe during times of religious persecution.) Sixty years later, Gwen's acquisitive Lockhart forebear added Geneva to his growing portfolio of Dominican estates. James Potter Lockhart became rich; the dispossessed Bertrands vanished from history. Rhys was still brooding on the Lockharts' takeover of Geneva when she gave the Bertrand family's name to the most heartlessly treated figure in her last and best-known novel. "Who would have thought that any boy could cry like that?" demands an uncomprehending Mr. Rochester when the gentle island-bred Bertrand, known to him only as "the nameless boy," weeps at being abandoned by the man he so admires: "For nothing. Nothing. . . ."[9]

Gwen hated everything Jane Woodcock told her about James Lockhart. Twice Governor of Dominica, the Scottish-born and London-bred businessman had made his fortune from the sugar mills that could crush a weary arm to pulp, and by the profitable trafficking of slaves

When Rhys was a child, she loved to visit her unmarried great-aunt Jane Woodcock (*right*), who lived at Mitcham House, Geneva with her sister, Rhys's grandmother. The third figure (*left*) is unidentified but may be Brenda Lockhart, Rhys's aunt. *(Hesketh Bell papers, Royal Commonwealth Society, Cambridge)*

from one island estate to another. Oil portraits of the white-haired planter and his pretty wife were prominently displayed in the dining room at Mitcham House; well out of view (and unportrayed) were the planter's two slave-mistresses and their dark-skinned descendants: Gwen's Lockhart cousins.

Jane Woodcock talked bluntly about an unscrupulous planter she had never known, whose fortune was made by driving harsh bargains during the last years in which slavery in the West Indies was still legal. Understandably, she spoke with more affection about James Lockhart's son Edward, the man who had married her sister Julia. Perhaps Jane had never been told the truth about what happened six years before Julia and she came to Mitcham House from St. Kitts in 1850. Gwen learned from her only that Edward Lockhart had valiantly rebuilt the house she knew after its precursor had been burned to the ground by a rebel workforce. She heard that her grandfather Edward was "a mild man" and a kind employer. None of these statements was true.

In June 1844, a British attempt to gather statistics for an island census had aroused understandable fears of some cunning new form of enslavement among Dominica's former slave population. When hints of a minor rebellion began to surface, suspected insurgents were brutally suppressed. One man was hanged for throwing a stone which had grazed the cheek of an estate owner. At Geneva, two women protesters were personally flogged by the sugar-mill manager, while "mild" Edward Lockhart joined forces with a local schoolteacher to vandalise the wooden fieldside homes of his workers. With Lockhart's approval, the severed head of one alleged rebel was displayed on a pike.

Inevitably, there were reprisals. Talking to Gwen, old Jane Woodcock painted a lurid picture of angry workers burning Mitcham House to the ground. But the house that the former slaves destroyed had in fact belonged to the sadistic sugar-mill manager. All that Edward Lockhart lost were some of his chattels (beds, chairs, two pianos), which were carried out of his home and burned within view of Mitcham's shuttered windows.

Dominica's press did not hold back about the barbarous flogging of two women at the Geneva estate in the summer of 1844. In London, a disapproving House of Commons heard reports of "most wanton acts of cruelty" undertaken by "an attorney" at Geneva.[10] (Edward Lockhart was a magistrate with legal powers.) Out on the island of Dominica, sympathy was in short supply for the destruction of Mrs. Lockhart's pianos.

THERE WERE ALWAYS two worlds in Gwen's life on Dominica and she made no secret of which of the two she preferred. It wasn't in the company of her family that she stood on the shivering edge of the island's treacherous Boiling Lake, where a volcanic underworld bubbled into view. Her mother could understand the Kwéyòl language, but it wasn't Minna Lockhart or Gwen's brothers who taught her the saucy words of local songs, or introduced her to the harrowing tales handed down by the French-speaking slaves of a former French colony to their freed descendants. Rhys may even have been drawing on a personal memory for her account of Antoinette Cosway running away as a child to live "with the fishermen and the sailors on the bayside," before she is brought safely home to Coulibri.[11]

Beyond the careful ritual of life in Dr. Rees Williams's townhouse lay the vivid and forbidden world of the islanders. Describing the outspoken Martinique-born Christophine (who functions as Antoinette Cosway's ally and spokeswoman in *Wide Sargasso Sea*), Rhys drew on personal memories of Anne Truitt, a tall, quiet woman who worked as a cook at Bona Vista—and later, at Mitcham House—until her arrest and conviction for practising obeah. Some form of voodoo was often secretly practised by the workforce of a colonial household in the 1890s; late on in life, Rhys casually remarked that Dominicans used to travel to Haiti to study obeah just as English students went to Oxford and Cambridge.[12]

Obeah was widespread in the West Indies during Gwen's childhood. Gwen could easily have learned about it from "Francine," the islandborn girl whom Rhys would later describe as the closest friend of her childhood. Francine, first characterised in *Voyage in the Dark* as a free spirit with an enchanting gift for storytelling, led Gwen into a world that was meant to be hidden from a girl of her own class and colour. The abruptness with which an adolescent Francine disappeared from Gwen's life was noted as sad, but unsurprising. An explanation, so Rhys opaquely commented in *Smile Please*, could be surmised. As with Elisa Farsa, a connection of the illicit kind practised by Gwen's hated greatgrandfather with his female slaves seems to be lurking here, just out of view. Was Francine compelled to leave after becoming involved with a male member of Gwen's family? It's far from impossible.

Part of Francine's attraction for Gwen lay in the fact that such inter-racial friendships were frowned upon by a mother who was mocked in the Dominican newspapers for her haughty ways. Minna wanted her daughter to mix only with the well-dressed English children who occa-sionally visited Roseau with their parents from abroad, or from other islands. The British-born doctor was swift to grasp what his white Cre-ole wife failed to understand: such aspirations were doomed to failure. Just as Gwen had been taught to keep her distance from village chil-dren, so visitors from England instructed their daughters to stay away from a mere colonial, a girl with a singsong accent, one who had never been to London and who actually enjoyed bathing naked in a river. The sense of not belonging—one which would become central to Rhys's work—was born in the cruel, caste-conscious little world of Roseau. The only certain refuge lay in the books which Gwen began to read—after a start so slow that her parents grew concerned—as soon as she could spell out the words on a page. From that moment on, there was no holding her back.

Floggings, School and Sex
(1896–1906)

"Will you dance Loobi Loobi Li
Will you dance Loobi Loobi Li
Will you dance Loobi Loobi Li
As you did last night?"

—Old island poem quoted by Jean Rhys, 1975[1]

NO RECORD SURVIVES of the books Gwen read as a child, other than those mentioned in the incomplete memoir she wrote during her eighties. *Smile Please* tells us that, before she went to school and started exploring the town library, Gwen devoured the books kept at her Roseau home in an unlocked glass cabinet. *Treasure Island*; *Robinson Crusoe*; *Gulliver's Travels*; a few volumes of poetry that included Byron and Milton: the brisk little list reveals that Rhys already preferred fiction to fact. The row of informative encyclopaedias on the bottom shelf were left untouched.

Books provided a silent but loving connection between Gwen and her Irish grandmother in Wales. Well-read and strong-willed, Sophia Rees Williams had paid out of her own pocket for her second and favourite son to get the medical education he needed to qualify and to travel abroad. Her clergyman husband cared nothing for Willie or his future; a startled Gwen once caught her habitually cheerful father

Bod Gwilym, the Roseau townhouse in which Rhys spent most of her childhood. Boarded up when she revisited the island in 1936, the house was demolished in 2020. *(Author picture)*

shaking his fist at a faded photograph of the crotchetty old Welsh grandfather she never knew.

Twice a year, Granny Sophia sent books to Dominica for a girl who was reported by a proud William to have inherited her own family's good brains. Right up to the last package sent shortly before she died in 1896—it contained the true story of Richard Brinsley Sheridan's romantic elopement with a beautiful young singer—Sophia always intuited just what was wanted.[2]

Gwen's mother took no interest in her daughter's passion for reading; Gwen's nursemaid, Meta, warned the child that her eyes would fall out if she didn't break the habit. It was from Meta, hard-fisted and always in a rage, that Gwen learned that a cockroach, if it flew into her mouth, would leave a bite that would never heal. The threat seemed more real because Gwen's mother would never enter a room where a cockroach had been glimpsed. A white girl like Gwen faced being taunted by passers-by in the streets of Roseau as a "white cockroach": an outsider; the wrong colour on an island which had a predominantly dark-skinned population.

Meta—given an entire chapter to herself in *Smile Please*—thrived on the manufacture of terror, telling stories of red-eyed women who crept into children's bedrooms at night and sucked their blood. Zombies, so Meta said, could open any door; you'd know nothing until a pair of hairy hands locked around your throat. "Meta had shown me a world of fear and distrust," Rhys wrote in her old age and added, pitifully: "I am still in that world."[3]

As with Meta, so it was with her mother. "How did it happen and why?" Rhys would ask herself years later in a private undated note, "that I gradually grew to love and trust my father. Not her."[4] Sharpest in her memory was the torment of being mocked. Meta, having noticed her charge's childish crush on the son of her father's colleague, enjoyed pretending that Willie Nicholls had just called at the Cork Street house, for the fun of seeing a flustered Gwen fumble with the elaborate hooks and buttons of her best frock before rushing downstairs, only to find an empty room. A letter of shy admiration that Gwen planned to send to one of her parents' male friends was opened by her mother, who expressed mocking astonishment: why on earth would a popular gentleman like Mr. Greig want a letter from such an ugly girl? Gwen's tribute was never sent.[5] The cruel putdown, to a girl too young and insecure to recognise her own uncommon beauty, was deeply felt.

There was worse. Meta, when angry, which was often, shook the child until her teeth chattered. Mrs. Rees Williams went further, flogging her daughter with a whip whenever Gwen did something to annoy her. The cause could be as trivial as taking part in an inappropriate game. ("*Will you dance Looby Looby Li, as you did last night?*" Gwen and her friends sang and acted out in a quiet corner of Roseau's ultra-respectable Botanical Gardens, vaguely sensing that they were doing something forbidden.) Often, Gwen was whipped for no reason at all. Years later, confiding her unhappy memories to a black exercise book still preserved among her papers at Tulsa, Rhys would write that her mother saw "something alien" in her daughter: in fact, "she couldn't bear the sight of me."[6] The whippings were still in full force in 1902, when Gwen was twelve years old. "I've done my best," she was told at this point. "You'll never be like other people."[7] An outsider might deduce that Minna Rees Williams was jealous of Gwen's closeness to a father in whose eyes his clever, ardent daughter could do no wrong.

Gwen would never have had an education if her mother had got her way. The Rees Williams boys (their mother's favourites) were sent away to boarding schools in England, returning home to Dominica only once a year. Gwen, aged nine, was sent on her father's insistence to Roseau's Catholic convent as a day girl. The convent's pupils wouldn't mix with the handful of white girls, among whom Gwen found it hard at first to make a friend; eventually, she teamed up with an exotic trio of fellow outsiders—the three South American sisters seeming scarcely younger than the exquisitely dressed mistress who accompanied their debonair father (and his pair of Cuban bloodhounds) on rare visits to the island from abroad.

Gradually, away from her mother, Gwen grew happier, sufficiently so that it didn't distress her, aged thirteen, to board for six months when her parents visited England during the doctor's official leave. The original convent, which survives as a retreat for priests, was based around a small, square-shaped house that still looks much as it did when Gwen arrived at its sturdy doors in 1899. There, taught by a group of intelligent and worldly nuns whose mother convent was located at Norwood in south London, Gwen studied piano and fell in love for the rest of her life with French poetry. Tucked away within the substantial archive of Jean Rhys's notes and drafts and letters held in the McFarlin Library at Tulsa, Oklahoma are a handful of tiny blue pages on which she wrote out—always in French—extracts from poems by Verlaine, Rimbaud, Baudelaire, Hugo, de Musset.[8] In moments of despair, Gwen would always return to poetry, and to the convent's maxims for comfort and encouragement. "Truth is great and will prevail" remained high among her favourites, but the proclamation that Jean Rhys would adopt as her enduring source of inspiration came from Saint Teresa of Ávila: "At the cost of a thousand sufferings, at the cost of a long death before the fact, I will find that country which is new and ever young. Come with me and you will see."

Gwen, when she first arrived at the Virgo Fidelis Convent, had never yet left Dominica. Aged eleven, she was taken by her Aunt Brenda to the town of Castries on Saint Lucia, where Acton Lockhart, head of the white side of Gwen's maternal family, was getting married. In *Smile Please*, Rhys would invoke the crowing of cocks to suggest the dawning of sexual awareness at Castries, where a daring girl trapeze artist from Havana captured all of her attention on a first delighted visit to a circus. At some point shortly after her return to Roseau, conscious of being watched by an admiring young Willie Nicholls, Gwen slid her body down into the green water that always filled the Rees Williamses' massive bathing trough. For the first time, she experienced the power of her physical beauty.

Aged twelve, Gwen was poised between childhood and adolescence. Some of the final whippings inflicted by her mother may have been a

The author in 2018, outside the original little Virgo Fidelis Roseau convent attended by Rhys. *(Author picture)*

punishment for the habit which now began and which the older Rhys buried in a private note, not intended for publication: "I remember that hot day when I locked the window and started. I remember when it got coarse and when it got too bad to bear and when it started to change . . . At last I would have [liked?*illeg.*] for it to stop. I closed my eyes. It helped me to sleep and I knew of course never to give way to despair. It is a sin."[9]

VISITING MITCHAM HOUSE in April 1902, Gwen was woken from sleep and silently led by her mother to watch a molten cloud bloom and spread above the distant hills of Martinique. The fiery cloud proved a harbinger; on 8 May, a massive volcanic eruption buried Martinique's cultural capital, pretty Saint-Pierre, and its forty thousand inhabitants, in burning ash. A few weeks later, Gwen's father joined a boat that went to inspect the devastation of Saint-Pierre—and to gather souvenirs. Dominica's thirty-eight-year-old French-born governor, Henry Hesketh Joudou Bell, brought back a china Madonna that he found clasped in a dead woman's arms: "a wonderful memento of the terrible catastrophe."[10]

Gwen's father returned home to Roseau with two church candlesticks, fused together by the heat and twisted into a single blackened trophy which he hung on a dining-room wall in Bod Gwilym as his own souvenir of the tragedy. To Gwen, the entire episode felt unreal, like something in a dream. Many years later, she would draw upon it for a story she called, simply: "Heat."

Shortly before Hesketh Bell's arrival on the island in 1901 for a happy six-year sojourn as Dominica's administrator, the island became a colony of the British crown.[11] Encouraged by Joseph Chamberlain at the Colonial Office and backed by his son Neville, the hardworking Hesketh Bell set himself the challenging task of restoring a white plantocracy. In 1903, Bell arranged for the crown to grant Dominica's indigenous people—then known as "Caribs," and now as the Kalinago—control over an unpromising tranche of hilly coastland on the island's eastern side, facing the Atlantic. At the same time, 100,000 acres of fertile land were put up for offer to British settlers with access via a magnificent new road from Roseau that—after encircling their properties—would return to the island's west coast.

Bell's project replaced an earlier and more benign administrator's plan to restore an old French paved track and from it create a bridle path across the island, for the use of all, not just the new settlers. Recalling tales about this earlier project, Gwen would later persuade herself that the Imperial Road itself had spanned the island, and that she had witnessed its ceremonious opening. The sad truth was that Bell's project for a circular Imperial Road ran out of funding after seventeen misguided miles. Gwen was present to witness the grand opening celebration in 1903, complete with trumpets and speeches and gold-braided epaulettes, of the opening of the Canefield Bridge, marking the point where the new road was to begin, three miles north of Roseau. The rebellious Gwen who yearned to become a free spirit, a girl of the island, was briefly displaced by an ardent young imperialist, waving her parasol and clapping her white-gloved hands on a day that marked her island's link to distant, glorious England as the seat of empire.

Impressed by Mr. Bell's appearance in a plumed hat and splendid uniform, Gwen was too innocent to understand that the handsome and unmarried administrator was homosexual. Aged fourteen in 1904, she gladly accepted an invitation to a Christmas fancy dress ball which Mr. Bell was hosting for an adored young niece whose parents, the Scullys, also lived on the island. Gwen's audacious plan to swagger into the Governor's House wearing the close-fitting blue jacket and scarlet bloomers of a Zouave officer was scotched by her conventionally minded mother. Deft-fingered Aunt Brenda came to the rescue, whipping up a sea-green costume with a tight bodice and a full skirt; the convent's nuns added a rustling hem, which they decorated with paper fish. Clothes would always be talismanic for Rhys; she attributed her triumph to the beauty of her dress when the chivalrous Mr. Bell invited her to partner him for the first waltz. He asked her to dance with him

Henry Hesketh Bell, as he may have looked when a shy Rhys encountered him after attending the Governor's fancy dress ball. *(Hesketh Bell papers, Royal Commonwealth Society, Cambridge)*

again and again. Skimming across the floor, watched by all, Gwen thought she had discovered bliss. Now, "I would always be happy."[12]

Riding out of town a few days later, Hesketh Bell spotted Miss Rees Williams ambling towards him on Preston, her favourite mount. He called out a friendly greeting. Overcome by shyness, she couldn't speak. Following a subsequent afternoon game of croquet at Roseau's carefully exclusive Dominica Club, Gwen's mother took good care to report home that Mr. Bell had used the occasion to poke fun at her daughter's timidity. Gwen never spoke to him again.

Self-consciousness was becoming Gwen's greatest enemy. It had given her real joy to be applauded for a piano recital ("the lights and the people clapping and the palm trees") that may have taken place during the visit to Castries with Aunt Brenda.[13] Back at home, more courage was required in order to volunteer herself as the accompanist when Mr. Greig, one of the men she most revered for his sensitivity and cultured ways, offered to play the violin to a group of friends assembled for a musical evening at the Rees Williams' home. Mr. Greig forged ahead; Gwen, unconscious of the significance of the *da capo* (repeat) sign, lost her way. Instead of helping her out, an icily impolite Mr. Greig laid down his instrument; to a mortified teenager, it was made clear that the fault was all her own. Meeting Mr. Greig by chance years later at a London restaurant, Rhys persuaded herself that he was still scowling with remembered rage. A searing awareness of herself and of how people responded to her would become a vital element in Rhys's later work as a writer; even as a young girl, such extreme self-scrutiny imposed a heavy burden.

Sexuality often runs just beneath the surface of what Rhys published about her early years. She described her father as a generous man adored by women; she also wrote of the pleasure he took in sharing small acts of intimacy with his favourite daughter. The doctor often asked pretty Gwen to light his pipe and mix his evening drink ("I measure out angostura and gin, feeling important and happy . . . "[14]). Her father's friends enjoyed it when she performed similar tasks for them. Sometimes, they beckoned the doctor's slender, large-eyed daughter to perch on their knees. "Baa baa black sheep," one of the first of the island's new settlers, Mr. Ramage, rumbled in Gwen's ear. Later, Rhys would shape for public view the true and strange story of how Mr. Ramage married an islander, became a hermit and once swam downstream to Roseau stark naked, with his clothes in a bundle on his head. But she chose not to tell the world about another house guest, Mr. Brown, whose waist-length beard tickled her tender skin and gave her nightmares in which tall, bearded men chased her down dark passages.

Conspicuous by its absence from the pages of *Smile Please* is a disturbing incident upon which Rhys would base "Good-bye Marcus, Good-bye Rose," one of her most autobiographical short stories. The names in the title of a short, often rewritten story about twelve-year-old Phoebe were among those young Gwen had fancifully selected for the children of the suitable marriage which was her expected destiny as a colonial girl. ("But she'd always doubted this would happen to her," says self-aware Phoebe. "Even if numbers of rich and handsome young men suddenly appeared, would she be one of the chosen?")[15] Well tutored in guilt by her Catholic teachers at the convent, Gwen construed her encounter with the sinister Mr. Howard (Captain Cardew in her published story about Phoebe) as evidence of her own innate wickedness. "He must know," states Phoebe of her "seducer." "He knew. It was so."[16]

Gwen was fourteen years old when the Howards—a handsome oldish man and his seemingly bored young wife—visited from a neighbouring island and made friends with her parents. In her private notes, Rhys recalled how she had first approached their distinguished-looking guest and offered to light his cigar, just as she had been schooled by her father. Invited to show the visitor around Roseau's magnificent Botanical Gardens, Gwen gladly agreed. The fictional Phoebe dresses carefully for the expedition in a white blouse, long white skirt, black stockings and black buttoned boots; clothes-conscious Gwen probably did just the same. In the story's published form, Captain Cardew surreptitiously gropes Phoebe's breasts after learning that she is twelve. An earlier exercise book version had revealed Gwen's actual age at the time of meeting Mr. Howard: "Fourteen he says, fourteen is old enough to have a lover . . . His hand of an old man on my breasts felt cold and dead." On the way home, this evidently practised predator talked calmly to her of casual things. "I hardly spoke."[17]

On subsequent visits to the gardens, Mr. Howard invited Gwen to consider herself his slave, ready to be carried off to a distant island where she would obey his every whim: she would be whipped, bound with ropes of flowers, summoned to wait, naked, upon his fully clothed guests. "It fitted like a hook to an eye," Rhys sardonically commented years later in one of four unpublished exercise books. "After all I'd been whipped a lot." Of Phoebe's strange suitor, she wrote that "Captain Cardew" dwelt on the many different ways of making love. "Violence, even cruelty, was an essential part of it."[18]

Precisely when Rhys first chose to record this act of sexual abuse remains unclear. Elsewhere in her private notes, she wrote that Mr. Howard grew nervous after his wife, realising what was going on, had blamed Gwen, calling her a bad girl. When she next offered to light his cigar, he pushed her away.

Recalling the night before the Howards sailed home, Rhys later remembered lying on her secret bedroom platform under enormous, glowing stars, imagining the moment when she, too, would leave the island. "And when I go what will happen to me? Strange treasures, carpets of the East, and the mountains always saying 'Temps perdi, temps perdi'."*[19]

———————

ESTABLISHING A CHRONOLOGICAL sequence for Gwen's last two years in the West Indies isn't easy. At the convent, the doctor paid for his brightest child to receive extra tuition in French and in music. At home, Gwen spent long hours lolling on the veranda of the new town library, built when she was eleven—energetic Mr. Hesketh Bell was drawing up plans for an even larger, better-stocked one to be funded by Andrew Carnegie—that overlooked Roseau's fishing harbour and the bay. And what did she read? Rhys says almost nothing in her late-written memoir, but it's reasonable to assume that the library introduced her to some of the stalwarts—Dickens, Thackeray, Walter Scott—which Edwardian colonial ladies and their daughters could read without a blush.

But the Victoria library's collection wasn't entirely conventional. Reminiscing in her old age, Rhys described a youthful penchant for stories about prostitutes. Was it here, in a library that collected books from the ships that paused at Roseau on their way to neighbouring French islands, that she first discovered a lifelong favourite? Pierre Louys's *Aphrodite* (1896) told the story, in gorgeously erotic prose, of a sculptor in ancient Alexandria and his passion for Chryses, a beautiful courtesan. If so, she kept quiet. Louys's extraordinary novel was never publicly mentioned by Rhys, despite her enduring love of it. Instead, recalling the little library's crowded, dusty shelves, she singled out Filson Young's *The Sands of Pleasure*, a hastily written 1905 bestseller about an Englishman's romance with a Parisian demimondaine.

These were not the kind of books a young lady was expected to read.

———————

* *Temps perdi*, in Dominica's French-based language, means time that is not "lost," but wasted.

Locked away in her room, dreaming of Parisian trysts, Gwen created more respectable dramas for home performance. Docile, sturdy little Brenda was usually cast as the speechless princess, while the young playwright played the swashbuckling villain.

Every good villain needs an accomplice; perhaps Gwen found a walk-on role for her beloved terrier in the (lost) scripts that she churned out. Heartbroken when Rex suddenly died from distemper, she was consoled with the present of a dress allowance from a doting father who indulged her passion for clothes. Minna Rees Williams, fretting ceaselessly about her husband's extravagance, disapproved; Rhys remembered an occasion on which her mother—while visiting a sympathetic island neighbour—broke down in tears over the family's shrinking resources. The doctor, although he grieved at having to sell Bona Vista, remained blithe and gay; Gwen herself worried more about the poverty that so evidently surrounded them everywhere in Dominica. Later, laughingly, she referred to a conscience-stricken early phase in life when the family nicknamed her "Socialist Gwen." Beyond attempting to teach their overseer to read, no evidence suggests that any of her planned social reforms were ever put into action. Rhys did, however, state in *Smile Please* that she had never been so happy as when, inspired by the sermons in the Anglican church and defended by a loving father from her mother's impatient protestations, she went through a period of doing good deeds.

WHITE CREOLE GIRLS from the Caribbean were traditionally sent to England in order to lose their lilting accents and thus become more eligible for marriage. Brenda, Gwen's younger sister, would eventually attend—war interrupted her progress—a respectably mediocre school in Bloomsbury. Several years earlier, in 1906, word reached Dominica from the doctor's widowed aunt, Jeanette Potts, that clever Gwen, unseen and untested, had been granted a place for the following year at Cambridge's distinguished and academically demanding Perse High School for Girls. In 1906, only one English girl in five was receiving a formal education. Here was a triumph: Clarice Rees Williams, visiting her brother's home from St. Asaph in South Wales early in 1907, volunteered to act as Gwen's chaperone to England.

Rhys would always retain vivid memories of her aunt's six-month stay on Dominica, and of the silent war that was continually being waged between Clarice and her sister-in-law over the doctor's affections. "Poor Willie," Clarice would sigh, hinting that a homesick brother had been kept abroad against his will. Mrs. Rees Williams struck back by retreating to her bed with an unidentified illness that kept her out of view, leaving the busy doctor to arrange picnics, excursions and even a farewell summer dance at the family's home in Roseau, all in honour of his adored—and adoring—daughter.

Minna, distracted by the unpleasing news that Owen, her second and favourite son, had recently fathered a child by an "island girl," had no time for farewells to Gwen. Her husband made up for her wounding indifference. After travelling with his sister and Gwen to Bridgetown in Barbados, the doctor escorted them onto the steamer and seized hold of his daughter in such a tight embrace that he crushed to pieces the little coral brooch that had been his last gift to her. "I had been very fond of it," Rhys later wrote with the calmness of hindsight: "now I took it off and put it away without any particular feeling. Already all my childhood, the West Indies, my father and mother had been left behind. I was forgetting them. They were the past."[20]

A concert was held on board to while away a tedious voyage. Boldly, Gwen volunteered to sing. A pretty voice compensated for a very un-English island lilt: the applause was loud. Elated, and perhaps encouraged by the glamorous accounts of theatre life that her Aunt Brenda had brought back from a recent visit to England, Gwen announced that she intended to go "straight on to the stage" as soon as they reached London.[20] Clarice laughed outright at such an absurd proposal: did her niece honestly imagine that the sober Perse School would tolerate such nonsense? What would her parents say?

Gwen was entirely serious. She felt no wish to return to Dominica or to continue her education. What she wanted was to become a great actress: Britain's very own Sarah Bernhardt. Aged just seventeen in August 1907, Gwen suffered from crippling self-consciousness and fits of anger and despair that she did not know how to control. The compensation came in the moments when, however briefly, she could believe in a glorious future.

II

ENGLAND:
A COLD COUNTRY
*Ella**

"Then, quite suddenly, it seemed, it began to grow cold."

—Jean Rhys, "First Steps," *Smile Please*

---

* A year after arriving in England in 1907, Gwen began to use her first given name: Ella. This was how Rhys would choose to be addressed in her private life during the next fifty years. Shortly after the publication of *Wide Sargasso Sea* in 1966, however, Rhys instructed her own daughter and grandchild to start calling her Jean, "because that is who I am" (Dr. Ellen Moerman to author, 23 January 2019).

3

Stage-struck (1907–13)

"I often wonder who I am and where is my country, and where do I belong . . ."

—Antoinette Cosway, *Wide Sargasso Sea*[1]

DREAMING IN A rocking chair on the broad veranda of the Victoria Memorial Library, set high above Roseau's glittering bay, Gwen Rees Williams had created an idealised Motherland from the books that she devoured. Snow—unimaginable in Dominica—would carpet the fields and "wolds" (whatever they might be). Fires would blaze in every grate. Bright trains, coloured like nursery toys, steamed into a theatre-filled London, a city where handsome gentlemen in gleaming top hats swept deep bows to beautiful ladies with rosy cheeks. A small but sturdy pink England presided over a reassuringly pink map of the world hanging on one of the library walls.

In the summer of 1907, a young colonial girl could confidently picture herself standing at the heart of the glorious Empire. For Rhys, the memory of that enchanting image would never fade. Writing about Antoinette Cosway, half a century later, she would confer on the Caribbean-born heroine of *Wide Sargasso Sea* (1966) precisely the same fantasies of "wolds" and a "rosy pink" Motherland that she would weave into her fragmented autobiography, *Smile Please* (1979).[2]

Arriving at the port of Southampton, Gwen peered out of her cabin's porthole and realised that her imaginary England was no more than a fairy tale: "looking at the dirty grey water, I knew for an instant all that would happen to me. . . ."[3] The train taking her up to London was brown and drab, as was—on an arid afternoon in late August—the great dusty city itself. The next day, disheartened by an early morning stroll around smoke-grimed Bloomsbury, Gwen decided to take a bath at the boarding house where she and Aunt Clarice were staying. Bathing reminded her of home and the pleasure of languid afternoons spent lazing with Francine in Dominica's shadow-spattered forest pools. But a real bath, with taps that ran hot water: this was a novelty. Immersed, she decided to keep the stream of warm water running in. Content at last, Gwen started to sing.

As an older, self-searching writer, Rhys would cite that act of innocent self-indulgence to illustrate how, right from the start, she was made to feel like an outsider in England. The landlady was furious, as was her mortified aunt. Baths were still a luxury in 1907, even among the rich; it's surprising that the boarding house even possessed one to offer to its lodgers. By using up an entire day's supply of hot water, and without seeking permission, Gwen had committed her first offence. How could she be so thoughtless! "I've already noticed," her aunt remarked tartly, "that you are quite incapable of thinking about anyone else but yourself."[4]

Later in life, Rhys would come to appreciate that Clarice Rees Williams had been a thoughtful chaperone to her limp and unresponsive niece. Conducted around the sights of London—Westminster Abbey, St. Paul's, the Wallace Collection, the Zoo—Gwen was unimpressed. How could a girl who grew up on an island alive with exquisite hummingbirds relish seeing those tiny symbols of freedom fluttering in a dark cage with a filthy floor? "The humming-birds," Rhys wrote in *Smile Please*, "finished me."

Gwen's introduction to London was brief. In September, she went as a boarder to the Perse. The school, established in a substantial Georgian villa that stood on Union Road in the heart of Cambridge, had been successfully run for over twenty years by a formidable principal. Katherine Street—always addressed by the pupils as "Madam"—was a handsome woman with an understanding expression and long, thickly waving grey hair which she plaited up into a bun worn like a crown. Fictionalising the school in later years, Rhys unsubtly changed Miss Street's name to Rode. "Miss Born" provided an equally thin disguise for Hannah Osborn, a sharp-faced retired teacher who would eventually share Miss Street's Cambridge grave as her "beloved friend."

Blanche Paterson ("Patey"), the relatively young teacher of classics, was Gwen's favourite among the Perse staff. Patey once took her to

The staff at Perse School in Cambridge, where Rhys attended through the academic year of 1907–8. The principal, Katherine Street, sits centre front with her lifelong companion, Miss Hannah Osborn, seated on her left. *(Used with permission of the Stephen Perse Foundation)*

visit Ely Cathedral, where Gwen was overwhelmed by the grandeur of
the stone arches that soared above her. Perhaps their majestic height
reminded a homesick girl of Dominica's tall forests; seated at a ceremonious tea intended by Miss Paterson as a treat to complete the day's
excursion, Gwen grew so emotional that she dropped her delicate china
cup and smashed it.

The teachers were kind, but Gwen's schoolmates proved either tactless or cruelly snobbish. Mocking her singsong Caribbean lilt, they
nicknamed the outsider "West Indies"; when *Jane Eyre* was announced
as a set book, much fun was had about the fact that Bertha Antoinette Mason, presented by Charlotte Brontë as a red-eyed, grovelling
maniac, was a white Creole—just like Gwen. It didn't help that a fire
broke out at the school, from a carelessly raked hearth, while the pupils
were reading about Bertha Mason's immolation of her husband's Yorkshire manor house. Snide comments were made. The insult to a sensitive spirit was never forgotten or forgiven.

CAMBRIDGE ITSELF LEFT little impression on the newcomer, other
than a faint enthusiasm for the Bridge of Sighs and a tender memory of the unknown young man who carefully helped pretty Gwen to
her feet when she fell off her borrowed bicycle. On Saturdays, when
she cycled out to visit her stately great-aunt's home on Trumpington
Road, Gwen was gently teased about her passion for poetry. White-
haired and black-eyed, the long-widowed and still captivating Jeanette
Potts—sister to Sophia Rees Williams—still retained signs of having
been a celebrated beauty. She told Gwen a strange story of once having
planned to leave her dour husband, a celebrated Cambridge mathema-
tician, for a lover until she glimpsed the devil in a mirror, leering over
her shoulder. Mrs. Potts unpacked her bag and stayed at home.

Gwen liked and respected Mrs. Potts, to whom she most likely owed
her introduction to the Perse. Later, writing fragments of recollection
in her notebooks, Jean Rhys would conflate this imposing representative of Cambridge's academic world with her beloved great-aunt, out

at Geneva. Jane Woodcock had been her loyal ally and favourite story-teller—and yet Gwen never again made contact with her, nor answered the old lady's fond, enquiring letters. Ill at ease though Gwen might have felt in England, she had consciously severed herself from her past.

Mrs. Potts, well connected in the academic world, held out high hopes for her great-niece. The Perse specialised in turning out fine teachers; with diligence, Gwen Williams might even rise to become a headmistress. There was no doubting Gwen's intelligence—she easily won the school's top prize for ancient history—but she was too much of a rebel to embrace a future in the academic world. Dismay was caused when she submitted an essay on *The Garden of Allah*, by Robert Smythe Hichens, for her exam in English literature. The novel, a turgid but surprisingly popular account of a thirty-year-old woman who seeks spiritual meaning during a long journey across the Sahara, was not one of which the Perse approved. Perhaps Gwen picked it on purpose to annoy. By the summer of 1908, she already knew what she wanted to become, and it was not a teacher.

Aged almost eighteen, Gwen remained determined to go on stage. She took confidence from the resounding applause for her perfor-mance, in front of the assembled Perse parents, as the playfully dis-honest Autolycus in *The Winter's Tale*. Playing a male role once again, she was praised for her lively impersonation of the honest provincial, Tony Lumpkin, in Oliver Goldsmith's *She Stoops to Conquer*.

"Overture and Beginners Please," a late Rhys story that began life as an autobiographical vignette, describes the startled pleasure that Gwen felt when a Perse housemaid complimented her performance in the Shakespeare play. But it was one of the mothers—if Rhys's fictional version can be trusted—who provided the necessary spur to action, asking her own daughter to tell the girl who had played Autolycus that she was "a born actress." And then: "She says that you ought to go on the stage and why don't you?"[5] Gwen had already taken that decision when she wrote home to Roseau and asked permission to audition for acting school.

While Aunt Clarice disapproved of Gwen's project as strongly as did Mrs. Potts, Dr. Rees Williams was pleased that Gwen had chosen a career for which she seemed to exhibit a genuine talent. Permission having been granted, the doctor's confidence was rewarded by the news that his talented daughter had won a coveted place at Sir Herbert Tree's new Acting School on Gower Street, the first of its kind in England. Today, we know that same school—greatly enlarged and modernised— as RADA.

A CAREER ON the English stage in 1909 offered enticing prospects to an ambitious young woman. The theatre certainly had its disreputable side, but no stigma attached to becoming a great actress—Ellen Terry, for example, or Mrs. Patrick Campbell—and Gwen was determined to become not merely good, but great. Aunt Clarice, while keeping a close eye on proceedings from a small flat that she had rented on Baker Street, soon found herself redundant. Gwen, having taken Bloomsbury lodgings of her own, was working hard. The school was coaching her in all the skills required for a stage career: gesture, fencing, and ballet. Elocution was taught by a gentle Mr. Heath until a snobbish senior student overruled his insistent mispronunciation of the word "froth" ("I'm not here to learn cockney," she shrilled, or so Rhys recalled, decades later)—and got him sacked.[6]

To Clarice, Gwen reported that her prospects looked good; still only in her second term, she was regularly playing the lead in rehearsal scenes chosen from Shakespeare and Oscar Wilde. She wasn't short of admirers. When a wealthy fellow student called Harry Bewes asked her to marry him, Gwen told her disconcerted aunt that she had turned the young man down in order to pursue her vocation.

Gwen's acting apprenticeship was brief. Money was increasingly scarce in the Rees Williams household and the Tree school charged high fees. In June 1909, the doctor asked the academy's head, Kenneth Barnes, for a candid view of his daughter's prospects. Gwen was paying a dutiful visit to the family of her father's older brother, Neville, up in Yorkshire when the bad news arrived. Equipped as she was with a seemingly ineradicable island lilt, Mr. Barnes had advised her father that Gwen could never achieve success as a serious actress. To continue with her lessons was—in Barnes's opinion—a waste of money. Writing to his daughter, Willie Rees Williams gently explained that the time had come to renounce her dreams and return to her home in Roseau.

At the time, Gwen was devastated. Later, Jean Rhys's chief concern would be to conceal the truth. Her father died the following year. By shifting the date of his death back to the previous summer—as she would do both in the story "Overture and Beginners Please" and in her memoir—Rhys managed to blame her swift departure from the acting school on Minna, the doctor's unsympathetic and financially straitened widow. She never mentioned the verdict of Mr. Barnes. But from this time on, she would train herself to speak in a soft, whispering voice that concealed her origins. That cultivated whisper made it all the more shocking on the occasions when a seemingly ladylike young woman lost control over it and vented her fury in a voice that ranted and raved like a daemonic alter ego.

While disguising the reason for her sudden departure, Rhys was honest about the anguish that leaving the Tree school caused her. Fleeing Uncle Neville's Harrogate home to take refuge at her aunt's cosier Welsh cottage, Gwen dissolved into sobs. "You cry without reticence," Aunt Clare remarks in "Overture and Beginners Please." By the time Miss Rees Williams and her downcast niece returned to London from the tiny cathedral city of St. Asaph—Clarice still lived touchingly close to the rectory where she and her brothers grew up at Bodelwyddan—Gwen's mind was already made up: whatever might become of her, she was not going back to Dominica.

Smile Please implies that Gwen's next step was taken on a last-minute impulse, but it's clear that she had formed a plan. While Clarice went shopping, her niece hurried off to London's best-known theatrical agency, Blackmore's, and requested an immediate audition. The approach, born of desperation, was audacious, but Gwen was exceptionally pretty and ready to display a fetching pair of slender ankles while forming the requested few dance steps.

Gwen left Blackmore's armed with a renewable contract and a freshly minted stage name: Ella Gray. She was given orders immediately to join rehearsals with Sir George Dance's second touring company. Her visit had been fortunately timed; the agents were giving the newcomer a chance to join the first summer tour of a musical comedy, *Our Miss Gibbs*, in which "Miss Gray" would form part of a chorus of implausibly glamorous shop assistants at "Garrods." A wage of thirty-five shillings a week was expected to cover her travel, food and lodgings. The gorgeous costumes (sweat-stained hand-me-downs from the dancers in the grander London production of the same show) would be provided free of charge.

Rallying to this abrupt change of direction, Clarice chaperoned her unnervingly determined niece to the designated rehearsal space, a dingy room at the back of a sporting club off Leicester Square. The other girls liked sturdy, old-fashioned Clarice; they weren't so sure about the pale, foreign-sounding girl she had brought along to join them. A friendly gentleman at Blackmore's had already warned Gwen to keep quiet about her aspiration to become a serious actress. Doubtless, he also advised her to set aside any fantasies about marrying a peer. An English lord might—and often did—propose to one of the celebrated Gaiety Girls who frolicked through the London musicals presided over by Mr. George Edwardes (the great impresario of the day). No aristocrat would offer his name to a girl he'd found dancing in the chorus of a mere touring production.

The agent could warn Gwen, but she'd read too many romantic stories for him to crush a young girl's hopes. Together with a small print of herself as a smiling young dancer (one who could also carry a tune), Rhys would lovingly preserve a photograph of pretty Nancy Erwin, a shrewdly knowing London chorus girl with a trademark quip. "My little bit of Scotch," Nancy liked to trill as she flourished a tiny plaid handkerchief. Nancy's marriage turned her into Lady Dalrymple Champneys, while pretty Rosie Boote became the Marchioness of Headfort. Constance Collier, once a Gaiety Girl, married two grandees in a row. Gertie Millar, a talented former mill girl (her first husband composed the songs for *Our Miss Gibbs*) became Countess of Dudley. "Ella Gray" might not be destined to become the next Sarah Bernhardt or Ellen Terry, but she could still look beyond the limited options of a touring chorus girl.

———————

IN 1977, WHEN Jean Rhys was old and famous, she asked a new friend, a respected young actor, to make up her face with grease paint. Peter Eyre did his best. Rhys, elegantly dressed and sipping a martini, watched him closely in the mirror. There was no small talk. She simply observed. And then, so Eyre recalls, she just as simply asked him to depart. "I left her there alone, staring at herself in the mirror. And honestly, I still don't have a clue what it was all about."[7]

Perhaps, contemplating her rouged lips and cheeks through the eyes of the newcomer to the stage that she had once been, Rhys was wondering at her stamina in having survived those early years on tour. Perhaps she was remembering the noisy camaraderie and saucy jokes that brightened life in the restricted number of provincial lodging houses open to touring actors, often regarded as both immoral and unreliable payers of their bills. Was she recalling a chivalrously paternal old admirer called Colonel Mainwaring who had carried her off for a countryside tour in his clanking prewar motor car? Or might a frail old woman have been remembering an incident—one which she included in *Smile Please*'s light-hearted account of her years on tour—when she and a dancer pal leaped out of a bedroom window into a snowdrift and ran away from their lodgings, to escape paying an overcharged bill?

Like Colette, of whose 1910 novel about life on stage, *The Vagabond*, she would later become an ardent admirer, Rhys often conflated fact and fiction. In *Smile Please*, Rhys denied that reading formed any significant part of her life as a chorus girl. "I never felt the least desire to read anything . . . I think this indifference lasted a long time."[8] Reminiscing to her daughter, however, Rhys recalled in 1959 that the best part of a drizzly afternoon on tour was to curl up with a book: "There is always a fog or mist, so that warmth and a book indoors are heaven. All this was long ago when I was young and tough."⁹

Rhys was a well-read woman, but she took peculiar care to conceal it. Writing her memoir, she would insist that she and the other chorus girls had spent their spare time reading one book, and one book only: *The Forest Lovers*. A hasty reader of *Smile Please* might assume that she was referring to an Edwardian page-turner of the frothiest sort.

Written by Maurice Hewlett, *The Forest Lovers* was nothing of the kind. A long, earnest and faintly ghoulish pastiche of a medieval romance, Hewlett's novel follows the woodland adventures of Prosper le Gai who, having rescued a country maiden from being hanged as a witch by the simple act of marrying her, compels the unfortunate Isolt to earn his love by undergoing endless acts of submission. Her acquiescence borders on masochism. Was Rhys making sly use of Hewlett's fiction to revisit Mr. Howard's abusive games of submission, out in Roseau, or did she feel some troubled affinity to Hewlett's compliant heroine? Impossible though it is to guess why Rhys singled out this justly forgotten novel for mention in her memoir, we shouldn't assume that *The Forest Lovers* was the only work she devoured during those drizzly afternoons on tour, when losing herself in a book was "heaven."

Our Miss Gibbs was not a production that demanded a great deal from its chorus. Lionel Monckton's songs were beguiling; the dance steps were uncomplicated. Gwen enjoyed the chance to experiment with make-up; the exquisite dresses and spectacular hats for which the production was celebrated confirmed her lifelong love affair with millinery and pretty clothes. In *Smile Please*, Rhys would write that the other young actresses had disliked her and that the wardrobe mistress hated her. The jokes and banter that she had evoked over forty years earlier in *Voyage in the Dark* suggest otherwise. Reminiscing to a theatre-loving friend in the 1960s, a septuagenarian Rhys could still warble a cockney ditty from Ella Gray's backstage days. It doesn't sound plaintive.

'E doesn't wear a collar
Or a shirt all white
'E wears a tidy muffler
And 'e looks all right
'E pays his little tanner
In the gallery with Anna.[10]

Ella—as the nineteen-year-old Rhys now became known to all her new friends—had been lucky to join Sir George Dance's second touring company in July, at a time when *Our Miss Gibbs* was about to start visiting seaside towns along England's sunny south coast. Ella's summers, always the jolliest season for the hardworking chorus girls, were followed by a retreat to Clarice's cottage at St. Asaph—or else to "The Cats Home," a dingy London hostel for actresses who were short of cash—until the onset of the gruelling winter tour. Oldham; Leeds; Manchester; Southport; Newcastle (where Ella, like Anna Morgan in *Voyage*, got sick with pleurisy and had to be left behind for a grim three weeks): Rhys had good reason never to return to the north of England after visiting Leeds and Newcastle with *Our Miss Gibbs*. She liked the company of the funny, tough-talking girls whose life she shared. She grew tired of wearing handed-down dresses and of being treated as a second-class citizen: in short, as a chorus girl acting in the provinces. The touring chorus was where Rhys began; apart from a moment of relative glory, when she played one of three bold Irish colleens who briefly share centre-stage with Miss Mary Gibbs and her suitor, Lord Eynsford, the chorus was where she would remain.

Why did she carry on? An abundance of youthful optimism was the answer that Rhys would offer in her memoir: "Going from room to room in this cold dark country, I never knew what it was that spurred me on and gave me an absolute certainty that there would be something else before long . . . I was so sure."[11]

A more prosaic reason for persisting with her chorus work was the sudden death of Dr. Rees Williams, her adored father, in the summer of 1910. Bereft of his presence in Dominica, Rhys had no incentive to return home and no hope of receiving help from a destitute and suddenly isolated widow who still had a fifteen-year-old daughter on her hands. Owen had left the island in disgrace after the revelation of his second family (by a young woman who worked at the Amelia estate); Edward was travelling the world as an army medical officer. In England, a conspicuously unsuccessful young chorus girl now stood alone, helped only by an occasional handout from her kindly aunt in Wales. Uncle Neville, up in Yorkshire, had already made his disapproval of her life plain by severing all connection to his niece.

Tenacity was a quality that would always enable Jean Rhys to survive. What she never admitted in her memoir was how hard she had to struggle to stay afloat during those early years. Unable to afford time off after her second summer season with *Our Miss Gibbs*, Ella Gray snagged herself a walk-on role in a London pantomime before reluctantly applying to join a music-hall company touring the north through the dead of winter. Her role marked a new low in Rhys's short-lived career on stage. For a sketch designed to entertain an undemanding audience, a comic twist had been added to *Chantecler*, a respected French play by Edmond de Rostand. "Chanteclair or High Cockalorum: a Feathered Fantasy in Three Fits" required the feather-costumed actresses to imitate hens. Audiences from northern England's coalpits and steelworks proved unappreciative; pretending to lay an egg onstage troubled Rhys less than the thump of clogs as dissatisfied gallery-goers headed for the exit. With unfortunate timing, one mortified "hen" turned tail and pattered off stage on the night that the show's manager was monitoring the performance. Sacked on the spot and despatched to London on the early morning train, a chastened Ella was taken in by the only member of the Rees Williams family who still had a genuinely soft spot for her: Clarice.

The future at that moment, early in 1911, must have appeared peculiarly grim. The contract with Blackmore's ensured that Miss Gray could, if she so wished, continue dancing in a travelling show for another twenty years. The option wasn't a tempting one. Desperate

Rhys identified this image of herself (*right*) in her touring days of the ill-fated *Chanteclair* production, but the pretty hats are more likely to have been worn for *Our Miss Gibbs*, a musical celebrated for gorgeous millinery, rather than for a sketch in which the chorus girls were dressed as hens. *(McFarlin)*

to avoid another brutal season of touring (one late story, "Before the Deluge," mentions the unfortunate chorus girls being shipped off to Cork on a cattle boat), Rhys jumped at the possibility of filling a tiny spot in the London chorus of Franz Lehár's charming new operetta, *The Count of Luxembourg*. Daisie Irving, a beautiful new friend who was standing in for the play's star (the dazzling Lily Elsie had been taken ill, according to Rhys's story), was willing to give the play's director a gentle nudge.

The part was hers. Rhys's appearance in *The Count of Luxembourg* marked the climax of her stage career. On the opening night in May 1911, Lehár himself was conducting the orchestra at Daly's Theatre, and King George V and Queen Mary were watching from the royal box.

Seated below them in the stalls was a forty-year-old bachelor, a highly successful stockbroker whose well-connected father had recently been appointed Governor of the Bank of England. His name was Lancelot Hugh Smith.

4

Fact and Fiction:
A London Life (1911–13)

"He was a dream come true for me and one doesn't question
dreams, or envy them."

—Jean Rhys, "The Interval," *Smile Please* (1979)

RHYS'S FIRST LOVER was named after one of England's best-known
eighteenth-century landscape designers. Lancelot "Capability" Brown
had laid out the gardens at Mount Clare, the handsome house at Roehampton in which Lancelot, third son of the Hugh Smiths, was born
in 1870.

Lancelot (always "Lancey" to his colleagues and clients), had grown
up in a world of order and great wealth. The closest friends of his parents were the Hambros and Junius Morgan, father of the legendary
John Pierpont Morgan himself. The Hugh Smiths were connected to
the Martin Smiths, the Ridley Smiths and the Abel Smiths: all were
members of a quietly powerful clan that helped to control, and even
to dictate, Britain's finances. Theirs was a world of cool discretion in
which a gentleman's returned cheque—as with Christopher Tietjens in
Ford Madox Ford's *Parade's End*—could immediately destroy his reputation. So might a misjudged marriage.

Writing her unpublished recollections of a flawlessly dull life, Lancey's mother Constance (Lady Hugh Smith) identified only one outsider

"Lancey" Hugh Smith
photographed with his dog
at a sports event a few years
before he met Rhys. *(Used
with permission of the Smith family)*

in the cosily integrated world of Surrey bankers who ranked among
her family's closest friends. Grove House—it adjoined Mount Clare—
belonged to the widow of Mr. Lyne Stephens, a banker who had left the
whole of his fortune to his wife. Her enormous inheritance included
a manor house in Norfolk, a magnificent home in Paris and a collection of art fine enough to rival those of the Wallace and the Frick.
The reason that nobody called upon the wealthy little widow was simply this: the former Yolande Duvernoy had once been a dancer. Occasionally, the Hugh Smith children skated—with the lonely old lady's
permission—upon her garden pond; breaking the strict code of ostra-
cism upheld by Roehampton's banking matrons in order to express her
gratitude, Constance thought she had never encountered a woman with
a sadder face than Yolande Lyne Stephens. Her funeral, which Lady
Hugh Smith described from hearsay, was singularly modest: nobody of
consequence had attended.[1]

Lancey was obsessed by Mount Clare (of which he would eventually
become the proud custodian) and by social position. The awful consequences of Mr. Lyne Stephens's imprudent alliance were still in his

mind when, as a middle-aged and cautious man of the world, he began
his own discreet courtship of a chorus girl.

————————————

DISCRETION WAS ESSENTIAL to a man with powerful clients; we need
not wonder why Lancey himself preserved no trace of an imprudent
love affair. Rhys destroyed everything except for a couple of affectionate notes despatched from the Bishopsgate office of Rowe & Pitman,
the stockbroking firm which twenty-six-year-old Lancey had joined
in 1895. Shrewdly, Rhys's first biographer Carole Angier connected
Mr. Hugh Smith to "Neil James," the affable former lover to whom
the perennially hard-up Julia Martin knows she can always resort for
a handout in Rhys's second novel, *After Leaving Mr Mackenzie* (1931).
While drawing more deeply upon memories of her first love affair for
Voyage in the Dark (1934), Rhys would remain carefully circumspect.
It was never her intention that Lancey's grand friends should identify
him as Walter Jeffries, the mildly seedy protector of Anna Morgan,
an innocent young woman who ends by sleeping with men for money.

Rhys's realistic description of Jeffries has nevertheless provided her
biographers and critics with a convincing story line. Reading *Voyage* as
autobiography, a reader can easily assume that the novelist herself had
first encountered a mildly sleazy financier while taking a day off from
performing at the King's Theatre in the summer of 1911, to stroll along
the promenade at jolly, raffish Southsea (a seaside extension of the naval
town of Portsmouth). It's at Southsea that an admiring Walter Jeffries
treats Anna Morgan to some cotton stockings before making his first
attempt to seduce her in a London brothel masquerading as a plush-
mantled restaurant. But Rhys flags up the contrast between Anna and
Emile Zola's worldly Nana on the first page. Nana is at ease in such
places. Anna—her name is a deliberately unsubtle anagram—is not.
And neither was Rhys. Restaurants of the kind described in *Voyage in
the Dark* had almost vanished from view by 1911, the year in which
the twenty-one-year-old Jean, still known to all her friends as Ella,
embarked on her first serious love affair.

Walter's encounter with Anna is a biographical red herring. A more convincing start to Rhys's own liaison emerges from "Before the Deluge," a short story that Jean only began to write many years after her lover's death. Rhys's stories contain far more autobiographical detail than her novels. Here, quite casually, the narrator lets drop the fact that her friend Daisie Irving often swept her off to the smart supper parties at which admirers feted the pretty stand-in star of *The Count of Luxembourg*. Rhys's official role was to carry Daisie's armful of bouquets, but she was also a welcome guest at the dinners held in Daisie's honour. Snobbish, conventional Lancey would neither have slummed it at Southsea, nor gone shopping for ladies' stockings. He certainly wouldn't have objected to escorting the star of a musical that had received the royal seal of approval at its premiere to a supper at Romano's or the Savoy, chaperoned by Daisie's pretty attendant.

As with Anna Morgan at Walter's "Green Street" home, it was probably in the bedroom of Lancey's Mayfair home at 30 Charles Street (now part of the Saudi Embassy) that Jean Rhys lost her virginity. Penniless, and with no home of her own, she had little option but to become a fond and generous man's kept mistress. ("He had money. I had none," she would bluntly explain, many years later, in *Smile Please*.) Settled by her lover into pleasant lodgings close to Primrose Hill, a lavish dress allowance enabled Lancey's pretty "kitten"—as he liked to call her—to dress in style for elegant suppers out. "I was for sleeping with—not for talking to," Julia Martin dryly remarks of her past affair with Neil James; Rhys herself remembered Lancey asking with genuine interest about her early life in the West Indies and (quite uselessly) attempting to act as her financial advisor. Bewitched by his courtesy and kindness ("He was like all the men in all the books I had ever read about London," she recollected in *Smile Please*[2]), Rhys saw nothing humiliating about the fact that she was never allowed to spend a night at Lancey's bachelor home, or to visit Mount Clare. "I was never envious," she would write with touching defensiveness in her memoir. "It was right, I felt."[3]

Voyage in the Dark offered readers a carefully misleading account of its author's first encounter with Lancey. Nevertheless, discreet though Rhys would always try to be for the sake of a shy, proud man to whom she remained enduringly attached, fictionalised accounts of actual events do appear within *Voyage*. It's here that we read of a romantic weekend for four spent at a hotel in Wiltshire's glorious Savernake Forest; remembering that escapade with Lancey and two friends (the tall green trees had reminded her of Dominica), the older Rhys would often reminisce to friends about the beauty of Savernake's glades and valleys.

Rhys's personal memories of the jaunt may have been pleasant. She kept until the end of her life a long, high-necked and clinging flower-printed dress that is fondly identified in *Voyage* as Anna Morgan's chosen costume for her first evening at the hotel. But the novel also makes the hotel at Savernake the place in which Walter Jeffries casually reveals that he and his young cousin Vincent will shortly be off to New York on a business trip. Vincent, rather than Walter, brutally advises a shocked Anna to start making plans for a life alone. "The new show at Daly's," he tells her in a slyly hidden authorial reference to the very theatre where Lancey had first seen Rhys dancing in *The Count of Luxembourg*. "You ought to be able to warble like what's her name after all those singing lessons."[4]

Whether or not the actual break-up began during a Wiltshire weekend, there's no doubt that Rhys based her portrait of Vincent on the only member of Lancey's family who knew about his affair. Julian Martin Smith, Lancey's handsome eighteen-year-old cousin and favourite protégé, was perceived by Rhys as her nemesis. Lancey, she would always persuade herself, had truly loved her. As the product of a rigidly conservative colonial world, she may for a time have aspired no higher than marriage to her wealthy and generous protector; a man of whose grand family home she had not been permitted so much as a glimpse. She would always believe that it was Julian—the look in Vincent's eyes is compared by a dispirited Anna Morgan to "a high, smooth, unclimbable wall. No communication possible"—who had destroyed their love affair.

Julian Martin Smith, Lancey's cousin and protégé. Rhys put the young stockbroker in *Voyage in the Dark* as Vincent. *(Used with permission of the Smith family)*

While it's unlikely that Lancelot Hugh Smith ever considered marrying Rhys—he remained a bachelor until his death—it's clear that he did recruit Julian Martin Smith as his broker and spokesman during the delicate process of disentanglement. Writing *Smile Please* decades after both Lancey and his young cousin were dead, Rhys described the condescending visits that Julian (whom she identified in print, but only by his first name) had made as Lancey's proxy. The sense of barely suppressed rage is almost palpable in Rhys's description of Julian's demanding the return of her lover's letters and smoothly producing in exchange the cash for an abortion (described in her memoir as "an illegal operation") to which she had already declared her opposition.

The rules of severance had always been explicit. When a Marylebone landlady ordered Miss Ella Gray to leave the elegant suite of rooms that Lancey had recently taken on her behalf—abortions were bad for business—Rhys obediently posted her forwarding address, not to the baby's father, but to Julian Martin Smith (who thoughtfully arranged a quiet seaside holiday at Ramsgate as a reward for her compliance). When a letter arrived to explain that she could rely upon a monthly stipend, a cheque payable via a solicitor's office, Lancey presented it as a joint decision, taken by Julian and himself. " 'We thought that perhaps this was the best way . . . (I thought: *'we*—yes, I thought so.')"[5] Explaining to readers of her memoir why she had accepted the pay-

off, the elderly Rhys justified the continued allowance as a symbolic
bond: "The man still cared what became of me and the bond was still
there."[6] Tellingly, when she came to write *After Leaving Mr Mackenzie*,
Jean Rhys named the least empathetic of her female protagonists "Julia
Martin." Reading his former girlfriend's novel, as we can confidently
assume that he did, Lancey must have winced at the memories revived
by her bold hijacking of his adored young cousin's name.[*]

"I KNOW HOW ghastly it is to be stranded when you're young," Rhys
would write to a woman friend in 1950.[7] In *Smile Please*, Rhys described
herself as withdrawing from the world during the autumn weeks that
followed her abortion and seaside recuperation. She went for long, solitary walks, neglected her appearance and slept for fifteen hours at a
time. Solitude and sleep; sleep and solitude. "I am talking," Rhys wrote
in the section of her memoir called "Christmas Day," "about sadness."
Anna, in *Voyage*, falls swiftly into prostitution after Walter Jeffries
rejects her final, desperate overture. All Rhys herself could remember
having done during those bleak months was to earn some money as a
movie extra: girls deemed to be pretty were always welcome for crowd
scenes in the early years of film-making.

Lancey, who still took his desolate girlfriend out to an occasional
supper, at which he talked and she cried, sent along a miniature star-
crowned tree for his Christmas gift at the end of the affair, laden with
prettily wrapped trinkets and accompanied by an unsigned card. The
reminder of happier times brought no comfort; after donating it to the
Children's Hospital on Great Ormond Street, Rhys sat alone in her
room, pondering whether life was still worth living. Later, Jean Rhys
would claim that she only once made a serious attempt to kill herself,
by slitting her wrists in a warm bath. On this earlier occasion, accord-

---

[*] Lancey's interest in the development of his former girlfriend's career as a writer
appears in two notes that Rhys preserved from 1927.

ing to *Smile Please*, one of the unhappy young woman's film-extra girl-friends, an artist's model, turned up in time to stop her jumping out of a window and to suggest—over a shared bottle of gin—the possibility of making a new start. Why stay in and mope when she could be out having fun in rackety, sociable Chelsea?

Not every detail of Jean Rhys's early life made its way into either her memoir or her fiction. *Voyage in the Dark* invites us to see her as having followed Anna Morgan's tragic course, sliding down the ladder of despair—from being Walter Jeffries' mistress, to a job as a hopelessly inept manicurist, before Anna finally sleepwalks into prostitution. *Smile Please*, in contrast, moves straight from the sad little episode on Christmas Day 1911 to Rhys's discovery of herself as a writer, while leading a solitary life in Chelsea. Neither version offers an accurate portrait.

It seems to have been around the beginning of 1912 that an enterprising Rhys tried her hand at manufacturing cold cream in her lodgings, before she took a job selling the pretty hats made by a deft-fingered girlfriend (identified only as Dawn). According to the story told by Rhys to her daughter almost forty years later, Dawn dispensed with her assistance after finding that her partner, instead of pushing the sale of their most expensive hats, was sweetly encouraging clients to buy only what they could easily afford.[8]

More significant, and more than a little puzzling, is the absence from any of Rhys's accounts of the fascinatingly odd man who befriended her during the year 1912. His memorable name was Arthur Fox Strangways.

Born in 1859, "Foxie," as a sensitive and intensely musical man was always known to his friends, was old enough to have been Rhys's father, and it was as a paternal figure that Rhys adored him. A respected public-school teacher at Wellington during the first half of his life, Fox Strangways retired early, after suffering a breakdown. Following a year in India, during which he became close to the Bengal-born poet Rabindranath Tagore, he returned to London late in 1911 and settled into a bachelor flat on King's Bench Walk in the Temple, just north of Blackfriars Bridge. When Rhys met him in 1912, Strangways had become a respected music critic, writing both for the *Musical Times* and the *Observer*, while acting as Tagore's representative in London.

Rhys's first biographer Carole Angier has speculated that the nymph-like "Ella" became Fox Strangways' mistress.[9] More plausibly, at a time when Rhys was still bruised and miserable about the end of her affair with Lancey, this touchingly old-fashioned Englishman offered the reassurance of a cultured and unthreatening friendship.

Questioned a little patronisingly in later years about her fondness for popular songs, Rhys murmured that she was "not quite indifferent to better things."[10] Stravinsky and Nijinsky were electrifying London audiences during the prewar years; Rhys's enduringly romantic taste suggests that Strangways took his young friend to hear the less revolutionary music that was usually on offer at the drab but acoustically superb Queen's Hall in Langham Place, first home of the Proms. As a man who counted George Moore among his close friends, "Foxie" may also have introduced an avid bookworm to one singularly bleak novel for which Rhys formed an abiding passion. Published in 1894, Moore's *Esther Waters* was years ahead of its time, with its story of a hard-working woman who bravely decides to keep her baby after an accidental pregnancy. Was Rhys's initial admiration for Esther connected to her own regretted abortion, or was it Esther's quiet courage which she always found so sustaining? In her old age, Rhys told friends that she could no longer recall how many times she had reread Moore's book.

DIANA ATHILL, THE editor whose difficult task was to chivvy along the memoir that Jean Rhys produced with painful slowness in her final years, thought the chapter of *Smile Please* set on the fringes of Chelsea and titled "World's End and a Beginning" was a triumph. So it is, if we are seeking only to know when Rhys felt herself ready to become a writer.

It was on the very first day that she moved into lodgings in Fulham, according to *Smile Please*, that Jean Rhys (still Ella to her London friends) set off to explore the neighbourhood and find a plant to brighten the work table in her room. Walking into a stationer's shop on the nearby King's Road, she impulsively purchased some thick exercise books, a handful of brightly coloured pens and nibs ("the sort I liked") and took them home. Following her habitual modest supper of bread, cheese and a glass of milk, Rhys felt a curious tingling in her fingers. "I remembered everything that happened to me in the last year and a half. I remembered what he'd said, what I'd felt. I wrote on late into the night . . ." After filling almost four exercise books, she set down a single, striking sentence that would later surface in the voice of Anna Morgan: "Oh God, I'm only twenty and I'll have to go on living and living and living."[11] Rhys herself, at the opening of 1913, was twenty-two.

There is no reason to doubt that this vividly described experience was largely true, as was the unanticipated sense of emotional release. (Rhys recalled that the irate lodger downstairs threatened to hand in his notice because of the sobs and laughs and pacing feet as she herself scribbled on late into the night, unconscious of the passing days.) But this discovery of a vocation was not all that occurred during Ella's stay in Chelsea. A glimpse of her lively social existence there emerges from the unpublished memoir written by the artist Adrian Allinson (and lodged at the McFarlin Library, together with Rhys's archive). In "A Painter's Pilgrimage," Allinson describes how he met "Ella, a fair young Englishwoman born in the West Indies" at a Chelsea studio party, and how affected he immediately felt by her "tender loveliness."

Chelsea, just before the outbreak of war, offered a headily adventurous experience to a young, single woman. The annual Chelsea Arts Ball, raising funds for artists' charities, was a famously riotous affair. Women were welcome at the Arts Club on Old Church Street, while a mass of new cinemas had recently opened, including two "Electric Theatres" and a "Palace of Varieties" on the King's Road. One of Allinson's fellow artists shot his young mistress in the Chelsea room they shared.

Life in Chelsea was unpredictable. Fresh from Adelaide and comfortably supported by a family allowance, Stella Bowen was startled to find herself living in a Chelsea flat where a late partygoer might casually scramble through her bedroom window at 3 a.m., having missed a late train to the suburbs. Stella soon settled in, teaching a nimble-footed Ezra Pound new dance steps and attending his weekly dinner club in Soho, while taking occasional lessons from Walter Sickert at the Westminster School of Art, chief rival to the Slade.[12] Nina Hamnett, renting her first Chelsea studio in 1911 when she was just twenty-one, would fondly recall a young Mark Gertler bringing to tea a golden-thatched Dora Carrington, wearing one red shoe and one blue; it felt, Hamnett reminisced, "as if I had invited a god and goddess . . . I preserved Gertler's tea-cup intact and unwashed on the mantlepiece."[13] A little later, Nina fell in love with Henri Gaudier-Brzeska—and wept after discovering that the fierce young woman who shared the French sculptor's penurious life in a Fulham Road studio was not his sister, but his mistress.

Sickert; Yeats; Epstein; Pound; Wyndham Lewis and even the theatrically creepy Aleister Crowley; these are the names that ripple through the pages of Hamnett and Bowen's recollections of prewar life in Chelsea and Fitzrovia (as the most consciously artistic quarter of Bloomsbury became known). This was the remarkable world into which Jean Rhys ventured in 1913. Adrian Allinson's recollection of meeting her at a studio party in Chelsea suggests that a shy and uncommonly beautiful young woman soon ceased to be an outsider.

Generous though Hugh Smith's monthly allowance proved to be, extra funds could always be raised by modelling for artists. Unfazed by posing nude for a "classical" work if no strings were attached, Rhys gladly agreed to model for the elderly and eminently respectable Sir Edward Poynter. Later, Rhys drew upon personal memories of her modelling work for the immensely successful and sexually unscrupulous Sir William Orpen when she wrote (in an early, unpublished work called "Suzy Tells" and then, "Triple Sec") about a flirtatious society artist whom she named "Tommie." After Tommie ardently embraces his alluring new model in a taxi, the narrator asks for money. Relieved by the modesty of the requested sum, Tommie obliges—and promptly resumes the attack. Ordered to stop, he withdraws. "I know now that I have a certain power," the narrator remarks, "and yet, how mean, how mean."

Was Rhys conveying outrage at an attempted rape in this early and unpublished work of fiction? With Jean Rhys—who would one day describe Mr. Howard as having recognised and responded to the secret fantasies of an adolescent girl's wicked self, in the Botanical Gardens of Roseau—it's impossible ever to be certain precisely where the blame is being laid.

5

London in Wartime (1913–19)

"I'm hanged if I didn't fall in love with her."

— Adrian Allinson, "A Painter's Pilgrimage"[1]

"I pulled a chair up to the table, opened an exercise book, and wrote: *This is my Diary*. But it wasn't a diary . . ."

— Jean Rhys, "World's End and a Beginning," *Smile Please*

NO EARLIER DRAFTS or manuscripts survive to contradict Jean Rhys's assertion in *Smile Please* that she first began writing seriously during her prewar life in Chelsea. Although she doesn't say what happened next, it is clear that these early writings continued through the war and that they were later cobbled together as the episodic, unpublished work named "Triple Sec" by Rhys's first literary patron after the dry, crystal-clear and unexpectedly potent French liqueur.

"Triple Sec," previously dubbed "Suzy Tells" by another of Rhys's literary mentors, is narrated by a young woman. While the tough but vulnerable Suzy speaks for her creator, certain true-life experiences that she undergoes have been embellished and rearranged to produce a fictitious outcome. "Triple Sec" cannot be treated as pure autobiography, but it does offer some helpful clues about Rhys's personal life before and during the war.

THE YEAR 1913 had been a testing time for Rhys, crushed by the sense, aged twenty-three, that she had failed in both her stage career, and in love. In April 1914, however, her life grew brighter after a clever and party-loving political journalist called Alan Bott (he later helped to create the Folio Society and Pan Books) enrolled his new friend as member of a private nightclub that had recently opened in Soho.

The Crabtree was founded as a congenial meeting place for his friends by the Welsh painter and draughtsman Augustus John, then at the height of his fame, and financed by John's affable and literary-minded patron, Lord Howard de Walden. Three rickety flights of stairs up from a narrow doorway on Greek Street, the little club was cheerily shabby. Stella Bowen, disapproving of the Crabtree's lack of formality (women wearing trousers, worryingly unmanly men and "*nobody* in evening dress!"), was equally unimpressed by its decor: "Beer marks on plain deal tables, wooden benches, and a small platform on which a moonfaced youth made music for a bevy of gyratory couples."[2] Informal boxing matches were sometimes held here; two good-looking singers of the time, Betty May and Lilliane Shelley, offered impromptu cabaret turns. On one occasion, a baffled Stella Bowen heard the futurist poet Marinetti orating one of his "zoom-bang" songs in Italian at the Crabtree; on another, one of the club's two rival crooners performed an early form of pole-dance by shinning up the wobbly fruit-topped post from which the club derived its name.

The Crabtree's scruffy furnishings were unimportant. Paul Nash, Henri Gaudier Brzeska, Wyndham Lewis, Nina Hamnett, Mark Gertler, Jacob Epstein, Marie Beerbohm, Henry Lamb, Compton Mackenzie: the list of its members reads like a guide to prewar bohemia. A crucial reason for the club's appeal to this youthful group was that basic food and hard liquor were cheap (an honesty box was provided by the door) and members could loiter until dawn—the Crabtree didn't even open its doors until midnight—to dance or to lounge and chat. In *After Leaving Mr Mackenzie*, Julia Martin and George Horsfield visit a club clearly based on the Crabtree. Julia settles in straight away and starts dancing with a stranger; sober George looks on, feeling awkwardly out of place.

Clubs were starting up all over London in an era when writers regularly lunched at Soho's accommodating Eiffel Tower (its sparsely furnished bedrooms were in great demand), while a skittish young Nina Hamnett swigged iced crème de menthe beneath the blind stare of the Café Royal's gilded caryatids. August Strindberg's widow presided over "The Cave of the Golden Calf" in a lavishly decorated basement near Piccadilly Circus, until it went bankrupt in 1914; Jean Rhys preferred the noisy little rooms high above Greek Street. I like to imagine seductive Ella whirling around the floor with my grandfather, the generous, art-loving peer whose deep pockets helped to keep that jolly little club afloat. More certainly, it was during an early visit to the Crabtree that the "tender loveliness" (Adrian Allinson's striking words) of Jean Rhys's appearance caught the eye of one of Alan Bott's fellow journalists.

Maxwell Hayes Macartney, an artist's son and the brother of a political historian, had trained as a lawyer, before switching professions to become a specialist on European affairs at *The Times*, where he worked alongside Bott. Ten years older than Rhys, Macartney was instantly smitten by the delicate features and wistful expression of a young woman who could imaginably have been painted by Botticelli. It was during a teatime feast in Macartney's rooms, where hot buttered toast and sponge cake were appreciatively consumed by a hungry visitor, that Rhys received an impulsive proposal of marriage. Acting from honour or reluctance, she discouraged her host with lurid tales of her life on stage and in Chelsea.* Despite his subsequent hesitation about setting a precise wedding date, Macartney persisted. An agreement to marry was reached, but theirs—so Rhys would nonchalantly comment in *Smile Please* (she never identified either Macartney or Hugh Smith by name)—would remain an "on-and-off" engagement.

Rhys was a little more forthcoming about Macartney (lightly disguised as "Ronald") in "Triple Sec." There, while describing the flat where she visits "Ronald" in the Temple, Rhys fused it with the

---

* "Triple Sec" includes a long confession by Suzy of her unworthiness to become "Ronald's" wife.

nearby home of Arthur "Foxie" Strangways. Located in an area popular with lawyers and conveniently close to Fleet Street for journalists, Macartney's Temple rooms were crammed with books, while signed photographs and informal sketches of Chesterton and Shaw hinted at illustrious friendships. Like the old-fashioned "Foxie," Macartney dressed in tweeds and washed his lean limbs in a tin hip-bath. Unlike Fox Strangways, he also played golf and expected to be cheered on by his sports-averse fiancée.

In July 1914, shortly after meeting her new beau, Miss Ella Gray returned to the stage, playing one of the besieged inhabitants of Renaissance Pisa in Maurice Maeterlinck's scandalous *Monna Vanna* (first performed in 1902). The source of outrage—and full houses—was a scene in which the playwright required Monna Vanna (played by a voluptuous Constance Collier in an all-concealing cloak) to appear naked onstage. A ban on evening performances—in case the mere thought of Collier's body beneath her strategic mantle might incite turmoil in the stalls of the Queen's Theatre—enabled Rhys to continue dancing and drinking long after midnight at the Crabtree. She was heading for the club with her fiancé on the night when they spotted, in Leicester Square, a news-stand poster announcing the assassination of an Austrian archduke at Sarajevo. The consequences of that disastrous event would sink in gradually, less when Macartney went out to France in November as a war correspondent ("Suzy" remembered sadly packing her fiancé's favourite tweed suit), than when Rhys's beloved Crabtree closed its doors in December 1914, "for the duration." We don't know if the news reached her, or whether she cared, that Lancey's adored young cousin Julian Martin Smith had been the first volunteer officer to die in action.

THE AGGRESSIVE LOYALTY to Britain and the Empire which Rhys displayed during the First World War suggests that she had always managed to maintain vestigial contact with her family in Dominica. Out in the Antilles, the belligerent jingoism of the white settlers was infectious. Only a few stalwarts of the all-white Dominica Club sailed home to enlist; it came as a shock to the patriotic village youths who signed up to fight for king and country when they found themselves assigned to an all-black West Indian regiment in an army that had promised equality to every creed and colour within its enlisted ranks.*

In London, Rhys felt strongly enough about the war to declare that any man who failed to fight for England was a coward. Her views helped to influence Macartney's courageous exchange of his role as one of the war's most respected correspondents—like the fictitious "Suzy," Rhys conscientiously followed her lover's bulletins in *The Times*—for that of a middle-aged soldier at the front.

Macartney's flat felt cosily safe from the German zeppelins which began to launch raids on London in 1915. (Nina Hamnett, who once narrowly escaped stepping aboard a bus that was promptly blown to bits by a zeppelin bomb, later recalled a night when she tiptoed ankle-deep through shattered glass along the Strand to keep a date at the Café Royal.3) Perhaps Jean grew guilty about lolling among her fiancé's volumes of Chesterton and Wells while, outside the flat's rattling Georgian windows, the city was besieged. Still aged only twenty-four, she volunteered to work long daily shifts at an army canteen that had been set up at Euston Station, where soldiers travelling down from Scotland and the north made their connection to Charing Cross for the last leg of their journey to the Channel ports.

Lightly though Rhys dismissed her war work in *Smile Please*, her self-imposed assignment was a tough one. Organised by a couple of formidable army wives, the Euston canteen's soberly dressed female staff (gloves and neat black hats were mandatory) committed themselves to frying up plates of hearty food and offering encouragement to their soldier clients. By early 1915, at least 600 men were being shunted

---

*   Most of the young islanders who enlisted were served up as cannon fodder. Dominica's most respected modern historian argues that it was the British Army's segregation of black recruits in the First World War which spawned the island's first move towards independence in the early 1930s (Dr. Lennox Honychurch to author, 15 February 2019).

through the station every day; on Platform 12, eighteen camp beds were kept ready for injured and disabled soldiers returning home. Anybody working at the canteen as Rhys did, for nine hours a day, over a period of almost two years, became a witness to the horrors of war.

———————

MACARTNEY'S LONG ABSENCES in France enabled Jean to take a relaxed view of what might be expected of herself as a deserted fiancée, living under his roof. In the summer of 1915, she gladly accepted an invitation from the lovesick Adrian Allinson to come and spend a few off-duty weeks at a cottage in the Vale of Evesham, deep in the bucolic Gloucestershire countryside and close to Crickley Hill. Sweet though Allinson's personality was, and greatly though she admired the earnest young man's uncompromisingly realistic paintings (he had helped to found the London Group, after studying at the Slade alongside Gertler and Stanley Spencer and spending two years on the Continent), Rhys felt no sexual spark. It was the prospect of free hospitality and fresh country air which made Allinson's suggestion irresistible, together with the news that their companion at the cottage would be Philip Heseltine. She may not have expected a brilliant young man, better known for his poetry than his music at that stage of his life, to be accompanied by his beautiful girlfriend, an artist's model called Minnie Channing.

Tall, fair and athletic, with exceptionally blue eyes and a disturbing reputation for physical violence, Philip Heseltine came from a privileged background of wealth, as did Allinson, with whom he had gone on several mountaineering expeditions during their prewar months on the Continent. Rhys was uncertain what to make of him, but the forcefulness of Heseltine's personality made him impossible to ignore. On one well-attested occasion, after dinner, Heseltine suddenly stripped off his clothes, jumped onto his motorbike and roared off, stark naked, up a moonlit Crickley Hill. In the moments when he wasn't squabbling with Minnie (known as "Puma" for her fierce temper), he might either whistle plaintively as a curlew, or serenade his housemates with some melody from Frederick Delius, a British-born composer with a

The charismatic young composer Philip Heseltine, who later took the name Peter Warlock, photographed at the country cottage which he shared with Rhys and two friends in the summer of 1915.

German mother, whose reputation was unjustly clouded by the war. Heseltine worshipped Delius, whom he had first met personally during his schooldays at Eton, and who treated him as a pet protégé. While Allinson was earning a living in wartime by designing sets for Sir Thomas Beecham's opera company and doing sketches for the *Daily Express*, Heseltine had taken a five-month job in 1915 as a music critic for the warmongering *Daily Mail*, largely in order to promote the temporarily banned compositions of his hero.

The best-known account of what happened during Rhys's stay at the Gloucestershire cottage would eventually be published in 1960, in a story which had passed through many stages of careful revision. "Till September Petronella" mixes fact with fiction as bewilderingly as does the account of this same country holiday that Rhys had earlier described in the unpublished "Triple Sec." Only by comparing both of these versions of events with a third—the more artless account offered

in Adrian Allinson's unpublished memoir, "A Painter's Pilgrimage"—
can we glimpse what actually took place at the crowded cottage.

"A Painter's Pilgrimage" records a memorably unsatisfactory episode in Allinson's life from the point of view of a half-German artist, a
sensitive and rather brilliant young man who shared his friend Heseltine's passionate hatred of war. Viewed with hindsight by Allinson, the
holiday was doomed from the start. Heseltine and Minnie Channing
formed an instant bond of dislike for Adrian's vociferously bellicose
girlfriend; urged to pack her bags and take her beastly opinions back
to London, "Ella" displayed what Allinson would describe as "a streak
of hard determination oddly at variance with her outer frailty." When
Philip and Minnie said they couldn't even bear to eat in her presence,
his guest calmly retreated to her bedroom, where she seemed content
to spend hours rubbing creams into her face, languidly combing her
hair and—as always when left on her own—reading. The more that the
couple attacked her, the more firmly Ella withdrew. When Allinson,
still a virgin at 24, sought sexual favours in return for his own resolute
loyalty, Ella coolly announced that she was tired—and closed her door.

"Triple Sec" is less trustworthy than "A Painter's Pilgrimage." The
relationship with Allinson is coyly presented here in the format of "a
semi demi love affair"; unlike Allinson's Ella, Rhys's "Suzy" walks out
on her squabbling housemates. On the contentious issue of war, however, "Triple Sec" proves enlightening. Confident of the rightness of
her views, Suzy becomes forthright and even rude. "Why aren't you at
the war anyway?" she demands; a white-faced Forrester (unmistakably
based upon Heseltine) leaves the room at once. Here, there is no doubt
that Suzy's own aggression was the cause for the "instantaneous and
violent" hostility to which she (like Rhys) has been exposed.

"Triple Sec" provided the embryo for one of Rhys's finest stories.
Parts of "Till September Petronella" are fictitious. Allinson's offended
girlfriend did not flee the cottage with the help of a sympathetic "Marston" (the name Rhys eventually picked for the Allinson figure in her
published story). Philip Heseltine ("Julian Oakes" in "Till Septem-

ber Petronella") may not have mocked Rhys's voice as "a female pipe," but certain of Julian's cruel remarks do sound authentic: the vicious-tongued Heseltine was entirely capable of having called Allinson's jingoistic girlfriend "a female spider" and even "a ghastly cross between a barmaid and a chorus girl." In Rhys's version of the past, Julian Oakes's hatred is fuelled by the suspicion that Petronella Gray is only interested in his pal (described here by Rhys as one of England's finest young artists) because of Marston's wealth. While it's beyond proof that Heseltine expressed such a cynical view at the Crickley cottage, it's certainly not beyond belief.

Rhys admired Heseltine's musical gift and—perhaps—his devotion to Delius. "He *is* the great Julian," she allows Marston to say in defence of his brilliant but volatile friend. "He's going to be very important, so far as an English musician can be important." But those words were written long after Heseltine, having renamed himself Peter Warlock in mocking acknowledgement of his interest in diabolism, had taken his life by gassing himself in 1930, aged only thirty-six. While Rhys's story recognises Heseltine's musical artistry, it also honourably records her absolute failure to please or impress him during the Crickley cottage holiday.

Returning to London from a disquieting month in the country, Rhys gladly resumed her perch in Macartney's flat during his own continued absence at the front. A restful home richly supplied with books offered a welcome refuge after her long days at the Euston station canteen. Or perhaps not: Julia, in *After Leaving Mr Mackenzie*, alludes to "the mad things one did" during the war. If Rhys, too, did "mad things," she kept them to herself.

ASSIGNING DATES TO Rhys's wartime life is difficult. Circumstantial evidence suggests that it was after the closure of the canteen in 1917 that "Ella Gray" contacted Blackmore's Agency once again, hoping for work in the surprisingly active world of wartime theatre. Soon after this, Rhys fell ill. Details are scant. "Triple Sec" refers only to "a slight operation," but it was serious enough to require three weeks at a London nursing home (for which Lancey Hugh Smith, still paying Rhys a regular allowance, may have footed the bill), followed by a short recuperative holiday in the country.

Despite the fact that "Triple Sec" expressed gratitude to the sister of Maxwell Macartney for looking after her during this second, convalescent stage, it was at this vulnerable time that Rhys's fiancé broke off their engagement. "Suzy" describes "Ronald's" haggard appearance when he returned on leave. Macartney may have been shellshocked: the effect of exchanging work as a prominent war correspondent for life under fire must have been devastating to a man in his mid-thirties. Accused of bringing "numerous men friends" back to her fiancé's flat, Suzy is brusquely ordered to get out. (So far as is known, Rhys herself never saw Macartney again.) In "Triple Sec," a narcissistic Suzy describes the impact on her own fragile sensibility. "I'm one of the weak ones and I'll always be hurt," she states, and—a few lines later: "Lay thinking of nothing at all—just tired. Self confidence blown out like a candle."

Rhys herself always responded well in a crisis. While still recovering from her "slight operation," she moved into cheap lodgings in Bloomsbury before making a final attempt to relaunch her stalled stage career. Suzy's dance teacher (Madame Zara) is sufficiently pleased by her pupil's progress to predict a bright future in "acrobatic" ballet (a form of near-nude but tastefully static classical dancing not far removed from Emma Hamilton's notorious "attitudes"). Rhys herself was still taking ballet lessons when she found more conventional work as a sifter of war-related correspondence at the newly founded Ministry of Pensions.

How did an untrained former chorus girl obtain such a job? The answer probably lies with the well-connected Lancey Hugh Smith. Operating out of the Royal Hospital in Chelsea, the government's brand-new ministry had been put in charge of organising the payment of pensions to members of families affected by the war. More employees were urgently required; Rhys was a well-dressed and softly spoken young woman who may have arrived carrying a personal recommenda-

tion from the influential Mr. Hugh Smith. She made a welcome addition to the busy team of sixty women whose challenging daily task it
was to read and assess the sackfuls of heartrending appeals submitted
by maimed soldiers and destitute widows.

The work was both hard and bleak. Britain's new coalition government favoured a more egalitarian approach, but the system of which
Rhys now gained first-hand experience still consistently favoured the
privileged above the deserving. The size of a widow's pension was dictated by her husband's rank, as were the education grants grudgingly
doled out to his sons. In the navy, only the widow of an admiral was
eligible for a government handout. In the army, a soldier's death from
disease was shockingly and regularly blamed on personal "negligence":
no question of a pension for *his* widow. The family of a soldier released
because of a war injury qualified for a pension only after—and if—he
died within seven years of his resignation.[4]

Such disillusioning daily employment, combined with the shabby
way she felt she had been treated by Lancey and Macartney, ended
Rhys's colonial fantasy of an innocent England. She didn't move to a
cheap attic room in Torrington Square for safety—a zeppelin bomb
destroyed lives in neighbouring Endell Street—but because the double-
fronted Bloomsbury lodging house was packed with refugees from
abroad; aliens, like herself. The landlady ran a tight ship; rebuked (once
again) for an excessive use of the household's hot water supply for her
baths, a mortified Ella was defended by a friendly fellow lodger.

Rhys would write with unusual tenderness in the English section of
Smile Please about her chivalrous supporter. Camille (the only name by
which we know him) was a university-educated émigré from Bruges.
Little jokes about robbing the bank for which he worked as a cashier
in order to fund their elopement were light-hearted banter between
friends; Rhys knew how devoted the calm, bespectacled Belgian was
to the elderly wife who co-hosted their weekly "nursery teas," held
in a welcoming room filled with interesting people. Camille, in his
spare time, was writing a book about the Noh theatre of Japan. One
guest was an Icelandic poet; another was a dark, tousle-haired and fine-

featured young man whom Camille introduced as Jean Lenglet (pronounced "Leng-lett").

Camille identified his twenty-eight-year-old friend as Belgian; Lenglet, a man of mystery from the very start, described himself as Franco-Dutch. Asked out to lunch, Ella decided that this intriguingly reticent man with sensitive hands was both kind—he rebuked her for using the chorus girl's cheap trick of drawing attention to a plainer woman in order to highlight her own attractiveness—and generous: years later, Rhys would fondly recall Lenglet's purchase of an expensive box of her favourite Egyptian cigarettes, a large bottle of exotic scent and—at her own special request—a glass pot of kohl with which to outline her immense blue eyes. Escorted back to Torrington Square, or possibly to a dance lesson with Madame Zara (he was sceptical about Ella's stage future), she was baffled when Lenglet simply shook her hand and left. Such sedate behaviour was unusual in wartime London. Lenglet's reticence greatly increased his allure.

Smile Please jumps straight from that memorable first date to Lenglet's proposal of marriage. Between times, Camille, Lenglet and Rhys often spent their evenings drinking at the Café Royal. Here, the seemingly wealthy Lenglet talked about himself, but only on prescribed topics. He captivated francophile Ella with stories of running away from his strict Jesuit school to become a teenage *chansonnier* in Montmartre; he may have mentioned penning the occasional article about Montmartre for the Paris-based *New York Herald Tribune*. But his story of leaving a family home in the Netherlands in order to join the French Foreign Legion failed to disclose that he had served for just one month. No explanation was offered for his presence in England; no mention was made of the second wife, Marie Pollart—he had married her predecessor in Antwerp in order to legitimise a baby son—with whom Lenglet lived in Paris until 1913, while sharing rooms with her widowed mother.

At the end of 1917, the landlady of Torrington Square invited her lodgers to a fancy-dress party. A scraggy roasted fowl was served as a suppertime treat. ("Don't laugh," kind Camille whispered to Ella as she began to giggle: "she's awfully proud of having got that chicken."⁵) The star of the party was one Simone David, a young Frenchwoman whose large bedroom on the first floor was filled with pretty clothes and dashing hats.* Perhaps it was Simone who loaned her admiring friend the black-and-white Pierrette costume that Rhys remembered having worn that momentous night.

In her memoir, Rhys would relate the evening's events in fairy-tale style. Leading her outside—where, naturally, a huge full moon waited to beam approval—Lenglet took Ella by the hand and asked her to marry him. Only because of her—he now explained—had he courted danger by remaining in London. He didn't say why he was in peril, only that he must leave the country the following morning. Later, when the war was over, he would send word for Ella to join him in his beloved Paris. Could she wait? "It came to me in a flash that here it was, what I had been waiting for, for so long. Now I could see escape." His gentle kiss seemed to promise an enchanted Rhys that she would be forever cherished by this romantic man. Her acceptance was unhesitating.⁶ Fuelled by fantasies of adventure and escape, she was impatient for her summons to come.

Not everybody shared the newly abandoned Ella's sense of excitement. At the boarding house, only Camille was encouraging. A three-page letter arrived from Rhys's younger sister, Brenda, out in Dominica, warning her against such folly.† It is unclear which members of the family actually succeeded in visiting her in London in 1918, or what was said, but it's evident that a mysterious stranger from the Continent was not regarded as a marvellous catch.

The end of the war ushers in a curious silence in Rhys's life. If a young woman disillusioned by her own work at the Ministry of Pen-

---

* The same attractive lodger would feature as "Estelle" in "Till September Petronella."

† In a later draft of "Leaving England" (a chapter in *Smile Please*), Rhys crossed out the word "sister" and bitterly substituted the phrase: "someone who didn't care whether I lived or died."

Previously thought to be of Brenda Rees Williams as a young woman at school in London. Brenda's schooling was cut short by the war. More likely, this dates from the year when Brenda wrote from Dominica to censure her older sister's choice of fiancé. *(McFarlin)*

sions chose to join the three days of celebrations when the Armistice was announced in November 1918, she kept that fact to herself. Early in 1919, however, as steamers began to resume their normal cross-Channel traffic, Rhys agreed to join Lenglet at The Hague. Joyfully, she wrote to tell Lancey to stop paying the solicitor's cheques.

The news that Lancey wanted an urgent meeting caused a flicker of apprehension. Aged twenty-nine, Rhys remained in awe of her first lover; reluctantly, she agreed to meet him for lunch at the smartly conventional Piccadilly Grill.

The cruelly premature death, back in 1914, of Julian Martin Smith had devastated Lancelot Hugh Smith. He himself had gone on to enjoy what is known as a "good" war. His negotiating skills had helped to keep Norway and Sweden free from the grasp of the Central Powers and in 1917, he became one of the very first recipients of a CBE. Politically, as in the world of finance, he was uncommonly well connected. Seen from the perspective of a nervous lunch guest—as Lancey steered a carefully neutral conversation towards her plans—Mr. Hugh Smith appeared to know everybody, and everything.

What emerges from this encounter—and from Lancey's urgent entreaties that "Ella" should break off her relationship with Jean Lenglet—is that this shrewd, conventional and quietly unhappy man remained on some deep level in love with his "kitten," the enchanting young woman he himself had refused to marry, and that Rhys herself had lost none of her reverence for him. Quietly, she listened as Lancelot revealed all that he had ascertained. None of his news was good. Lenglet's passport was invalid (due to the critical loss of his Dutch citizenship when he had impetuously joined the French Foreign Legion). In England, he had apparently been working as a spy for the French. Several of his friends had been arrested; Lenglet had fled from England at the close of 1917 only because the police were after him. By marrying such a man, Rhys would be putting herself at grave risk.

The one thing Lancey seems to have chosen not to convey to his guest—perhaps he was unaware of Lenglet's second marriage—was that her fiancé had a wife still living in Paris; perhaps, he thought enough had already been said. Rhys, to his astonishment, was undeterred. Risks, as she calmly reminded him, were what she most enjoyed. Didn't he remember that she thrived on danger? "He gave a little nod." Only after Lancey had gained her promise to stay in touch—and then kissed her goodbye—did she break down. Rhys wrote in her memoir that she went home in tears.

Danger did excite Rhys; Hugh Smith's warnings were all ignored. In the spring of 1919, too overjoyed at the prospect of escaping from a country she had grown to detest to care about any possible mishaps, Jean Rhys set sail for the Netherlands—and the start of a new European life.

III

A EUROPEAN LIFE
Madame Jean Lenglet

"He [Jean Lenglet] influenced me greatly and for keeps . . . Far more than anyone else ever has done, or will do."

—Jean Rhys to Francis Wyndham, 5 June 1964, *Letters*

6

A Paris Marriage (1919–25)

"From 1917 onwards a gap. He seemed very prosperous when I
met him in London, but now no money—nix. What happened?
He doesn't tell me."

—Jean Rhys, *Good Morning, Midnight*, Part Three (1939)

ON 30 APRIL 1919, in front of two local witnesses at The Hague, Ella
Gwendoline Rees Williams married Willem Johan Marie Lenglet ("of
no fixed profession"). Lenglet saw no need to explain to his bride why
the ceremony needed to be conducted outside France—where Rhys's
bridegroom remained the legal husband of the abandoned and presumably uncontacted Marie Pollart.

Knowing only that she had married a man who loved poetry, sang
charmingly and with whom life always felt exciting, Jean Rhys was
happy in the five months that she spent living with Lenglet in the
pretty old town of The Hague. She kept the photographs that prove
it; little black-and-white images showing the Lenglets larking about
on Scheveningen Beach, together with a burly male friend. One snap
shows a demure Rhys kneeling down in a neatly pleated skirt as she
waits for Lenglet to place an imaginary crown on her head; in another,
the couple pretend to be having a fight. They both look marvellously
carefree.[1] Before the Lenglets left for Paris—her longed-for Paris—
Rhys knew that she was pregnant.

The news that her husband's lack of a valid passport meant they

Marked by Jean in her old age as "Austria," these happy snaps more convincingly belong to the Lenglets' honeymoon months at The Hague, when Scheveningen beach was nearby. Their friend is unidentified. *(McFarlin)*

would be entering France illegally came as a shock. In *Good Morning, Midnight*, for which Rhys would draw upon her early memories of The Hague, Sasha Jensen undertakes a similarly illicit journey, curled up like a cat on a third-class luggage rack in order to escape attention. ("I didn't think it would be like this," she sighs.) Recording her own journey in one of her coloured exercise books, Rhys would remember Lenglet's insouciance and her own terror. How could they possibly escape being captured by patrolling guards? As always, her husband had the answer ready: "How? Just by walking over the frontier. By walking along the road between quiet rows of poplar trees at night. A quiet night with the moon up. Walking along until you get past the sentry & finding yourself in Dunkirk in the early morning and so tired so tired . . . And the fear. . . ."[2]

By early September, safely arrived in a Paris that had just liberated itself from the massive encircling stone walls erected in the previous century, the Lenglets had settled into a low-ceilinged fourth-floor hotel room on rue Lamartine, in the pleasant area south of Gare du Nord known—ever since the arrival of the flamboyant Palais Garnier—as Opéra. Today, still sporting an entrance door crowned by reclining nymphs, the Lenglets' first French home has become part of the Hotel des Plumes, although Rhys's name does not yet feature among the famous writers—Verlaine, Rimbaud, Wilde— proudly recorded in its brochure. An old-fashioned spiral staircase leads up to the couple's snug home; beyond the bedroom window, overlooking a nineteenth-century *école de filles*, a hotel guest can still glimpse the narrow iron balcony on which the newlyweds used to drink white wine and smoke Jean's favourite Egyptian cigarettes. The room itself was simply furnished (the largely fictitious *Good Morning, Midnight* provides the lovers with a large bed and a cosy red eiderdown), but it became a happy nest for two people who were very much in love. The Lenglets returned there whenever they could afford the hotel's modest charges.

For Jean Rhys, born on an island where a creolised form of French was in daily use, Paris felt like a homecoming. She loved the pink glow of the long summer days and the subtler menace of the sea-blue dusks when tugboats whistled to each other along the Seine; she instinctively preferred the casual commerce of quiet neighbourhood bars to the noisy self-consciousness of the big brasseries of Montparnasse that were already being taken over by tourists from abroad. Each day, she revelled in her escape from the invisible social traps of London, a chillier, greyer city that had always seemed to Rhys to be intent upon crushing the spirit of a sensitive outsider.

Once, sitting alone in a boulevard cafe, an intrigued Rhys watched a Creole girl—"a lovely, vicious little thing"*—break away from her older, more sedate companions. "*J'en ai marre*" (I'm fed up), the girl shrilled as she whirled herself into a dance. Carelessly, she lifted her skirt: "Obviously the red dress was her only garment; obviously too, she was exquisite beneath it." Delighting in how the girl strutted around to the song, listening to the seductive and familiar lilt of her island-bred

The balcony of the Lenglets' beloved attic bedroom in Paris on rue Lamartine. (*Author picture*)

---

* "Vicious" is used here in its French sense, *vicieuse*, meaning depraved, amoral (Jean Rhys, "Trio," 1927, in *Collected Short Stories*, Penguin).

voice, Rhys felt a moment of secret affinity. In London, she had struggled to repress her emotions in order to fit in. In Paris, she and this
fiercely independent youngster had found their home.

Rhys's time was not all her own. Shortly after arriving in Paris
with her husband, she answered an advertisement in *Le Figaro* for a
teacher of English to children. Asked to call at 3 rue Rabelais, just off
the Champs Elysées, a mildly awed Rhys was ushered by a uniformed
maid into the presence of a slight, dark-haired and smiling woman.
She introduced herself as Germaine Richelot, unmarried aunt to the
four little cousins with whom Madame Lenglet would be expected to
converse only in English, a language with which the young Bragadirs
and Lemierres were already familiar. Rhys's acceptance was seemingly
taken for granted; invited to stay for a family lunch, she was instantly
welcomed as a friend, not an employee.

Rhys's recollections of her three months working for the family of
Dr. Louis Gustave Richelot, a respected figure in the French medical
world, carry no barb or hint of discontent. Each day, she dined with the
family in a room hung with beautiful tapestries and guarded by one of
the doctor's greatest treasures: a serene wooden Madonna. The mornings were reserved for English conversation with the children; during
the afternoons, Germaine insisted that the pregnant "Ella" should rest
herself in one of the Richelots' favourite rooms, a light-filled studio.
Sometimes, she heard Germaine's musical sister, Yvonne Bragadir,
practising for a concert off in some distant room, or softly chatting
with the young women's third sister, Jeanne Lemierre, the wife of an
eminent physician who lived in a neighbouring street.[3]

Rhys liked and admired all the Richelot family, but it was Germaine
who sought to become her particular friend. Germaine confided that
she was a secret socialist. She longed to get rid of the family Daimler. Covertly, she attended political meetings. During the war, she had
learned terrible things from her voluntary work as a *marraine de guerre*
(a soldier's correspondent and comforter). Germaine talked; Rhys, so
it seems, was usually the listener in the intimate discussions that continued until, eight months into her pregnancy, the long daily trek from

rue Lamartine became too demanding. Gratefully, Rhys promised to stay in touch, and always to consider herself one of the family. Since Dr. Richelot was a gynaecologist, it is to be supposed that this generous family helped to locate (and perhaps even paid the bills for) a hospital suitable for the birth of Rhys's first child.

Born on 29 December 1919, William Owen Lenglet was proudly named—though not baptised, since Jean Lenglet did not believe in baptism—after Rhys's late father, and after Owen, the brother closest in age to herself. Perhaps the attic bedroom at rue Lamartine was draughty; the baby caught pneumonia. On 19 January 1920, the Lenglets' small son died, aged just three weeks, at a convent hospital in rue Denfert-Rochereau.

Later, recalling the tragedy in *Smile Please* with an undertow of self-reproach that no careful reader can ignore, Rhys wrote that she and Lenglet had been patching up a quarrel (about her desire to baptise her sick baby) by drinking champagne with a friend at the *exact* moment that their tiny son had died, alone. "We were all laughing," she wrote. The nuns at the hospital had told her, when she asked, the precise hour of the baby's death. "He was dying, or was already dead, while we were drinking champagne."

Rhys could not forgive herself. She had not been there and she had let her little boy die bereft of proper religious rites. The convent sisters assured her that a baptism had taken place; how could she be certain that they weren't simply consoling her? The baby was hastily buried at Bagnieux, just outside Paris. Privately, Rhys attempted some form of atonement by writing—the date is unknown—a poem which she named "Prayer to the Sun."

A wistful short prayer to a higher power, Rhys's unpublished and affectingly bleak little poem (it consists of fifteen short, unrhymed lines) refers to the loss of a child; a loss for which the poem's author seeks absolution. The speaker is imprisoned within a coffin-like chamber. Poignant allusion is made to the absent consolation of trees, tranquillity, and running rivers. Outside the door, the city continues on its indifferent way; "alien voices" provide a remote background noise.

Beginning and ending with a prayer for deliverance, the poem suggests that Rhys did not recover quickly from the death of her first-born child. She always initially wrote by hand, but this little poem has evidently been revised and typed out in what may have been a final form.[4]

A swift change of location was welcome at such a desolate moment; the Richelots stepped in to help by finding Monsieur Lenglet (whom they had never met) a lucrative position as interpreter for the Japanese section of the Inter-Allied Commission being hastily set up in devastated postwar Vienna. The job required the bereaved father to leave Paris at once; Rhys's distraught state is apparent from the fact that, having found herself another English-speaking job to earn some money before following Lenglet to Vienna, she somehow managed, on her first day of employment, to lose her way from child-friendly Parc Monceau back to her pupil's nearby home on avenue Wagram. That particular stroll takes a pedestrian less than three minutes; Rhys ended by dragging a weeping little boy halfway across Paris before flagging down a taxi to take them home. Refunded the fare by the child's angry mother, Rhys was also sacked on the spot. A week or so later, Germaine waved her sad-faced friend off on the train to Vienna.

THE LENGLETS, PARTLY due to some quiet currency trading of the sort that became common after the war, now grew rich. The citizens of "Red Vienna," so named for its vigorous new postwar policy of social reform, were starving; Rhys, for once, was on the winning side. While the Japanese officers took up residence at Sacher's Hotel, the Lenglets and their friend "André" (Rhys's pseudonym for a romantic young French bachelor regarded as the Inter-Allied Commission's wild card), moved into the Imperial, after lodging with a family of Austrian aristocrats who had lost everything but their grand address on the elegant Favoritenstrasse. You could always tell what a lady Madame de Heuske was, Rhys would confess with self-damning insouciance, from "the faraway look" with which she complied with Madame Lenglet's request for a restorative personal massage of her back and chest.[5] The hypersensitive Rhys was conscious of an implied criticism of herself in the fact that the de Heuskes forbade their daughter Blanca to apply cosmetics to her own fine, transparent skin. Rhys, by contrast, dyed her hair red and paid weekly visits to a beautician. Passers-by, so she would sardonically recall, sometimes compared her to a doll made from the purest white Saxon china ("*la poupée de porcelaine de saxe*").

"Funny how it's slipped away, Vienna," Rhys would ruminate in the marvellous short story "Vienne," which she would write during the next few years. Living in a world that placed a high value on looks, Rhys lingered on the extraordinary beauty of a Viennese dancer coveted by the city's visiting officers, who nevertheless fear that she may be "too expensive."

> A fragile child's body, a fluff of black skirt ending far above the knee. Silver straps over that beautiful back, the wonderful legs in black stockings and little satin shoes, short hair, cheeky little face . . . Ugly humanity, I'd always thought. I saw people differently afterwards—because for once I'd met sheer loveliness with a flame inside . . . Finally she disappeared. Went back to Budapest where afterwards we heard of her . . . Married to a barber. Rum.[6]

For the dancing girls, as Rhys was quick to recognise in a passage that suggests the influence of Colette on her early work, the visiting officers represented only money; a way out of poverty. For Rhys herself, the city offered an escape from the swift and painfully remembered death of her baby son. "Vienne" describes 1920 as a time when "Frances" (or "Francine") feels "cracky with joy in life"; a later and far more elaborately constructed story titled "Temps Perdi" catalogues every one of the ravishing dresses that a newly rich Lenglet had personally selected for his wife's Austrian wardrobe. Ruffled white muslins; rustling organzas; brilliantly coloured prints in cornflower blue and buttercup gold: all that Rhys would omit from that loving retrospective inventory was a magnificent astrakhan coat, purchased to keep out the bitter cold of Viennese winters. The coat from Vienna would haunt the future novels of Jean Rhys as a symbol of bad times (when it went to the pawn shop) and adventurous times (when it cloaked what Rhys once privately and savagely described as her treacherous body's "little trot" along the sidewalk, nostrils flared, picking up the scent of sex in the spring air: "Trust me, trust me, says the body—But trust it, never."[7])

The Inter-Allied Commission remained in Vienna for over a year. On Rhys's thirtieth birthday, the Japanese officers held a splendid dinner in honour of "Ella et Jean," from which she preserved an autographed menu card, one which would earn a brief mention from Julia Martin in Rhys's second novel. The city enchanted Rhys; she was disappointed to learn in 1921 that it was time for the commission to move on to Budapest where—following two waves of terror, during which many Hungarians had fled abroad—a regent, Miklós Horthy, had replaced an exiled king.

Rhys in Vienna, wearing what may have been the famous fur coat which would feature in her novels, where it sometimes acquired an astrakhan collar.
(McFarlin)

As with Vienna, Rhys experienced Budapest from within a cocoon of wealth. Jean Lenglet had profited handsomely from his currency transactions back in Vienna. Rhys kept a photograph of the couple's Austro-Daimler with their uniformed chauffeur chubbily ensconced behind the wheel; it was—did the thought ever cross her mind?—precisely the kind of car that Germaine Richelot despised.

It is likely that the Lenglets were housed in Pest, the livelier of the yoked cities that confront each other across the Danube; certainly, they felt at home in a shadily romantic city crowded with leafy little squares and Parisian-style cafes. The Hungarian women were beautiful, but none were lovelier—as doubtless Lenglet reassured his wife—than her own petted and cherished self. It may have been a desire to flaunt that shapely, well-dressed body before the sceptical Lancey Hugh Smith that caused Ella Lenglet, during the late summer of 1921, to make an impulsive brief visit to London.

The Lenglets at home during their year with the Inter-Allied Commission in Vienna and Budapest.
(McFarlin)

The conjecture that Rhys was seizing an opportunity to parade her successful marriage to a mistrustful former lover is prompted by her choice of hotel. The Berkeley stood within spitting distance of Lancey's own discreet abode in Charles Street: the home in which a conventional man had never permitted his young mistress to spend a single night. It's unlikely that Rhys was invited to do so now. The friendship survived, but their affair was over.

Rhys may also have been summoned to London by a needy family. Following the death of Dr. Rees Williams, his widow had fallen on hard times in Dominica. By the summer of 1921, there were no white Lockharts left on the island. Proud Minna, having grown up in the Great House at Geneva, was living in cramped conditions at 28 Woodgrange Avenue in Acton, west London. Crowded in beneath the same gabled roof were Minna's unmarried twin, their widowed sister, two daughters and a devoted nurse companion called Miss Woolgar. By 1921, Jean Rhys's mother had already become bedridden; by 1927, the year in which she died, a series of strokes had rendered Minna Rees Williams unable to communicate, or even to sign her own name.

The account of an awkward family reunion which Rhys would put into her second novel, *After Leaving Mr Mackenzie*, appears to draw upon and combine two separate visits to Acton, of which this was the first. Grudgingly conscious of her younger sister's stoic heroism, Julia Martin compares Norah Griffiths to a character in an unidentified Russian tragedy, "moving, dark, tranquil, and beautiful, across a background of yellowish snow." Entering the bedroom in which her mother now lies prostrate, every day, all day long, Julia imagines that she has attracted a flicker of recognition: "Then it was like seeing a spark go out and the eyes were again bloodshot, animal eyes."[8]

Rhys's description of Julia Martin's cool reception by her family at Acton may only slightly exaggerate the contempt with which selfish, well-dressed "Gwen" was received by an impoverished family of reluctant exiles. Julia, however, is broke and importunate. Rhys, in 1921, was riding high.

Back in Budapest for her third autumn out of England, Rhys discovered that she was once again pregnant. Shortly afterwards, Lenglet confessed that he had gambled and lost a small fortune embezzled from his superiors in the commission. Now, penniless and terrified of arrest, he was ready to kill himself.

In life, as in the short story "Vienne" that she would soon base upon her continental adventures, Rhys took pride in her cool-headed behaviour in times of crisis.[*] Loyal Lancey would never let his erring kitten down: "My plan of going to London to borrow money was already complete in my head," Rhys makes "Francine" say in "Vienne." "One thinks quickly sometimes." The need to escape from Budapest was imperative—but not before a last celebration. Like Lenglet, perhaps, "Pierre" in "Vienne" orders a last, splendidly ostentatious bedroom dinner of wild duck and two bottles of champagne; touching Pierre's arm as if to draw his newfound bravado into herself, Francine feels her own courage wane. "Horrible to feel that henceforth and for ever one would live with the huge machine of law, order, respectability against one. Horrible to be certain that one was not strong enough to face it."[9]

Preparing to leave London for The Hague, back in the early spring of 1919, Rhys had boasted to prudent Lancey that she revelled in taking risks. Fleeing from Hungary in 1921 in the Daimler driven by their stolid chauffeur, her relish for danger was put to the test. "Vienne" fictionalises a frightening moment in the Lenglets' flight at the Czech border, where Pierre is taken into a patrol hut for interrogation. Emerging at last, he shouts to the chauffeur to get moving. "The car jumped forward like a spurred horse," Rhys recalled in her story. "I imagined for one thrilling moment that we would be fired on . . ." On they flew, towards Prague—and then off again.

> "Faster! Faster! Make the damn thing go!"
> We were doing a hundred . . .
> "Get on! . . . Get on! . . ."

---

[*]   The autobiographical nature of "Vienne" is confirmed by the fact that the protagonists were initially named "Ella" and "Jean."

We slowed up.

"You're drunk, Frances," said Pierre severely.[10]

"Vienne" ends breathlessly in November 1921 outside Prague, on the verge of a last flight to England ("It was: *Nach* London!"). At this point, Rhys's private life vanishes from view until the birth, on 22 May 1922, of Maryvonne Lenglet, in Ukkel, Belgium. By July, following a further request to Lancey for help and a subsequent seaside holiday at Knokke-sur-mer, the vagabonds were safely back in their attic room at the little hotel on rue Lamartine. This was no place in which to bring up a child. Helped by Germaine Richelot, the Lenglets reluctantly arranged for Maryvonne to be cared for at a series of baby shelters or orphanages (each bore some saccharine name like "The Cradle"), from which she could be whisked back home at whim. This seemingly heartless practice was not uncommon. By 1922, two years before he encountered Jean Rhys in Paris, the English novelist Ford Madox Ford had deposited his adored baby daughter by Stella Bowen in a damp little cottage on the edge of the city, where Julie was cared for by a nurse while her unmarried parents resided in Montparnasse.

In the autumn of 1922, a further catastrophe struck the Lenglets when the French police showed up at rue Lamartine, demanding Lenglet's immediate return to his lawful wife. Loyal though Rhys would remain to a husband who seemed habitually to live on the wrong side of the law, the revelation of his bigamy marked the beginning of an erosion of trust from which the couple's relationship would never entirely recover. Over the next two years, Lenglet occupied the twilight world of a fugitive, one from which he would sporadically emerge and seek Rhys out; essentially, she faced life alone.

Other than the saintly Richelots and an occasional handout from Lancey (with whom she remained in irregular contact until at least 1925), Rhys now had no resources. Her story "Hunger" dryly reports the number of days—five—for which a young woman in similar circumstances can survive on bread and coffee.

"Hunger" and the three bitter stories which follow it in *The Left*

Bank, Rhys's first published collection, may well be based upon actual memories of this challenging period. In the first of the three, the narrator withholds her pity from a starving friend who not only continues to rouge her lips and to wear silk stockings, but dares to be flippant about it. ("What did you say?" the narrator asks before repeating the starving woman's retort in dull disbelief: " . . . You cannot buy special clothes to starve in. Naturally not.") In the next, "A Night," where the (once again) penniless narrator wonders whether a lover's tenderness might be enough to keep her from killing herself by drowning or gunshot, Rhys uses the speaker to voice the nonspecific hatred which will become a feature of her work: "It is as if something in me is shivering right away from humanity. Their eyes are mean and cruel." In the third and least successful, "In the Rue de l'Arrivée," a stony-broke and slightly drunk Englishwoman learns to accept pity from someone even unluckier than herself. "*Pauvre petite, va*," murmurs the sinister-looking man who might have been about to pick her up or murder her, after he catches sight of her face. That night, in Miss Dorothy Dufreyne's troubled dreams, the same stranger returns disguised as an angel, about to carry her off to hell: "But what if it were heaven when one got there?" Sentiment still smudges the sharp edges of Rhys's prose, but here, very faintly apparent, are the first traces of Rhys's fourth and finest novel, *Good Morning, Midnight*.

How *did* Jean Rhys survive two years—autumn 1922 to the autumn of 1924—of poverty and unwelcome independence? The wealth that Lenglet had accrued in Vienna and Budapest had vanished, leaving only a cupboard filled with exquisite clothes to inspire "Illusion," one of Rhys's most whimsical early stories (about an outwardly dowdy English woman whose Parisian wardrobe is filled with improbably exotic dresses that include "a carnival costume complete with mask"). Scraps of paper surviving from that bleak period bear the names of various Paris hotels, often in grim areas like the then-notorious wasteland of Place Dauphine. Did Rhys prefer to hole up in some hideaway where she could read and write, to begging from the small group of expatriate friends who had known her in London, before the war? Was this the time when she began to read Colette (for whose early books about the great novelist's years in vaudeville Rhys would retain an enduring admiration) and the remarkable Pierre Mac Orlan, whose stylistically brilliant and often witty Parisian novel about a modern-day Faust and a pure-hearted prostitute, *Marguerite de la Nuit* (1924), became one of her most cherished volumes?

Rhys's only known employer during a period of daunting challenges (met with characteristic defiance) was Violet Dreschfeld, a Jewish sculptor living in Paris. In *Quartet*, Rhys's first and most directly autobiographical novel, Dreschfeld is represented by the gauntly anxious Esther de Solla; in *After Leaving Mr Mackenzie*, a similar character called Ruth owns a Modigliani print—a tigerish, lounging nude with which Julia Martin feels a troubled affinity. Esther and Ruth are mature women, but Violet was close in age to Rhys herself. Their personal relationship is unclear, but Rhys—who would preserve almost no souvenirs from this period of her life—did keep one small photographic record of Violet's work; it presents a modestly dressed "Ella" seated on a rock, her head bowed in thought. Dreschfeld never married and seems to have formed no other significant relationships. We can't know whether she became Rhys's lover for a time, or simply provided a bit of badly needed income, or both. Rhys's relationships with women remain one of her best-kept secrets, but she writes about the female body with an appreciation of physical beauty that seems to go well beyond self-regard.

IT WAS DURING the last quarter of 1924 that a dramatic change occurred in Rhys's life. Lenglet had managed to rejoin her in Paris. Money remained desperately short. It was her own idea (or so Rhys would recall in *Smile Please*) to turn her husband's colourful past to commercial use. Lenglet had worked both as a journalist and a singer in his prewar life; Mac Orlan had written about his own experiences as a chanteur at *Le Lapin Agile*; surely it wouldn't take her husband long to dash off a few racy vignettes about his nights as a teenage heartthrob

at Montmartre's famous club? Lenglet complied. Theirs would always
be an affectionately collaborative partnership where writing was concerned; after translating and sharpening her husband's submissions,
Rhys took them along to the offices of the Continental *Daily Mail*.
Courteously informed that Lenglet's anecdotal pieces were a bit old-
fashioned for the *Mail*'s readers, Rhys rejected the compensatory offer
made to herself on the spot to become an interviewer of celebrities,
working from the paper's office in Rome.

In Rhys's retrospective account of the sequence of events, it was an
editor at the *Daily Mail* who then suggested that she might show her
husband's stories to Helen Pearl Adam, an American journalist whose
husband had previously worked in London alongside Maxwell Macartney at *The Times*. "I was very nervous as I'd only met Mrs Adam once,"
Rhys would write in *Smile Please*, "and I wondered if she'd remember
me."[11] Pearl was already aware of Rhys's ambitions as a writer, however;
she may even have been told about a work in progress. And so, having
rejected Lenglet's anecdotes, Adam apparently asked to see something
written by Rhys herself. Playing her cards with care, and conscious of
the urgent need to show something marketable to a seasoned journalist, Rhys held back the accomplished stories that she had been working
on in Paris during Lenglet's long absences. Instead, she handed over
the raunchier and still unnamed episodic novel that had started life in
Chelsea in a handful of large-sized notebooks, a year before the war.

Pearl Adam liked what she read, enough so to offer to edit the material and give it a catchy title. "Suzy Tells" would offer a knowing nod
both to one of Paris's best-known drinks (a "Suze Fine" was Pernod-
based) and to Suzy's, a famous brothel that was celebrated later by the
photographer Brassaï.

What happened next would change Rhys's life. Having divided
"Suzy Tells" into sections, each headed by a man's name, Pearl Adam
decided that Rhys's scandalous manuscript was original enough to
interest Ford Madox Ford, editor of Paris's respected literary magazine for English-speaking expatriates, the *transatlantic review*. She

was right; Ford was intrigued. Nevertheless, a few days after reading "Suzy Tells" and then renaming it "Triple Sec," Ford set the typescript aside. Instead, he told Pearl Adam that he wanted to see more of this writer's work. Moreover, he wanted to meet such a gifted young author in person.

7

"L'affaire Ford"* (1924–26)

> " 'The snow was all over Ireland, falling on the living and the
> dead.' Who used to read James Joyce to me? I forget."
>
> —Jean Rhys, misquoting in her old age a line from the famous
> closing paragraph of Joyce's story "The Dead," from *Dubliners*[1]

RHYS HAD MOST likely first met Ford's partner, Stella Bowen, in London, shortly after her arrival from Adelaide, Australia. Back before the war, Bowen and Rhys briefly belonged to the same Chelsea-based group of bohemians. Stella was studying art; Rhys was beginning to write "Triple Sec," while picking up cash by posing as an artist's model. In 1918, the year after the twenty-eight-year-old Rhys met Jean Lenglet in London, Stella, aged twenty-four, fell for Major Ford. A highly educated officer, half German on his father's side, Ford had recently returned to England from a war that left him temporarily shellshocked and suffering from memory lapses.

Nobody has ever described Ford as handsome, but nobody who knew him has questioned his ability to charm women, or his gift both as a writer and editor, one who had collaborated with Joseph Conrad and who published his own widely admired novel, *The Good Soldier*, in

---

* The phrase used by Rhys for a long retrospective account of her relationship with Ford, to which she referred when dictating the Paris section of her memoir to the novelist David Plante (McFarlin, 007-14.5.f5).

1916. Ford's generous nature had never been constrained by a perpetual lack of funds; neither had a concern for facts impeded his genius for telling stories. At work, he pumped out what were often magnificent novels at the rate of some manic teleprinting machine. Winding down at night, he knocked back red wine with as much gusto as he (very badly) danced and (very enchantingly) talked. Like his own most auto-biographical creation, Christopher Tietjens in the sequence of novels called *Parade's End*, Ford would always seem larger in spirit than the world he was obliged to inhabit.

"Silenus in tweeds"—according to the great war artist Paul Nash, who knew him pretty well—Ford was too gentle in manner ever to appear predatory.[2] Stella, a darkly attractive and culture-hungry young woman with a talent for organising other people's lives, found this brilliant and deceptively helpless man irresistible. An age gap of twenty years was vaulted as easily as the fact that her lover was still entangled with the writer Violet Hunt (for whom Ford had previously abandoned

Stella Bowen (*left*) lived in Chelsea at the same time as Rhys and visited the Crabtree Club with considerably less pleasure. Later, she formed a relationship with Ford Madox Ford (*right*) and moved to France.

his wife and two children). Two years later, Stella gave birth to Julie (Ford's adored "*petite princesse*"), with whom the couple migrated in 1922 to the south of France—and who was later left to the care of a dependable nurse in their country cottage close to the capital. Often though the "Fords," as the unmarried couple were always known in France, would return to the then unspoiled Riviera coast, Paris exerted a powerful attraction over an astonishingly well-read francophile who thrived on discovering talented new writers.

By the autumn of 1924, when Jean Rhys entered his life, Ford stood at the heart of the expatriate and (thanks to spectacular exchange rates) uncharacteristically affluent literary world that thronged the brasseries of Montparnasse. Ford himself, despite regular injections of funds from Stella's Australian investment trust, was always strapped for cash, in part because of his generous impulse to subsidise needy poets like the reticent Ralph Cheever Dunning, a starving opium addict whose sour warning against the acceptance of charity was taken by Jean Rhys as the prefatory heading for her own first novel, *Quartet*. By September 1924, the imminent closure of Ford's cherished year-old creation, the *transatlantic review*, was already on the cards.

After their fashion, Stella and Ford did their best to economise. In the country, they rented the stone-walled labourer's cottage at Guermantes where little Julie was lodged; in the city, they occupied a minute apartment at 16 avenue Denfert-Rochereau. Meanwhile, Ford encouraged his magazine's illustrious contributors to buy their own drinks at the impromptu weekly evenings he hosted at the Bal du Printemps, a tiny cafe-restaurant squirrelled away in the winding streets behind the Panthéon. More student-style partying took place in the dungeon-like premises that the *transatlantic review's* headquarters shared with Bill Bird's illustrious Three Mountains Press on Ile Saint Louis's quai d'Anjou. The setting was as dingy as the menu, but the dancing was wild and the guests included everybody from Ernest Hemingway to a majestic Gertrude Stein. Hemingway, Ford's first and prodigiously gifted literary beneficiary in Paris—he was even allowed to edit an issue of the magazine in which Ford published the young American's work—paved the way for Jean Rhys as she joined this exhilarating coterie, shortly after her first encounter with Ford in September 1924.

Recalling the events of the next two years in her memoir, *Drawn from Life* (1941), Stella Bowen would describe an unnamed but entirely identifiable Rhys as having first appeared on their doorstep toting a battered suitcase that contained "an unpublishably sordid novel." Bowen's recollection doesn't square with the account in *Smile Please* of Pearl Adam having already edited and submitted "Suzy Tells" to Ford; what Rhys had produced from her shabby holdall at that first meeting with Ford was the manuscript of a recent—and far more accomplished— short story. Reading "Vienne," Ford thought it so remarkable that he instantly offered to publish the opening six pages (unpaid, of course) in the final, December issue of *transatlantic review*. He might have published more, but Rhys, while willing to undergo another change of name—"Ella Lenglet" did not meet with her new patron's approval— insisted on withholding the part of the story dealing with the couple's ignominious flight from Budapest. The rapid choice of the name "Jean" for herself—no other explanation sounds convincing—may have struck Ella as a way, following the embarrassing rejection by the *Mail* and Pearl Adam of her cultured husband's own, less remarkable stories, to grant Monsieur Jean Lenglet a role in her new literary life.

For Rhys, the news could not have been better. The extract from "Vienne" was to appear in Ford's distinguished magazine alongside contributions from Hemingway, Stein, Tristan Tzara, Robert McAlmon and Ford himself (publishing a tender homage to his old friend Joseph Conrad, who had died in August). No aspiring young writer could have hoped for a more auspicious debut.

Rhys's good fortune seemed infectious. In that same month, September 1924, Lenglet obtained a well-paid job with Exprinter, a Paris tourist bureau. Elated, the Lenglets took their two-year-old daughter out of her latest foster home and away to Tours for a celebratory holiday. Many years later, Rhys would tenderly remind a middle-aged Maryvonne of the visit to Tours with "my sweety pie baby." An informal snap from the trip, presumably taken by a fond Lenglet, shows

Rhys laughing up at the photographer as she nuzzles the elegant canine snout of a new friend's German shepherd. Aged thirty-four, Rhys still looked like a carefree twenty-year-old, one whose serene features belied the writer's evident familiarity with a world of fathomless darkness. It's easy to see why both Ford and Stella were intrigued and—from the very start—a little smitten.

Throughout that golden autumn of 1924, a triangle was established from which Jean Lenglet's demanding new job excluded him. Later, Jean Rhys would say little about this period. It is possible that the relationship between herself and Ford—and possibly Stella—was sexual from the start. Publicly, nothing was said by anybody. It was Stella herself who later coined the phrase "Ford's girl" to suggest how scornfully the gifted intruder was regarded by their friends. Hemingway, who attended the same parties, and worked on editing the *transatlantic review* alongside one of Rhys's new chums, the Midwestern poet, Ivan Beede, never mentioned Rhys once. James Joyce, indebted to Ford for his unfaltering support in publishing the Irish novelist's most experimental work, recalled only having been asked to zip up Miss Rhys's dress while sharing a lift. A lift? An unzipped dress? Clearly, Joyce was flagging up an assignation at a hotel, but Ford is not named, only the vulnerable young outsider from whom a slightly malicious Joyce had nothing to fear.[3]

Ignored in the memoirs of the novelists and poets and painters who flocked to Paris during the 1920s, Rhys herself would maintain a maddening discretion. She didn't want to betray Ford and Stella, her friends and patrons. She hated the idea of dropping famous names. Years later, when asked about Joyce, Rhys acknowledged having met him, but not that Ford had taught her to read his early stories as carefully as she would do *Ulysses* and *Finnegans Wake*. Asked for anecdotes about Ernest Hemingway, the older Rhys recalled an unassuming young man who came to life only when he was dancing. Subjected to more persistent interrogation, she grew vaguer still. *Had* Ford really introduced her to Gertrude Stein? She might have visited. Miss Stein's companion, Alice Toklas (Rhys added with an almost wilful satisfaction at her own elusiveness), had certainly made herself friendly.[4]

The newly named writer "Jean Rhys" at the time of her affair with Ford. Out of sight at her side here is Germaine Richelot, among the most loyal of Rhys's friends in Paris. (*McFarlin*)

Always evasive in public about what was clearly a passionate love affair ("I love him. Terribly," Marya Zelli says about Hugo Heidler in Rhys's unashamedly autobiographical first novel, *Quartet*), Rhys never failed to honour Ford as her literary mentor. Rattling off a florid introduction in 1927 to his brilliant protégée's first publication, a collection of short stories, Ford himself was equally careful to distance himself, pointing out that Miss Rhys had always known better than to take his advice. Rhys, while she didn't disagree, credited Ford with broadening her knowledge of the great French and Russian authors from whom she learned so much.

The absence of almost any documentation before 1931 in the form of letters makes it nearly impossible to chart Rhys's reading habits in Paris during the Twenties. Then, as now, books were always easily available from the *bouquinistes* beside the Seine, but it's likely that Ford, a widely read man who treated Rhys as his pupil, gave her access to his own extensive library. Her husband, the ardent admirer of one of France's most revered modern novelists, had already introduced Ella to the novels of Anatole France, whose vast public funeral the couple attended in 1924. French poetry had come into her life through the nuns at the Virgo Fidelis convent in Roseau. Adoring Mallarmé and Rimbaud, Rhys's strongest affinity was still with Baudelaire, in whose sensual but also condescending celebrations of his beautiful Haitian-born mistress, Jeanne Duval, she perhaps sensed the beginning of her long journey to reclaim a place in history for Mr. Rochester's mis-treated Creole wife, the madwoman in the Thornfield attic of *Jane Eyre*. Perhaps: we can only conjecture.

Ford made Rhys aware of some of the writers who would become her touchstones as she strove to create a style—and a world—of her own. Her admiration of Guy de Maupassant, frequently mentioned in her later letters as a master storyteller, is apparent in "La Grosse Fifi." This story of an older woman's brutal murder by her young gig-olo lover stands alongside "Vienne" as a minor masterpiece in Rhys's early work. Maupassant's influence was still in evidence in the 1950s, when she planned to call a later story "Fort comme la Mort" in homage to Maupassant's work of the same name. The novella, about an older man's passion for a much younger woman, had been Ford's favourite of all Maupassant's writings. But Ford also introduced Rhys to the novels of his cherished colleague, Joseph Conrad, and to the Russian writers, often in translations made by his friend Constance Garnett. One of the bleakest moments in Rhys's later life would come when a shortage of money and space obliged her to sell her treasured Russian novels. Put-ting them up for sale in the 1950s, she got only a few pounds in return.

WHILE RHYS WAS being introduced to a world of writers, poets and painters in the halcyon autumn of 1924, her husband made a reck-less attempt to improve their family circumstances by speculating with money that had been entrusted to him by the tourist agency, earmarked for a specific commercial transaction. Arrested for an *abus de confiance* (premeditated felony) and taken on 28 December to the grim Pari-sian holding prison of La Santé, pending his trial, a distraught Lenglet begged Germaine Richelot to help him to get legal assistance. Curiously, he made no mention of Rhys, although Germaine's swift response expressed a pointed concern for "your poor little wife." It's possible that Lenglet already felt confident that Rhys would be protected by her powerful new friends.

Quartet, the novel published by Rhys in 1928, relates how a dismayed Marya Zelli is abruptly summoned into the back room of the cheap hotel in Montmartre where she and her husband have been staying. Informed by the hotel's owners that the police have taken Zelli to an undisclosed address, Marya remains in Paris. Rhys herself did not. During the late afternoon of 28 December (the very day of Lenglet's arrest), Ford chaperoned his protégée to the Gare de Lyon; there, the two of them were observed having a heated argument in the station brasserie. It seems likely that Rhys was disputing Ford's hasty decision to get her out of Paris before news of the scandal broke. Later that same evening, a wheezing Ford clambered onto the night train to the French Riviera to beg a favour of the artist Paul Nash and his remarkable wife, Margaret Odeh, a Jerusalem-born radical feminist with—it was said—clairvoyant powers. Ford may not have known that the Nashes had witnessed his quarrel with Rhys; now, he wanted to know if they, too, were travelling down to Cros de Cagnes? If so, could they take care of the suitcase keys which his young friend had inadvertently left behind her in the brasserie as she rushed to secure a seat—somewhere; he couldn't find her—on the Riviera-bound train? The Nashes knew Ford well enough to conclude that the lost passenger was a cast-off mistress. They gave him their word.

Settled into the main hotel at Cros de Cagnes, the Nashes waited for Ford's mystery friend to appear. When Rhys arrived, pale with dismay after spending the night at what she had assumed to be a pension (it proved to be a brothel) the Nashes invited her to supper and arranged for a room: "*Ah, les anglaises,*" tittered the hotel manager, swiftly assuming that Nash was sleeping with both women. No sooner was Rhys settled in than she asked Margaret to cover the cost of her return ticket to Paris. And that was that: the young woman "disappeared from our lives in the same ghost-like way in which she had appeared," Margaret Odeh Nash wrote in her unpublished memoir.[5]

Confirmation of the encounter at Cros de Cagnes—and evidence of Rhys's discomfort—would later surface in an unflattering portrait of the Nashes as the stiffly correct Olsens in "La Grosse Fifi," a story which Rhys wrote in the mid-Twenties and set on the French Riviera. "How rum some English people are!" the central character, Roseau, exclaims. "They ask to be shocked and long to be shocked, but if you really shock them . . . how shocked they are!"[6] The Nashes had not been shocked, but they were certainly intrigued. Setting out the subjects for a future chapter of his marvelous and sadly unfinished memoir, *Outline*, Paul Nash made an opaque reference to a Riviera encounter with the "blonde legacy from Ford."

Seeing her convicted husband was a prime reason for Rhys's return to Paris and she visited Lenglet as loyally as Marya Zelli would do in *Quartet*. At that stage, however, there was nothing Rhys could do for Lenglet (and almost as little to help herself). Like Marya, she sold her pretty Viennese dresses; possibly, Rhys begged assistance from her Aunt Clarice in Wales and received a modest sum, together with advice to seek help from some British clergymen settled in Paris. ("You could easily find out the address of one of them, or I could find out and send it to you," counsels Marya's kindly aunt, Maria Hughes, in *Quartet*.) Marya is taken to live with the Heidlers in their village home at Brunoy; Ford swept Rhys off to the cold little cottage at Guermantes where—as he disclosed to his new agent, William Bradley—the poor young woman became too ill even to work on her writing. Stella was also reported to be sick; a resigned Ford found himself acting as cook, cleaner and nurse, all amidst struggling to complete the second part of his great tetralogy, *Parade's End*.[7]

On 10 February 1925, Rhys learned that her husband had been found guilty of the planned felony charge. Jean Lenglet was condemned to spend two years in the notoriously brutal prison of Fresnes, and then to depart from France. Germaine Richelot advised Rhys to seek a divorce;

instead, a destitute Rhys turned for help to her new patrons. According to Stella Bowen's recollection, their unfortunate friend possessed only a few francs along with her precious writings; there was no question but that they would take her in. The flat on avenue Denfert-Rochereau contained a small spare room; there, Rhys could sleep and write while, for the foreseeable future, Ford and Stella acted as her providers and joint guardians. All they asked in return was that she should be compliant and discreet. As Rhys would later remark of this humiliating episode in her life, she really had no other option.

———

AS WITH MARYA ZELLI, Rhys's life now developed its own melancholy pattern. Once a week, she went to Versailles to visit little Maryvonne at the most recent orphanage to have been located by Germaine Richelot. Once a fortnight, she took a tram out to Fresnes. Seated opposite Lenglet in one of the square booths that reminded her of roofless telephone boxes, Rhys noticed how thin and nervous her husband had become. They still cared about each other; it was a fact which nobody else seemed to understand.

But Rhys had also fallen in love with Ford, and he with her, as he helped her to revise the short, almost sketch-like stories that she was writing about Paris and Dominica. Sometimes—which gave her pleasure—Ford would snatch up one of her pencilled scrawls and read it aloud, shaking his head when he stumbled over a banality ("Cliché! Cliché!") and putting on a solemn voice for passages that he admired. The praise felt good, and so did the reassurance of being loved. Stella worked on a portrait of their guest; Ford praised her mind and took her to bed with comforting enthusiasm. If Stella knew—as, despite her later, published protestations of ignorance, she probably did—she turned a blind eye to an affair which she had no power to prevent. Sometimes, when Rhys drank too much and felt that the couple were playing a cruel game of their own with her emotions, she lost control and screamed or even spat. This aspect of their emotional guest alarmed her hosts. Neither Ford nor Stella relished the dramas upon which Rhys seemed to thrive. Their highly strung protégée could write as much as she pleased about violence and despair without bringing her anger into what was, despite their bohemian friendships, an outwardly conventional household. They didn't want a fuss. Tensions grew.

Lenglet's prison sentence was shortened, due to good behaviour and the need for space in the large but always overcrowded prison of Fresnes. Released after four months, a shivering ghost of his former charming self, he was granted a few days of freedom before his enforced departure from France. In his largely autobiographical novel *Sous les verrous* (Under Lock and Key) published in 1933, Lenglet described Stania and Hubner (Rhys and Ford) coming to the station to wave him off to Belgium: Hubner, eager to see him gone after sitting through one disastrous dinner out for the four of them, even paid for his rival's rail ticket. Legally, Lenglet was exiled for life. The risks he took to return to his wife speak for the strength of his love for Jean.

And what, meanwhile, was to be done with "Ford's girl" and her inconvenient rages? Ford was still like a man under a spell, but Stella, on whose financial support and organisational skills he relied, was sick of being expected to play the calm, capable wife, as opposed to Rhys the victim—"the poor, brave and desperate beggar who was doomed to be let down by the bourgeoisie."[8] Their experimental ménage à trois had failed, and—as even Rhys had become aware—"it was high time I got away from Montparnasse."[9]

The solution arrived in the form of a potentially undemanding job in the south of France. Winifred Shaughnessy Hudnut, the languidly elegant wife of America's first cosmetics magnate, was the mother-in-law to Rudolph Valentino and—thanks to Hudnut's well-marketed products—the proud owner of the palatial Château Juan-les-Pins on the French Riviera. She was also an ardent spiritualist. In the summer of 1925, Mrs. Hudnut despatched a representative to Paris to seek out some writer gifted enough to assist her in writing a book about the importance of dressing in the spirit—so to speak—of one's previous incarnation.

The energy with which both Stella and Ford represented Jean Rhys as the perfect candidate for Winifred Hudnut's bizarre project reveals how eager they were to be rid of Rhys. Stella provided a glowing character reference for their friend; Ford went further and actually forged a couple of stories intended to showcase Rhys's vast knowledge of the eighteenth century (Mrs. Hudnut's favourite period) and of Russian folklore. (Ford's faux-Serbian folk tale has not survived, but doubtless contained much about reincarnation.) Their efforts were rewarded: on a hot afternoon in July 1925, for the second time in five months, Ford escorted his protégée to a train that was bound for the Riviera.

IT'S A SHAME that Ford kept none of the lively letters in which Rhys regaled him with tales of chateau life at Juan-les-Pins, but her two fictional accounts offer rich compensation. "At the Villa d'Or," a story published in Rhys's first collection, lightly disguises the lecherous and sprightly Mr. Hudnut as Robert B. Valentine, a vegetarian plutocrat who hatches plans to seduce his guest, a curvaceous young singer named only as "Sara of Montparnasse." The ethereal Mrs. Valentine, fiddling with her long strings of beads while she lolls on a cushioned sofa among her pekineses, ponders the merits of rice over ham ("I'm dead sick of rice, Bobbie"); Charles, her obsequious manservant, is fashionably English ("like the armchairs"). Sara, the Rhysian visitor, revels serenely in the chateau's luxury: "Very nice too," is her calm response to an opulent bathroom glittering with crystal bottles of scents and oils.

A Riviera palace had no place in the despairing life Rhys constructed for Marya Zelli in *Quartet*. A decade later, however, Rhys would return to her sojourn with the Hudnuts in *Good Morning, Midnight* (1939). There, in one of her fourth novel's most oddly tender scenes, Sasha Jensen and her suitor, René (a quick-witted gigolo whose history and appearance bear a striking resemblance to those of Jean Lenglet), share a moment of emotional connection in the discovery that they have been guests at the very same chateau: "Here are the palm trees. Here are the entrance steps. That terrible English butler they had—do you remember?" Briefly, Sasha and her dubious companion become cheerful allies in their memories of an absurd but privileged life.

Rhys's three months at Château Juan-les-Pins were far from wretched. Winifred Hudnut took her to Monte Carlo to hear the ageing Russian bass, Chaliapin, growling his way through a concert, while her husband preferred to take an attractive young woman to watch her lecherous host gambling at the casino. During the day, when not required to assist with Winifred's writing project, Rhys retired to her room to work over the collection of stories for which Ford had promised to find publishers in England and America. Sometimes, she went wandering. It was during an impulsive excursion to the deserted nearby beach at La Napoule that Rhys experienced a rare moment of bliss; a feeling of being at one with the world and filled with joy, "not only for me, but for everyone." Such moments never fooled Rhys for long; later, reshaping her exquisite epiphany as a story in draft form, she cynically named it: "The Forlorn Hope."[10]

Rhys's abrupt return to Paris was engineered by Ford. Winifred Hudnut had been displeased to learn from a sharp-eyed chauffeur that her husband had been coaxing kisses from their guest during their drives to Monte Carlo; what vexed her more was a complaint from Ford that a gifted writer was being asked to work unpaid on Winifred's second literary venture. Rhys had grumbled to her mentor about the lack of payment; she had not expected Ford to seize an excuse to summon her back to himself. Escorted to Paris by her irate employer, Rhys was greeted at the station by a beaming Ford. As for her own feelings: conducted by Ford to a grim hotel near Gare Montparnasse: "I thought of the Chateau Juan les Pins and very nearly burst into tears."[11]

"GOD SAVE ME I perish SOS SOS I am so alone."[12] That heartfelt wail most convincingly belongs to a period that would be vividly evoked in *Quartet* when Marya moves from the Heidlers' home into the Hotel du Bosphore, a sour reference by the well-read Rhys to the archly self-forgiving title of Ford's "Mr Bosphorus and the Muses."

At the chateau, Rhys had grown accustomed to luxury; in Paris, she became a poor dependent, isolated from the literary world to which Ford had introduced her, confined to a lonely room in which she wrote and drank and drowned herself in narcotics-induced sleep. Ford moved her to a nearby hotel on rue Vavin. He visited her once a week; he paid the bills. Rhys had become his part-time mistress—his private toy. It was better than nothing for a woman who remained, as *Quartet* would make painfully apparent, in love with this improbable Casanova. Her role now was that of the grateful dependent. Her lover called the shots. Plausible public encounters were conducted for Stella's benefit, to keep up the pretence of a conventional friendship between the three of them. Later, Rhys would remember the humiliation of being ordered by a lofty Stella to sit on the *strapontin*, the inferior seat, her back to the carriage driver, whenever the three of them shared a cab. Showing a quiet face to the world, she burned with rage and wounded pride.

Alone, Rhys visited her daughter. Occasionally, she ventured out with Ivan Beede, the friendly young novelist and poet from the American Midwest who had worked as Ford's assistant on the *transatlantic review*. Beede disapproved of what he saw as Ford's manipulative hold over Rhys. If *Quartet* can be believed (Beede appears there lightly disguised as "Cairn"), he was even prepared to borrow funds and give them to Rhys, simply to get her out of Ford's clutches. Marya Zelli turns Cairn's offer down. Jean Rhys did not stop seeing Ford.

At the centre of Rhys's life—throughout the bleak months that followed her return to Paris—stood her writing, a resource that is entirely absent from the lives of the women she describes in her novels. Glimpses of the world through which she drifted—a flâneur's habit that Rhys shared with her female protagonists and borrowed from Baudelaire—appear in the stories that now began to take their final form from pages of urgently scrawled notes. Sometimes, as in "Mixing Cocktails"—one of two sketches about her Caribbean childhood—she looked back, remembering the melancholy mountains of Dominica, the hammock where she lay dreaming at Bona Vista, the chirping voice of her visiting aunt, Clarice ("That *sea* . . . Could anything be more lovely?"). Sometimes, evoking Parisian life among the down but not quite out, Rhys trained a cold stare on her present self, mocking Miss Dorothy Dufreyne of "In the Rue de L'Arrivée" as the fallen "Lady" (Rhys's own awkward term) who drinks a brandy and soda at every second cafe she passes, while erroneously congratulating herself on not yet—despite the waiters' "curious stares"—appearing to be entirely drunk. Sometimes, as in "The Sidi," Rhys would crib and recreate a story from one of Lenglet's eloquent accounts of his terrible four months at Fresnes. She knew he wouldn't mind. Their shared passion for writing (and above all, for *her* writing) would always remain a bond. Lenglet was yet to understand how devastated his wife had been to see her attractive husband transformed into the trembling ghost of himself that he became at Fresnes, or how intense and complex were her feelings for Ford.

STELLA AND FORD were away at Avignon in July 1926, when Jean Lenglet stole back across the French border to secretly rejoin his wife in Paris, while hiding away in the quiet suburb of Clamart. The Lenglets had evidently remained in touch during his absence from France,[13] and it's clear from the clandestine reunion that Rhys still cared about a husband who was willing to take such risks to be with her.

On 4 August, Lenglet was hunted down and once again expelled from France (following a further miserable week-long stay at the fortress-like prison of La Santé). In mid-September, spurred by the fear of losing his wife, Lenglet returned once more. Ford now tried yet again to ship an unhappy Jean Rhys off to the Riviera, out of the reach of a man he believed was endangering his protégée's literary future. She refused to go. According to the fictional accounts subsequently provided by both Lenglet and Rhys herself, this was the moment when Ford announced that he had personally endured enough. As a writer, he would always support her; as a lover, he could take no more drama. Rhys must have been distraught; ordered by a hysterical Lenglet to choose between her lover and her husband, she refused to renounce Ford.

Quartet, at this moment of climax, permits an enraged Stephan Zelli to murder his wife with a cool "*Voila pour toi*" and then flee, accompanied by another, intriguingly available woman. In reality, a distraught Lenglet armed himself with a revolver and raced off with the crazed intention of killing his portly rival. The police had already learned enough to intercept the would-be assassin. Briefly thrown back into La Santé on 16 September, Lenglet was released only when he promised to leave France for ever.[14]

How had the gendarmes known where to find Lenglet, or that he planned to murder Ford? The most likely source of information was Stella Bowen, whose jealous anger still rang out when she described Rhys, in a memoir written fifteen years after these events, as a "doomed soul, violent and demoralised . . . She nearly sank our ship!"[15]

If Stella did go to the police, Ford did not discourage her. Emotionally, he was done with both women: as Ford sailed away to undertake a lucrative American lecture tour, Stella was left to comfort herself with a flowery public assurance of his enduring devotion. (It took the form of a dedicatory letter prefacing Ford's own new French translation of his finest novel, *The Good Soldier*). Professionally, as Rhys was aware, her faithless lover was still determined to promote her career. The difficulty that Ford now faced was how to offer continued literary support while closing the door on what had proved to be an exhausting and sometimes alarming love affair. It wouldn't be easy.

8

Hunger, and Hope (1926–28)

> "The cardinal fact is that a woman cannot earn a decent living . . . I'm going into wages and facts. They are utterly dependent on their sexual attraction for salvation."
>
> —Patrick Hamilton to his brother Bruce Hamilton, May 1927[1]

RHYS WOULD OFTEN write about women who sold their bodies for sex. By the time that her affair with Ford had ended, she already knew that writing—not sex—was going to be her own salvation and that Ford, fuelled by guilt in addition to his unswerving belief in her talent, would do everything he could to help her obtain it. And he did. When Rhys travelled to London in the autumn of 1926, she had in her pocket two important introductions. One was to Joseph Conrad's devoted friend Edward Garnett, the éminence grise of Jonathan Cape, who—advised by Garnett—expressed a gratifying willingness to publish an unknown writer's collection of stories about low life in Paris, especially since they came with the guarantee of a preface by Ford, one of the most respected writers of the day. The second letter was to Leslie Tilden Smith, a publisher's reader and freelance editor who had written to Ford in Paris, asking for the names of any up-and-coming authors whom he might represent as their agent in London. Ford had promised to put him in touch with Jean Rhys.

In Paris, anxious to distance his own name from that of Rhys, Ford arranged (with Stella's reluctant consent) for Germaine Richelot to post

copies of their talented friend's stories to a handpicked group of newspaper editors in the city: he knew that the advance publication of a tale
in the fiction pages of a respected paper would help to promote Rhys's
work, ahead of her British debut. The responses were respectful. One
letter, which Richelot passed along to Rhys at her latest Montparnasse
address (6 rue du Maine), came from Valentine Williams, the Paris
editor of the *Daily Mail*. Writing back to praise the unnamed author in
January 1927, Williams singled out Rhys's gift for sharpening descriptions by focusing on "unusual features." Perhaps Williams remembered
Rhys visiting the *Mail* with her husband's stories and guessed at Ford's
involvement; slyly, he suggested—at a time when Ford was commuting
between Chicago and New York—that the most likely takers would be
the *Chicago Tribune* and the *New York Times*.[2]

In America, where the promiscuous Ford had wasted no time in
embarking upon new romantic liaisons, he made contact early in 1927
with a Chicago publisher, Pascal Covici, about a daring new novel.
Perversité had been hopefully presented to Ford by its author, Francis Carco, just before his autumn departure for America. Ford liked
Carco, a former wartime lover of Katherine Mansfield's; he admired
the poems and novels in which Carco—like Pierre Mac Orlan, the
writer so admired by Rhys—dealt with themes of passion, exploitation
and abuse, set in a Parisian underworld. *Perversité* tells of a brother's
incestuous desire, which ends in murder. It's uncertain whether the
novel was discussed in the (presumably) professional letters which Ford
continued, from abroad, to exchange with Rhys, but it is clear that he
believed his hard-up protégée would make a sympathetic translator.
Covici, who assumed that Ford himself would be doing the translation,
was willing to pay a generous $250 in two instalments. Ford, although
he could ill afford it in the early spring of 1927, advanced the entire
sum to Rhys from his own pocket, while pretending the payment had
come from Covici.

Ford's munificence was based on a shrewd calculation. Before leaving Paris, he had persuaded Stella Bowen and Germaine Richelot to
collaborate on a discreet plan to assist the penniless Rhys after her

husband's final banishment from France. From October 1926 until at least the end of February 1927, when Ford returned to France and cut off the payments, a weekly cheque for 400 francs was paid by Stella and transmitted to Rhys by Germaine.*³ As Ford hoped, Rhys assumed that she was being helped out by the kind-hearted Richelots. The translation payment was intended by Ford to fill the gap left by the terminated allowance.

Ford's keenness to stop subsidising Rhys was sharpened by his having to deal with Stella's suspicions. Dutifully forwarding Rhys's unopened bulletins to Ford's New York address, Stella told him that she imagined Rhys's report of her visit to London contained "a good deal" that was not professional. He made no response. A week or so later, Stella raised the subject with Ford once more ("You might let me know something of the affairs in that quarter"); sending along what she surmised was yet another billet-doux, she reproached Ford for remaining so annoyingly uncommunicative "on that subject." Close to the start of his American trip, Stella had pointedly hoped that Ford wouldn't bring home any more blondes: "I can't bear any more Fair Hair," she told her philandering lover. There wasn't much comfort in learning that a buxom and newly bewitched Mrs. Rene Wright was a brunette.⁴

Visiting London in the autumn of 1926 (as Ford sailed to New York), Rhys had kept away both from Lancey and from her unhappy family in Acton. This was to be a business trip. While Ford prevailed on Harper and Row in the US to publish his protégée's collected stories in the autumn of 1927, Rhys introduced herself to Edward Garnett. Having established that Jonathan Cape would publish *The Left Bank* in the spring of 1927, she arranged to meet Leslie Tilden Smith. Her arrival proved timely. Leslie, who worked for the Curtis Brown agency alongside his wife, Katherine Millard, had recently been left by Katherine for another man. In the autumn of 1926, a still devastated Tilden Smith was working for Hughes Massie, a split-off from the Curtis Brown

---

*   In 1927, 400 francs was equivalent to just over £180 today. As a point of comparison, Ford and Stella were paying their daughter's full-time nanny 500 francs a year.

firm, while sharing a modest flat in west London with his seventeen-year-old daughter, Phyllis Antoinette.

Rhys's chief model for the gentlemanly George Horsfield in *After Leaving Mr Mackenzie*, Leslie Tilden Smith was the well-read and Oxford-educated son of a clergyman. Leslie's pale skin and an unexpectedly wide, white smile would lead Rhys, late in life, unkindly to compare him to the villainous and whitely smiling Mr. Carker of Dickens's *Dombey and Son*. (Rhys called her story about Leslie "The Joey Bagstock Smile," but it's clear that Rhys was remembering the odious Mr. Carker rather than roguish Major Bagstock, a character singular for the fact that he laughs, but never smiles at all.) Back in 1926, Rhys noticed Leslie's marmoreal skin and arctic beam less than his admiration for her work and his readiness to support her in a male-dominated publishing world where she could no longer depend upon Ford.

Leslie himself was enchanted by Rhys. So was his pretty daughter, especially when Rhys presented the teenage Antoinette with a ravishing black dress from a suitcase filled with Parisian clothes. Rhys's outward appearance, chic as a fashion model, formed a poignant contrast to her unconcealed anxiety about the cost of London hotels. A chivalrous Leslie insisted during this first visit both on finding his new client lodgings and paying for them himself; later, as they embarked on what Jean coyly described as a "50–50 affair," Tilden Smith invited her to treat his London home as her own.

In London, conscious of her indebtedness to Ford for the all-important introduction to her first publisher, Rhys managed to keep her anger under control. Back in Paris later that autumn, and unaware that Ford and Stella were paying her allowance, her rage finally bubbled over. In a fury fuelled by the alcohol upon which she was becoming increasingly reliant, Rhys dashed off a ferocious little story. "Houdia," which remains unpublished, tells of a sculptor who uses her sharp chisel to stab the eyes of her creation before attempting to shoot the sitter, her married lover. Rhys then set about turning her experiences with Ford, Stella and Lenglet into a play about which, in late November 1926, she sought the opinion of her old friend, Pearl Adam. Pearl, conscious of

Rhys's recent relationship with Ford, expressed herself with caution. She thought that "Iris" (representing Rhys herself) should be made more helpless; the portrait of Stella (as the knowingly deceived wife) was deemed too insubstantial to convince.[5]

Here, in a play now lost or destroyed, Rhys planted the bitter seeds from which her vengeful first novel would grow. The high degree of drama in *Quartet*, as compared to its relatively plotless successors, owes much to the fact that Rhys imagined it being performed on stage. Impossible though it is to prove—she kept none of Lenglet's letters from that time—Rhys's hostile attitude to Ford and Stella was likely to have been encouraged and stimulated by her absent husband.

Jean Lenglet's whereabouts during the autumn of 1926 remain unknown. In February 1927, however, he at last regained the Dutch citizenship that had been forfeited when he joined the French Foreign Legion. After months of extreme poverty, Lenglet thus became eligible for state care in the Netherlands and able to enter the country's equivalent of a workhouse. A man possessed of immense charisma and determination, Lenglet improved his position with remarkable speed. By the end of April, he was in charge of the poorhouse's library; by the end of the summer, he had been placed in charge of the institution itself.

Lenglet had not forgiven Ford. To him, it seemed clear that his marriage had been undermined by a powerful man's determination to seduce his wife; he was haunted by the memory of the deliberately humiliating occasion (Rhys would make good use of it in *Quartet*) on which Ford and Bowen had invited the couple to a restaurant dinner, during which he had been treated—as both the Lenglets agreed—like a common felon. Ford and Bowen had stage-managed Lenglet's final arrest; together, they had destroyed his happiness. When Rhys consented only to visit the poorhouse for a single late-winter fortnight—the paupers were enchanted by their visitor's wistful grace—Lenglet found himself once again, however irrationally, blaming his former rival. He was only partially comforted to learn from Rhys that Ford was in America and that she foresaw no likelihood of ever meeting him again.

Early in 1927, Rhys travelled to London for her mother's funeral. No details survive of the occasion. In *After Leaving Mr Mackenzie*, published four years later, Rhys offered an unsparing portrait of Julia Martin's shift from emotional breakdown during the crematorium service to a truculent verbal attack, back at the family house in Acton, on her sister, Norah. "You're jealous of me, jealous, jealous," Julia screams at the quietly provocative Norah, before informing their complacent Uncle Neville, who has just finished lecturing his bereaved nieces about, life, literature and Dostoevsky, that he himself is "an abominable old man." Later, seeing Julia walking jerkily down the road in a way that attracts curious looks, Uncle Neville wonders what will become of her. "And with decision, he crossed over to the other side of the street."[6] An exaggeration, no doubt, but it may have been how Rhys recalled a bizarre day on which she herself had relished the chance for a battle with Brenda, the younger sister whom she had grown to both despise and envy.

Rhys spent most of the early spring of 1927 in Paris translating *Perversité*, a short novel by a writer whom she admired and with whose world, as Ford had been quick to appreciate, her own writings shared an affinity. She herself would almost certainly have written the book from the perspective of Irma, the doomed prostitute who is murdered by her brother, but Carco's nocturnal world of gaudy fairgrounds and seedy bars, similar to that depicted in Mac Orlan's wittier novel, *Marguerite de la Nuit*, was one on which Rhys had also drawn for her first Parisian stories.

Rhys's treatment of Carco's *Perversité* provides valuable glimpses of her own development as a novelist. She took artistic liberties, breaking Carco's twenty-two chapters into four parts—much as she would do in her own fiction—with subtitles emphasising a unifying element within each section. She strengthened Carco's menacing emphasis on the colour red—symbolising bloodshed—and his powerful use of shadows. Songs were left in the original French, as in "La Grosse Fifi," a tale in which Rhys had imbued Carco's fictional world of violence and sudden death with her own sardonic wit.

She worked fast, completing the translation of Carco's novella of 127 pages in under six weeks. The pride Rhys took in her achievement is clear from the fact that she allowed Germaine to read chapters of her work aloud to an admiring old Madame Richelot before the finished work was despatched to Ford. In March 1927, on the verge of her own first book's publication in England, Rhys experienced a moment of calm satisfaction. She had done well to be chosen by Jonathan Cape and to find herself an agent who was prepared to type out her manuscripts while offering shrewd advice and—as part of a seemingly affectionate sexual transaction—free accommodation. Translating a fine and intriguingly dangerous writer would do no harm at all to her burgeoning career.

Rhys had already received her payment in full. She was not to know that Ford would hang onto *Perversity* for three months. In June, while passing it along to Covici from the French summer home that he still occasionally shared with Stella, Ford casually announced that he himself had given the translation a few tweaks. Ford's intentions remain ambivalent, but it was just what an unscrupulous publisher needed to hear. Jean Rhys was unknown; Ford Madox Ford, in 1927, was one of the most celebrated writers in North America. Ford, not Rhys, would be announced from its first publication until the present time as the sole translator of Carco's novel.

THE LEFT BANK: Sketches and Studies of Present-Day Bohemian Paris was published by Jonathan Cape in March 1927. The announcement "With a Preface by Ford Madox Ford" dominated a stark cover which presented the black-and-white image of a dejected tramp seated beside the Seine. Turning the page, the reader found sixteen pages of meandering evocation, not of Rhys's Paris, but of Ford's own, rifled from his recently published collection of memories: *A Mirror to France*. Instead of praising Rhys's stories, Ford entertained Jean Rhys's first readers in England with his musings on the Parisian underworld, complete with a Carco-esque recollection of being chased home one night by a gang

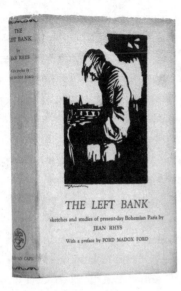

Jonathan Cape's cover for Rhys's first published work was resolutely downbeat. The artist is unknown.
(Used with permission of Peter Harrington Antiquarian Books)

of thugs. A braver editor might have told Ford to quit writing about himself. Unfortunately, neither Jonathan Cape nor Edward Garnett possessed sufficient gumption.

Twelve pages in, and still on a roll, Ford finally recalled the purpose of his preface. "Coming from the Antilles," he wrote:

> Miss Rhys has let her pen loose on the Left Banks of the Old World—on its gaols, its studios, its salons, its cafes, its criminals, its midinettes . . . One likes [. . .] to be connected to something good, and Miss Rhys's work seems to me to be so very good, so vivid, so extraordinarily distinguished by the rendering of passion, and so true, that I wish to be connected with it.

The author's vivid style and subject matter, as Ford was keen to explain in his interminable preface, were far from his own—"No! . . . Her business was with passion, hardship, emotion." Unlike himself, although similarly possessed of "remarkable technical gifts" and a "singular interest for form," the exotic Miss Rhys had a "terrific—an almost lurid!—passion for stating the case of the underdog."

So far, so painfully condescending. But Ford did admire Rhys's work, and he concluded by expressing the hope that when "hundreds of years hence!—her [Rhys's] ashes are translated to the Pantheon . . . a grain or so of my scattered and forgotten dust may go too, in the folds." Such extravagant hyperbole failed to sweeten Rhys's bitterness.

Rhys, still unaware of the fate of her translation of Carco's novel, felt swindled by Ford's hijacking of her collection of stories to promote his own work. Nevertheless, Ford's long-winded introduction drew attention to an unknown author whose "sketches and studies" might otherwise have sunk without trace. *The Left Bank*'s English reviewers didn't go overboard, but they were willing to allow that Miss Rhys's depiction of the underworld of Paris was alarmingly convincing. Hints were dropped that her subject matter was not quite ladylike, but her prose was praised for its originality. "Vienne" and "La Grosse Fifi" attracted particular praise in England. The *New York Times*, reviewing the Harper's publication towards the close of 1927, opined that her style was "singular." A little surprisingly, not one of the reviewers drew comparisons to Katherine Mansfield, a writer to whose more conventional stories of Paris Jean Rhys had been introduced by Ford.

Coming from Jonathan Cape and heralded by a tribute from Ford, *The Left Bank*'s resolute determination not to glamorise Paris helped to place Jean Rhys's name on London's literary map, during the year that Virginia Woolf published *To the Lighthouse*. In May 1927, Rhys received a letter from an old friend, who addressed her as "My dear Kitten," before carefully folding down the top of his note to conceal that tender endearment from the eyes of his work colleagues.[7]

Clearly, the former lovers had maintained some degree of communication; Lancey knew Rhys's French address and regretted not having seen her over Easter, when he had spent a day in Paris. "Is all well [*sic*] write and tell me Lancey." Writing again three weeks later and signing off with "Great Affection," Lancey expressed his frustration at not having yet read her allegedly daring book. "Has it [*The Left Bank*] been stopped by the Censor?" he wondered. "Anyway I am longing to see it. One day you will tell me about the past two years . . . "[8]

Did she? No evidence of a further correspondence has survived, but the presence of a Lancey-like figure four years later in *After Leaving Mr Mackenzie* (1931)—affably remote, but always ready to sign a cheque when required—suggests that the former lovers remained in touch. Rhys's portrait of Mr. Neil James, a connoisseur of fine art, courting Julia Martin's opinion on his most recent acquisitions, makes sad fun of a mismatched affair which had led, in life, to an abortion, an attempted suicide and the humiliation to a proud but poor young woman of being paid off. "[Mr. James] was anxious because he did not want to love the wrong thing," Rhys wrote, mocking Lancey. "Fancy wanting to be told what you should love!"[9]

By May, Rhys had resumed work on *Quartet*. The novel's chief character, Marya Zelli, lives in seedy hotels; Rhys's working conditions were far less bleak. In the autumn of 1926, she had occupied a room on rue du Maine; Lancey wrote to his "kitten" the following May at 9 rue Victor Cousin. These were pleasant side streets in Montparnasse; Germaine was probably paying the rent. The Richelots never lacked money; Germaine took pleasure in helping a friend in whose ability to write a great novel she had complete faith—"even if" (as she gently teased) "you do prefer short stories."[10]

For Rhys herself, it took a long struggle to advance beyond creating a simple record of the past. All she knew was that her novel—she toyed with calling it "Masquerade"—would explore the predicament of an impoverished young woman whose husband is jailed and whose protectors betray her. In the summer of 1927, her puppets had not yet wriggled free of their strings. Her progress—when she was not half-heartedly working in undemanding jobs at fashion houses or cosmetics stores, obtained through glowing testimonials from Germaine—remained slow.[11]

The reason why Germaine and Rhys fell out remains unclear. One cause was Rhys's discovery of her friend's compliance in hiding the source of an allowance that had been paid to Jean for six months by Ford and Stella. But Germaine could also be controlling. It wasn't agreeable to be lectured on the need to obtain a divorce from Jean

Lenglet, for whom Rhys's feelings remained both loving and protective. Neither was it easy for a proud woman to accept that Germaine was both choosing the series of Catholic orphanages at which little Maryvonne still regularly lodged, and paying for the child's clothes and uniforms. The Richelots had even ventured to raise the possibility of adopting Maryvonne themselves. Putting aside her troublesome novel for a few weeks, Rhys vented her altered feelings about the Richelots in a savage little story. Provisionally titled "Susan and Suzanne," it presented a young mother (Susan Helder) who is mistakenly shot while attempting to steal jewellery from her employer. The employer, who adopts Susan's orphaned child, is called Madame Brega. Germaine's sister was Madame Bragadir.[12]

Though it's unlikely that Rhys showed this particular unpublished story to her friend, she certainly made her anger felt. In September 1927, Germaine made a dignified attempt to put things right. "I see that you still have much bitterness against me," she wrote after receiving what appears to have been a grudging apology. But: "My dear Ella, I have nothing to forgive (had I anything to forgive you would be forgiven long ago, as you are unhappy, and because I did love you)."[13]

Jean Lenglet left his job on the same September day that Germaine despatched her kindly message to Rhys. Sacked for appropriating funds intended for the poorhouse library, Lenglet returned to The Hague where—somehow—he acquired a pleasant home at 3 Esdoornstraat, close to the city's broad beaches and nature reserve. This, from October 1927 until early the following year, was the home of the reunited Lenglets and their five-year-old Maryvonne. The reunion, though relatively brief, was evidently successful, since they repeated it in the summer of 1928.

Rhys was still with Lenglet at The Hague when news reached her of what appeared to be an act of incredible treachery. *Perversity* had been published in the US in her translation, but under Ford's name. She may never have known about the frantic letters of protest that Ford had fired off to Covici, but the apparent betrayal stoked a fierce resentment that Lenglet did nothing to dampen as his indignant wife worked on *Quartet*, with her husband at her shoulder.

Was Lenglet a sympathetic listener, or was he himself contributing to the novel? The question arises because Lenglet would later surprisingly claim in the Dutch press, where his word was accepted as the truth, that he had co-written Rhys's first three publications. Certainly, their relationship as writers had always been one of friendly collaboration. *The Left Bank* had included "From a French Prison" and "The Sidi," based on Lenglet's account of the tragic death of a sensitive young Arab at Fresnes. Yet Rhys would always state that it was she alone who wrote her books, and there's no reason to doubt her. What Lenglet did contribute to the writing of *Quartet* was faith in his wife's ability, combined with a shared memory of key moments—like the restaurant encounter with Ford and Stella that had followed his release—on which his wife intended to draw.

"MASQUERADE" REMAINED THE working title for a darkly satiric novel about appearances and their deceptions. Visiting a new restaurant, Marya Zelli finds "no *patronne*, but the patron was beautifully made up." Warning Marya against the English in Paris, the friendly artist Esther de Solla tells her: "They touch life with their gloves on. They're pretending all the time."[14] Rhys's prose glitters with irony on every page, especially when she writes about Stella Bowen, easily recognisable as the opinionated and commanding Lois Heidler. The angry contempt of Bowen's subsequent portrait of Rhys in *Drawn from Life* was an understandable response to the vicious way that Stella had found her cultural aspirations lampooned in *Quartet*. Here, in one of the milder passages, Lois is painting Marya, her guest. Lois, as usual, is holding forth:

> The movement of her head was oddly like that of a bird picking up crumbs. She talked volubly . . . and it was evident that she took

Montparnasse very seriously indeed. She thought of it as a possible stepping-stone to higher things and she liked explaining,
classifying, fitting the inhabitants (that is to say, of course, the
Anglo-Saxon inhabitants) into their proper place in the scheme
of things.

Ford is more gently treated. We see Heidler striding "masterfully" up
and down the room as his amiably elephantine contribution to a dancing party given by his alter ego, Mr. Rolls. Later, Heidler asks Marya
(his mistress) to save Lois from embarrassment by pretending to maintain a friendship: "You've got to play the game." Heidler lays out his
conditions—the helpless Marya will be cared for, and loved, so long as
she agrees to abandon her convicted husband. In the end, it is Marya
whose heart is broken, when Heidler leaves her and returns to Lois.
"I loved him too," Marya proclaims to her husband in the awkwardly
melodramatic last pages of the book.[15] Rhys herself remained publicly
silent about her feelings for Ford throughout her life.

What evidently bothered Rhys most about her relationship with
Ford and Stella, as she worked on *Quartet*, was the persistent recollection of being robbed of her freedom. Released from prison, Stephan
Zelli describes liberty as an illusion: "When you come out—but you
don't come out. Nobody ever comes out." Ordered back into captiv-
ity with the Heidlers by their friend Miss Nicholson, Marya identifies her own situation with that of an entrapped fox. "Up and down it
ran . . . Up and down, up and down, ceaselessly. A horrible sight, really.
"Sweet thing," said Miss Nicholson."[16]

The novel which Rhys brought back to London from Holland in
the summer of 1928 was typed out from her habitual scrawl by a pains-
taking Leslie Tilden Smith. Offered to Jonathan Cape, it was rejected
on the grounds that Rhys's portrait of Ford Madox Ford as Heidler
was libellous. Jonathan Cape's nervousness was understandable; he was
already taking a considerable risk in publishing Radclyffe Hall's sensational lesbian novel, *The Well of Loneliness*, over which he would lose an
expensive lawsuit later that year. Rhys's novel also contained troubling

hints of same-sex relationships; reassuring her jealous husband about the way Lois clasps her hand beneath a restaurant table, Marya shrugs it off: "Oh, she often does that."[17]

When Jonathan Cape turned Rhys's book down, his colleague Edward Garnett stepped in to recommend her novel to Frank Swinnerton, his discerning colleague at a rival firm. Retitled *Postures* to highlight her treatment of disguise and pretence, Rhys's first full-length work of fiction was published in the autumn of 1928 by Chatto. Friends were enthusiastic. Germaine Richelot hurried to congratulate Rhys: "I know enough of your life, dear Ella, to feel I was "reliving" it with you as I reread the book."[18] Ivan Beede praised the novel's poetic language. Like an admiring Leslie Tilden Smith, Beede was put in mind by Rhys's Paris scenes of T. S. Eliot's ability to conjure up the echoing vacancies of a nocturnal metropolis; Beede mentioned Eliot's "Portrait of a Lady," while Tilden Smith compared *Postures* (favourably) to "Prufrock."

The reviewers—they were predominantly male—hedged their bets. Admiring Rhys's laconic style and the originality of her voice, they deplored—as in the *Left Bank* stories—the way she dwelt upon "squalor." True, the glamorous Kiki of Montparnasse (Alice Prin) and her lover, Foujita, could be glimpsed in a passing reference to "Cri-cri" with the Japanese companion whom Lois Heidler longs to lure to her parties. But where was the exhilarating city of Josephine Baker, and frantic jazz and flirtations? What were they to make of a protagonist who brazenly declared her intention of becoming "so drunk that I can't see"? Wasn't Heidler stating the obvious (Rhys's irony went clean over their heads) when he said that "nobody owes a fair deal to a prostitute. It isn't done"?[19] While conceding with majestic reluctance that the author was "an artist," the *Manchester Guardian* opined that "a great deal depends on what she does next."[20]

For the 1928 reviewer, knowing nothing about Jean Rhys's life, it would have been impossible to appreciate the art with which Rhys had transferred her own experiences into the life of a less educated heroine. By excluding the literary aspect of her own connection to Ford from the novel, Rhys was able to alter the relationship between the characters. Marya has only her body to offer, as a model for a bewitched Lois, and as a mistress for a quietly oppressive Heidler. Far more passive than her creator, she is as much of a prisoner as her incarcerated spouse. Only occasionally—it seems to be an authorial lapse when Marya quotes Edouard Dujardin's famous novella's title "*Les lauriers sont coupés*" (usually translated as "We'll go to the woods no more), as Heidler prises open her bedroom door—does the sophisticated sensibility of Jean Rhys glint through the simpler, sadder personality of a young woman whose increasing reliance upon alcohol is firmly connected by Rhys to Marya's relationship with the worldly, hard-drinking Heidler.

Quartet is by no means artistically perfect. The shifts in points of view are executed as unsubtly as the moments in which Lois expresses her jealousy of Marya ("she ought to sing for her supper; that's what she's here for, isn't it"),[21] or when "HJ" (Rhys seems to be mocking Ford's reverence for Henry James) bluntly spells out the novel's theme of imprisonment by remarking that: "One's caught in a sort of trap." Nevertheless, Rhys had taken a remarkable leap forward from the sharply observed sketches of 1927 to the well-planned structure and confidently ironic tone of 1928. Leslie Tilden Smith now felt ready to devote himself entirely to encouraging and promoting such an exceptional talent.

Shortly after reading the reviews of *Quartet*, Rhys carried Maryvonne away from her father in Holland for a promised three-month holiday, beginning with a happy stay at Bandol in the south of France. It was the first time since leaving Paris that Rhys had been alone with her daughter. Lenglet, regarding himself as the more devoted parent, criticised her for negligence. "*Elle desire jouer, courir, discuter meme* ['She needs to play, run about, chat']," he scolded his wife on 21 February 1929. Given that Lenglet himself welcomed Maryvonne back to Holland by installing her at the home of a certain Madame van der Heyden, this seems unjust.[22]

Tireless though both Rhys and Lenglet now became about creating delightful stories for their daughter's amusement (several of Lenglet's

Maryvonne Lenglet and her father in Holland, c. 1929. Dutch was her first language, and would remain so. *(McFarlin)*

small hand-bound texts survive, as do Rhys's regular gifts of classic children's books like *Treasure Island*), they had abandoned Maryvonne during her early years. More lavish presents helped assuage Rhys's conscience. Such indulgence became easier for Rhys in 1929 after Simon & Schuster agreed to publish *Postures* in America, where they retitled it *Quartet*.

Why the sudden transatlantic interest in an almost unknown writer? It is possible that Ford (perhaps still feeling guilty about Covici's blushless naming of himself as the translator of Carco's novel) mentioned Rhys to the literary agent Paul Revere Reynolds, a shrewd, slow-spoken

New Englander who had represented everybody from Joseph Conrad
to Lytton Strachey, and who now, unexpectedly, took Jean Rhys on as
his client.

Reynolds was famous for getting good deals for his authors. Encouraged by their own inhouse reader's praise for the newly named *Quartet*
as a work of "Flaubertian economy," Simon & Schuster offered a generous advance which also owed something to their hope that Rhys's daring novel would follow the runaway success of *Bad Girl*, Viña Delmar's
racy 1928 tale of life in Harlem.[23]

By the summer of 1929, Rhys was finally enjoying the ease of a little financial freedom with which to work on a second novel. Not yet
wholly committed to a personal relationship with Leslie Tilden Smith,
she used her American advance to return to Paris.

IV

THE RHYS WOMAN
Jean Rhys

"Every day is a new day. Every day you are a new person."

—Jean Rhys, *After Leaving Mr Mackenzie*

9

Two Tunes:
Past and Present (1929–36)

"When you were a child, you put your hand on the trunk of a
tree and you were comforted . . . you knew that it was friendly
to you, or at least, not hostile. But of people you were always a
little afraid."

—Jean Rhys, *After Leaving Mr Mackenzie* (1931)

AFTER LEAVING MR MACKENZIE was written in Paris and London over
a period of two years from 1929. During that time, Rhys unexpectedly
found herself having to care for Maryvonne on her own for several
months while Lenglet—no explanation was provided for his abrupt
departure—disappeared from Holland. Much though Rhys loved her
solemn little girl, the frustration proved considerable of having to
combine child care with the demands of writing a novel. Thankfully
returning to Leslie Tilden Smith's mews flat in Holland Park from the
hated south London convent school at which she briefly boarded (it was
the mother branch of the Virgo Fidelis convent formerly attended by
Rhys in Dominica), Maryvonne witnessed enough drama to decide that
she herself would never attempt to become a writer.[*]

***

[*] "This was idiotic of me," Rhys later told Sonia Orwell of the impulsive decision
to send her daughter to the school in South Norwood. "Because I'd liked my convent

Rhys's difficulties with producing her second and more carefully crafted novel are still apparent in the draft that survives at the British Library. Sometimes, only a few words were scribbled across a sheet of paper; insistent repetitions and carefully indicated gaps show how fully the novel needed to take shape in Rhys's mind before she felt ready to commit any readable writing to a page.

Although less directly autobiographical than its predecessor, *After Leaving Mr Mackenzie* contains many links to Rhys's own life. Some are easily spotted: Julia Martin, the narrator, remembers having been frightened and fascinated by masks as a child growing up in a hot and distant country. Her family live in Acton. She has had two unsatisfactory love affairs. She even occupies rooms in a cheap hotel on the Quai des Grands-Augustins, where Rhys began working on the novel in 1929. Unlike Julia, however, Rhys was typing out an English student's doctoral thesis in order to pay the rent.[*] Mr. Mackenzie is a pompous caricature of Ford, but Rhys is playing games with the reader by allowing Julia to discover him tucking into a dish of veau Clamart: Clamart was where Lenglet had skulked while hiding from the Paris gendarmerie. Another example of Rhys's layering and game-playing is the way in which she signals *Mackenzie*'s debt to Katherine Mansfield's "The Daughters of the Late Colonel" (especially in the portrayal of Julia and Norah as two fatherless sisters well past girlhood). Rhys winks her acknowledgement to Mansfield's story when Julia's cautious admirer, George Horsfield, follows the announcement of his father's military rank with a troubling non sequitur: "Pa was a colonel. I was

---

I imagined that a convent was a kind and pleasant place to be" (Jean Rhys to Sonia Orwell, 3 May 1971, McFarlin 2.8.f6).

[*] In 1929, Elsie Phare (later Elsie Duncan Jones) spent a few months in Paris, where she met Samuel Beckett and also Jean Rhys, who unexpectedly volunteered to type out her dissertation on English Royalists in exile. Later, Elsie blamed Rhys's abysmal typing for her failure to gain a fellowship (Elsie Duncan Jones obituary, *Independent*, 23 October 2011; Professor Peter Davidson, her former pupil, confirms the details: Davidson to author, 20 December 2020).

seduced by a clergyman at a garden-party. Pa shot him. Heavens, how the blighter bled!"[1] Mansfield's story of a colonel's two daughters had appeared in a collection called *The Garden Party* in 1922.

Finding the biographical clues hidden within a Rhys novel is always fun. Echoes and parallels can be filleted out; resemblances and points of difference can swiftly be established between the fiction and the life of its creator. Entertaining though the enterprise may be, it's a pursuit which undermines appreciation of Rhys's uncanny ability to engage with readers who know nothing about her personal circumstances.

While connected to *Quartet* in its use of the third person and abruptly shifting points of view, Rhys's second novel is more sophisticated in the way that it separates the imagined Julia from the actual Jean. Although close to Rhys in her obsession with appearance, her vulnerability, lightning rages and casual reliance upon alcohol for a boost, Julia Martin—like Marya Zelli—is neither a writer nor even especially cultured. The "Rolling down to Rio" rhyme that haunts Julia—and neatly flags up her Brazilian childhood—comes from Kipling's popular children's book, the *Just So Stories*. Modigliani's brazenly exposed nude, with which Julia registers a disturbing affinity when she first sees it, is feebly described by her as "a rum picture." A reference to Joseph Conrad's early novel, *Almayer's Folly*—to which Rhys had been introduced by Ford—arises from the consciousness not of Julia, but of her quietly valiant sister, Norah Griffiths. Julia—it's clear—wouldn't know who Conrad was. Unlike Rhys, who hated the sense of being indebted, Julia Martin is a habitual parasite, a woman who takes money without shame from anyone she can persuade to bestow it. (She meets her match in Uncle Griffiths, the affluent but tight-fisted relative who stumps up a pound, but only to ensure his embarrassing niece's immediate departure from England.)

Rhys's genius—still not fully flowered in her fortieth year, but growing at an astonishing rate—lay in her unfailing ability to create, within fewer than 150 pages, a world that is both uniquely alien and recognisably mundane. The grim outline of Julia's future life is visible from the bald opening statement ("After she had parted from Mr Mackenzie, Julia went to live in a cheap hotel on the Quai des Grands Augustins"[2]) to their second farewell at the novel's disturbingly inconclusive ending:

> "Goodbye," said Mr Mackenzie.
> The street was cool and full of grey shadows. Lights were beginning to come out in the cafes. It was the hour between dog and wolf, as they say.[3]

RHYS WOULD SOMETIMES describe *Mackenzie* as her best novel. The unshowy but always telling vocabulary (Uncle Griffiths sounds "alarmed and annoyed"; Julia speaks to her inert mother in a "frightened, hopeful" voice) reminds us that Ford had introduced his protégée to the early work of James Joyce; she could always quote lines from *Dubliners*. Shafts of sardonic wit lighten the darkness: a landlady is briskly skewered on her notion of acceptable behaviour in a female lodger: "A man, yes; a bottle, no,"[4] while Mr. Mackenzie's tips are "not always in proportion with the benevolence of his stomach."[5] Julia's stingy uncle greets his penniless niece with utter disbelief: "as he might have said: 'A zebra? A giraffe?' "[6]

Of less interest to her first readers than to students of literature is the way in which—far more than in *Quartet*—Rhys held herself apart from the imaginary Julia Martin. Rhys's appearance remained exceptionally youthful and attractive. It is unlikely that any man reacted to her as a hopeful stroller does after a swift backward glance at Julia's haggard face in the novel's closing chapter, "Last." ("*Oh la la*," he said. "*Ah, non alors*"). Rhys's sharp eye, not Julia's, notices how the host of a certain Parisian restaurant always positions himself on the kitchen stairs, in order to leer up the skirts of female customers. Rhys, not Julia, undercuts the consideration shown by Mr. James (modelled upon the business-like Lancey) when he announces the precise number of minutes he can allot to a meeting with his former mistress. ("I've got loads of time—heaps of time. Nearly three-quarters of an hour.")[7] Rhys, not

Julia, skilfully prefigures a suicidal moment beside the Seine through a deftly planted reference to Mr. James's vase of drooping tulips.* Dying, "with curved grace in their death,"[8] the flowers will return as sirens of the night river, shadows that "thrust out long, curved, snake-like arms and beckoned."[9] Here, far more than in *Quartet*, Rhys's prose approaches poetry in its evocative use of images—like the suggestive vase of tulips—to conjure up Julia's thoughts.

———————

JONATHAN CAPE PUBLISHED *After Leaving Mr Mackenzie* early in 1931. The times were commercially challenging; the novel's jazzily bright pink and yellow jacket—it showed Parisian-style houses bordering the Seine—was directed at a broader market than *The Left Bank*'s heroically gloomy cover (from the same publishing house).

American publication by Knopf followed in June, but only after Rhys's unflattering portrait of Ford, a major figure in the States, as Mr. Mackenzie had caused a nervous Max Schuster to reject the novel which his publishing firm had been keenly anticipating since 1929. Reviewers were unanimous in praising the exceptional quality of Rhys's writing: the critics for the *Observer* and the *Daily Telegraph* described it as "flawless" and "superb," while America's *Saturday Review* astutely praised Rhys's prose for possessing "the balance and beauty of verse."[10] Militating against any hope of popular success on either side of the Atlantic for Rhys's second novel were the vociferous objections made to a morally dubious heroine and—once again—a "squalid" tale. The point was rammed home when *The Times* and the *Times Literary Supplement* simultaneously published an anonymous review in which *Mackenzie* was dismissed as "a waste of talent," expended on "a sordid little story."[11] Rebecca West, while assuring readers of the *Telegraph*

———————

*   Rhys's first working title, "Wintry Orchids," hinted through its glacial invocation of a famously sexual flower (the courtesan Odette in Proust's novel wears a corsage of orchids) at Mr. James's chilling kindness to Julia, his former mistress. Possibly, a vase of orchids had preceded the drooping tulips she sees in her lover's Mayfair home after he—once again—bails her out.

that Rhys was among the finest writers of her generation, regretted that such an interesting writer should be "enamoured of gloom to an incredible degree."[12]

By 1931, Leslie Tilden Smith was working in a freelance capacity for his friend Jamie (Hamish was his given name) Hamilton's new London publishing firm, with connections in the States provided by Hamilton's second job as a scout for Cass Canfield, head of Harper's. Editors and publishers talk among themselves; overheard trade gossip may have led even Rhys's devoted supporter at home to question the darkness of her subject matter. "My father had tremendous faith in her writing . . . he did all the typing and correcting," Leslie's daughter would inform Diana Athill in 1967.[13] Within the privacy of her notebooks, however, Rhys jotted angry notes about observations made by a certain "Mr Smith," who considers that the only kind of writing to succeed "is written to make money," and that authors who "drink and starve and all the rest are mad." Elsewhere in the same black exercise book, Rhys recorded a quarrel during which "L" warned her that "a writer is always to be identified with the kind of person he or she writes about." Defending herself, Rhys had begun to shout. "Well then said L, enjoying himself in his quiet way . . . Yes he said now don't get excited and don't use that awful language."[14]

Behind what read like fragments from actual discussions lies the

Leslie Tilden Smith, Rhys's second husband. (McFarlin)

sense of Rhys's personal anxiety. She didn't need to be warned that novels like *Quartet* and *Mackenzie* would never make her rich. The problem of distinguishing herself from the women about whom she wrote would become a lifelong concern. She was, and still too often is, judged by the fictitious alter egos whom she created, but only in part resembled.

In 1929, when Rhys started work on her second novel, one of the few fictional characters comparable to Rhys's wayward Marya Zelli and Julia Martin was the surrealist poet André Breton's Nadja, a woman who (in Breton's words) "enjoyed being nowhere but in the streets, the only region of valid experience for her." Breton had published *Nadja* in 1928, just before the UK publication of *Postures* (*Quartet*). It is unclear when Rhys first read the book, but she could still hold a discussion with a fellow admirer in her eighties about the merits of *Nadja*.[15] Writing to a new American friend in June 1931, Rhys confessed that she liked *Mackenzie* above anything she had yet achieved. Seeking a French publisher, she sent a copy to Ford's Paris agent, William Bradley.* Her pride was justified; *Mackenzie* reached a significant group of admirers. They included a talented Irish writer whose own wild personality matched that of Rhys at full tilt, but Norah Hoult—unlike Peggy Kirkaldy, Evelyn Scott and Norah's own husband, Oliver Stonor, a novelist writing under the pseudonym of a Devon village, Morchard Bishop—was never to become a personal friend.

Peggy Kirkaldy (born Margaret Jacks) was a tiny and kind-hearted woman with a hot temper, a weakness for the racecourse and a devastatingly sharp tongue. Among writers, she was on good terms with Elizabeth Bowen, Jocelyn Brooke and Denton Welch, but her closest and most long-standing literary friendship was with Dorothy Richardson, author of the *Pilgrimage* cycle of novels. Always hopeful of becoming a writer herself, Peggy divided her time between socialising

---

* Bradley's friendship with Ford did not stop him talking to Rhys, when she visited Paris in September the following year, about a publisher for "Triple Sec." Rhys excused herself, claiming that she had "borrowed enough" from it for her work-in-progress (*Voyage in the Dark*) to render the original unsaleable (JR to WB, 3 February 1931; 21 September 1932; 1 October 1932, William H Bradley papers, HRC).

at her London house, and self-imposed seclusion—she felt that solitude helped her writing—at an isolated home on the Norfolk Broads.

By 1931, when Peggy first made contact with her, Rhys was living with Leslie Tilden Smith in Elgin Crescent, west London. Peggy paid a visit to the flat; the two women hit it off. Growing chummy over a glass—or two or three—Jean discovered a sympathetic listener to whom she could groan about Leslie's sporadic attempts to restrict her drinking. Writing to Peggy later, Jean was treacherously frank about Leslie's gift of an "awful" hat during a damp, joint excursion to Cambridge. Conscious that Peggy had smart friends, Rhys put on airs. Cambridge was described as "rather a darling place"; one early letter was signed *"A bientot,* as they say" (this from a woman who spoke impeccable French). More candidly, Rhys expressed her urgent hope of making some money with a third novel, one on which she had just embarked. Income was needed; when Rhys first met him, Leslie was already running short after borrowing heavily against his future inheritance (his clergyman father planned to divide a modest legacy equally between a prudent daughter and a spendthrift son). Freelance editing for a burgeoning publisher, however kind-hearted a one, was not well paid.[16]

The friendship which Rhys formed with the strong-willed and beautiful Evelyn Scott and her second husband, John Metcalfe, promised to be more important to Rhys's career. A respected novelist and exceptional critic, Scott's literary fame by the late Twenties was so great that her reader's report on William Faulkner's *The Sound and the Fury* (1928) had been published as a preface to a limited edition of the novel, together with its editor's prediction that Mr. Faulkner's star might one day rise high enough to glitter alongside Scott's own. James Joyce had personally written to thank Evelyn for a discerning early review of *Ulysses* in *The Dial.*

Scott's private life was equally remarkable. Three years younger than Rhys, she had eloped in 1913, aged twenty, swapping a shabbily grand life in Tennessee for a lonely hut in the wilds of Brazil. While there, Scott's unhappy mother showed up and stayed on to create a

An arresting portrait of Rhys's influential American admirer, the novelist Evelyn Scott. *(Used with permission of Denise Scott Fears)*

threesome with Evelyn and her married—and much older—partner from the South, a promiscuous author, playwright and physician in tropical medicine called Frederick Creighton Wellman. Returning to New York, her affairs with Waldo Frank and William Carlos Williams had done nothing to hinder Evelyn Scott's ascent in the literary world before her second marriage, in 1930, to the English-born Metcalfe.

In June 1931, writing to Rhys from the steamer bound for New York aboard which she and Metcalfe had been devouring *Mackenzie*, Scott announced her intention of winning American recognition for such a "rare, subtle and sensitive talent."[17] For a writer who had just begun work on her third novel with no certainty of which brave editor, during increasingly straitened times, would publish another unsparing tale of life on a downward curve, this was splendid news. Rhys wrote back on the same day that she received Scott's enthusiastic letter, expressing gratitude and pleasure. The exchange marked the start of a friendship based upon mutual admiration: "My God, what a fine writer you are," Rhys would exclaim after reading Scott's fiercely strange novel, *Eva Gay* (1933). More than warm-hearted Peggy Kirkaldy, Scott became a valued literary advisor, while John Metcalfe (himself a writer of fascinatingly macabre short stories), a man who lived predominantly in

England, would quietly establish his own close friendship with Rhys and Tilden Smith.

———————————

WRITING AN AFFECTIONATE letter to Leslie Tilden Smith's daughter in 1968, Maryvonne described how dependent she had been upon Leslie's kindness during the childhood holidays she spent with her volatile mother. He was "a marvellous man . . . I really loved him," Maryvonne told Antoinette.[18] But this declaration was made to Leslie's own loving daughter. Elsewhere, Maryvonne would go out of her way to explain what fun her mother had been as a companion on the riverside excursions and camping holidays which formed a regular feature of Maryvonne's annual summers in England. In 1931, when Maryvonne turned nine, the trio left London for a long summer spell at a rented bungalow beside the River Wye. Rhys was always happy in the Welsh borderlands which reminded her of her father's attachment to Wales; the chuckle of the Wye's clear water flowing steadily over a stony bed reminded a homesick writer of Dominica's enchanting rivers. By the autumn, however, Maryvonne was back in Holland; shortly before Christmas, Rhys visited Lenglet and Maryvonne in Amsterdam.

The presence of Jean Rhys in her estranged husband's home was unusually welcome. Jean Lenglet had spent much of his year of absence from Holland working on *Sous les Verrous* (Under Lock and Key), his own take on the Ford affair. "I found him . . . very unhappy," Rhys remembered later. "He'd finished this very long and, yes, autobiographical mostly, novel in French, but made no attempt to publish it. So I took the mss back to London and worked at it with rage, fury and devotion."[19]

Rhys went over her husband's novel (which Lenglet, contrary to her later recollection, had already translated into awkward English), with all the scrupulous care she had lavished upon Carco's *Perversité*. The use of prison imagery in her own *Quartet* inspired her choice for its English title: *Barred*. Honourably, since the novel did not present Rhys herself in a glowing light, she made only a few alterations to

Lenglet's portrait of his wife as Stania, a weaker and more subservient character than *Quartet*'s Marya Zelli. Rhys did, however, take care to establish that Stania never lived with her "protectors," the Hubners, as she herself had lived with Stella and Ford. Given the libellous portrait that Ford had painted of Rhys as Lola Porter, a tempestuous and highly sexed Creole writer, in his most recent book, *When The Wicked Man* (1931)—and it's difficult to suppose that the well-read Rhys was unaware of such a sensational fiction—she was generous to tone down the harshness of Lenglet's portrait of her former lover.* Perhaps Rhys was seeking to redress what she later described remorsefully as the "spite" of *Quartet*.

Published in the spring of 1932 by Desmond Harmsworth (following a string of rejections), *Barred* inspired a rave from Compton Mackenzie and drew respectful reviews from J. B. Priestley, Frank Swinnerton and one of Rhys's most ardent admirers, Norah Hoult. Rebecca West declined to supply a review, pointedly saying that she looked forward soon to reading another of Jean Rhys's *own* works. Rhys's involvement in her husband's novel was no secret: Lenglet had added a touching foreword under his pen name of Edouard de Nève, in which he thanked Jean Rhys, as the author of two "beautiful" novels, for sparing the time to foster "this gloomy child of mine."

Translating *Barred* drew Rhys away from working at her third novel. Provisionally, she named it "Two Tunes," a reference to its dazzlingly persuasive exposition of her growing belief that the dreamworld of the past and the activity of the present co-exist, simultaneously, within a single conscious realm. In *After Leaving Mr Mackenzie*, Julia Martin vividly recollects a moment from her Brazilian childhood (the memory, of course, belonged to Rhys's own and ever-vivid Domini-

---

* Rhys's first biographer, Carole Angier, suggests that Ford's curious novel *When The Wicked Man* (1931) balanced his vicious fictionalisation of a creole character who displays all of Rhys's intemperate violence and rage with a gentler presentation of her, within the same novel, as Henrietta Felise. Ford's biographer, Max Saunders, has convincingly since shown that Henrietta Felise was based upon Ford's later lover, Elizabeth Cheetham (Max Saunders, *Ford Madox Ford*, Vol. II, OUP, 1996, pp. 296–7).

can past) when a terrified child scents invisible danger in a sunlit forest glade. Now, in the novel that would become *Voyage in the Dark*, Rhys dived more deeply into her Caribbean past, exploring the episodes and images that she could best employ to haunt—and eventually, overwhelm—young Anna Morgan. Rhys's use of the first person marked a technical advance in her ability to forge an immediate connection with her reader. The eerie authenticity of Anna's voice conceals from our eyes the chasm that lies between Rhys, the creator, and the tragic, untutored girl.

Voyage in the Dark was written during the long aftermath of the US stock market crash when Leslie became almost as penniless as Rhys. Money problems were behind the couple's impulsive decision to move to Berlin; in Germany, the exchange rates would work in their favour. The plan fell through when the Tilden Smiths' Jewish contact ominously vanished from view. As a result, Leslie and Rhys were still living in London early in 1933, when Lenglet asked for a quick divorce in order to marry an attractive and intelligent Dutch writer. Well regarded as a novelist in her day, Henriëtte van Eyk shared Lenglet's admiration for Rhys's work.

Rhys gave her consent, but not without reluctance. Lenglet had been the first to encourage her to write. He was part of her life, the father both of her lost baby son and of the living, loving Maryvonne. Granting a divorce felt especially strange at a moment when she had just finished translating and revising *Barred*, Lenglet's own account of their shared past.

The news of Lenglet's marriage plans came at a time when Rhys was struggling to maintain authorial control of the emotions stirred up by her deep immersion in the past. Before *Voyage in the Dark*, Jean had never written with such passionate intensity about Dominica, an island which grew ever more alluring to her amidst the angry despair and cynicism of England in the early Thirties. "It was as if a curtain had fallen," she wrote in *Voyage*'s opening line, recalling London's cool disdain for a gauche little girl newly arrived from an outpost of the

Empire. A few pages later, Rhys used the same consciously dramatic image to set her two stages, past and present. "A curtain fell and then I was here."[20]

The dipping, gliding past–present progress of *Voyage in the Dark* is impeccably managed from the first moment of shy embarkation—the pick-up of a couple of chorus girls on a promenade at an English seaside town—to its unflinchingly bleak destination. "This thing here—I can't believe it's the same sun, I simply can't believe it," Anna tells herself in the midst of remembering how, as a child whose closest friend was a free-spirited black girl, she had hated the colour of her own white skin.[21] Taken to England's Savernake Forest by her well-meaning lover—Walter Jeffries imagines it will remind her of the tropics—Anna does indeed slip back into her earlier life on the edge of a wilder, virgin forest in the Caribbean. ("We used to sit on the veranda with the night coming in, huge. And the way it smelt of all flowers.")[22] Finally, as Anna undergoes a botched abortion—the operation would end Miss Morgan's short life in Rhys's preferred first version—the past sweeps the present away in a bravura passage which runs all Anna's distant memories together, pulling her under while the treacherous voice of her protector rings like a hollow bell through the rising dark. "*My darling mustn't worry my darling mustn't be sad . . . he said it's nearly four o'clock perhaps you ought to be going . . . You ought to be going he said.*"[23] Rhys's debt to James Joyce, as apparent here as in the extraordinary conclusion to her fourth novel, *Good Morning, Midnight*, reminds us that an early section of *Finnegans Wake* was published as "Work in Progress" in the *transatlantic review*. Copies of Ford's cherished magazine had been Rhys's intimate companions for at least a year during her affair with him in Paris.

In later years, trying to explain her writing process, Rhys cited Charlotte Brontë's famous description of the novelist (or poet, since Brontë was thinking of her sister, Emily) whose duty it is to work passively, "under dictates you neither delivered nor could question."[24] Omitted from this romantic view of inspiration guiding the pen was the considerable emotional strain that writing imposed. *Voyage in the Dark* would become Rhys's finest achievement yet; it was also by far her most demanding.

Drink, always a reliable source of brief good cheer, impeded the novel's progress towards its end. Desperate to reach completion, Rhys turned down an invitation to join Lenglet and Maryvonne for a last family week in Holland during the spring of 1933. Instead, leaving Leslie to spend some welcome time with his own daughter at the still unmarried couple's new flat on Adelaide Road, just north of Regent's Park, Jean retreated alone to the quiet Sussex seaside town of Rottingdean.

As a cure for booze and the blues, Rhys's industrious month in a room above a seaside teashop was a success. Having arrived "crazy with depression," she slept well in the sea air and read nothing more stressful than P. G. Wodehouse's latest contribution to the Blandings Castle series while she worked at *Voyage*. "If I could make one more effort I could finish it I think," she wrote to a sympathetic Evelyn Scott. "One more—You know—You do know don't you."[25]

Scott, a heavy drinker herself, did know, and sympathised. "Haven't touched a drop for a month," Rhys bragged at the end of her seaside vacation—but then undercut the boast: "Won't it be fine when I do."[26] Rhys never concealed her fondness for alcohol and she never renounced it for more than a few weeks—just long enough to demonstrate her iron will.

The Thirties was a decade remarkable for the heaviness of the drinking that went on, especially in Prohibition America. Nobody thought any the worse of Rhys for getting drunk, until drink unleashed her demons. "I'm not one to whine like some women do," she told a writing friend in later life: "I attack."[27] Attacking could mean delivering a punch, a string of expletives or a sudden disgusted jet of saliva. Leslie, a heavy drinker himself, tried to subdue her by silent disapproval, a tactic which Rhys angrily described as "his hanging judge's face."[28] When that failed—and it invariably did—Tilden Smith reverted to screaming back at her. Sometimes, their verbal battles ended in blows. "She [Rhys] and my father had terrible rows," his daughter later confirmed.[29]

In September 1933, the Lenglets' divorce was finalised. Tilden Smith would wait until February 1934 to propose. Rhys, who accepted at once, remembered both the proposal and the quiet ceremony at a London registry office as times of rare, unqualified joy. While marriage did not mark an end to her professional relationship with Lenglet, an active supporter of her writings, the wedding signalled Leslie's personal commitment to his Ella as a beloved partner, as well as a writer of extraordinary talent. Their squabbles continued. Until the very end of her long life, Jean Rhys preserved an undated scrap of paper recording the conclusion to one of the many physical and verbal battles that rifted her marriage to Leslie, but never broke it. "To an afflicted one," it read. "Nothing have I to give for you. Only my heart, my true heart—forgiving and loving Leslie."[30]

LESLIE, WHO TYPED out the new novel, faced the difficult task of finding a publisher for a work which demonstrated that Jean Rhys had defied the requests of her reviewers for a little less squalor and gloom. Jonathan Cape rejected *Voyage* (still called "Two Tunes" at that point) as too depressing, while Jamie Hamilton—despite an enduring respect for Jean's work—asked for cuts that Rhys felt would wreck her delicately calibrated book. As a devoted supporter of Patrick Hamilton, the hard-drinking author best known today for *Hangover Square*, Michael Sadleir of Constable was used to publishing bleak books: his friend's most recent fiction had borne the unappetising title: *Plains of Cement*. Sadleir took Rhys's novel, scheduling it for the autumn of 1934, prior to the US publication in March 1935. He imposed two conditions: he wanted 2,500 words cut from the elaborate Joycean sequence at the end and he wanted Anna Morgan to be kept alive.

Rhys complied about the deletion, but it seems likely that—after preserving and obsessively revising the original manuscript—she later made use of the omitted pages for her descriptions of madness in *Wide Sargasso Sea*.[31] She disagreed more strongly with the publisher's insistence that Anna should survive her last grim ordeal. Artfully, she subverted Sadleir's wishes by her deft use of the ray of light—a crucial last image—that is visible from Anna's sickbed. To Anna, the light appears as a sword: "the last thrust of remembering before everything is blotted out." In the novel's closing words, she weighs hopefulness against despair. "I lay and watched it and thought about starting all over again. And about being new and fresh. And about mornings, and misty days, when anything might happen. And about starting all over again, all over again . . . "[32]

As Rhys's revision subtly intimates, death has already reached poor Anna and death will strike her down.

WHILE LESLIE SEARCHED for a willing publisher, the couple's resources dwindled. It was not for family feeling alone that—shortly after their winter wedding ceremony—Rhys introduced Leslie to her favourite brother, Owen Rees Williams, who was back in London after unsuccessfully attempting to set up a fruit farm in Australia. Charmed both by Rhys's delicate beauty and by her unexpected willingness to sit down on the floor and play trains with their small son, Owen's wife Dorothy revised her initial opinion when Rhys asked for a loan. Speaking to Rhys's first biographer, Carole Angier, Dorothy Rees Williams recalled how she had warned her easy-going husband that she would walk out on him rather than give his sister a single cent. ("If you send that woman one penny I go out that door and never come back.")[33] Dorothy, the most forthcoming interviewee that Angier spoke to in Jean's family, missed no opportunity to condemn her sister-in-law after that first unfortunate encounter.

Leslie and Rhys had never lived grandly. In the first months of their marriage, they struggled to cover the modest rent for two adjoining bedsits in Bloomsbury's dilapidated Brunswick Square. During the summer of 1934, they took a further step down the property ladder by moving out of town to "Luxor," a tiny bungalow near Shepperton, on muddy little Pharaoh's Island (presented to Horatio Nelson as a fishing retreat on the Thames after his victory on the Nile). "Luxor" lay between "Rameses" and "Assouan." Writing to Evelyn Scott on 10 June, Rhys playfully commented on a disrespectful homage to the Egyptian gods: an image of Osiris painted by a previous inhabitant onto their new home's lavatory door.

To Maryvonne, now twelve, this was a time of uncomplicated happiness. Her mother had married a kind and affectionate man; she liked living at Luxor; a late summer camping excursion to Wales's Brecon Beacons was remembered for wonderful family games of charades. It might be hard to imagine—Maryvonne would proudly comment on a radio programme, almost fifty years later—just how brilliant her late mother had been at playing roles. She could even do Long John Silver! But "you can't imagine her like that. No, she was an actress really."[34]

Constable paid only £25 for "Two Tunes" in July 1934, but the death of Rhys's maternal Aunt Brenda netted her a welcome £100 (most of Brenda's modest legacy went to the younger niece and namesake who had taken care of her in Acton), while the death of Leslie's mother at the end of that same summer produced a welcome financial injection of £2,500 (£180,000 in today's money). Always materially generous when she could afford to be, Rhys lavished treats upon her daughter—"everything a child could wish for," Maryvonne later recalled: "books and ballet, music, pantomime and circus."[35] Shortly before Christmas, Rhys went into Harrods, bought smart pyjamas for Leslie and a much-coveted mouth organ for her daughter—and then forgetfully left them behind, on a cloakroom chair. Not surprisingly, they disappeared. And her thoughtful gifts were to have been such a surprise! Twenty years later, Rhys still felt mortified.

Lost presents sound like an oversight, but Rhys's mind may have been unsettled by disappointment. The autumn reviews of *Voyage in the Dark*, the most compassionate, understanding and tragic portrait of a woman that she had yet created, were the best and most extensive that Rhys had so far received. One perceptive fellow novelist, Clemence Dane, writing in *Dublin Magazine* (January 1935), singled out the author's power "to express the emotions and bewilderments of the inarticulate" which is central to Rhys's presentation of Anna, the most innocent of her heroines. Nevertheless, while *The Lady*'s reviewer (8 November 1934) believed it would give that magazine's readers a clearer understanding of how even a "nice" girl might be driven into prostitution, regret was still persistently being expressed at such a fine female writer's obsession with "dreadful" and "difficult" subjects. For the future, Rhys's own literary voyage looked to be heading into uncharted waters.

A more likely explanation for Rhys's odd act of carelessness in Harrods was that she had begun drinking so heavily during 1934 that she couldn't write.[36] And without her writing, she went to pieces.

Rhys's distraught state militated against new opportunities to establish herself in the London literary world. Rosamond Lehmann was among the keenest admirers of *Voyage in the Dark*. At the beginning of 1935, Lehmann wrote Rhys a flattering letter, suggesting that they should meet. This was an opportunity that was not to be passed up. Lehmann's own first novel, *Dusty Answer* (1927), had been an instant bestseller; since then, she had become a force to be reckoned with in the publishing world. Invited to visit the Oxfordshire home which Rosamond shared with her husband, Wogan Philipps, and their baby girl, Rhys was initially hesitant. Reassured by Leslie that the meeting would be well worth the difficulties of an elaborate cross-country journey by train and bus, she agreed to make the trip.

Eagerly anticipated by Rosamond, Rhys's visit to Oxfordshire was a disaster. All ready with their questions, Rosamond, her actress sister Beatrix, and their friend, the widowed, elegant and sharply intelligent Violet Hammersley, together let fly like a firing squad. An unnerved Rhys, fidgeting unhappily with the gloves which she considered essential for a lady's social visit, provided her terse responses in a carefully enunciated whisper. After an awkward hour, she asked to be taken back to the railway station.

Rosamond's second attempt to befriend Rhys was equally unsuccessful. Set for May 1935, it conflicted with celebrations being held to honour George V's twenty-fifth (and penultimate) year on the throne. Rhys, whose face bore alarming bruise marks from an unmentioned battle with Leslie when she finally showed up, seemed obsessed by the pros and cons of showing the royal procession to the nation on Pathé newsreels. Books, to Lehmann's disappointment, were not discussed, and neither were the bruises. A further encounter, scheduled for 14 June at the popular Café Royal, brought a new setback when a dishevelled Leslie Tilden Smith shambled through the cafe's elegant doors to offer Rosamond a rambling tale about a car crash. Although unharmed, Rhys was said to be too distraught for a social outing. Empathising— she, too, had recently been in a motor accident—Lehmann sent best wishes for a speedy recovery.

Plainly, Rhys liked Rosamond or she would not herself have proposed a further attempt at establishing a friendship. Invited for an early autumn visit to the flat on Bury Street, just off Piccadilly, into which the Tilden Smiths had recently moved from their faux-Egyptian bungalow on the Thames, Rosamond was greeted by a wan-faced Leslie. Ushered in, the immaculately dressed visitor found herself staring at a dishevelled Jean, sprawled across a sofa, glass in hand as she taunted her silent husband for looking—as well he might—downhearted. "Poor Leslie," she kept saying, "poor, poor Leslie. He looks so miserable and wretched and ill. . . ."[37]

Departing as swiftly as she could, Lehmann felt more sympathy for an embarrassed Leslie than his intoxicated wife. She didn't know the couple well enough to wonder whether perhaps Leslie had been playing an unkind game of his own when he ushered her into the flat, rather than sending their visitor away with a polite excuse. If his wife shamed him, so could he shame her.

Lehmann never learned the truth about that second cancelled meeting with Rhys at the Café Royal. There had been no car crash. On 13 June, the Tilden Smiths had been arrested for causing a disturbance (by fighting each other) in Soho's shabby Wardour Street at four in the morning. It seems that the gentle Leslie could hit back. The mutual damage inflicted by punches and flailing fists was bad enough for a

doctor to be called to the police station where the couple were jailed for
the rest of a short night. Charged at Bow Street the following morning, Rhys pleaded not guilty to the charge and signed herself as "Ella
Tilden Smith, Journalist" before a thirty-shilling penalty was handed
down. Leslie, after chivalrously taking full responsibility for the incident, paid the fine.

Twenty years later, Rhys would combine the jubilee celebrations of
1935 with her humiliating arrest as she set to work on one of her finest
short stories: "Tigers are Better-Looking." But it was the Leslie-like
"Mr Severn" whom she chose to despatch to prison for a night, adding
only a cryptic "GR" on the wall of his cell to signify his creator as the
former Gwen Rees.

———————

A COMPLETE ABSENCE of documentation in the form of letters or diaries makes it impossible to know how much responsibility for the couple's rows can be assigned to Rhys, and how much to her outwardly
calm husband. Confirmation of Rhys's own volatility emerges earlier
in 1935, and from an unexpected quarter. Bringing his daughter to
England for the Easter holidays, Jean Lenglet had spent a few days at
"Luxor." Any ménage à trois is risky; emotions at the house ran high.
Fictionalising the occasion in a 1937 novel, *Schuwe Vogels* (*Shy Birds* was
not published in England and may never have been seen by Rhys), Lenglet characterised Rhys as a violent and obscene-tongued wife whose
alcoholic depression culminates in her death (by drowning in a river).
Tilden Smith's daughter, Antoinette, who visited the island hideaway
during Lenglet's stay, later confirmed that tempers had indeed run
high. Peace was temporarily restored after Lenglet's departure; back in
England for the summer holidays, Maryvonne was carried off to south
Wales's beautiful and isolated Gower Peninsula in a newly purchased
car for what she would remember as an idyllic week alone with her
mother and Leslie.

The death of Leslie's father in September 1935 unlocked the remaining portion of his son's inheritance. "Luxor" was promptly abandoned

for the Bury Street flat—just off Piccadilly—to which Rosamond Lehmann paid her memorable visit. The flat was well located, but neither
a new home nor Leslie's decision to spend his newfound wealth on
taking his wife back to the Caribbean could shake off Rhys's despair.
The drinking continued—and so did the rows. Jamie Hamilton, acting
in his capacity as Leslie's part-time employer, visited discreetly while
Rhys was on her own. He mentioned remarks that had been made at
the office about Leslie's battered face; prospective clients were not
favourably impressed when greeted by bruises and black eyes.

The hint of a threat hung in the air. Reluctant to sack an excellent editor and literary advisor, Hamilton decided instead to provide
a diversion. In June, he had asked Leslie to edit a memoir written by
two nephews of Winston Churchill. Based in part on their recent
experiences of public school, and laced with anecdotes about an eccentric upbringing, *Out of Bounds* was co-authored by Giles and Esmond
Romilly. Leslie and young Esmond had got on rather well. It was Hamilton's idea that Esmond should become a paying guest at Bury Street.

Aged seventeen, their new lodger enchanted Rhys. Handsome, wilful and clever enough to dazzle her with his political views, Esmond
had recently got himself thrown out of a fascist rally for causing a disturbance. Later, he would elope with Oswald Mosley's adamantly left-
wing sister-in-law, Jessica Mitford. Rhys was working on an early draft
of "Till September Petronella" when Esmond arrived at Bury Street.
Might her characterisation in that long short story of the charismatic
composer Philip Heseltine as the captivating but also dangerous Julian
Oakes offer readers a glimpse of the way Rhys responded to wild young
Romilly? Working on her fiction always improved her spirits, but it's
likely that Esmond himself helped to effect a change of mood as the
year drew to a close. But the real boost for Rhys came from the prospect of returning, at last, to her island birthplace.

VOYAGE IN THE DARK had provided the spur to Leslie's generous impulse
to splash out on a Caribbean adventure. How could anybody who

had lived at Rhys's side as she lovingly recreated a Caribbean past for
Anna Morgan not believe that a return to Dominica would make her
happy? First-class tickets were purchased for a passenger ship leaving
Southampton in February 1936. Just back from seeing her sick daughter (Maryvonne had contracted measles) at her new convent school in
Holland, Rhys wrote a farewell from Bury Street to Evelyn Scott. As
usual, all was in chaos. A fused light had plunged the couple into darkness; they were packing by the erratic glimmer of a few candles that
Leslie had wedged into a biscuit tin.[38]

Rhys's letter to Scott doesn't disclose whether Esmond was still with
the Tilden Smiths at the time of their departure from England; by the
time they returned, the young man had left England himself, to fight
against Franco in the Spanish Civil War. It's unknown whether Rhys
read at the time of his premature death in 1941, when Romilly's plane
vanished over the North Sea while undertaking a raid on Germany, but
she always spoke of him with tenderness. Her own son, had he lived,
would have been just two years younger than Esmond.

10

A la recherche, or *Temps Perdi* (1936)

"I suppose going back to Dominica is foolhardy but I want to
so much—I can't help risking it. You can imagine the wild and
fantastic plans and hopes."

—Jean Rhys to Evelyn Scott, December 1935[1]

WAVING THE TILDEN SMITHS off at Southampton—the port where
Rhys had first stepped foot on English soil nearly twenty years earlier—
were members of both their families: Leslie's recently married daughter
arrived with her husband, while Rhys was given bouquets of flowers
by her two sisters and brother, Owen (Edward, the eldest, was still
working abroad as an army medical officer). Rhys struck them all as
unusually animated and happy; judging by her boast to Evelyn Scott of
"fantastic plans and hopes," she may have dreamed that day of returning to Dominica for good.

Most of what we know of the couple's journey comes from two long
typewritten letters sent by Leslie to his daughter back in England. He
reported the voyage out as tranquil, marred only by Rhys's suspicion
that one of the SS *Cuba*'s passengers, a boisterous young Italian woman,
was making fun of the Tilden Smiths. After steaming through the Sargasso Sea, rank with the floating brown *sargassum* weed from which
it takes its name, the Tilden Smiths disembarked at the exuberantly

colourful town of Fort-de-France in Martinique, where they met up with the Irish novelist Liam O'Flaherty, "typing away for dear life," Jean reported to Evelyn, "and delighted with the West Indies, the only place left not yet written up he said."[2] The following week, the couple sailed on to St. Lucia, where the widowed Evelina Lockhart—a cherished young bride when Rhys last saw her—welcomed them to the little hotel which she was being paid to run by its absentee owner.

Leslie's letters read as though he would gladly have prolonged their stay at Hotel Antoine, where Rhys showed at her best as a valued literary advisor to a mildly eccentric young cousin, Emily (always known as Lily) Lockhart, who proudly displayed a magazine to which she herself was the sole contributor.[3] But Rhys, understandably, was impatient to reach Roseau. She hadn't been home for twenty years; how much would remain unchanged?

To Leslie, settling into the best rooms at the La Paz—the town's only hotel—Roseau appeared charming, with its wide harbour, busy market square and the tranquil Botanical Gardens. To Rhys, change was visible everywhere. Her family's house was boarded up; Kingsland House, the elegant former home of her father's medical colleague, Sir Henry Nicholls, had been converted by his daughters into a pension from which—to Rhys's dismay—a visiting lady writer despatched invitations for literary chat. The haughtily exclusive Dominica Club looked but a ghost of its former self; almost all the white pioneer settlers who had once regarded themselves as lords of the island had sold up and left. One resident told the visitors the curious story of Mr. Ramage (someone whom Rhys had known as a child), who was found dead at his remote property during the 1920s, still clasping a shotgun. Mr. Ramage's mysterious death followed a mob attack, allegedly triggered by the frightened crowd's ghostly encounter with a "white zombi."[4] The eerie image of a tall, pale old settler, brandishing a gun, stayed with Rhys. It seems to lie behind her account of the English Mr. Mason's confrontation with an angry mob of arsonists in one of the most dramatic scenes in *Wide Sargasso Sea*.

Alone, Rhys visited the old Victoria library where as a girl she had loved to sit reading on the shady veranda; here, a distant cousin still wearily presided over the massive desk to which books were brought by the island's schoolchildren to be stamped. The building, although unchanged, was overshadowed by the larger and adjacent Carnegie-funded library which had been built during the year that Rhys left the island to the design of Dominica's former administrator, Sir Henry Hesketh Bell. Alone still, she visited her former school to take tea with a greatly aged Mother Mount Calvary, the nun who had formerly been in charge of the convent. Here, too, everything—including her welcoming hostess—seemed diminished. Wishing to please an elegant visitor dressed in her best hat and gloves for the occasion, the old lady reminisced about the various ways that Rhys's father had always assisted the convent. Later that day, standing beside the Celtic cross that marked his neglected grave in the nearby churchyard, the doctor's daughter thought of the many ways in which kind, easy-going Willie Rees Williams had helped islanders and settlers alike. Nothing was recorded; all was forgotten. In her memoir, years later, Rhys confessed that she had shed tears that day.

Creating a careful map of the island for his daughter's benefit and his own amusement, Leslie had to rely upon Rhys's memory for the accurate placing of his two careful "x's," marking her father's two hill-country estates up on the island's west coast. No one could direct the Tilden Smiths to Amelia, nor Bona Vista; the little plantations of Rhys's girlhood lay buried under two decades of luxuriant, smothering forest. But Geneva: surely Mitcham House must survive? Having hired the grandest available car in Roseau for a pilgrimage to the old Lockhart home, Rhys was advised to employ a guide. "I thought, "A guide to Geneva for me. How ridiculous." However, there was a guide, we went quickly by car, and he seemed to know exactly where to take me."[*][5]

It may have been from their guide that Rhys first heard about the

---

[*] Leslie's retrospective account to his daughter suggests the Geneva visit took place towards the end of their stay, but it's hard to believe Rhys had resisted the temptation while staying in Roseau.

ruinous changes that had taken place on the island. Some of these distressed her more than others. Hurricanes and crop disease had devastated Dominica's fragile economy during the postwar years; growing racial anger had been fuelled by the brutally insensitive act of segregation meted out by the British Army to the black islanders who had crossed the world in 1915 to fight—and die—for Britain and the Empire. Rhys was surprised but relatively unconcerned to learn that a new non-white middle class had taken charge of the island, while the white plantocracy, its regime never so secure as those of the sugar barons of Barbados and Jamaica, had shrivelled away. Phyllis Shand Allfrey, the niece of Rhys's childhood sweetheart Willie Nicholls, had briefly returned to Dominica in 1931 only to discover, as she would write in her autobiographical novel, *The Orchid House* (1953), that her own class had become "the poor whites, we no longer have any power."[6]

The chief cause of distress for Rhys came from discovering the recent fate of her own family home. Four years before her return, there had been outrage when it was discovered that the British Colonial Office was increasing taxes on the island's black population to subsidise generous salaries paid to the handful of white officials who remained at Roseau. Following a mass resignation by the angry members of Dominica's legislative (all black) council, the British administrator invited two white planters to take their place. Within a month of his new appointment, Rhys's cousin, Norman Lockhart, the white owner of Geneva, was taught a harsh lesson when Mitcham House was raided and torched.

Some tokens of the old Geneva estate survived for a shocked Rhys to see: a mounting block; a few blackened walls; the sugar works' massive iron wheel, shipped out in the 1820s from Derby, England. The rest had gone: "There was nothing, nothing. Nothing to look at. Nothing to say. . . ." When Rhys knelt by a river to scoop a palmful of clear water into her mouth, the guide warned her: "Very dirty, not like you remember it."[7]

Following this wrenching experience, Rhys found it distressing to remain close to the places she had remembered best. A Lockhart connection still carried weight among the island's tiny white community. Strings were pulled; funds were tendered: by the end of March, the Tilden Smiths had bought themselves six weeks of isolation on a partly abandoned estate in the far north of the island, complete with maid, cook and overseer, and its own spectacular beach. The estate was called Hampstead.

WRITING *WIDE SARGASSO SEA* two decades later, and conflating the ruined Geneva of 1936 with the events that she believed had taken place there back in the 1830s, Rhys would also draw upon other and far less melancholy memories, of Hampstead. For here, to her astonishment, she discovered an almost exact replica of her lost home. Even the history carried startling echoes: once again, the Swiss family of Bertrand had been supplanted by members of the Lockhart family. Inscribing each of the little holiday snaps taken by Leslie of his wife (flaunting a faultless figure in her chic one-piece bathing suit), Rhys carefully recorded the fact that the beautiful beach at Hampstead was still called Bertrand Bay.

Despite Hampstead's isolated position, it was within reach of a couple of white families who were keen to welcome visitors from England. The Aspittels of Melville Hall proved pleasant but unexciting; a more interesting encounter was promised by an invitation from the Napiers of Pointe Baptiste.

Rhys had been fascinated by the exotic past history of Evelyn Scott. She showed less interest in the backstory of headstrong Elma Gordon Cumming, daughter of one of Scotland's largest landowners, who left her husband to run away with Lennox Napier, a literary-minded outcast from her own world who had spent time in Tahiti. Disgraced by their notorious affair, the Napiers had fled from England, eventually settling in Dominica because—in part—of their need for a warm climate. (Lennox was more fragile than his sturdy wife.)

Pointe Baptiste, the house that the Napiers had lovingly created to overlook twin beaches—one was of black sand, one of the finest pale coral—was and is like nowhere else on Dominica. Distinguished visitors—from Noël Coward to Patrick Leigh Fermor—would fall under the spell of the immense sea-facing veranda that fronts a light-filled, beautifully proportioned house packed with unexpected treasures: carved masks from Tahiti; a screen painted by the polymathic French chef Marcel Boulestin; a library stocked with French literature, including (the small volumes still sit on the library shelves) a well-thumbed first edition of Proust's *A la recherche du temps perdu*. Here, surely, Rhys would feel herself perfectly at home?

The reason for the Napiers' hospitality soon became clear. Elma Napier was in search of a publisher. Jamie Hamilton had sent her—at the autocratic Mrs. Napier's insistence—the negative fiction-reader's report on which his rejection of her recently submitted novel, *Duet in Discord*, had been based. Mrs. Napier had since gleaned that Leslie Tilden Smith was an editor (but not that he worked for Hamilton); Leslie, not his wife, was the object of Elma's lavish attention during the Tilden Smiths' visit to Pointe Baptiste. The price of a delicious lunch was made explicit: Mr. Smith must provide a glowing report for Mrs. Napier to flourish before reluctant publishers. It's unclear whether Leslie complied, but Elma's novel was published by Arthur Barker—under the pseudonym Elizabeth Garner—a few months after their encounter.

Rhys was understandably displeased by Mrs. Napier's attentiveness to Leslie, while ignoring his wife. Unburdening herself in a letter to Evelyn Scott, she wrote with withering scorn of a neighbour who is "by way of being literary" and who has "done her war dance at me. (Tomahawk in hand, smile on face)." There was one piece of good news: "She's going to England next week thank God."[8] Elma Napier was equally scathing. Responding over a decade later to a query from Alec Waugh about Rhys's literary reputation in Dominica, Elma promised to "try and read her. None of us has ever heard of her."[9] The hiss of poison-tipped arrows is almost audible.

Rhys's happiness at Hampstead glows out of Leslie's tender photograph of his wife gazing down at him from a tree-strung hammock. A continued exchange of friendly cards between Rhys and Dora, the

Rhys at Bertrand Bay, now known as Hampstead Bay (*left*), and relaxing in
a hammock (*right*). Leslie was the admiring photographer. *(McFarlin)*

Hampstead housekeeper, suggests that a comfortable relationship had
been established; Leslie's lengthy letters to his daughter communicate
an ease-filled sense of peace. Ella was working again, he reported with
evident relief, adding that she was really well (his code for sober) and
"simply loving the place."[10]

Rhys, nevertheless, had set her heart on undertaking two major
expeditions during their long stay in the north. She wanted to visit
the territory that had been granted to the island's earliest settlers—the
Amerindian Caribs now known as Kalinago—back in 1903. And she
wanted to cross the island on the great Imperial Road which everybody
claimed (wrongly, so a stubborn Rhys would enduringly assert) had
never been completed.

Ever since childhood, Jean Rhys had been intrigued by the fate of
Dominica's earliest surviving inhabitants. Following her return, she

had learned about the Caribs' recent exposure to what they reasonably perceived as insulting behaviour. In 1930, after two Caribs were erroneously shot for suspected smuggling, their people's compensation had been, not the badly needed hospital they requested, but a police station from which to spy on them. When a handful of angry protesters burned the station down, the British navy retaliated by flashing searchlights across the Caribs' terrain each night from the deck of an offshore warship. Feelings of resentment ran high.

It's reasonable to suppose that Rhys gave an accurate account of her visit to the Carib community in "Temps Perdi," a story she first began to contemplate during her final weeks at Hampstead. Arriving on horseback at a circle of thatched Carib huts, the Tilden Smiths were advised on how best to conduct themselves:

> "There is a beautiful Carib girl," the policeman said, "in the house over there—the one with the red roof. Everybody goes to see her and photographs her. She and her mother will be vexed if you don't go. Give her a little present, of course. She is very beautiful but she can't walk. It's a pity that."[11]

Anger at the policeman's condescension simmers beneath the surface of Rhys's prose. Later, the disillusioned visitor tells the reader that a stiff drink helps fend off any compassionate impulse. After a swig of rum, "nothing dismays you; you know the password and the Open Sesame. You drink a second; then you understand everything—the sun, the flamboyance, the girl crawling (because she could not walk) across the floor to be photographed."[12]

Rhys's second expedition, with a compliant Leslie tagging along behind their two local guides, began with a drive south down the island's east coast to Hatton Garden, one of the island's many abandoned estates. It was here, a few miles beyond the site of the modern airport, that Rhys believed the final stretch of the Imperial Road had emerged from the tropical jungle. Signs of an old *pavé*, or paved track, a leftover from Dominica's eighteenth-century French past, strengthened her argument. Off the travellers set, plodding alongside the brown–green waters of the winding Pagua river, advancing ever deeper into the island's seemingly impenetrable forest. Leslie grew silent. Rhys fell and twisted her foot. Relentless rain poured down from a dark sky. The sense of her own folly grew unbearable, but Rhys could not bear to yield: "Nothing left of the Imperial Road? Nothing? It just wasn't possible."[13]

It seems that Rhys did convince her husband of the road's existence, however irritable the long-suffering Leslie must have grown during a pilgrimage along muddy paths that had to be hacked out of the jungle by the cutlasses wielded by their quietly disdainful guides. Seventeen miles short of Roseau, the exhausted group finally reached the original road's end at Bassinville; and still, Rhys remained adamant. Completing his island map and anxious not to anger his wife, Leslie dutifully represented an Imperial Road that had almost spanned the island.[14]

Back in Roseau, and on the verge of making their first—and last—visit to America, the Tilden Smiths were called upon by the island-born children of Rhys's brother Owen. Leslie was proud to report to his daughter that Rhys had confronted an "awkward" family situation with uncommon grace. Approached by Ena, the oldest of her unknown nieces, his wife had been affectionate and—insofar as Leslie's rapidly shrinking funds permitted—generous. Oscar, the oldest boy, asked for more. He had grown "downright beastly," but Rhys had "marvellously kept her temper." Bringing the interview to an end, Ella had presented Oscar's younger sister with a generous handful of notes and coins. "And you," she had instructed her disgruntled nephew, "can go."[15]

EN ROUTE TO New York in the early summer, the Tilden Smiths were full of hope. Evelyn Scott had already helped Rhys to move from Paul Revere Reynolds (with whom she had fallen out) to another leading American agent, Carol Hill; writing to Leslie, Scott had expressed a determination to do her very best for the writer whom she felt most proud to know. It's probable that the two women had met up in England during 1935, when Evelyn was spending much of her time with John Metcalfe at a Suffolk cottage in Walberswick (affectionately known at the time as Bloomsbury-by-the-Sea); by February 1936, Scott had temporarily rejoined her previous husband, Creighton Wellman, in New York. Since then, she had been urging Rhys to visit and promising to arrange useful introductions. Having helped John Metcalfe only a couple of years earlier to whip through a windfall legacy of £20,000, Evelyn was unlikely to have encouraged the Tilden Smiths to curb what had become an enjoyably spendthrift existence.

Arriving in New York in June for a three-week stay, the Tilden Smiths rented a suite at the top of a charmingly Frenchified hotel near Washington Square. Rhys got all her teeth crowned and went shopping for the expensive clothes which always provided her protective armour against a (seemingly) critical world. Evelyn, meanwhile, arranged a cavalcade of social events, leaving little time for the quiet restaurant suppers which were an unsociable writer's preferred form of entertainment.

Having stumbled and twisted her ankle while trying to find the Imperial Road, Rhys now suffered a second and more serious fall. It seems likely to have taken place during the very last days of her visit to New York, when she was increasingly relying on alcohol to get her through the ordeal of a hectic social schedule. Groups, however courteous their intentions—and the New Yorkers were eager to welcome Evelyn's friend—always frightened Rhys. ("The damned way they look at you, and their damned voices," she had made Anna Morgan say of the English in *Voyage*.) Performing on stage had never inhibited her (except, understandably, when she was asked to mimic a hen laying an egg). The prospect of putting herself on display in society required courage of a kind Rhys lacked: "as a well-trained social animal I'm certainly not the goods," she would ruefully confess to Evelyn after her return to England.[16]

It may have been the combination of physical pain, drink and nervousness that caused Rhys's volatile temper to erupt during the final week of her visit. Piecing together what happened from the few letters that Evelyn Scott and Rhys exchanged thereafter, it seems that the Tilden Smiths were invited to Evelyn's home for a farewell family supper. Evelyn believed that she heard Rhys say something casually brutal about the misshapen hand of Manly, Wellman's son; Rhys remembered only that Manly had been combative and that Evelyn took his side. "So I blew up," Rhys wrote in the plaintive half-apology she sent from London in August, and "once I got going old griefs and grievances overwhelmed me."[17]

The explosion may not have been entirely Rhys's fault. In 1936, Scott herself was going through a personal crisis, exacerbated by the fact that her much-loved second husband John Metcalfe, back in England, had entered a period of severe depression. Money was short and—following a cool reception for her most recent novel—Scott was fighting her own emotional battles. During the same year of her rift with Rhys, Evelyn also quarrelled with one of her closest American friends, Lola Ridge. Writing to Emma Goldman during the following spring, Scott acknowledged with sorrow that, "between the near tragedies in personal affairs, the intensive labour and pressure about livelihood, I have simply dropped interchanges of correspondence with even my dearest friends."[18]

It seems that both Rhys and Scott were at fault. Their friendship, one of the most significant in the prewar period of Rhys's literary life, was never resumed, after a last volley of angry exchanges in the late summer of 1936, and by 1942, Scott, suffering from increasingly severe bouts of mental illness, had almost no allies left. To those who remained, including her loyal husband, Evelyn Scott always expressed pride in having known and helped such a remarkable writer as Jean Rhys.

11

Good Morning, Midnight (1936–39)

"It is only lately that I answer unkindness with a raving hate—because I've got weaker. My will is quite weakened because I drink too much."

—Jean Rhys, Green Exercise Book[1]

DEFENDING HER OUTBURST in Evelyn Scott's apartment in a letter sent from London in August 1936, Rhys admitted to her friend that she had drunk "a hell of a lot" during the last days of her stay. Reminiscing about that same New York visit many years later, Rhys said that she hadn't been sober in Manhattan "for one instant."[2] It's quite likely that she did the damage to her foot in New York through a tipsy stumble, but it's also conceivable that she was given an angry shove after launching into one of her unpredictable and vitriolic tirades. The injury, following her tumble while searching for the Imperial Road on Dominica, was serious enough to confine her to the Tilden Smiths' twin-bedded cabin on the liner transporting them home to England.

Back in London by early June, Rhys found that the persistent physical pain of a badly swollen foot did nothing to improve her mood, nor to reduce her reliance on alcohol. While holidaying in her beloved Wales with Leslie and Maryvonne in late July—Lenglet had meanwhile joined the anti-fascist cause in Spain as a reporter—Rhys was rushed into a tiny local hospital: a "most alarming experience." Back again in London, Leslie settled his wife into an expensive (and alcohol-free) nursing home off the Cromwell Road: "of all terrible streets," an unappreciative Rhys complained. Depressed by her surroundings ("grim, clean, hard, cheerless, smug, smirking etc.") and the unwelcome absence of drink, Rhys mordantly quipped to Evelyn that amputation would save trouble, while doubtless adding to "my chic. . . ."[3]

Leslie, meanwhile, was forced to face the consequences of their extravagant holiday. By the late summer of 1936, the legacy from his father had almost run out, as had the Bury Street lease. Fortunately, the prudent and relatively wealthy Muriel Tilden Smith was ready to support her improvident but beloved sibling. By mid-August, Rhys was able to exchange her nursing home for the snug Chelsea flat which, thanks to Muriel's discreet generosity, Leslie and his wife would occupy for the next three years.

A blue plaque now records Rhys's residence at 22 Paultons House, which was then a smart new building in bright red brick that stood at the shabbier end of the King's Road in Chelsea. Today, Rhys sleuths may savour her posthumous blue-plaqued proximity to the smart townhouse in Paultons Square where Lancelot Hugh Smith's favourite niece—a sculptor—has added some of her own equestrian bronzes to a legacy of her uncle's collection of eighteenth-century porcelain and paintings. This was never Lancey's home; back at the time when Rhys lived at Paultons House, her former lover had recently exchanged his family's mansion in Roehampton for Garboldisham Hall, a handsome old Norfolk manor house within easier reach of Sandringham. While an ageing bachelor entertained the young princesses whose royal parents had been grateful beneficiaries of Lancey's shrewd financial advice, Rhys found solace in strengthening connections to her Creole past.

———————

IN AUGUST, ENGAGED in a war of words with Evelyn Scott, Rhys was told by a still furious Scott that she held a "distorted" view of how people behave. Responding on 10 August, Rhys carefully excluded Evelyn and her American friends before launching into a ferocious condemnation of English society's "mean bloody awful hatred of everything that isn't exactly like your mean self."[4]

Rhys had picked quarrels with many friends since her return to England. She was also anxiously adrift in her search for a subject for her next novel. Installed at the new flat, she felt the daily reproach of a private study and writing desk that a thoughtful husband had provided for her use.

Two women provided consolation to Rhys during this fallow and unhappy period; it's striking that they both had deep connections to the West Indies, where women were not judged irrational—or even insane—if they had a temper that sparked out like a lightning flash: "like a hurricane like a creole" as Antoinette Cosway remarks of her mother in *Wide Sargasso Sea*.

Phyllis Shand Allfrey, a generation younger than Jean Rhys, was the granddaughter of Dr. Rees Williams's medical colleague, Sir Henry Nicholls; her 1953 novel, *The Orchid House*, would take its name from Sir Henry's abiding passion for growing orchids. Back in 1936, returning to England after a short time in America, Phyllis became an assistant to Naomi Mitchison, the formidably well-connected author and activist through whom she met many left-wing intellectuals (including George Orwell), while becoming a regular contributor of poetry and articles to the new Labour Party-sponsored magazine, *Tribune*.

Years later, as founder and editor of the *Dominica Star*, Phyllis would appoint herself as Rhys's personal Caribbean informant. Back in the Thirties, however, politics played little or no part in their friendship. Admiring Phyllis's slender fairness and quiet elegance without sharing her political views, Rhys was delighted to find a London neighbour with whom to share her memories of the vanishing Dominica of her youth. Phyllis enjoyed telling island stories of her own; possibly, some of these tales inspired Rhys's plans for a historical play set in Antigua, the island where Robert Shand Allfrey, Phyllis's disappointingly unemployable white husband, had grown up.[5] Rhys herself had briefly visited

Antigua during the voyage out to Dominica: just long enough to decide that it was both flat and dull: "*not* a beautiful island."[6]

Questioned in her later years about the writer whose literary fame—a little to her mortification—by then far outshone Phyllis's own, Allfrey gave nothing away about Rhys's drinking and her temper, preferring to recall the ballet treat her friend had bestowed on a thrilled seventeen-year-old Maryvonne by sweeping her daughter off to Moira Shearer's stage debut in *Endymion* in 1939. Phyllis did, however, let slip one incident which betrayed—as she was perfectly aware when she disclosed the episode—Rhys's enduring social insecurity. Invited to dine at Paultons House one night, Phyllis had dropped some casual remark about the commonness of the name Smith; a standoff about what was perceived to be a deliberate put-down of the Tilden Smiths (and perhaps even of the Hugh Smiths) had ended with Rhys's angry refusal to cook dinner for their honoured guest that night.[7]

It would seem obvious for Rhys to have discussed with Phyllis her brother Owen's mixed-race children, as three of Phyllis's uncles, including Willie, Rhys's childhood beau, had been rebuked or exiled for fathering children by island women. The likelihood is that Rhys preferred to discuss Owen's illicit relationships with Eileen Bliss.

Rhys always described this as her favourite photograph of Maryvonne, her uncomplaining and long-suffering daughter. *(McFarlin)*

Unlike Phyllis, who never forgot the social superiority of Sir Henry Alford Nicholls to a mere Dr. Rees Williams, Eileen was a woman with whom Rhys could reveal and revel in being her own true self.

The initial approach had been made by Bliss, an admirer of Rhys's novels who obtained a personal introduction by applying to Horace Gregory, a scholarly poet and translator who had successfully experimented with reading sections from Rhys's prose work aloud to his American college students at Sarah Lawrence.* In September 1936, shortly after the Tilden Smiths moved to Paultons House, the thirty-three-year-old Bliss paid Rhys her first visit. The friendship that instantly sprang up between the two women would prove robust enough to last a lifetime.

———————

ELIOT BLISS (Eileen renamed herself in homage to George and T. S. Eliot) was born and bred to English parents in Jamaica before moving to England, where the publication of her second novel, *Luminous Isle* (1934), had been sponsored by Vita Sackville-West.

A volatile depressive who suffered from long periods of illness, Bliss was a lesbian who wore her hair in an unfashionably close-cut crop, and who wrestled, like Rhys, with yearnings for a Caribbean world in which, as both women were acutely aware by the time they met, they possessed no authentic home. "When I try to explain the feeling I find I cannot or do not wish to," Rhys once confessed to her orange exercise book, although she was happy to describe in her memoir the desire she had felt to lose her own pallid skin tone along with her inhibitions when she watched, as a child, the dark-skinned carnival dancers leaping and prancing along the streets of Roseau.[8]

Phyllis Shand Allfrey regarded herself, always, as Rhys's social and intellectual superior; Eliot, from her very first encounter with Jean

———————

* Gregory evidently appreciated the kinship to poetry in Rhys's prose. His students were fortunate; her work is best experienced when read aloud, either in English or French.

Rhys, was a shamelessly adoring fan. Everything about the writer and her Chelsea home had been perfect, Bliss told Rhys's first biographer back in the 1980s, from the green bedsheets to the lovely portraits of Jean that decorated the walls; from the evident devotion of a tactfully invisible husband to the tasteful hair rinse (blue) that complemented the chicly dressed Miss Rhys's sapphire eyes. Rapturously, Eliot reminisced to Angier about the delicious Caribbean meals cooked by her hostess; ruefully, she admitted that Rhys often drank more than was prudent. Perhaps unwisely, Bliss also recalled that kind Leslie had always been on hand to scoop the ladies off the floor at an evening's end and carry them safely off to bed. Further details were neither sought nor provided.[9]

"GREAT IS THE truth, and truth will prevail," Rhys inscribed in the copy of *Quartet* which she gave to Eliot Bliss, echoing the dog-Latin motto she had once drunkenly scrawled for Eliot across a bedroom mirror at Paultons House. This was Rhys's abiding creed: *to tell the truth*. She saw it as her only chance to draw upon and survive the growing darkness within her: "the bitter peace" that she would describe in *Good Morning, Midnight* as standing very close "to hate," and even, to death.[10] The feeling was there; what eluded Rhys still, in the summer of 1937, was the way in which to give form to that theme.

"It's hard to harbour illusions in a room by the month hotel." That line might have come from *Good Morning, Midnight*, in which Rhys's ageing avatar hides from the cruel eyes of Paris in just such a room. Rhys herself had read it in Louis-Ferdinand Céline's first novel, published in 1932. *Voyage to the End of Night* became one of her touchstone books; it was one of the few that she would always keep close to her.

Céline's reputation as a racist bigot has obscured the wit, humanity and elan of his earliest work. Celebrated for the dazzling originality of Céline's style, *Voyage to the End of Night* takes its readers into the depths of Paris and its heights. From the gloomy grey piers of the old encircling city walls, up to a Walpurgis Night fantasy above Sacre

Coeur, out to the bravura description of the Seine and its fleets of tug-boats with which the novel ends, Céline reinvented a Paris that Rhys drew upon as she created her own extraordinary version of a city that is both real and imagined. But it may also have been Céline's use of a compellingly intimate narrator's voice that Rhys was hearing as she began to think of how Sasha should speak. Fiercely; bitterly; wittily; suspiciously: it was Céline's Bardamu who taught Rhys the difficult art of shifting moods in the space of a sentence.

Diary of a Country Priest, the novel written in 1935 by one of Céline's greatest admirers, Georges Bernanos, exerted a more direct influ-ence on the creation of Sasha's personality than elements of Rhys herself. Recommending one of her most cherished French books to a literary friend in 1953, Rhys quoted Bernanos on an author's need for scrupulous honesty. *"Il faudrait parler de soi-meme avec un rigueur inflexible"*—"It's essential to be inflexibly truthful about oneself"—the lonely parish priest writes in his self-excoriating diary. Rhys's patron saint was Teresa of Ávila, with her clarion call to rise above despair; the priest's touchstone is Saint Thérèse of Lisieux, who preached the doc-trine of universal grace. "Grace is everywhere," are the young priest's dying words; reaching up for the final embrace of a sinister lover whose white dressing gown is insistently compared to a priest's robe, Rhys's narrator is allowed to find her own cruel form of grace in death.

Rhys went to Paris alone in the autumn of 1937, while she was still planning her unwritten novel. She was just in time to catch the tail end of the International Exhibition that was housed in and around the new Palais de Chaillot. Today, the 1937 world fair is best remembered for *Guernica*, Picasso's passionate elegy for the massacre—in the anni-hilation of an entire town—of his Basque compatriots. At the time, the crowds were drawn to an art-deco railway pavilion and a hangar-like Palais de L'Air, rather than to Le Corbusier's city of the future by Porte Maillot, or the looming symbols of Nazi Germany (Speer's gigantic tower crowned by eagle and swastika) and of Soviet Russia (two massive farmworkers). Rhys arrived in October, just as the fair was starting to close down. She returned to London with a portrait of a melancholy-eyed banjo player painted by a new friend, Simon Segal: the Russian-born émigré had sold everything he put on show in Paris in 1936 to a single buyer, an achievement which Rhys's novel fondly recorded for her "Serge Rubin." But Rhys also brought back to London a unifying image for her book. The International Exhibition provides a ghostly backdrop to a key scene in *Good Morning, Midnight*, but what is on show instead throughout the novel is Mrs. Sasha Jansen, formerly "wild Sophia": the woman who—ludicrously, unflinchingly and entirely self-aware—escorts the reader to the dreary, predestined setting for her death.

Marya Zelli died at the end of *Quartet*; no hope gleams from the knife-like band of light that shines under Anna Morgan's door at the end of *Voyage in the Dark*. Older, better-educated and superficially more worldly than her predecessors, Sasha Jansen is shown sleepwalking through a dying world—Rhys was not oblivious to international events—towards an equally bleak conclusion. ("So good night, Day!" is how the second stanza of Emily Dickinson's 1838 poem "Good Morning, Midnight!" ends, in a gloom that leaves no room for doubt that it has reached its terminus.)

Rhys herself evidently knew Dickinson's work well. Mrs. Jansen never mentions the poem, but it's made apparent that she's aware, from the moment that she chooses a hotel that overlooks a dead-end street ("an impasse"), precisely where she's headed. ("Quite like old times," the room seems to jeer. "Yes? No?"[11]) The question Sasha faces is merely of method: how to reach her own dead end without too much indecorum, without too many of the sobbing fits that can never bring adequate relief. Her survival of a difficult past has evidently owed more to luck than to will: when she speaks of the good fortune of being saved ("rescued, fished-up, half-drowned, out of the deep, dark river").[12] Sasha already knows that "the real thing," when it comes, will be when no friends are on hand to help: "When you sink you sink to the accompaniment of loud laughter."[13]

Raw-nerved herself, Rhys endowed Sasha Jansen with her own paranoia. Everything and everybody becomes Mrs. Jansen's cold-eyed judge. A clock, seeming to belch, giggles at her; windows distort into sneering eyes. It's a shock to discover that she, in her once elegant fur coat (the coat from Vienna was becoming Rhys's literary trademark), has faded into the shabby old soak perceived by others as "*la vieille*": age haunts her like a vengeful spectre. Mirrors are as pitiless as the judging gaze of strangers: "Fly, fly, run from these atrocious voices, these abominable eyes. . . ."[14] But Mrs. Jansen always holds the advantage over her perceived judges. Sometimes, she uses a witty form of mockery to strike back. "He arrives," she comments of the man who will cause her to be sacked from her job at a fashion house, "Bowler-hat, majestic trousers, oh-my-God expression, ha-ha eyes . . . I know him at once."[15] Sometimes, as with the quietly spoken Rhys herself, Sasha's anger knocks the reader backwards with the force of a physical blow:

> One day, quite suddenly, when you're not expecting it, I'll take a hammer from the folds of my dark cloak and crack your little skull like an egg-shell. Crack it will go, the egg-shell; out they will stream, the blood, the brains. One day, one day . . . One day the fierce wolf that walks at my side will spring on you and rip your abominable guts out . . . One day, one day. Now, now, gently, quietly, quietly . . . [16]

While it's not difficult to identify the resemblance to Rhys in Mrs. Jansen's savage self-knowledge and the violence of her imagination, it's naive to attribute to the author herself what Judith Thurman once interestingly described as a "squalid complicity" between Rhys's narrator and Sasha's predators: "their company, their protection, their money—in exchange for the pleasure she can give them as a victim."[17] Another early feminist critic, Judy Froshaug, proved equally illuminating when she praised Rhys's uncanny understanding of minds that teeter on the border of insanity: "women who spend their lives balanced between despair and a sort of frantic hopefulness, women alone, women who beg to be loved but expect to be rejected."[18] For this aspect of Sasha, Rhys was drawing upon the darkest aspect of the only person of whom she knew enough to tell the truth: herself.

While Mrs. Jansen's final days in Paris place her at an unquestionable distance from her creator, elements of Rhys's own experiences are apparent throughout the novel. An account of Sasha's loss of her baby boy enables us to glimpse how deeply Rhys grieved when her own son perished. The retrospective narrative which comprises Part Three of the adroitly structured four sections of *Good Morning, Midnight* summons up all the tenderness, innocence and anxieties of Rhys's early married life with Jean Lenglet (the Dutchman Enno Jansen in the novel) in Paris and at The Hague.

Beyond all this, however, it's rash to read *Good Morning, Midnight* as an artless account of Rhys herself, or even as a vision of the woman she feared she might become. Like her predecessors, Sasha Jansen is, rather, that ideal surrogate memorably posited in Rhys's private exercise books as the damaged spirit to whom we can all relate: "the I who is everybody." The casual reader might suppose that Rhys—who relished her comforts and liked pretty surroundings—had visited the Paris Exhibition while spending her nights among the brooms and mops of the servants' floor at a down-at-heel hotel. ("*Quatrième à gauche*, and mind you don't trip on the hole in the carpet. That's me," says Sasha.")[19] The likelihood is that Rhys stayed with a disapproving but always loving friend. Germaine Richelot is recognisable in the novel as Sidonie, whose kind attempt to find her hard-drinking friend a suitable room is interpreted by thin-skinned Sasha Jansen as condescension. ("God, it's an insult when you come to think about it!")[20]

Deceptively concise—a mere 190 pages—*Good Morning, Midnight* reveals better than any other of Rhys's novels the chasm that divided Jean's chaotic life from the disciplined clarity of her writing. Behind *Good Morning, Midnight*, even more skilfully concealed than in *Voyage in the Dark*, lies the wealth of a cultivated mind. "*Belle comme une fleur de verre*" . . . "*Belle comme une fleur de terre*,"[21] the words Sasha casually summons to describe two young fashion models, first appear in a poem by the surrealist writer, Robert Desnos. Rhys's startling image of mascara-fringed, staring eyes, set on a whirling wheel of lights, is placed towards the end of the novel, presaging Sasha's self-sought death. It derives from Man Ray's *Les Larmes* (1932), the Paris-based artist's close-up photograph of a heavily lashed eye weeping glass tears. Sasha's long nocturnal strolls remind us of Rhys's admiration for Baudelaire, Céline and George Moore, in whose finest novel, *Esther Waters*, she had read of the "strange mingling of enchantment and alienation that people experience in the city streets."[22] Rhys herself was also recalling the wanderings of the ghostly woman at the centre of *Nadja*, André Breton's avant-garde novel of 1928. Rhys, not Sasha, was quietly referencing both Bernanos's gift of universal grace to his dying priest and Molly Bloom's celebrated monologue in *Ulysses*, in the final affirmative that the less literary Mrs. Jansen whispers as she reaches exaltedly up from the darkness of her bed for the last time: "Then I put my arms round him and pull him down on to the bed, saying: "Yes—yes—yes . . . "[23]

A Beckett-like vein of black comedy and occasionally, pure slapstick, provides a steady counterpoint to the vortex of Jansen's descent. Its presence is evident from Rhys's opening page, when Sasha encounters a woman cheerily humming the tune of "Gloomy Sunday" while reading its score and tapping out the song's rhythm on the tabletop. In 1939, Rhys didn't need to inform readers that the melancholy Hungarian hit song of 1932 (later recorded by Billie Holliday) was known as "The Suicide Song." At times, the jokes in *Good Morning, Midnight* are delightfully silly: "Very light," remarks a chambermaid as she flicks on the switch in a sombre little room that faces an exterior wall. (Jansen had requested "a light room.")[24] "They add, of course, a macintosh,"[25] Sasha quips when describing the penchant of Englishmen for making love while fully dressed. René, the gigolo with whom Mrs. Jansen develops an unexpectedly satisfying relationship, describes to her a house so grand that even the lavatory chain, when pulled, plays a tune. "Rich people," he sighs. "You have to be sorry for them."[26] Dropping her guard for just one moment, Sasha laughs with him, not at him.

Briefly, their author permits two characters to enjoy a moment of perfect harmony.

––––––––––––

BACK AT PAULTONS HOUSE early in 1938, Rhys began work on the novel almost at once. She kept at it for just under a year. Simon Segal wrote to urge his new friend (it's unclear whether they had become lovers in Paris) not to despair and to keep in mind Baudelaire's words about the strength born of grief. *"Moi aussi je souffre souvent—toujours, beaucoup, croyez moi,"* he comforted her. *"Mais je l'aime, cette souffrance, car elle seule ne me trahit jamais, me donne courage et la belle colère . . ."* ['I too suffer often—all the time, and deeply, believe me . . . But I love my suffering, for alone of all things it never betrays me, it gives me courage, and my blessed rage'].[27] Rhys's magpie mind seized upon the quotation and compulsively twisted it into another maxim, muttered by Sasha as she sits alone with her ghosts in her room, after turning down a promising teatime date at the Dome: *"La tristesse vaut mieux que la joie"* ("So sadness has it over joy").[28]

Distractions were few, but it was impossible, living in London in 1938, to be unaware of the shocking events that were taking place in Europe, or of the growing inevitability of war, something that can only have darkened the mood of a woman whose only child lived for much of the year on the Continent. Neither Rhys nor her daughter attended the funeral of Rhys's Aunt Clarice, who died that year, but Maryvonne still enjoyed the long school holidays she spent travelling and camping with Leslie and her mother in Scotland, Wales and—just the once—Ireland: holidays on which her volatile mother, with her writing set to one side, always seemed to be happy and relaxed. Maryvonne would also remember 1938 as the year in which she was finally introduced to her mother's wistful sisters: Minna, by then suffering from advanced Parkinson's disease, was being looked after in Acton by the same sturdy nurse who had nursed Minna and Brenda's mother, and who still shared their home. It's unclear whether Maryvonne also met luckless Owen and his hardworking wife, or her great-uncle, Neville, husbanding his frugally issued pennies up in Harrogate.

Replying years later to one of *Good Morning, Midnight*'s most ardent admirers, Rhys recalled that ending the novel had been her greatest challenge: "I tried and rewrote and rewrote but no use." A bottle of wine had, so she airily claimed in 1956, produced the solution "from Heaven knows where" in the form of "the Man in the Dressing Gown."[29] It's a warning never to take writers at their word about the mysteries of the creative process. In fact, the sinister role that Sasha's top-floor neighbour would play had been woven into the fabric of Rhys's novel from its opening pages, when his "immaculately white robe" presents him both as "the ghost of the landing" and "the priest of some obscene, half-understood religion."[30] His significance as a bringer of death is intentional, and clear.

Always a perfectionist, Rhys was reluctant to let go of her novel. Furious arguments took place. At one point, having threatened to destroy the manuscript, she hurled Leslie's typewriter out of a window. Smith only dared carry the pages to the waiting publisher, Michael Sadleir of Constable, after his wife had fallen asleep. When Sadleir sent a contract for her signature, the couple were still quarrelling, or so Rhys would enjoy telling the story to close friends.[31]

Published in April 1939, on the eve of war across Europe, *Good Morning, Midnight* received dismal reviews. In America, it was summarily rejected and remained unpublished until late in Rhys's life. Jean Lenglet, who admired the novel enough to translate it into Dutch, secured his former wife a valuable new critical admirer in Victor de Vriesland. In France, however, both Lenglet and Rosamund Lehmann's brother John failed to find Rhys a publisher. Editors at Plon and Stock were not alone in raising their hands in horror: *"le sujet (en ce moment surtout) effroye tout editeur"*—"The subject matter (especially at this time) appals them all"—Lenglet wryly reported to his former wife. In England, Frank Swinnerton expressed his distaste for a novel which neither Norah Hoult nor Rebecca West, two of Rhys's most loyal admirers, were prepared to review. "Oh dear—how sad, how painful it is to read," Violet Hammersley protested to Rhys on 22 May.[32]

Today, Rhys's fourth novel is regarded by many as her finest work. Touchingly, the only two men who seem to have recognised *Good Morning, Midnight* as a work of genius at the time of its publication were its author's husbands, both present and past. Home comfort was not enough. Almost thirty years would pass before Rhys would feel able to relinquish a novel into the hands of a publisher.

A FEW PERCEPTIVE reviews might have made all the difference to the career of Jean Rhys. In 1938 she had begun to collect ideas for a next novel. The fascinating evidence survives, both in a group of fictional recreations of her childhood that she scrawled within a much-used black exercise book, as well as in a seven-page typescript dating back to 4 December 1938. Revised over a period of almost three decades, "Mr Howard's House" was typed on the onion-skin reverse sheets of what seems to have been Rhys's final draft of *Good Morning, Midnight*. Here, in the cold cruelty of "Mr Howard," and in a troubling dream of sacrifice and rejection, were planted the seeds of *Wide Sargasso Sea*. Rhys called this group of fictionalised childhood memories, simply "Creole."[33]

Rhys's return to Dominica in 1936 had stirred up many of her old memories. Buried deep within *Good Morning, Midnight*, one of Sasha Jansen's strangest recollections is a reimagining of fourteen-year-old Gwen Williams's encounters with her parent's married friend, "Mr Howard," in the Botanical Gardens at Roseau:

> A man is standing with his back to me, whistling that tune and cleaning his shoes. I am wearing a black dress, very short, and heel-less slippers. My legs are bare. I am watching for the expression on the man's face when he turns round. Now he ill-treats me, now he betrays me. He often brings home other women and I have to wait on them, and I don't like that.[34]

Unpursued in *Midnight*, this same trauma of sexual coercion resurfaced in the notes for "Creole"; it is possible that the account that Rhys gave here of her abuse by "Mr Howard" caused an older Rhys protectively to scribble across the top of "Creole"'s opening page: "Don't on any account," and then, with unexplained relief: "Thank God."

The episode which follows directly on from "Mr Howard" in Rhys's exercise-book notes towards "Creole" reveals that, long before Rhys began work on her fifth and final novel, she was pondering the injustice done by Charlotte Brontë to Mr Rochester's first wife, a "mad" Caribbean heiress, in *Jane Eyre*. Her emotional return to Dominica in 1936 had provided a possible title from her voyage across the treacherous waters of the Sargasso Sea.

Rhys had first read Brontë's novel as a schoolgirl at the Perse. She read it again in 1938. Pondering "Creole," Rhys began to blend elements of the sinister Mr. Howard with "Raworth," her own interpretation of Edward Rochester. Privately, she set down her idea of a troubling dream in which a young girl sees herself in bridal white, trustfully following a beckoning gentleman into a forest. Within the wood, without warning, the man turns on her; his face is "black with hatred." The dream ends abruptly as the girl's mother rouses her daughter from sleep.

Over three decades later, following the publication of *Wide Sargasso Sea*, Rhys acknowledged that she had embarked upon a first version of that novel (provisionally named "Le Revenant") before the Second World War, commenting that Leslie had been very excited by what he then read. In October 1945, Rhys confided to Peggy Kirkaldy that she regarded "Le Revenant" as "the one work I've written that's of much use."[35]

"Revenant" is generally taken to mean somebody who has returned from the dead: a zombie. All that survives from another idea Rhys had in the late Thirties, "Wedding in the Carib Quarter," is a one-page plan of headings for chapters. A hint of that vanished work's transgressive content survives in the words Rhys scrawled across the head of the page: "& a fearful warning too! That was! It went for keeps." She added what seems to have been a similar warning to her future critics and biographer: "Attention Miss! Or Madam. No playing around with ME."[36]

"Le Revenant" vanished—ripped up during a marital squabble, Rhys would sometimes claim—but it's significant that she squirrelled away two chapters for future use. One contained the dream encounter in the forest which had found its first form in the notes towards "Creole." Eventually, that dream would play a crucial role in *Wide Sargasso Sea*.

HOLIDAYS HELPED ASSUAGE the bitter disappointment with which Rhys read the reviews of *Good Morning, Midnight* in April 1939. Following a visit to Wales and a brief summer sojourn at Taplow, a sleepy little town beside the Thames, she and Leslie returned to Chelsea. Seventeen-year-old Maryvonne was staying with them when war was announced by Neville Chamberlain on 3 September. Offered the choice of remaining in England or rejoining her father, she opted for Holland. Appreciative though she was of Leslie's kindness and of her mother's affectionate impulses, Maryvonne's first language was Dutch and her first loyalty, at a time of potential crisis, was to the father she adored.

The farewells between mother and daughter were not dramatic: in the early autumn of 1939, nobody could imagine what horrors lay ahead.

V

DARKNESS AT NOON
Mrs. Max Hamer

"A harsh word could kill her, imagined insults lurked in
chance encounters. A vulnerable complex organism,
she was made to be hurt.'

—Peggy Kirkaldy, "Portrait of a Lost Friend"[1]

12

At War with the World
(1940–45)

"Pressed flat against the cellar wall, they listened to the inexorable throbbing of the planes. And above them, the house waited . . . "

—Jean Rhys, "A Solid House"[1]

AGED FIFTY-FIVE IN 1940, Leslie Tilden Smith was too old to fly combat aircraft as he had done in the first war. Gallantly determined to do his bit for England, he volunteered and was commissioned as a pilot officer, a modest desk job ranking just above a midshipman in the naval equivalent. Evelyn Scott's middle-aged English husband followed the same patriotic route: it's possible that the Tilden Smiths met up with John Metcalfe after their move in February 1940 to Bircham Newton, an RAF base in the flatlands of north Norfolk. It was there, three months later, that Jean Rhys learned of the fate of the Netherlands.

Rhys had remained in touch with her daughter and Jean Lenglet for some months after Maryvonne's return to Amsterdam in the autumn of 1939. Lenglet's regretful letter about his failure to secure a French publisher for *Good Morning, Midnight* reached his former wife early in 1940; probably, he added a copy of an article written the previous summer in which "Edouard de Néve" (Lenglet's pseudonym) had praised

Rhys as a shamefully unrecognised novelist, one who regarded isolation as essential to her work: *"cette solitude imposée à elle-même."*[2]

Lenglet had approved of Maryvonne's return from England shortly
after war was declared, believing that his own country was safe. On 10
May 1940, Hitler invaded the Netherlands. By the end of the month, the
German occupation of the country was complete and all lines of communication were abruptly severed. Jean Rhys now daily faced the possibility that both her adored first husband and her only child were dead.

The first sign that Rhys was under stress emerged at Bircham Newton shortly after news of the German occupation of Holland. Laura,
the protagonist in one of Rhys's wartime stories, "I Spy a Stranger,"
violently rounds on an officious male visitor for claiming that the
WAAFS up at the station smelled. Rhys's fiery real-life response to
such an offensive comment may have been what proved her undoing.

No details survive, but while Leslie remained at the base, Rhys was
hastily banished to West Beckham, a pretty little north Norfolk village situated close to woodlands and the coast—and also to a bomber-
detecting radar station. Three village houses had been requisitioned for
military use; Rhys was consigned to the former home of the housemas-
ter at a local school. She was living there alone in the summer of 1940
when the first German bombers streamed overhead, targeting Norwich. Gazing upwards, how could Rhys not think of the bombs that
Hitler had already dropped on Holland? Watching her—as wartime
villagers would have watched the solitary, book-reading woman who
now lived at the schoolmaster's house—how could they not become
suspicious?

Rhys had lived within the comforting anonymity of cities for all of
her adult life. Even at Bircham Newton, however out of place she had
felt there, she occupied the protected role of a spouse attached to the
glowingly patriotic world of the Royal Air Force until—for whatever
reason—she had disgraced herself. At West Beckham, Rhys felt more
under scrutiny than Sasha Jansen had ever sardonically perceived herself to be in the Parisian bars of *Good Morning, Midnight*. Laura, spo-

ken of as "that crazy foreigner" in "I Spy a Stranger," suspects passing strangers of stopping to "gape" at her house and peer into her room ("or I think they can"). At West Beckham, Rhys shut herself in, closing the window curtains and—more practically—draping blankets over the doors: even in summer, Norfolk's east wind carries the sting of a salted whip. She could not rid herself of the sense that the villagers, and even the house itself, were watching her—"seeing me as I really am."[3]

The growing darkness of Rhys's mood in 1940 emerges from the jungle of angry notes which she jotted to herself while living at the village house she renamed "Rolvenden" in the story "Temps Perdi." One furious outburst was triggered by a cleaning woman's failure to return Rhys's greeting: "servants are much the worst, I always think," snapped the thin-skinned colonial outsider, adding that "90% of the English have the souls of servants and the manners too." Elsewhere, Rhys cursed the entire nation of England—"rot its mean soul of shit"— before trying to obliterate words that, if discovered, might incriminate her as the enemy. In three disjointed pages, headed: "The Kingdoms of the Human Ants, part of a lecture delivered when I was drunk from sadness," she bitterly compared the innocence of young women ("beautiful & eager with a touching humility and charm") to the harridans they must become: "drab spiteful cruel . . . you think how can I let these girls grow into these women." Confiding her thoughts to these same private pages, Rhys noted her consciousness of being disliked and added a final prayer: "Let me not be like my father and mother do let me not they were so unhappy so dead. I want to be happy."[4]

Later, reworking these thoughts into stories that were among the best she ever wrote, Rhys would acknowledge that most of her suspicions were groundless. "They don't think or say anything that I would imagine they think or say," she admitted of her West Beckham neighbours in the finished version of "Temps Perdi." But the hostility that she sensed was real. On 1 August 1940, a Norwich newspaper published a tasty snippet about a woman who had pleaded guilty to the charge of behaving in a drunk and disorderly fashion on a public highway. Rhys's married name was given in full; so was the location. So was the fact that an upstanding member of the West Beckham community had doused the obstreperous female with a bucket of cold water.⁵

Looking down at the soberly dressed woman in the dock, the magistrate heard that Mrs. Tilden Smith, prior to her arrest, had proclaimed herself a proud West Indian and denounced the English as "a b——— mean and dirty lot." A compassionate man, the justice gathered that she was distraught about the fate of her daughter, out in Nazi-occupied Holland. He imposed no fine. Rhys's punishment was bad enough: she must continue to live among the villagers who had witnessed her arrest—and who noted that Mrs. Smith's husband seemed in no hurry to join his wife.

In February 1941, following a modest promotion to the desk-bound rank of flying officer, Leslie was relocated to work with the radar-detection unit near West Beckham. By March, for undisclosed reasons, Rhys had moved to lodgings in the Chapelfield area of Norwich. It was to escape her seemingly self-imposed isolation that she impulsively travelled south to the Colchester home of her old friend Peggy Kirkaldy.

The visit was not a success. Some friend of Peggy's let slip a malicious comment about the Jamaican-born Eliot Bliss as exuding a certain odour. Eliot was a friend of Peggy's, but it was Rhys who took loyal offence at a blatant ethnic sneer about her Caribbean compatriot. Evidently, there was a heated exchange with her hostess; certainly, by the time Rhys wrote to plead for understanding, and to lament her "hideous" life in Norfolk, Peggy felt no duty to respond. The result would be four years of silence.

Rhys returned to Norwich from Colchester on 20 March. Reading *The Times* a few days later, she came across a respectful obituary of one of the country's leading financial figures. Lancey had played no part in Rhys's life in Norfolk, where he himself lived in old-fashioned splendour at Garboldisham Hall, but she was still in possession of his friendly notes to her in Paris. She kept a couple of them, along with a flowing, high-waisted and prettily flowered robe to which she had granted a brief appearance in *Voyage in the Dark*, as Anna Morgan's din-

ner-gown at the hotel in Savernake Forest. The dress, still in her wardrobe when Rhys reached her eighties, was a last reminder of the days
when young Ella had imagined herself becoming Mrs. Hugh Smith:
a genuine English lady; the cherished spouse of a rich and generous
English gentleman: his petted kitten. Another time; another world.

Rhys would always maintain discretion about her periods of mental
crisis. Some partly destroyed letters, drafted into the back of a diary
that she kept after the war, suggest that she held her younger sibling
Brenda responsible for despatching her to an asylum on the outskirts of
Norwich.[6] It's conceivable that Rhys—like Laura in "I Spy a Stranger"
and Teresa in "A Solid House"—had deteriorated enough by April
1941 to have been briefly committed by Leslie, with the consent of
Rhys's sister, to the gloomy mental hospital of St. Andrew's in Thorpe,
although the hospital had largely been handed over for the care of
injured soldiers. No records survive from this period of the hospital's
history to allow Rhys's claim to be checked.*

Rhys was either due for release from St. Andrew's, or was lodging
elsewhere in Thorpe, when she begged her practical and well-connected
friend Phyllis Shand Allfrey to find her some quiet sanctuary, away from
a city under siege from the air. Phyllis gave the request careful thought
before recommending an unusually literate Norfolk vicar, whose family were already housing several evacuees. His name was Willis Feast
and his abiding interest was in modernist poetry. An informal drawing
of Feast in 1940 by Wyndham Lewis (held in the Norwich Gallery
Archive) shows a quizzical, intelligent-looking young man with slanting
eyes set above high cheekbones and a narrow-lipped, appealing smile.

Phyllis had probably warned the Feasts that her friend was in need of
a rest. It's unclear whether she herself knew about the gravity of Rhys's
breakdown, but the Feasts went out of their way to make their visitor
feel welcome. Rhys was housed in the best bedroom at Booton rectory,

---

* Some of the diary's torn pages were addressed to Edward Rees Williams. Evidently,
Rhys intended to share her suspicions of Brenda with their older brother, following his
return from service in India as an army medical officer.

its long windows overlooking an old-fashioned garden shaded by the tall green trees that always reminded her of Dominica. Meals were brought to her room on a tray so that she could work in solitude. Later, in the afternoons, the visitor lounged under the low boughs of a garden elm (according to the recollection of Barbara, the vicar's thirteen-year-old daughter), slowly leafing through *For Whom the Bell Tolls*, Hemingway's newly published novel about the Spanish Civil War. A cake was baked at the rectory to honour a birthday which the age-conscious and still girlish-looking Rhys is unlikely to have admitted was her fifty-first. Young Barbara Feast thought that a real lady would have buttoned her dress a little higher when visitors dropped by. She wondered, as all the household did, how anybody should be so astonishingly languid.[7]

Rhys's indolence was not the only cause for concern at the rectory. Mr. Feast's gentle enquiry about her real reason for going into the garden one day provoked a burst of rage that escalated to hysteria until the vicar's wife, acting with imaginable satisfaction, gave their unapologetically contrary guest a hard slap across the face.[8] By the middle of September, Rhys was back in Norwich, where a vicar from one of Willis Feast's neighbouring parishes was taken to visit her. Although "hellishly angry" when the two priests arrived, a shared bottle of gin had apparently worked wonders. Rhys, after a drink or two, proved to be irresistible. Departing in a spirit of genuine regret, Eric Griffiths felt that he understood why Willis had been looking so dreamy of late: he had been hosting an enchantress.[9]

Rhys remained alone in Norwich throughout the autumn of 1941, dependent on the goodwill of hard-pressed and sharp-tongued wartime landladies, a breed whom she detested in part because she always felt that they were judging her. Teresa, in Rhys's story "A Solid House," is transfixed by "the hard bright glitter" of her landlady's eyes; the English can seem friendly, Teresa reflects after a conversation with her fellow lodger, Captain Roper: "but hidden away, what continents of distrust, what icy seas of silence. Voyage to the Arctic regions. . . ."[10] Teresa is said to be recovering from an attempt to kill herself; of Rhys, we know only that she was being seen by a doctor during her last months in Norwich. Louis Rose had trained as a doctor, but by 1940, he was living in Norwich while working as honorary psychiatrist to the Lowestoft and North Suffolk Hospital.[11] Rhys's striking description of the twin spirits, one passive and meek, the other discordant and angry, who wrestle within two of the women in her wartime stories, Audrey in "The Insect World," and Inez in "Outside the Machine," suggests that a professionally trained view of her personality may have influenced the writer's view of herself for a time. If so, it didn't last.

In February 1942, Leslie and Rhys were reunited at West Beckham just long enough for Rhys to get her husband into serious trouble by shouting "Heil Hitler" while drinking in a country pub. Her outburst, especially shocking for emerging from such a reserved, softly spoken woman, was reported. Leslie's superiors promptly removed him from Norfolk, packing him off to Bristol and then to picturesque Ludlow, once the capital of Wales. It seems that he was asked to leave the RAF; nevertheless, spending a summer holiday together at Oxwich Bay on the Gower Peninsula, Leslie and Rhys enjoyed a rare period of untroubled serenity. This particular part of Wales could always cast a spell: straying one summer afternoon into a field thick with golden cowslips, Rhys felt that she never wanted to leave.[12] A month later, the Tilden Smiths moved back to London.

———

FROM THE AUTUMN of 1942, Leslie and Rhys occupied (Leslie's loyal sister, Muriel, paid their rent) an airy top-floor flat on Steele's Road, a broad and pretty street near Primrose Hill in north-west London. Leslie resumed his old freelance job as a publisher's reader for Jamie Hamilton. Rhys was still drinking heavily; while nervously discouraging his married daughter from paying visits, Leslie represented himself to an impressed Antoinette as "working for the Air Ministry."

Primrose Hill wasn't a reassuring area of London to inhabit during wartime. Long-barrelled defence guns, mounted on top of the ancient hill, offered scant protection from the bombs that regularly fell on neighbouring streets. Rhys was evidently recalling one of these devastated locations when she described Audrey in "The Insect World" as walking home past a ghostly street of "skeleton houses," where front doorsteps "looked as though they were hanging by a thread."[13] At night, blackout curtains kept out the light, but not the sound, of a besieged city under fire.

It was during the two years that the Tilden Smiths spent together at Steele's Road that Rhys resumed her writing. Work continued on "The Revenant," but her chief preoccupation was with an auto-biographical group of stories, each of which examines the fate of a vulnerable woman—always alone; always adrift—trapped within a wartime world where anything less than noisy patriotism will be perceived as treachery; it's a world in which they have no place and can find no refuge.

Rich in black humour, Rhys's wartime stories focus on the experience of exclusion. While "A Solid House," "Temps Perdi," "The Insect World" and "I Spy a Stranger" are the most well known of the group, the behaviour of Inez Best in "Outside the Machine," which takes place in the women's ward of a hospital near Versailles, suggests that this story, although set in an earlier time, was also written or intensively revised at Steele's Road. Inez exhibits all the resentment and barely contained fury of Rhys's wartime women. Like them—and like Rhys herself—she exults in every chance to speak her mind. "Don't underrate me," Inez thinks as she listens to two of her condescending fellow patients calling for another member of the ward to be hanged (for the crime of trying to kill herself): suddenly, Best lets fly, calling them out as "a pair of bitches":

"Who was speaking to you?" Pat said.

Inez heard words coming round and full and satisfying out of her mouth—exactly what she thought about them, exactly what they were . . .

"Disgusting," said Mrs. Wilson. "I *told* you so," she added triumphantly. "I knew it. I knew the sort she was from the first."[14]

A simmering rage bubbles through these stories, boiling into eruption when least expected. "Damn you don't call me that," shrieks twenty-nine-year-old Audrey when innocently addressed by her cheery flatmate as "Old Girl" in "The Insect World." "Damn your soul to everlasting hell *don't call me that*. . . ." In "I Spy a Stranger," Laura—the most akin to Rhys herself of all the author's wartime women characters—explodes with more justification when her cousin's husband tries to hustle her out of their house and off to an asylum:

> "Come along, old girl," Ricky said. "It's moving day." He put his hand on her arm and gave her a tug. That was a mistake . . . It was when he touched her that she started to scream at the top of her voice. And swear—oh my dear, it was awful. He got nasty, too. He dragged her along and she clung to the banisters and shrieked and cursed. He hit her and kicked her, and she kept on cursing—oh, I've *never* heard such curses.[15]

Truths were being told and Rhys went out of her way to signal her own connection to the wilful, violent-minded women she described. Packing her cherished possessions to leave her cousin's home, Laura even provides the reader with an italicised inventory of Rhys's most sacred personal treasures ("the bracelet bought in Florence . . . the old flowered workbox with coloured reels of cotton and silk"). Having mentioned a jewellery box with a golden key, Laura/Rhys adds a blatant pun on the Lockharts' family name: "I'm going to lock my heart and throw away the key." Nothing here is accidental; every connection is intended. *Here I am*, the author seems to say. Make of me what you will. It's all in view, but on my terms, reader, never on yours.

SOMETIME IN 1944, Leslie and Rhys walked up Primrose Hill together and said a prayer—although neither of them was conventionally religious—for the safety of Maryvonne Lenglet.

And sometime in the spring of 1945, Leslie felt confident enough about his wife's improved behaviour to permit his married daughter to pay a first visit to the flat in Steele's Road. (No mention is ever made either by Leslie or Rhys of the son, Anthony, who had taken his mother's side in the Tilden Smiths' divorce.) To Antoinette's relief, Rhys greeted her cheerfully before showing off a room which she had been painting—she intended it to become Leslie's study—in a blaze of vibrant colours.

What was going on?

A plausible guess might be that Leslie had decided it was safe enough for his daughter to visit after his wife's dark mood had been lifted by unexpected and joyful news from the Netherlands: a letter had arrived explaining that Maryvonne was safe, well—and a married woman with a husband she adored.

The fuller story which reached Rhys later—direct communication with the Netherlands remained difficult throughout 1945 and Maryvonne was slow to reveal all the details—filled her with wonder and pride. In 1941, aged nineteen, Maryvonne had gone to work for the country's resistance movement, contributing to *Vrij Nederland*, an underground paper, while her father, one of the best brains of the Dutch resistance, daringly helped at least thirteen RAF pilots to evade capture and return safely to England. Within five months, both of the Lenglets were arrested. Lenglet, due to the swift intervention of Henriëtte van Eyk's brother, had been able to escape death by pleading insanity. His colleagues were shot. All that Maryvonne knew in 1945 was that her father, having escaped from an asylum and then a series of Dutch prisons, had eventually been deported—twice—to Sachsenhausen, one of Germany's most brutal concentration camps. His son, Maryvonne's older half-brother, had meanwhile fought on the side of the Nazis.

Lenglet's ultimate fate was still unknown to his daughter when Maryvonne first managed to get a letter to London. It's unclear when Rhys learned the fact that her first husband, having survived the camp's notorious death march from Sachsenhausen to the north-west of Germany in the spring of 1945, had rescued a destitute Polish aristocrat who—following Lenglet's swift divorce from Henriëtte van Eyk—became this remarkable man's fifth and final wife. Reporting the brief fact of her recent marriage to Job Moerman (on Valentine's Day), Maryvonne omitted to mention that the risk for two resistance workers of being recognised by a German registrar had been so great that the bride smuggled five grenades into the ceremony in her pocket, while Job carried a pistol under his jacket. Later, Rhys would learn that her heroic daughter, released shortly after her arrest in 1941 on account of her youth, had continued her father's work of helping downed British pilots evade capture. She performed this task while sheltering with a beloved family friend, a woman who was shielding twenty-five Jews in her Amsterdam attic. (Henriëtte, who was also working with the resistance, but on a different basis, had been nervous of the consequences of taking Maryvonne back into her home.) It was during this period that Rhys's intrepid daughter had met Job Moerman, an undercover expert in the gathering of intelligence about the enemy.[16]

What mattered most to Rhys in the final months of war was to learn that her lost daughter was safe. Peace was announced on 2 September. It's reasonable to suppose that the Tilden Smiths were feeling happy, relieved and in need of a rest when they decided to spend the month of October at a rented property on Dartmoor.

THE COTTAGE, ALTHOUGH set in a beautiful landscape, close to one of Dartmoor's many rivers, was remote and spartan. The journey had been long and the middle-aged Tilden Smiths were both in poor health. Rhys was recovering from a summer bout of flu; Leslie, now sixty, looked pale and gaunt. Writing to her husband's daughter a short time later, Rhys said Leslie kept remembering his mother's sudden and premature death; Rhys herself was full of unease. Fictionalising the Dartmoor visit in one of her most troubling tales, "The Sound of the

River," she made use of a brooding landscape, the wind, dark trees and a silent river which finally gushes free of its banks, to create a haunting sense of inevitability.

The end came with terrible swiftness on 2 October 1945, the first full day of their visit. Leslie had seemed fragile when they arrived; now, he complained of spasms and violent pain in his chest and arm. By the time Rhys had returned from her second anxious trek to the hostel where their landlord was staying nearby, having broken a glass pane in the front door in order to reach the telephone and summon medical assistance, Leslie was dead.

> "Wake up," she said and shook him. As soon as she touched him her heart swelled till it reached her throat. It swelled and grew jagged claws and the claws clutched her driving in deep. "Oh God," she said . . . and knelt by the bed with his hand in her two hands and not speaking not thinking any longer.[17]

To some, such a sudden and isolated death from a heart attack (the cause given on the death certificate) did not look natural in a man of only sixty. Rumours buzzed. Leslie's daughter told the doctor who had eventually visited the cottage that she believed Rhys might have killed her father; Rhys's unsympathetic younger sibling imagined that her sister had calmly sat by, doing nothing, while Leslie died in the adjacent room. Writing to a shocked Antoinette to explain that she would not attend a London memorial service, Rhys was devastatingly candid. Yes, she had often treated Leslie badly when she was working on her books. "I did love him though," Rhys wrote, adding wistfully that she thought her husband had "sometimes" been happy in her company. She was being honest—not intentionally cruel—when she told Antoinette that her chief sensation during the Devon cremation had been of empathy and even gratitude: "I had all the time the feeling that Leslie had *escaped*—from me, from everyone and was free at last."[18]

But Rhys's feelings ran deeper than this. "He was smiling as if he knew what she had been thinking," she wrote (in "The Sound of the

River"), when describing her husband's last living look at his wife.[19] Praising Leslie's gentleness and patience to Peggy Kirkaldy—it was the first time Rhys had communicated with her friend since their falling-out in 1941—Rhys allowed her misery to show in a sudden outburst of candour: "Oh Peggy I'd give all my idiotic life for an hour to say good-bye to him."[20] Years later, however, Rhys would use "The Joey Bag-stock Smile" to portray Leslie, not as Dickens's slyly lecherous Major Bagstock in *Dombey & Son*, but as Mr. Carker, the novel's pallid-faced and perpetually smiling villain. The sense of a meditated payback is strong; the reason for Rhys's grudge towards a man who had devoted himself unstintingly to the service of his wife and her fiction remains a mystery.

THE DEVON DOCTOR shared the dark suspicions of Leslie's daughter. He may have insisted upon a post-mortem only because Rhys freely admitted to having tried to ease Leslie's pain with her own prescription pills, but he had also heard gossip from the couple who lived in a neigh-bouring cottage. They stated that a quarrel had taken place on the first evening of the Tilden Smiths' arrival; the noise had been loud enough to penetrate their own closed doors and thick stone walls. More tell-ing, and in Rhys's favour, is the fact that these same loquacious neigh-bours took Rhys in for the first night after Leslie's death and—at her request—contacted Leslie's devoted sister, Muriel, and Edward, Rhys's eldest brother. The fact that they did so without hesitation hardly sug-gests that the couple saw their unhappy guest as a murderess.

Evidently, Rhys knew where her long-absent brother now lived; was Edward's presence in Devon the reason that the Tilden Smiths had elected to take a holiday on nearby Dartmoor? Desperate for money, it's entirely possible that Leslie and Rhys had hoped to obtain a loan; childless, retired from his career as an army medical officer and com-fortably established in the family home of his well-off wife, Gertrude, at Budleigh Salterton, Rhys's eldest brother might command resources upon which less well-heeled relatives could conceivably draw. (Rhys's younger sister had made a similarly late and far more prosperous marriage during the war, but by 1945, Rhys was conscious that Brenda's goodwill was no longer to be relied upon for further handouts.)

Colonel Edward Rees Williams was a man with a strong sense of duty. It was he who paid the outstanding month's rent on the Dartmoor cottage, arranged for Leslie's cremation, escorted Rhys to the ceremony and then drove her back to Knottsfield, Gertrude's house in Budleigh Salterton.

Interviewing various members of the Rhys family in the 1980s, Carole Angier was offered a lurid account of Rhys's short, unhappy stay at the home of a stiffly respectable sister-in-law determined, however reluctantly, to behave well in difficult circumstances. Leslie's son, Anthony, had visited Knottsfield for just long enough to note that his (almost unknown) stepmother was lolling in bed, while Colonel Rees Williams meekly gathered up her dirty laundry for the wash. Rhys herself was desperate not to be sent away: "I've a *horror* of London," she wailed to Peggy Kirkaldy. "I will go to pieces there." Another family connection told Angier that—rather than leave—Rhys had actually used the bedsheets to fasten herself to the bed. Edward lost his temper; Rhys produced one of her terrifying screaming fits; the police were called in.[21] True? The details are eerily close to Laura's wild behaviour in the story "I Spy a Stranger," when her cousin's officious husband tries to bundle her out of the house. Rhys was never afraid to draw upon shaming episodes in her life if she saw a chance to make them serve her art.

Undoubtedly, Rhys's sudden widowhood presented her family with a problem. Leslie's will bestowed nothing but debts; Rhys had no money of her own. Usefully, Edward Rees Williams persuaded his sister Brenda's rich and fair-minded husband, Robert Powell, to contribute to a small weekly allowance for his sister, while Muriel Tilden Smith volunteered to cover the rent on Steele's Road for a few more months. Given the difficult circumstances—a coldly furious wife (Gertrude Rees Williams apparently refused ever again to have Rhys in her home), and the harsh austerity of postwar Britain—the long-suffering Edward must have felt that he had done his best by an errant sibling whom he had not set eyes on for forty years. And so he had: in later years, Jean Rhys would always praise her brother for his kindness.

————————

EDWARD HAD NO knowledge as yet of his sister's remarkable capacity for survival. Paying a short courtesy visit to an unknown mother-in-law during the summer of 1946 (Maryvonne had remained in the Netherlands), Job Moerman was intrigued to be greeted at the door of 3 Steele's Road by a short, lively and sturdily built man. He said that he was helping Mrs. Tilden Smith to smarten up the flat. Rhys introduced this cheerful individual to Job as her late husband's cousin and executor. His name was Max Hamer.

13

Beckenham Blues (1946–50)

> "If the law says you're dangerous, you're dangerous. If the law
> says you're mad, you're mad. Then God help me."
>
> —Jean Rhys, Orange Exercise Book, c.1950[1]

FEW COUSINS CAN have had less in common than Leslie Tilden
Smith and Max Hamer. Leslie was bookish and—except when he
got drunk and quarrelled with his wife—quiet; Max was outspoken,
exuberant and—when he first met the widowed Rhys—unashamedly
indifferent to culture. A good raconteur in possession of a pack of
yarns, he regaled Rhys with comic stories about the early years he had
spent at sea before his embarkation (following a decade of unemploy-
ment) on a less adventurous career as a trainee solicitor. It was probably
Max's employers who had encouraged a somewhat imprudent man in
his mid-fifties, equipped with a wife and young daughter, to invest in
property. And so, at some point between 1930 and 1938, Max Hamer
took out a mortgage in order to purchase a three-storey gabled Victorian house in the new south London borough of Beckenham, formerly
a village in Kent. Plans to move there were forestalled by war: Beckenham lay on "Doodlebug Alley," a firm favourite with the Luftwaffe.

Like Leslie, Max had signed up once again, despite his mature
years, to do his bit against Hitler. (Max was eight years older than
Rhys, although he may never have known it.) In 1945, the sixty-three-
year-old Lieutenant Commander Hamer's impressive title concealed a

Rhys's third husband, Max Hamer (pronounced "Hay-mer"), was a cousin of Leslie Tilden Smith, a roguish charmer who made Rhys laugh. *(McFarlin)*

humdrum job supervising the issue of barrage balloons and kites from HMS *Aeolus*, a warehouse staidly anchored behind the high street of Tring, in Hertfordshire.

The attraction of Max as a potential husband—he was not forgiven by his wife of over thirty years for starting divorce proceedings shortly after he met Rhys—was considerable. Dapper, funny and well spoken, he was a far more sexual man than Leslie. On a more practical level, he owned a house; Rhys, when her sister-in-law ceased to pay the rent at Steele's Road, was going to be without a home. But what a shy, introverted woman, one who was prone to despair and self-doubt, valued above all in Max Hamer was his unquenchable cheeriness. He made her happy.

Max's optimistic temperament meant a lot to Rhys in 1946, the year in which she turned fifty-six. The end of war had ushered in a period of continued rationing and relentless hardship for most of the British population, half a million of whom lost their uninsured homes to bombing raids. Rhys's own spirits were not lifted by the difficult task of revising her wartime stories, among the darkest that she would ever write. Pushing herself even harder, she was determined to create a fictional record of the mysterious portents that had preceded Leslie's sudden death.

Writing "The Sound of the River" so soon after the loss of her husband brought Rhys close to a complete breakdown: she told Peggy Kirkaldy that she couldn't even bear to listen to certain music or to read her favourite French poets. She believed this story to be among her best work. She showed her faith by insisting that "The Sound of the River" should provide the title for the short and stark collection that she proudly submitted in March 1946 to Michael Sadleir of Constable. "It's been the hardest thing I've ever done in my life," Rhys had admitted to Peggy in February. By July, the publisher had turned it down, and hope had fled. "No one does believe in me," she sadly wrote.[2]

Sadleir's response was dismaying, but understandable. Having already been burned by the poor reception and negligible sales for *Good Morning, Midnight*, he shunned the patent risk of publishing an even more disquieting production, and in bleaker times. In 1946, English book-buyers wanted entertainment, not anguish. Crime fiction sold well (Sadleir's own historical thriller, *Fanny by Gaslight*, had recently been filmed); war-weary readers lapped up the romantic novels being written by Georgette Heyer and Daphne du Maurier. How could Jean Rhys's savage vision of a country at war, observed by her group of vociferously unpatriotic outsiders, hope to match the sales of Elizabeth Goodge's sweetly fantastic *The Little White Horse*, or even Nancy Mitford's acidly funny portrait of the declining ruling class at play, *The Pursuit of Love*?

Widowhood; lack of money; rejection; the encroaching spectre of old age: for all these reasons, an always reckless woman embraced the comforting attentions of a sensual, entertaining and delightfully hopeful man. Job Moerman, preoccupied by his postwar work with British intelligence—he would spend the following year back in the Netherlands, teaching the art of information-gathering to army officers stationed at Breda—didn't have time to fret over why a singularly well-read novelist was living with a man who shared none of her intellectual curiosity.[3] (Rhys had begun the year by lending Peggy a smuggled copy of *Tropic of Cancer*, while begging for its return.) Reporting back to a relieved Maryvonne, Job merely said that Rhys—still always referred to as Ella by her family—seemed in good heart.

Max asked Jean to marry him even before he became free; Rhys bridged an awkward hiatus by changing her legal name to Hamer by deed poll. By the time her third marriage took place on 2 October 1947 (two years to the day after Leslie's death, and just two weeks after Max obtained a divorce involving substantial alimony payments), Rhys had already exchanged her flat on Steele's Road for life on the breezier heights of Beckenham.

———

BACK IN THE 1940s, the proud new borough of Beckenham was an exceptionally decorous suburb. Civic parades were opened by sensibly shod ladies with large hats and double-barrelled names; the local tennis club and sports grounds, sponsored by Beckenham's sturdy new row of provincial banks, were well attended. So was the old grey church of St. George's, which stood guard high above Beckenham's winding hillside high street. No church-goer herself, Mrs. Hamer's preferred weekly appointment was with the local hairdresser to whom she repaired for a shampoo and set whenever a disquietingly flirtatious husband seemed about to stray.

The trouble with Max, as Jean later explained to Peggy Kirkaldy, was that while she herself might often "look potty, he *is* potty."[4] Evidence of her partner's unreliability became apparent as soon as they moved into 35 Southend Road. The house itself was large but damp; a rickety iron balcony overlooked the fruit trees and brambles in a small, neglected garden at the back. A cavernous cellar had become a wartime home to an army of rats, while the cast-iron water pipes were rusted beyond use. A builder selected by Max for his friendly manner requested a down-payment of £400 in cash (£15,000 today) and promptly disappeared. Max's postwar return to work as a solicitor had been short-lived. Newly unemployed, he decided to raise money by joining forces with a well-spoken former jailbird who urged Max to take a punt on nightclubs. Such a speculative investment naturally required many evenings of careful research; Rhys was left at home, alone. "Clinging vines aren't in it," she later sighed to Peggy when reviewing her passive acceptance of her fate.[5]

Rhys wasn't drinking much during her first months at Beckenham. The chief consolations of an often solitary life were her cherished collection of English, French and Russian books, her writing (however unpublishable) and the company of her three cats. Black-coated Mr. Wu was a sleek and fiercely handsome fellow, closely followed in his mistress's affections by pretty Gaby and, lastly, Mi-Kat, a keen mouser who kept the cellar rats at bay. When the next-door couple's guard dog killed both Mr. Wu and Gaby, Jean reacted with predictable fury. Summoned to Bromley magistrates' court in April 1948, she was charged with throwing a brick through her neighbours' window and threatening to do so again.[6] Found guilty of having wantonly destroyed an apparently historic piece of stained window-glass, Rhys was ordered to pay £5 (£175 today) compensation to Mrs. Hardiman, proud wife of a respected shoemaker and a figure of conscious importance in Beckenham society.

Characteristically, Jean Rhys would soon put her legal defeat to good use: Selina Davis, a free-spirited mixed-race woman living in Notting Hill, is found guilty of precisely the same crime in one of Rhys's best-known postwar stories, "Let Them Call It Jazz." At the time, however, Jean simply retreated behind a set of newly ordered Venetian blinds, which she kept pulled down all day. Screened windows only provoked further suspicion; from April, until the day of her ultimate departure from Southend Road, Mrs. Hamer was kept under close scrutiny by the local residents.

Larger worries than dead cats or hostile neighbours were preying upon Jean's mind in the summer of 1948. Maryvonne, bringing along her baby girl for a first visit to Southend Road, broke to her dismayed mother the news that the two of them, accompanied by Hock, their pet chow, were about to follow Job out to Java. Born in Indonesia, Job Moerman had gained a position as clerk to the largest Dutch shipping line in the East Indies. The post was a risky one since it was offered at a time when Indonesia was seeking to assert independence from the Dutch empire, and when armed combat was threatened. Maryvonne did her best to make light of the potential danger. Nevertheless, having so recently become accustomed to the fact that her daughter was still alive and well, Jean grew anxious. Six months later, while making light of friction with her Beckenham neighbours (the court case went unmentioned), she apologised to Maryvonne for having been so poor a mother, one who had never "helped you enough or been the right sort of person for you."[7]

WRITING TO PEGGY KIRKALDY in 1950 about her unhappy life at Beckenham, Rhys explained that it was then, when she went "all of a doo-dah," that she had once again started to drink.[8]

One theory about Jean Rhys's hard-drinking habit holds that it was driven by her body's need for a sugar boost; Rhys's granddaughter, Dr. Ellen Moerman, points to the fact that her own mother, during her later life, was diagnosed with diabetes.[9] While it's true that Rhys favoured sugar-laden drinks and often drank sweet wine early in the day, an unidentified diabetic condition would have made it unlikely for her to go at times for several months without a drink, while betraying no signs of ill health or unusual lassitude. In calmer periods, Jean was often happy only to sip a glass or two of wine at supper and exhibited no ill effects; when anxious or unhappy, alcohol comforted Rhys and she drank fast, in order to get drunk. Despite the pride she always showed in having a strong head, it never took long.

By the end of her first year at Beckenham, Rhys needed the comfort of drink to blot out her worry about Maryvonne, out in the East Indies, and to deal with the grim realisation that her hopeful, gullible Max was an easy target for any silver-tongued crook whom he happened to meet. By the autumn of 1948, she was threatening to leave him; instead, Max made a surprisingly practical suggestion. The house on Southend Road was built for family use; why not raise revenue without risk by renting out the underused upper floors? Two couples, the Bezants and the Daniells, moved in during November. Recent Jewish emigrants, the new tenants may already have been friends when they arrived at Southend Road; if not, they certainly became so during their stay. An in-house alliance of refugees from Germany boded less than well for a temperamental landlady who had already been cautioned in Norfolk for saluting Hitler.

The comforting prospect of a steady rental income was offset for Rhys by the news that her enterprising husband had discovered a new route to prosperity. The source was to be a certain Mr. Roberts, an inventor whose plans required investment in the form of substantial loans from his new partner. More reassuringly, Max found himself a day job in March 1949, working as managing clerk for a family firm of solicitors. Cohen & Cohen were an unusual outfit (the father lived at a hotel on Park Lane, while his playboy son preferred chasing women to pursuing legal cases) and Max's work proved undemanding. Unfortunately, his new annual salary of £400 attracted the keen interest of Mr. Roberts, a man who, like Max's previous business partner, preferred to do business after hours. Left alone all day and for a great many evenings, Rhys continued with her project for a prequel to *Jane Eyre*, with Bertha Mason as the central character. In the spring of 1949, she planned to locate "The First Mrs Rochester" (as Rhys now named the reworked "Revenant") at the ultra-English naval port that she had already used for a discarded historical screenplay set on Antigua and titled "English Harbour." The period in which to set her "West Indian" story remained unsettled; in October 1949, Rhys told Peggy Kirkaldy that she was considering placing "a novel half done" in the 1780s. The rest, she believed, was "safely in my head."[10]

Work never calmed Rhys; in the spring of 1949, she was still worried about Mr. Roberts' money-making schemes and terrified by the dangers to which Maryvonne, and her year-old granddaughter, might be exposed in politically turbulent postwar Java. She was already drinking heavily when her first serious confrontation took place with the upstairs tenants. The fault was largely Jean's own: writing a long confessional letter to Peggy Kirkaldy, she later admitted "I couldn't have behaved worse or with less tact."[11]

The trigger seems to have been an evening party held in the Bezants' flat on 11 April, in rooms just above where Rhys was trying to write, despite a racket which distracted, irritated and finally maddened her. The guests left an hour before midnight. A few minutes later, Rhys stormed up the stairs, shouted at Mrs. Bezant and then slapped—or perhaps punched—her husband. When the angry couple called in the police, as the tenants were always quick to do when she flared up, Rhys rashly called the constable "a dirty Jew." After hitting and even biting him, she accused the bewildered officer of belonging to the Gestapo.[*]

Max, a former solicitor, represented his wife at her second appearance in Bromley magistrates' court on 25 April. (Rhys had been bailed after pleading not guilty at the first.) A fair-minded magistrate awarded £3 to the injured policeman and a pound to Mr. Bezant. Mrs. Hamer was put on warning to keep the peace for a year.

Peace lasted less than a day. Back at Southend Road after her trial (Max had gone straight from the courtroom to the Cohens' city office), Jean found that she had locked herself out of the house. A helpful policeman fetched her a plank of wood, via which she managed to clamber in through an open window, but not before taking a tumble. Humiliated, bruised and distressed by her morning at court, Rhys found herself confronted by all four of her tenants. A golden opportunity to point out that Mrs. Hamer's saviour had been a member of the very constabulary she had recently abused was doubtless seized. The result was that Jean flew at Mr. Bezant.

Back in court on 6 May 1949, Rhys again pleaded not guilty. A claim that she had attacked Mrs. Bezant and Mrs. Daniell was briskly dis-

---

[*] Jean Rhys's insults were frequently anti-Semitic but almost always inconsistent and contradictory. Six months after her row with the Bezants in April 1949, she described her Jewish tenants to Maryvonne as "a little nest of Nazis" (Rhys to Maryvonne, 24 October 1949, in Francis Wyndham and Diana Melly (eds.), *Jean Rhys Letters*, André Deutsch, 1984, p. 265).

missed; the charge of an assault on Mr. Bezant was allowed to stand. As with the magistrate on the occasion of her wartime summons in Norfolk, the prosecuting council sympathised with the gentle, well-spoken lady in the dock. Agreement was swiftly reached that a token fine would be paid and that a psychiatrist would provide, at the end of three weeks, his assessment of the defendant.

On 27 May, Mr. Bezant appeared in court to declare that he had heard "nothing but screaming, shouting and abuse four times a week from this woman."[12] A warrant was served in her absence for Mrs. Hamer's arrest. On 24 June, Max informed the court that his wife was not well enough to undertake the ten-minute bus journey to Bromley. Three days later, having finally complied with the psychiatrist after over a month's delay, Mrs. Hamer showed up at the gloomy red-brick court building in person. It sounds as though Rhys had primed herself for the ordeal with a drink. "He [the magistrate] asked me if I had anything to say," Jean later told Peggy Kirkaldy. "So I said it." Having begun by objecting to being called hysterical by the psychiatrist, she found herself unable to stop. ("I hear myself talking loud and I see my hands wave in the air," Selina says in "Let Them Call It Jazz.")[13] Rhys was finally silenced by the magistrate who abruptly sentenced her to five days in Holloway prison's hospital wing, pending two years on probation and a further medical report. It's unclear whether Max was present to see his sobbing wife led out of court and taken away in a black police wagon.

RHYS ENTERED HOLLOWAY through what appeared to be the gate-house of a fortified castle; above the smoke-blackened archway, an inscribed motto prayed to God that *this place be a terror to evil doers.* Her experiences as a prisoner provided first-hand material for "Black Castle" (later retitled "Let Them Call It Jazz"), the story which Rhys began to write soon after her release. Her talismanic cosmetics and jewellery were removed; her clothes and shoes were replaced by flat brogues and a loose black tunic that distinguished the prisoners from the trimly pinafored female guards.

Being sent to prison was a terrible humiliation, but Rhys was not cruelly treated and the wing reserved for mentally and physically sick inmates was situated far away from Holloway's "lifers"—although not far enough to block out the sobs and shrieks that haunted a newcomer's nights. The dreariness of a postwar prison diet was compensated for by the opportunity to read—Rhys had learned the value of prison libraries from Lenglet—and, curiously, to rest.

Rhys got on well with the prisoners whom she met in Holloway. A cheerful old lag introduced her to the art of collecting "doggins" (the "dog-ends" or stubs of discarded cigarettes) and reminisced about her former life outside in "the Smoke." A seasoned younger inmate advised Rhys to say as little as possible about herself to the woman doctor in charge of her case. Like Selina in her short story, Jean seems to have heeded a prudent warning.

It was the misery that got under Rhys's skin during her stay at Holloway. "But oh Lord why wasn't the place bombed?" she wrote that autumn to Peggy Kirkaldy: "If you could see the unfortunate prisoners crawling about like half-dead flies you'd understand how I feel. I did think about the Suffragettes. Result of all their sacrifices? The woman doctor!!! Really human effort is futile."[14]

Selina contemplates killing herself by jumping off a high wall into the prison's drill ground. If Rhys had similar thoughts, she suppressed them. Writing to Maryvonne on 10 July, during the week that she was pronounced sane and fit for release (although in prescribed need, for two years, of psychiatric observation), Jean mentioned only that she had been briefly in hospital. Brightly, she wrote of sitting out with Max on their little iron balcony and of picking fruit and berries in the neglected back garden. If Maryvonne was puzzled by her mother's insistent tone when Rhys wrote on 16 August 1949 that "*I am all right dear*," heavily underlining her words of reassurance, there was nothing that a faraway daughter could do.

The shock and disgrace of imprisonment had been too great for a brief summer jaunt out of town to raise Rhys's spirits. Writing to Peggy on 4 October, Rhys confessed that she had temporarily lost the will to write. To Maryvonne, she had already confided her fears about Max's most recent friend, a man who was promising him "heaven and earth."[15] Max, unknowingly, had met his nemesis.

WHAT MICHAEL DONN lacked in integrity—and it would seem that he had none—was masked by an abundance of charm. Young, charismatic and unscrupulous, he had no difficulty in persuading the gullible Max Hamer to find him a job with Cohen & Cohen. Convinced by his personable manner, the family lawyers took him on. Rhys, to her credit, was never deluded for a second about Michael Donn's criminal streak, but Max started to behave with increasing recklessness, disappearing to Paris with Donn for five days before returning home via Jean's bedroom window, late at night. Maryvonne heard that Max was "very optimistic"; sometimes, longing for a happy outcome, Rhys allowed herself to share her husband's fantasies about finding a crock of gold which could be used to help poor, faraway Maryvonne and her baby daughter. Writing again provided a more reliable source of comfort; on 24 October, Jean urged her daughter to keep a diary or a notebook, adding that "writing can be (among other things) a safety valve."[16]

Rhys liked to claim that it was only left-wing Max who read their weekly copy of the *New Statesman*; (Hamer often teased his wife about her old-fashioned conservative views). If so, it may have been Max who, on 5 November 1949, found in the magazine's back pages a small announcement requesting "Jean Rhys" to contact a certain Dr. Hans Egli in Hampstead. Dr. Egli proved to be the London economics correspondent for the Swiss newspaper *Neue Zürcher Zeitung*; it was Hans's actress wife, Selma Vaz Dias, who had placed the advertisement and who instantly responded to Rhys's letter.

Jean must have felt dazed when she read in Selma Vaz Dias's bold hand that the actress had come across *Good Morning, Midnight* in Paris,

The *New Statesman* advertisement which changed the course of Rhys's life. *(McFarlin)*

read it and fallen instantly in love with the book. As a first step towards performing it on the BBC (Miss Vaz Dias enclosed her adaptation, written for a single narrating voice), she was giving a ticketed reading to a carefully selected audience on 10 November. An admired actress and gifted promoter of new European playwrights to English audiences, Selma did not need permission to give a reading. What she had sought to discover before approaching the BBC with her project was whether Jean Rhys was still alive.

We don't know whether it startled Rhys to learn that she was assumed to be dead. We do know that she liked the adaptation; the news that Selma also intended to talk about her earlier novels on the BBC reduced an emotional woman to tears. Writing back on 9 November, she told the gratified Vaz Dias that the actress had worked a miracle; such discerning enthusiasm had lifted "the numb hopeless feeling" that had paralysed her for so long. Now, filled with fresh hope, she could return to work.

Rhys blamed flu rather than nerves for her absence from the powerful reading that Selma gave to an appreciative audience—it included an admiring Max—at the Anglo-French Centre in St. John's Wood. She was not too ill to proclaim her triumph in disdainful Beckenham. Haughty Mrs. Hardiman, still nourishing a grudge against her brick-throwing neighbour, promptly spread the word that Ella Hamer, a common criminal, was pretending to be a famous writer. Doubtless, she shared the joke with Rhys's tenants; it's clear that they seized the chance to have some sport.

On 16 November, Mrs. Daniell, having barged her way into her landlady's bedroom at midday, offered her thoughts about the fact that the supposed great writer was still lolling in bed with a drink in her hand. Jean screamed at her. When Mrs. Daniell responded by tipping a rubbish bin—perhaps it was only a wastepaper basket—over Rhys's head, Jean lost any last shred of prudence. Still in her nightclothes and clutching Selma's letter as proof, she ran out into Southend Road, proclaiming her identity and shouting that her work was going to be performed on the radio.

Back at Bromley Magistrates' Court, on a charge of causing a public disturbance and holding up traffic on what was never a bustling thoroughfare, Jean was ably defended by Max. The case was dismissed. Rhys's tussles, however, were making excellent copy for the local press. "Mrs Hamer Agitated" ran the headline in bold black print which appeared on 24 November in the *Beckenham and Penge Advertiser*; as luck would have it, this was the very day on which Selma had arranged to visit her heroine in Beckenham.

Selma did not see the newspaper article, although she might have wondered why her distracted hostess poured out a cup of boiling water when her visitor had asked for coffee. Unconscious of the undertow of anxiety, Selma stayed on late into the evening, praising Rhys's work and promising her a golden future. Everything, in Selma's breezy view, was going to turn out splendidly. The Hamers, both of them, were enchanted by their new friend.

———

WHO WAS SELMA? Why were the Hamers so enthralled? Tara Fraser remembers her grandmother well enough to conjure up Selma's throaty announcement to Rhys as she first sailed into view: "Darling, I want to be the first to tell you: your work is *glorious!*"[17]

Jean Rhys's biographers and editors have been harsh judges of Selma

Selma Vaz Dias, the charismatic woman who entered Rhys's life in 1949.
(Used with permission of Tara Fraser)

Vaz Dias. The time has come to redress that critical imbalance and to understand why Rhys was enduringly grateful and loyal to this extraordinary woman.

Born in Amsterdam in 1911 (Selma's old-fashioned Dutch was good enough for her to attempt to correspond with Maryvonne in Mrs. Moerman's first language), Selma Vaz Dias had suffered a tragic loss during the Second World War when her adored brother Sieg was executed for his courageous work with the Dutch resistance. Exotic, passionate and widely read, Selma had won her first major role—acting alongside John Gielgud in a Russian play, *Red Rust*—at the age of sixteen, straight out of RADA, where she had been awarded the prestigious annual Gold Medal. Married since 1936 to a respected journalist, a dapper president of the Foreign Press Association known for his vehemently anti-Nazi views, Selma's bright star was still in the ascendant when Rhys entered her orbit.

Today, it's difficult to appreciate that Selma, back in 1949, appeared a far more significant figure than Jean Rhys. Since the war, she had been working closely with the BBC on plays and short stories selected and often translated by Selma herself, while introducing English audiences to the work of Genet and Lorca through the readings in the original languages that she regularly gave at the prestigious Anglo-French Centre. Shortly after meeting Rhys, Selma would join forces with Peggy Ramsay (not yet the formidable theatrical agent she would become), in order to form the First Stage Society.

Like Rhys, Vaz Dias possessed a volatile personality. Her brother's death had triggered a breakdown, leading to electroshock treatment. On the day of her Beckenham visit, however, the actress was elated by the warm reception that had been given to her latest reading. Having described her triumph to Rhys, Selma expanded on her plans to perform *Good Morning, Midnight* in her own adaptation, on the Third Programme. BBC radio drama was still in its first decade and the idea of one woman occupying airtime for almost an hour was unthinkable. But Selma's faith in her project was absolute. The play would happen. She knew it.

And so, having painted her bright vision and filled Rhys with hope, Selma swept splendidly away into the night.

———————

THE EXCITED EXPECTATIONS aroused by Selma's predictions were short-lived. On 14 January 1950, Max Hamer was charged with attempted fraud for abetting the stealing of seven cheques, to a value of £3,000 (£105,000 today), from the offices of Cohen & Cohen.

After months of worrying about the hold that Michael Donn appeared to have exerted over her naive husband, the awfulness of the reality caused Rhys's fragile control to snap. On the same night that Max was charged, she squabbled with the most belligerent of her tenants, Mr. Daniell; the following day, a furious Rhys was thrown out of Beckenham police station after referring to Daniell as "a dirty, stinking Jew."* Fined only £1 on this occasion, she was back at Bromley Court within days, following further allegations by her tenants of offensive behaviour.

On 30 March, Bromley Court decided to adopt the drastic course

———————

* Mr. Daniell was still nursing a grudge against Rhys thirty years later, when he wrote to her editor, having read of Rhys's death, to inform Diana Athill of his former landlady's insulting behaviour.

of banishing a conspicuously absent Mrs. Hamer from living in Beckenham. The mortgage company had moved more swiftly. By the end of March 1950, 35 Southend Road had been repossessed. All that was left in the Hamers' former home, as the magistrates now learned, were two Chinese vases, a divan bed and the quietly vindicated (or perhaps noisily triumphant) tenants.

The owners themselves had disappeared.

14

The Lady Vanishes* (1950–56)

"Her life was tragic; her courage quite indomitable."

—Peggy Kirkaldy to Selma Vaz Dias, 4 May 1957

IN THE EARLY spring of 1950, the mortgage company's repossession of 35 Southend Road left Max and Rhys without a home. The couple had not been entirely friendless in Beckenham: the last to survive of Jean's cherished trio of cats was hastily bestowed upon a good-natured young neighbour, while another local resident provided temporary storage for her clothes and—crucially—shelf space for a few favourite books. Selling off the majority of her books in order to raise money was a far more painful process for Rhys than it had been to relinquish (for the same purpose) Leslie's library after his death. Later, she recalled having had to part with the bulk of her cherished French and Russian novels. They fetched almost nothing. Among the handful that she kept back—they included works by Sartre, Beckett, Bernanos, Colette and Céline—was *Esther Waters*. The calm and stalwart Esther was always Rhys's touchstone in trying times: in 1953, she would tell one friend that she had read Moore's novel sixty times.[1]

---

* Selma Vaz Dias had appeared in cameo as a train passenger in the film *The Lady Vanishes* in 1938, but Hitchcock's title also seems fitting for Jean Rhys's disappearance from public view after Max's trial.

From March 1950 until Max's trial at the Old Bailey in May, the Hamers rented a single room at a London boarding house in Stanhope Gardens, South Kensington. When Max was not being summoned to meetings by the ever-optimistic and persuasive Michael Donn, the couple wandered like strangers through the unfeeling and stony (as Rhys felt it to be) city. Forlorn and guilt-ridden, Max allowed himself to be dragged by his culture-hungry wife to a film-showing of Jean Cocteau's *Les Parents Terribles* and on tours of London's monuments. Visiting Westminster Cathedral, Rhys fantasised about seeking refuge in a kindly Catholic retreat. "I'm so tired," she sighed to a sympathetic Peggy Kirkaldy that March.[2] Drifting through the Victoria and Albert's echoing galleries, she drew comfort from the archaic smile of a wooden Madonna; it revived happy memories of the Richelots' charming home in Paris (usurped and looted, as a shocked Rhys would overhear by chance in a hairdresser's salon one day, during the Nazi occupation of her favourite city).

The Madonna's smile offered private solace to Rhys at a time when her cheerful husband was understandably edgy and bad-tempered. A domestic row at the National Portrait Gallery about the relative merits of Jacob Epstein (intriguingly singled out for praise by Max) and James Tissot's gentle paintings of Parisian scenes (admired by romantic Rhys) ended with Max flying into a rage about Winston Churchill: "so it all ended badly as usual," Jean confided in one of the long confessional letters within which, during this sojourn in a London limboland, she unburdened herself to Peggy.[3]

An unexpected source of relief during a miserable three months arrived in the form of a mysterious benefactor. A letter from a London firm of solicitors announced that a modest sum of money would be provided to Rhys for an undetermined period; while this form of charity was not entirely welcome to a woman who hated to feel indebted, the Hamers were undeniably short of ready cash. Max thought that the anonymous donor might be the altruistic Earl of Listowel, Secretary of State to the Colonies, with whom the Hamer family claimed some distant link. Lord Listowel was well known for his charitable deeds;

nobody else comes to mind unless kind-hearted Peggy Kirkaldy was trying to help without offending Rhys's prickly sense of pride.

On two points, Rhys did not waver. Maryvonne was not to be told the truth and Max was not to be abandoned: "I couldn't give Max away," Jean told Peggy, and again, in the same letter of 21 April: "I don't want to leave Max (Mrs Micawber)."[4] Rhys could—and did—often quarrel with Max, but her loyalty to him never faltered.

On 22 May 1950, following a public trial at the Old Bailey that lasted a fortnight, Max Hamer, aged sixty-eight, was found guilty: his two-year sentence was to be served at Maidstone Prison in Kent. Michael Donn, already in possession of a substantial criminal record, was given four years at a different jail. Despite all that she had suffered through Max's association with Donn, Rhys warmed to the young man's mother: "a very simple, kind soul [who] says this is killing her," she told Peggy, adding that Mrs. Donn, who spoke almost no English, looked very frail.[5]

Max, to his wife's astonishment, wanted her to share a home with Mrs. Donn; instead, Rhys went to ground for several months at an old-fashioned Welsh inn owned by Peggy Kirkaldy's bookish friend, Edith Colley. "He [Max] doesn't know how I like trees, shadows, a shaded light," she had lamented to Peggy during her pre-trial sojourn in west London.[6] Staying at the Half Moon Inn in Llanthony, Rhys enjoyed a tranquil view of the misleadingly named Black Mountains' leaf-green hillsides; perhaps they reminded her of Dominica.

Far from London and the shock of Max's harsh sentence, Rhys took stock of her situation. She stopped drinking. And, despite her keen and recent interest in the story of an heiress with a "defective mind" who is locked away by her husband to slowly starve to death (Jean had been reading Elizabeth Jenkins's fact-based gothic novel, *Harriet*), Rhys set aside her own plans for a book about the imprisoned first wife of Charlotte Brontë's Mr. Rochester.* Instead, haunted by the loss of her own pre-

* Jenkins's well-received novel was based upon an actual case, but her debt to Brontë's *Jane Eyre* is apparent. What clearly interested Rhys about a book she called "a horrible and sinister thing" was that—unlike Brontë's crude characterisation of Bertha

cious library, Rhys began work on the story of how two Roseau childhood friends, a girl and a boy, rescue just two books from suffering a similar fate. The boy's "coloured" mother sets about the destruction of the library acquired by her late husband, a condescending white man. The books that are saved are revealing. The boy, modelled upon a sickly, studious child whom Rhys had befriended during her own childhood in Roseau, rescues Kipling's *Kim*, a favourite with Jean's father. The girl snatches up *Fort comme la Mort*, the novel by Maupassant from which Rhys had taken the idea of an older lover's passion for a younger partner for an earlier story: "La Grosse Fifi." Maupassant ended his short novel with a letter-burning scene; perhaps it was that conflagration which suggested to Rhys her own eventual title for a story called "The Day They Burned the Books."

By March 1951, Rhys had moved from Wales to Maidstone, the county town of Kent, better known then for the nauseatingly sweet smell of its toffee factory than for the faux-medieval prison building within which Max started saving up his prisoner's rations to buy choc-olates for the sweet-toothed and loyal wife he must have feared he had lost.[7] Rhys changed lodgings twice more before finally settling into rooms above a friendly Maidstone pub.

As at the Welsh inn, the fragile-looking Rhys was welcomed with genuine kindness. The family who owned the Ropemakers' Arms sometimes got on her nerves (Jean grumbled in her journal that the innkeeper's daughter-in-law always sang as she went about her house-hold chores: "that dreadful sobbing break in the middle of the voice"), but the proprietor's wife was quick to realise that their softly spo-ken lady lodger was something out of the ordinary. On one occasion, returning from "my obligation walk," Rhys found that her sitting-room table had been spread with books evidently bought from a local stall; none was to her taste, but she appreciated a thoughtful gesture. (Rhys's private reading at the time included Sartre's witty plays and Koestler's *The Age of Longing*, a futuristic novel set in Paris). Guiltily, she with-

---

Mason—Jenkins represented the unfortunate Harriet as a sympathetic character, one with whom the reader could identify.

drew her grumbles about the singing daughter-in-law—"as a woman, she is much better than I am. That girl who yowls so horribly is neat, clean, hardworking . . . She runs lightly up and down the stairs without touching the bannister. Light of foot and heart is she!"[8]

That passage appears in a remarkable document that was eventually employed to bulk out Rhys's posthumously published memoir, *Smile Please.* Written in a small brown exercise book, "The Rope-Makers' Arms Diary"* opens with the enigmatic words: "Death before the Fact," remembered by Rhys from a favourite passage in Teresa of Ávila's *Meditations.* The diarist then instructs herself: no chance will be permitted to revise or to have second thoughts. "Down it shall go. Already I am terrified."[9] What follows takes the form of a day in court, with Rhys challenging herself as she stands in the dock.

Trials and confinements had, over the past few years, played an increasingly significant role in Rhys's life; here, however, she took control of her fate. At first, the questions are put by an anonymous interrogator; later, a knowing prosecutor (*"There you are! Didn't take long, did it?"*) is replaced by a more understanding counsel for the defence (*"Did you in your youth have a great love and pity for others?"* Yes, I think so. *"Especially for the poor and the unfortunate?"* Yes.) These external voices are replaced by that of the author as she searches for a reason to go on living—and finds it in her writings.

Phrases in what was evidently always meant to be a private piece of work ("Oh the relief of words," and "How clumsily I'm writing. Start again") suggest that this extraordinary confessional marked Rhys's first nervous step towards resuming literary work since her arrival in Maidstone. Writing, she told herself in the journal, was what she must do in order to justify her existence. "If I stop writing my life will have been an abject failure," she wrote. "I will not have earned death."[10]

---

* "Diary" is an inexact description. Rhys interspersed the fictional trial of herself with personal responses to her life in Maidstone (the audience at a cinema matinee; the owners of the pub; her rooms) and sudden time shifts into reminiscences of Dominica and her first years in England.

Much emerges from this intimate, heroically honest document. It's clear that Rhys had not lost her sardonic sense of humour ("O.K. O.K. That brings me to my bedroom in waltz time") or her courage, presented in the half-remembered words of her beloved Saint Teresa: "At the cost of a long death before the fact, I shall conquer this world that is ever new, ever young. Dare to follow me and you will see." She isn't afraid here to convict herself of all the mortal sins—drunkenness is included—except for one that she adds only to clear herself of the charge: coolness of heart. Neither will Rhys permit the probing voice in her head to convict her of committing what she terms, in the Catholic fashion learned at her convent school, "the venial sins." After identifying these lesser, forgivable sins as spite, malice, gluttony, envy, avarice, stupidity, caution and cruelty, the diary-keeper sweeps her self-made list of minor crimes away, more grandly than any judge: "I cannot any longer accept all this. *Do you mean that you are guiltless of the venial sins?* Well. Guiltless!"

The evidence that Rhys never intended to publish such a private record is clear: she used that same small exercise book to draft—and then tear out—the letters that accused her sister of trying to lock her away in an asylum. But Diana Athill was right to add "The Ropemakers' Arms Diary" to her author's posthumously published memoir; nothing Rhys ever wrote was more bravely revealing.

DISGRACED AND PERMANENTLY disbarred from his profession, Max Hamer was an unemployable man of seventy when he walked out of Maidstone prison in May 1952. His wife, aged almost sixty-two, had not published a word for thirteen years. Their mysterious benefactor's assistance had ceased. Rhys was living on the modest allowance provided by her surviving siblings,* to which members of the Hamer fam-

---

* Edward Rees Williams had prudently invested a small sum in government gilts in order to provide his sister with a reliable source of income; Robert Powell (married to Rhys's younger sister) was also continuing to make regular contributions.

ily added a small annual payment in compensation for the modest naval allowance that was cancelled when Max was convicted. (Typically, for an always improvident man, Max Hamer had no pension.)

Life in the centre of London was beyond the Hamers' economic reach; instead, they squeezed themselves into a couple of small rooms in a shared house on Milestone Road in Upper Norwood, just north of the enormous, landscaped park that surrounded the burned-out remains of Joseph Paxton's Crystal Palace.* Writing to Maryvonne in June, and again in August, Jean was valiantly cheerful. A Polish co-tenant was doing a splendid job on the minute garden. The pond was filled with goldfish and the roses were glorious. Just one heartfelt state-ment offered a glimpse of what Rhys had endured during her husband's prison sentence: "I like so much not being alone."[11]

Rhys's response to a change of home was always the same. Begin-ning in euphoria, she rapidly plunged into gloom. Six months after their move to Norwood, Max—he was almost certainly prompted by Jean—sought advice from the former husband of Norah Hoult, one of his wife's earliest literary admirers. Oliver Stonor had remarried and moved to Devon, where the cost of living was low when compared to London. Did "Mr Bishop" (Stonor's literary pseudonym) remember having praised Miss Rhys's work? Max wondered. Now, his wife had a new novel "all planned out" and needed only a quiet country home in which to write. Might Mr. Stonor know of such a place in Devon?[12]

Sadly, Oliver Stonor was unable to help, and Jean's prudent older brother ruled out hare-brained plans for the couple to live in a caravan. Nevertheless, Rhys struck up a literary correspondence with Stonor who, as she was quick to appreciate, was an unusually well-read man. (He had recently published a short and erudite study of William Blake.) Max was not greatly interested in books; Rhys's letters to Stonor glow with all her old passion for the one world—other than her Dominican girlhood—in which she could always take refuge. Here was a man who

---

* Space restrictions at Milestone Road are apparent from Rhys's doleful references to "The Iron Maiden," a fold-up bed which frequently threatened to trap her fingers.

shared her admiration for the technique of Maupassant's short stories and understood why, in January 1953, she rated Hemingway's 1927 short story "Hills Like White Elephants" above his highly praised and recently published novella, *The Old Man and the Sea*.[13]

Hemingway had become one of the world's best-known writers. Rhys's novels were known only to a discerning few. On 5 March 1953, while confined to her bed by flu, she comforted a despairing Stonor about the future of his own work: "You have fifteen long years probably to be still at your best," she reassured him. "As a writer longer." All that really matters, as she was well positioned to advise her friend, is to endure: "I don't believe in the individual Writer so much as in Writing. It uses you and throws you away when you are not useful any longer. But it does not do this until you are useless and quite useless too. Meanwhile there is nothing to do but plod along line upon line."[14]

Apologising for her earnestness ("Max says I alarm people because I am so serious"), Rhys turned down Stonor's suggestion that the two of them should meet. "I'm a bit afraid of people now," Jean confessed, before slipping away into chatter about her cousin Lily, now living in London and composing Creole calypsos and songs "better than anyone . . . a natural born money maker 1953—I feel it in my bones."[15]

THE ABSENCE OF an obvious market may have contributed to Rhys's decision to drop work on a Caribbean prequel to *Jane Eyre* (the novel which Max had confidently described to Stonor as "all planned out"). Instead, she turned her thoughts to radio plays.

Back in the early 1950s, growing rivalry with television was making BBC radio hungry for innovative new work. The pay was generous and a successful drama was usually granted a paid repeat. Rhys herself had no connection with the BBC, but she knew someone who did. Selma Vaz Dias's career had been prospering since her well-remembered visit to Beckenham. She had played a leading role in the London-based French production of Jean Genet's *The Maids* in 1952; in 1953, Selma was booked to appear both on stage at the Embassy Theatre, and on the radio as Lady Macbeth. Her influence within the BBC at that time was considerable.

From January 1953, Jean Rhys spent six months pursuing Selma with an urgency that betrays how badly she needed to earn some money. A promised dramatisation of *Quartet*, with a role for Selma herself, was followed by a flood of poems and stories, including some very early work ("Houdia" and "Susan and Suzanne" both pre-dated *Quartet*) and the more recently completed "The Day They Burned the Books" (for which a nervous Rhys expressed little hope since "most people find it dull."*)[16] All came to nothing; by June—having also failed to interest the BBC in Lily Lockhart's calypsos—Selma was forced to discourage her. Rhys struggled to sound insouciant: "Really I am not worried about the BBC. It would have been a miracle if they approved of anything I write or wrote and I do think you were a heroine to try. Thank you." Rhys's appeal for communication ("Ring me up if ever you feel like it") seems not to have evoked a response.[17]

Consolation arrived in September in the form of a long-promised visit from Maryvonne and Job Moerman with their five-year-old child. The Moermans were briefly back from Jakarta and spending time in Holland with a fragile Jean Lenglet, to whom a concerned Rhys sent her "best love," and his equally frail Polish wife, Elizabeth Kassakowska.[18] Rhys plotted out their route for a quick late-summer tour of England, ensuring that her little family saw Cambridge and Ely cathedral as well as Savernake Forest and the pretty village of Burford, wistfully remembered by Jean for its exceptional tranquillity. The Moermans also made time for two expeditions to Milestone Road. "I was bursting with pleasure, my darling," Rhys wrote after their first visit and, following their second: "I send hugs and kisses as many as you want, and my best and deepest love."[19] However poor a mother Rhys judged herself to have been, she never lacked affec-

---

* Rhys's reference to the number of people to whom she has been showing her work reminds us that she was never so entirely out of touch with the literary world as her myth suggests.

tion for a daughter to whom she regularly wrote two or three letters a week.

In October, the Hamers undertook a disastrous experiment. Yacht *Atlast*—permanently moored at Haverfordwest in a remote and very English corner of south Wales—took their fancy because of the Welsh location and because the rent was low. The reason swiftly became apparent; the boat's only habitable cabins were buried in a dark hold at the foot of a rope ladder, within a space dimly lit by a series of unworkable gadgets. The washbasin taps didn't function; for company, the unhappy tenants had a frisky troop of mice. Rhys, clambering down the swaying ladder one night, missed a rung and fell. By January 1954, the couple were back in central London; by April, Rhys was airily joking to her daughter that she looked (in the opinion of one candid doctor) as though a horse had stamped on her face. Her fall had been serious; back problems would plague Rhys for many years to come.[20]

While the Moermans returned to the East Indies and to an even more dangerous posting—Makassar, capital of the island of Celebes, was notorious for its violence—the Hamers themselves settled in the spring of 1954 at a shabby, half-empty London hotel on Lancaster Terrace, close to Hyde Park. Charges were modest in an area that had been badly damaged by wartime bombing. Rhys blocked out a view of blitzed house fronts with bright yellow window curtains; two cherished blue-glass fish were placed where they could best catch the light. The Hamers remained at the Elizabeth Hotel for a year and a half; the need to live even more economically took them next down to Cornwall, where they settled close to Bude, near the Devon border, in the autumn of 1955.

The move to Cornwall's rugged north coast was not an immediate success. After six chilly months in an isolated clifftop bungalow intended for summer lets (the sea view across the aptly named Widemouth Bay was spectacular), "Bellair" was hopefully exchanged by the Hamers for "Garden Bungalow" at the nearby hamlet of Upton. Here, gardenless, and under constant patrol from a vigilant landlord, the carless couple still had to take a mile-long windswept walk along the cliffs in order to shop at Bude. By July, Rhys and Max had moved again. Their new home consisted of two rented rooms and a kitchen at 4 Cartaret Street—a small and featureless hilltop road close to the post office, Somerleaze Downs and Bude's most recently added attraction, a vast concrete "seapool" for outdoor swimming. Perhaps Jean sauntered down from Cartaret Street to bathe there (Rhys always firmly distinguished "bathing," which she loved, from swimming, which she disliked) while listening to the mighty roar of Atlantic breakers, out beyond Bude's expansive tidal beach. The sound brought back memories of when she first heard that same majestic Atlantic roar competing against the soft sigh of the Caribbean, on either side of a narrow isthmus jutting out from the south-west coast of Dominica at Scott's Head.

Rhys had learned that her daughter was ill, but not that she had been taken into hospital while out in the East Indies. (Tuberculosis was diagnosed later, following the Moermans' return to Holland.) Not worrying Maryvonne was, nevertheless, an evident objective of the long, chatty letters that Jean regularly despatched from Bude to distant Makassar. Nothing too negative was mentioned; instead, Rhys joked about their Cartaret Street landlady's persistent attempts to sell her untreasured knick-knacks to a reluctant tenant. Painting in words a comic picture of her own ageing self as she scuttled along a cliff path in a high wind, "chasing my poor old hat, swearing all the time," Jean went out of her way to praise Max for his irrepressible kindness and good cheer.[21] Sometimes, between grumbles about the dismal supply of books available at Bude's railway bookstore—there was no other—she mentioned what she was reading. In 1955, she had taken the trouble to post Maryvonne one of her own firm favourites, Stevie Smith's *Novel on Yellow Paper*. Published in 1936, Smith's first novel shared Rhys's unusual combination of a poet's ear with a bleakly sardonic perception of the difficulty for an outspoken, strong-willed woman to inhabit a world of conventional views. "We carry our own wilderness within us," Smith remarked in her second novel, *Over the Frontier* (1938). Rhys would have agreed.

And, at last, in the autumn of 1956, there was good news to report.

The BBC had succeeded in making contact with Rhys about the long-deferred adaptation of her novel; Sasha Moorsom, a talented young poet and producer, and an ardent fan of Rhys's work, was eager to bring her finest novel to a wider audience.

"I feel sure that I have to thank you," an excited Rhys wrote to Selma Vaz Dias on 16 October; six days later, she reported the change in her fortunes to Maryvonne, by then living in Surabaya. "It *has* come off! The BBC are going to do *Good Morning [Midnight]*. Just in time! I was nearly done."[22]

Rhys's gratitude to Vaz Dias was not misplaced. In the autumn of 1956, nobody at the BBC seems to have known whether Jean Rhys was still alive or—if this were the case—where to find her. Neither, when Moorsom contacted the actress, who was then appearing in the first English production of Jean Genet's *The Maids*, did Selma.* On 19 October, Vaz Dias revealed to Rhys the various routes by which she herself had fruitlessly tried to track down her elusive friend for Miss Moorsom. A letter to Lily Lockhart was returned unopened from an out-of-date address; Rhys's most recent publisher, Constable, thought she was dead; Peggy Kirkaldy hadn't heard a word from Rhys for four years, after refusing her request for a loan. Finally, Selma had suggested that Miss Moorsom might place an advertisement in the *New Statesman*, just as she herself had done seven years earlier. An unnamed friend of Rhys's had noticed the ad and had passed along the news to Bude.[23]

Selma's generous warmth—and the knowledge that she had not, after all, been quite forgotten—filled Jean with hope and energy. Between October 1956 and February 1957, Rhys advised Selma on how best to shorten her adaptation of *Good Morning, Midnight* for its airing in May. Their correspondence was outspoken, but companionable. When Selma insisted on using the word "rustle" for the swish of a silk

---

* Selma was reprising the performance as Solange (in English) that she had given (in French) in 1952. This was her Genet moment; in April 1957, she played Madame Irma in the world premiere of *The Balcony*, directed once again by Peter Zadek.

dressing gown, as Sasha Jensen's sinister last lover slips into her darkened hotel room, Rhys raised only a tentative protest ("she must *hear*
it and it isn't quite right for a man's dressing gown somehow. Do you
think?") before deciding to let Selma have her way.[24]

Towards the end of February 1957, just as the Hamers were at last
preparing to move out of their town lodgings and into a more remote
home of their own on the far side of Bude's tidal beach, news came of a
preliminary reading—the first of two—which were to be given at the
BBC. Rhys was determined to be present; a gratified Selma invited the
Hamers to dine with her family at home after the performance.

The lengthy preliminary reading—in 1957, it was the longest play
ever to have been performed on radio by a single actress—was a success. Always easily moved to tears, Rhys wept as she listened to the
caustic, insidious murmur with which Vaz Dias seemed to inhabit
Sasha Jansen's personality, body and soul. Rhys often told Selma that
she thought of *Good Morning, Midnight* as belonging to them both.
Having listened, mesmerised, to the recording of Selma's extraordinary interpretation which survives in Tulsa's McFarlin collection, I can
understand why.

Seated in the Eglis' cosy Hampstead kitchen later that same evening while Selma's family toasted the actress's successful rehearsal
performance, Jean Rhys spoke as if for the very first time of her ideas
for a novel that would explore the earlier life of Jane Eyre's Creole
predecessor, the mad first wife whom Mr. Rochester had locked away
in a Thornfield attic. And so it was, as both Selma and Rhys would
always agree, that *Wide Sargasso Sea*—still provisionally named "Mrs
Rochester"—came into being at the candlelit table in the Eglis' kitchen,
assisted by a sense of tremendous good cheer about the BBC's production and by liberal quantities of Hans Egli's wine: "it's the nicest thing
that's happened to me, for years and weary years," Rhys wrote to Selma
from her new home in Bude on 7 March 1957.

Excited though Rhys was ("I came back [from London] brimful of
ideas," she told Selma on 18 March), she still hesitated before committing herself to the novel that she had been pondering for so many

years. Instead, eager for another radio success, Rhys sent Selma her old idea for an eighteenth-century naval drama set at Antigua's English Harbour, suggesting its suitability for broadcasting, while presenting it as a current work which "ought to be ready in a day or two."[25] Silence followed: evidently, neither Selma nor Sasha Moorsom was keen to pursue the project.

ON 3 MAY, a week ahead of the public broadcast of *Good Morning, Midnight*, the *Radio Times* ran a puff piece by Selma under the enticing title: "In Quest of a Missing Author." Nobody could have known how close its content was to the impassioned piece that Selma had been preparing to write back in 1949, before she first made contact with Jean Rhys. Five days later, Rhys opened a letter from an eloquent admirer who had read Selma's article. His name was Francis Wyndham and he wanted to know whether Miss Rhys might have a work in progress. If so, might she care to grant an option on it to the publishing company with whom he worked?

Wyndham's timing was impeccable. Selma's broadcast on 10 May— repeated the following evening—was widely heard and admired. Within days, Rhys had heard from several fans and another interested publisher. But Wyndham had got there first and the prospect of being paid for an option on the spot was irresistible. So Rhys said yes.

On 1 June 1957, Jean wrote to thank Francis Wyndham's female colleague at André Deutsch for the cheque which sealed her commitment. Twenty-five pounds was a paltry sum to offer for the rights to an unsubmitted work, as Diana Athill, the colleague in question, would later readily admit. On the other hand, Jean Rhys had published nothing for a very long time. Rhys herself was delighted. Having assured the unknown Miss Athill that her new novel was already progressing well, she promised to deliver a completed manuscript before the end of the year.

VI

THE PHOENIX RISES
Jean Rhys

"With this eye I see and no other. I cannot see with other
people's eyes. With my own eyes I must see. I cannot help what
I see . . . When I let go of what I have seen I am lost in a world
so black and deadly that I am crazy with fear."

—Jean Rhys, Green Exercise Book[1]

15

A House by the Sea (1957–60)

"The shadow is yourself that follows you, watching."

—Jean Rhys to her daughter, Maryvonne,
14 January 1958, quoting from her own unpublished
fragment of a children's story for Maryvonne

Rhys's view from Rocket House, Bude: the causeway which connects Breakwater Road to the Atlantic. What inspiration did Rhys draw from seeing views like this while she worked on early drafts of *Wide Sargasso Sea*? (*A souvenir postcard owned by the author*)

AT THE TIME that Francis Wyndham's letter reached Jean Rhys, the Hamers had been living for three uncomfortable months at Rocket House, their new canal-side home in Bude.[*] Rhys had been initially attracted by the little modern house's romantic perch against a wall of black rock; just beyond it, the narrow strip of Breakwater Road broadens into a causeway of large, smooth stones, built to hold back a fierce and often dangerous sea. The large windows on the lower floor of Rocket House offered dramatic views across broad, sea-swept sands to a towering cliff and, set into the protective curve of a hillside, the town of Bude.

The move to Rocket House had started badly when Max slipped and cut open his head on a steep flight of stone steps leading up to Breakwater Road from an iron bridge that crosses the canal. In May, when Francis's letter arrived at this challenging abode (the Hamers only remained at Rocket House for as long as they did because the rent was so low), Max was still slow on his feet and troublingly shaky.

Rhys's excitement about her new home was short-lived. After three months at Rocket House, she began complaining to faraway friends and family—never to her West Country neighbours—about the house's chief drawback for an antisocial woman. Bude, in the days when it was easily reached by rail, was a popular seaside resort. From May through until the end of summer, Breakwater Road—leading up to the pretty and popular cliff route to Widemouth—offered one of Bude's favourite walking paths for holidaymakers and day-trippers. The windows which offered fine views across the beach also offered a chance for curious passers-by to peer in.

By 1957, many of Rhys's friends had died. One of the few who remained was Peggy Kirkaldy, with whom Rhys had recently renewed contact, but Peggy had terminal cancer. Cheerful as ever, Mrs.

---

[*] "Rocket House" suggests that the site had originally been used to alert the local lifeboat service when a ship was in distress. The house still stands, above the broad canal along which mineral-rich sea sand used to be carried inland, to use as a fertiliser for fields.

Kirkaldy wanted to know how Rhys's unwritten novel was progressing. "Dear girl you *must* do your book," Peggy wrote, urging Rhys not to fight against the impulse to settle down to work: "it is not to be denied." We no longer possess all the kind letters from Rhys in which, in turn, she tried to prepare her dying friend for the inevitable. "You comfort me," Peggy told her on 4 September, adding, pathetically: "—I am so scared."[2]

The late 1950s proved to be one of the most challenging periods in a life that was seldom easy for Rhys. True, Selma Vaz Dias's broadcast had been widely heard and admired; true, it had inspired a brief flurry of interest and curiosity about an author widely assumed to be dead: "very *tactless* of me to be alive," Rhys dryly commented to Selma in November 1957. "No *savoir faire*. (Dam [*sic*] little *savoir vivre* either.)[3] In 1957, Rhys herself was sixty-seven years old. She was poor, she was isolated—and she was burdened with the care of a seventy-five-year-old man whose health was failing. A friendship of the quietly nurturing kind that Francis Wyndham now began to provide offered her a lifeline.

Rhys was not a habitual preserver of other people's letters: a shame, since her lost first exchanges with Francis Wyndham might have told us how much her new friend disclosed about the long history of his interest in her work. Wyndham's introduction to it had come back in 1948, while talking with two artist friends, Anne Dunn and Lucian Freud; Dunn had read *Voyage in the Dark* in Paris, before reading it aloud (in Ireland) to an enthralled Freud and then sharing their excitement with Francis.[4] Copies of Rhys's novels had become rare during the postwar years, but in 1949, another close friend of Wyndham's, Jennifer Fry, picked up for him (once again, in Paris) a used copy of *Good Morning, Midnight*, a novel to which she also introduced her husband, Alan Ross.

By the end of the Forties, a discriminating clique of admirers of Rhys's work had formed (another fan was the novelist Julian Maclaren-Ross); encouraged by them, the twenty-six-year-old Francis Wyndham decided to draw attention to a forgotten—and possibly dead—writer, one whose work he had come to revere. His essay, "An Inconvenient

Novelist," published in December 1950 in *Tribune*, remains one of the shrewdest appraisals of Rhys that we possess and the first to point out how integral a blackly deadpan, self-decrying wit is to *Good Morning, Midnight*, the darkest of Rhys's novels. Having hidden herself away in Wales after Max's conviction, Rhys had been unconscious of that generous appreciation before she started, seven years later, to correspond with its author.

As meticulous as Rhys herself, and even more restricted in his output (a novel, a collection of essays, two books of short stories), Wyndham was a writer and editor who almost seems destined to have become Rhys's staunchest ally. A carefully critical reader, he shared Rhys's passion for French literature. (Wyndham's Francophile great-uncle, Sydney Schiff, translated the last volume of Proust's masterpiece under the pseudonym Stephen Hudson.) Having joined André Deutsch as a literary advisor shortly after the firm's modest birth in 1954, Wyndham, by 1957, had persuaded Deutsch—as well as André's long-suffering

An uncharacteristically dapper Francis Wyndham, teacup in hand. *(Used with permission of James Fox)*

colleague (and former lover), the steely and intelligent Diana Athill—to publish the first works of another Caribbean writer, V. S. Naipaul. Much though Athill often later liked to claim the credit for discovering both Naipaul and Rhys, the original impetus had come from Francis; it was Wyndham, rather than Athill, whom Rhys would slowly learn to regard as her most trusted literary confidant.

Looking back on his long friendship with Jean Rhys after her death, Wyndham fondly recalled the shared—and sharply ludicrous—sense of humour which lay at the heart of his relationship with a woman easily old enough to have been his mother. Only in her correspondence with Francis—to whom amphetamines were as much a daily necessity as whisky had become to Rhys—could Jean feel free to be smartly flippant about her life in Bude. In one characteristic letter, she compared Carson McCullers's celebrated novel to dismal Rocket House (a very sad former cafe indeed), before pondering how best to conceal a recent and substantial deposit of empty whisky bottles from public view. Diana Athill would prove to be patient, thoughtful and talented; (her well-received collection of short stories and her fine first memoir of a doomed wartime romance, *Instead of a Letter*, would be published before *Wide Sargasso Sea* appeared). But it was to Francis, between jokes and confidences, that Jean Rhys first began unfolding thoughts and ideas about how best to shape her own slow-growing novel, almost as if in conversation with a second self.

By March 1958, a year after the move to Rocket House, a little progress had been made with Rhys's still untitled work. "Mr Wyndham" was informed that the first two parts would be set in the Caribbean, shortly after the abolition of slavery: "Part III England. Grace Poole, the nurse or keeper speaking." The voices were still eluding Rhys, but she was evidently optimistic about the unwritten novel's progress: "Can you give me this year?"[5] Francis's response does not survive, but it's certain that he remained encouraging rather than directive. As a younger protégé of Wyndham's would later explain, what really mattered was to earn his approval: "his praise, his excitement and his responsiveness to the book meant more than anything."[6] Wyndham's responsive and unstinting support for what would sometimes seem to be a hopeless project meant everything to Jean Rhys.

The news that Francis was to leave Deutsch in 1959 was far from being the devastating blow that an apprehensive Rhys initially supposed. Employed for five years at *Queen*—where he doubled as both theatre critic and literary editor—before joining the newly formed *Sunday Times* magazine in 1964, Wyndham made use of his formidable array of friendly connections to operate as Rhys's unpaid agent and publicist. Rosamund Lehmann's brother John, editor of the *London Magazine*, was already himself a warm admirer of Rhys's work. To Francis, it was clear that the publication in such a respected literary magazine of a handful of Rhys's short stories—a genre in which he rightly felt that she excelled—would help to ensure a warm future reception for her still unfinished novel. For Rhys, the fact that John Lehmann was ready to pay her forty guineas for a single story would prove especially alluring.

The only other source of money to be looked for in hard times was the BBC. Even after the 50 per cent division of proceeds with Selma Vaz Dias (a division which both women considered fair), Rhys's share of the performance and repeat of *Good Morning, Midnight* had been handsome. Jean may have wondered why Peggy Ramsay thought Selma (her client) should be identified as the work's sole author for a German production the following year.* What mattered in the immediate future was that Selma, possessed of invaluable contacts at the BBC, was willing to act as her advocate.[7]

These were still the honeymoon years of Rhys's complex relationship with Vaz Dias. While she readily supported Selma's plan to adapt another of her already published novels (*Voyage in the Dark*) for a radio performance, her friend's persistent interest in the unwritten *Wide Sargasso Sea* was becoming more problematic. Rhys herself never doubted

---

* The 1958 Radio Bremen production was rewritten and shaped for performance by a large cast.

that what she was writing would be a novel, but Selma always insisted on seeing "Mrs Rochester" as a work for radio, with herself in the leading role. These contrary perceptions of what Rhys was engaged in doing are apparent in the ongoing correspondence between two strong-willed women; so is the fact that Jean was anxious to do almost anything to avoid a confrontation. Somehow, she evidently hoped, the predicament would resolve itself. Selma would adapt *Voyage*; Rhys, meanwhile, would complete her novel: all would be well.

Writing about her personal life to Selma, Jean confessed her despair about the dire living conditions (damp was the worst problem in a concrete-walled building) at Rocket House. Writing to her beleaguered daughter in Amsterdam, she struggled to sound cheerful. Job Moerman's abrupt decision to leave his final posting to Surabaya in July 1957 had been well advised; a few months later, 40,000 Dutch citizens were expelled from the newly independent Indonesia by President Sukarno. The price of that hasty departure was the loss of Job's employment and all sources of income, while treatment for Maryvonne's recurrent lung disease incurred substantial medical bills. By 1958, when Job finally found work in Rotterdam, the Moermans were penniless; Maryvonne started working night shifts at a mail sorting office, while caring for a nine-year-old daughter and helping Jean Lenglet's ageing Polish wife to nurse her ailing husband. (Lenglet never fully recovered his health, following his experiences during the war.)[8]

In the autumn of 1957, shortly before her hospitalisation, Maryvonne managed to save enough money for a short visit to Rocket House, just long enough for a relieved Jean to report to Selma that her long absent daughter was "nice and not a bit like her mum—*thank God*."[9] In her subsequent letters out to Rotterdam, Rhys stayed carefully light-hearted. Playfully, she lamented the absence of warmth on what she mistakenly called the "Cornish Riviera," or else shared the wonders of a new hair cream with a daughter whose own thatch of light brown hair had begun to turn grey as she neared forty.[10] Mocking her own folly, Rhys described her just reward for buying herself a cheap sundress to bask in an English summer: "at once the sun went in and a wind blew

from the Arctic—(Good morning midnight!)'[11] Cheerfully, she relayed
Max's endearing naivety about her use of hair dye. "This morning the
first thing he said was "Your hair is getting back to its natural colour.
Thank heaven"! Natural!! So I shook the bottle and put on some more
natural brown."[12]

When thinking about her granddaughter, Rhys always identified little "Ruthie" with her own younger self. "About Ruthie, she's there in
my head all the time," she told Maryvonne (much as Julia Martin had
remarked of her own remembered childhood in *After Leaving Mr Mackenzie*). Learning in the spring of 1958 that a new school in Amsterdam
would expose her grandchild to an unknown group, this sense of empathy overpowered her. "I hate them," she wrote back to her daughter in
April (meaning not friends, but groups) "and fear them like I hated ter-
mite nests at home."[13] On such occasions, Maryvonne refrained from
comment. Perhaps, she understood how impossible Rhys found it ever
to banish the memory of childhood terrors which time had magnified.

Surviving letters do not suggest that Maryvonne heard much about
her mother's new novel. Francis Wyndham, during the late 1950s,
received sporadic progress reports. Selma, alone, was allowed an occasional glimpse of the truth. "I will not disappoint you," Rhys had reassured her in the spring of 1958.[14] Nine months later, she had settled
into a bizarre but productive working routine: "One day drunk, two
days hangover regular as clockwork." The result—at last—was a first
draft: *The first draft*, you'll think. After nearly two years." Regrettably,
no early draft survives.[15]

In March 1958, while asking Francis if she could defer submission
for another year, Rhys had described the embryonic book as being
divided into three parts, the first two of which would be set in the
West Indies during the 1840s. By May 1959, she had changed her mind.
Part Two had shifted to the attic at Thornfield Hall in which Antoinette Cosway, like Bertha Antoinette Mason in *Jane Eyre*, is eventually
incarcerated. Rhys now envisaged this central section as an episode of
ominous darkness: " 'the slow approach of night' in that awful room,"
Rhys wrote to Selma, casually misquoting Milton.[16]

Rhys's dark vision of Part Two owed something to the atmosphere of gloom at home. Two years on, Max had not recovered from his plunge on the steep stone steps below Rocket House; in June 1959, Rhys gratefully assented to Selma's offer to nurse him back to health for a fortnight at the hospitable Eglis' London home, a suggestion which Max—he hated ever being separated from his wife—firmly declined.[17] Instead, acting on the persistent prompting of her brother-in-law, Rhys offered Selma the more congenial task of acting as a literary advisor to the charming and quietly ambitious Alec Hamer.

Two years younger than his brother Max, and often confined to his London home by the need to care for a disabled daughter, Alec had kept well clear of the Hamers during Max's imprisonment at Maidstone. Alec nurtured writing ambitions of his own, however, and it may have been the broadcast of *Good Morning, Midnight* which caused him to renew the fraternal connection. By January 1959, the relationship had grown friendly enough for Alec Hamer to offer to act—and to be accepted—as Rhys's informal editorial advisor.[18] Rhys clearly valued Alec's judgement; he would be the first person permitted to read the first (lost) draft of *Wide Sargasso Sea*. When her brother-in-law asked for help in getting some of his own stories adapted for broadcasting, Rhys didn't hesitate. Selma never did succeed in getting any of Alec's works on air, but the two of them became close friends. "Fred"—the name by which Frederick Alexander Hamer was always known to Vaz Dias—became such a regular feature of Selma's letters to Rhys that it's tempting to wonder about the exact nature of the relationship between an aspiring London-based writer and a glamorous actress whose marriage (according to her daughter and granddaughter) had never been exactly monogamous. Certainly, when Selma visited her in the summer of 1963, Rhys thought it quite natural to suggest that she should bring along Alec, not her husband.

A pleasing distraction from Rhys's struggle with the novel emerged towards the end of the summer of 1959; Francis was able to report that John Lehmann was eager to publish "Till September Petronella." (It appeared in the January 1960 issue of the *London Magazine*.) The novel-length story Rhys based upon her awkward 1915 holiday with Adrian Allinson, Philip Heseltine and Philip's girlfriend had already been drastically cut by Rhys. Heseltine had died back in 1930, but Rhys took care to protect the reputation of his surviving fellow pacifist and conscientious objector by pre-dating events to the summer of 1914. Francis, meanwhile, seized the opportunity offered by Lehmann to publish an accompanying glowing tribute to the story's author. Sent a first draft of Wyndham's introduction, Rhys offered only one proud correction: "I am not a Scot at all. My father was Welsh—very."[19]

By December 1959, Rhys had returned to plotting (and re-plotting) her novel. Scant but intriguing evidence that she had consciously begun to connect her own Lockhart ancestry to the life of Antoinette Cosway emerges from the compelling fact that she suddenly sent Selma a Christmas clutch of annotated photographs of Bertrand Bay, dating from her stay at the Hampstead estate, in the north of Dominica, in 1936. It is from the ominously deserted huts of former slaves at "Bertrand Bay" that Antoinette and her stepfather, Mr. Mason, ride back at sunset to Coulibri, the house that will be destroyed by fire that night. The house at Hampstead, rather than the charred remains of Geneva, offered Rhys her blueprint for Coulibri, the troubled, atmospheric island home in which readers first encounter the young Antoinette. Progress, however gradual, was being made.

———

IN FEBRUARY, 1960, the Hamers left Rocket House for good. The final straw had come the previous spring when a local woman suddenly dug up all the pretty wild flowers that Rhys had loved to see growing close to her door. "Oh she's a devil," an indignant, nature-loving Rhys wrote to her old friend Eliot Bliss. "How glad I shall be to depart."[20]

Fifty miles south-west of Bude, along the north coast of Cornwall, lies Perranporth, the home of Winston Graham, who was putting the little seaside resort into his fourth novel about Poldark during the unhappy six months that Rhys and Max spent as his neighbours. Graham never met the Hamers, and thus escaped the potential difficulty of being entertained in a minute and pitifully inadequate house that poor Rhys once jauntily compared to a horsebox. Unheated, "The Chalet's" sole washing facility was a small handbasin. Outside, cold March rain fell in driving sheets onto flat land which—as Rhys discovered with dismay—had recently been approved for a social housing development. A modest row of village shops lay half a mile away, at the far end of a muddy track across treeless fields.

This was not what advertisements for a sunny and warm garden home had led the ever-hopeful Hamers to expect. To Selma, Jean admitted that "a terrible weariness" was preventing her from working on the novel; to Francis, while hoping for his eventual opinion on "a chapter here and there," she only sighed about the incessant wind and rain. Maryvonne, approached as a potential typist for the ten-year-old story which her mother had partly set at Holloway prison (John Lehmann, having accepted both "Till September Petronella" and "The Day They Burned the Books," was eager to publish more of her work), heard about Rhys's terror of causing a local scandal: "the people here are terribly narrow-minded," Rhys confided to her daughter, "and they gossip like crazy."[21]

Four months at Perranporth drove Rhys, in final desperation, to seek help. Edward and Gertrude Rees Williams, arriving in May after a testing hundred-mile drive from Budleigh Salterton on tiny, winding lanes, found the Hamers penniless and on the verge of collapse. Rhys was in tears, Max was ill and the Chalet's roof was leaking.

Edward Rees Williams was not an imaginative man, but he did have a strongly developed sense of duty. Rhys was taken out to a comforting lunch in Perranporth by Gertrude, who then delighted her sister-in-law by buying her a pretty broad-brimmed hat; Edward, meanwhile, sat down for a manly chat with Max. Before returning home, Rhys's brother gave her his solemn promise of help, an oath which he made good on within a month. By July, a home for the Hamers had been purchased on the outskirts of Cheriton Fitzpaine, a rural north Devon village lying within an hour's drive of Budleigh Salterton.

Economy, as well as the need for rapid action, had influenced

Edward's purchase. Six Landboat Bungalows was a bargain only because it had recently been deemed unfit for habitation, a flaw which Edward promptly set out to remedy. Jean, learning that she would soon have her own kitchen and even a bathroom, grew as happy as a child. The yet unseen bungalow was immediately renamed "The Ark." Joyful letters were despatched to Selma, Francis and Maryvonne about romantic plans to embellish "The New Jerusalem" with sumptuous bargain fabrics of crimson and gold. "I do think Edward has been kind," Rhys enthused to Maryvonne in October 1960, adding what now became the mantra of her letters, that a perfect nest had been provided in which to complete the hatching of her novel.[22]

The novel's progress at Perranporth had not only been delayed by poor accommodation. In May 1960, just before Edward's errand of mercy, Rhys had suggested that Francis might show the London Magazine "Let Them Call It Jazz," "a bit of a crazy story" which she artlessly represented as a new work. A delay in revisions, together with the magazine's dismaying loss (by Charles Osborne, an office junior with a bright future) of another submission, "Tigers are Better-Looking," meant that neither story would appear in the magazine until 1962. In the meantime, Rhys's spirits were lifted by the news that Francis had successfully placed another story, "Outside the Machine," in a respected annual collection called Winter's Tales. William Sansom, a writer whose style Rhys admired, had apparently sent Francis an enthusiastic letter about "Till September Petronella." The poet and highly regarded founder-editor of New Verse, Geoffrey Grigson, intended to include Rhys in a new twentieth-century survey of world literature.[*] Better still, over in the US, both Simon & Schuster and Viking had expressed an interest in acquiring Good Morning, Midnight.[†]

"I don't know how to *start* thanking you, but I do indeed feel so very grateful," Rhys wrote to Francis on 31 May, before blithely

---

[*] Grigson's ambitious project seems not to have been completed.

[†] US interest evaporated and Good Morning, Midnight remained unpublished there until 1970.

announcing that she intended to set the novel aside and to work, instead, on a series of Caribbean stories set in the time of her childhood.[23] An old and frequently rewritten story about her father's former friend, Mr. Ramage—eventually to be published under the ironic title "Pioneers, Oh, Pioneers"—was now presented as a recent discovery among her papers.[*]

Francis Wyndham rarely put his foot down, but he did so now. On 14 July 1960, while still living at Perranporth, a chastened Rhys promised to desist. "I do understand that the book 'Sargasso Sea' is what is wanted," she wrote. "As soon as I am safe and sound" (at the bungalow purchased by Edward), "I will work very hard and finish it. Not too late I hope." As for writing a collection of Dominica-related stories: "I won't talk about it any more."[24]

---

[*] Nine years later, Wyndham negotiated the story's first appearance (as "My dear darling Mr Ramage") in *The Times Saturday Review*, 28 June 1969.

16

Cheriton Fitzpaine

"More discontents I never had
Since I was born, than here,
Where I have been, and still am, sad,
In this dull Devonshire . . . "

—Robert Herrick, "Discontents in Devon," *c.*1640[1]

JEAN RHYS SPENT her first seventeen years in Dominica because that was where her family lived. But what persuaded her to spend the last nineteen years of her life in a village of which she spoke to her London friends with a gloom to match that of the London-bred Civil War poet Robert Herrick? If she hated life at Cheriton Fitzpaine so much, why did she choose to remain there?

IMAGINING CHERITON FITZPAINE from afar, you should place this north Devon village midway between the towns of Tiverton and Crediton. Narrow the focus; cradle it amidst small, hilly fields, of which the nearest to the village are separated by narrow and winding lanes guarded by towering hedges. Out beyond the fields, to either side of this landlocked world of farming communities, lie the high and open heathlands of Exmoor and Dartmoor. Within, it's hard to shake off the feeling of having entered a parallel universe, one in which time remains suspended somewhere between the wars. Driving down the

steeply twisting little roads that lead the visitor past a neat row of former almshouses to the church, the open green and the long, thatched
schoolhouse that lie at the centre of Cheriton Fitzpaine, you wouldn't
feel surprised to encounter a gaunt young farm-boy, limping home
from the trenches of 1918.

Visiting to form my own impressions of the village in which Edward
Rees Williams purchased a home for his sister in the summer of 1960, I
met a rosy-cheeked man who'd liked growing up here enough to move
back to Cheriton in early middle age. Roy Stettiford was among the
youngest of a family who lived in the single-storey house next to the

Cheriton Fitzpaine, the secluded Devon village in which Rhys spent the
last nineteen years of her life. *(Used with permission of Piers Howell)*

Hamers for many years. He remembers peeping through their window one day and seeing Rhys (an old lady, in his child's eyes) sitting
in front of a television and drinking, straight from the bottle, all by
herself. "She were hard on her husband, we thought," remains his only
criticism. Roy's memory of Max Hamer is of a friendly, pale, shortish
man with a white forked beard "like a nanny-goat," whose wool beret,
pulled low over a balding pate, gave him a bit of a foreign air: French,
they thought.[2]

The most radical change about life in Cheriton Fitzpaine—after
Bude and Perranporth—was that on Cornwall's north coast, the
Hamers had lived among people who were used to the regular influx of
strangers who visited every summer. Cheriton has never—until Rhys
became famous—attracted tourists. Here, Jean and Max found themselves dwelling among conservative Devon families of modest means,
people who tended to view as an outsider anybody who came from
farther away than Exeter or Plymouth. The Hamers' nearest neighbours felt at home living alongside the fields that belonged to Landboat Farm, owned and run by the Carrs, a staunchly Methodist young
couple who didn't drink and who cared about land, not books. Max and
Jean thought differently. They were, and would remain, apart.

Edward Rees Williams had seen no reason to brief anybody other
than Cheriton's vicar about his sister's unpredictable moods. The sudden bursts of rage that Rhys's drinking habit often engendered shocked
her new neighbours and sometimes frightened them. Many stories are
still recalled of the kindnesses that were regularly performed for the
Hamers, especially as Max became increasingly infirm and his wife less
able to care for him at home. Nevertheless, it remains an uncomfortable fact that a handful of village families did encourage their small
sons to persecute an elderly woman whom they regarded as a stranger
and a witch. "I am envied and hated," Rhys reported to Selma Vaz Dias
in the autumn of 1963, adding, two months later, more nervously: "the
gossip is dreadful. . . ."[3]

Viewed on a bright summer morning, the centre of Cheriton Fitzpaine looks idyllically pretty. The long walls of the schoolhouse gleam

white under its steep roof of thatch; standing beside the rectory, a visitor can easily spot where the tower of St. Matthew's rises into view, solid and reassuring. Walking beside me along a hillside lane flecked with mud and cow dung, Roy Stettiford talks in a soft Devon accent about the village his parents first knew. Back then, Cheriton Fitzpaine was a thriving little community with its own post office, butcher's and grocer's shops. Hard times had shrunk the village; arriving in the late summer of 1960, Rhys and Max found themselves dependent for all necessities on two pubs and a small store for general supplies. For books, Rhys relied for several unsatisfactory years on the fortnightly visits to the village of a mobile library van.

I hadn't expected Cheriton's rectory to be so old or so appealing, but Roy Stettiford explains that the house was once home to the Arundells, a family of public-minded rector-squires who put on plays for the village and rewarded good Sunday-school pupils with an occasional outing to the Tiverton picture house. An older villager, Ken Sanford, remembers games of tennis, always in whites, taking place on the high flat lawn that lies behind the rectory; Roy remembers scrumping for apples in the orchard. In 1964, Rhys told Selma Vaz Dias of the pleasure she always derived from watching the huntsmen trotting past on a bright winter's morning; a last trace of the days when the Arundells hosted the Eggesford Meet, an annual gathering of hounds, horses and their riders that took place in the heart of the village.

The rectory played an important role in Rhys's life at Cheriton. By 1960, the Arundells had been replaced by Alwynne Woodard, the only person among the villagers who swiftly understood that an exceptional writer was living in their midst.

Woodard was a remarkable priest—"a dear, the real McCoy," as Rhys gratefully wrote to Diana Athill in the late summer of 1963.[4] The grandson of a Victorian canon who had founded a group of evangelical schools, Alwynne was educated at one of them, Lancing. Returning there as a young schoolmaster, he taught classics and English to Evelyn Waugh. Unjustly dismissed by a headmaster who was then himself forced to leave, Woodard spent many years doubling as a rural dean

The Reverend Alwynne
Woodard, the cultured,
compassionate and broad-
minded vicar who came to
Rhys's help while she was
struggling to write *Wide
Sargasso Sea*.

and the well-liked chaplain to a psychiatric hospital in Surrey, before
settling into the less demanding role of vicar to a tiny parish of which
only a small percentage were regular churchgoers.

A bookish, dreamy man, Woodard was married to a conscientious
and necessarily patient woman who supervised weekly basket-weaving
classes in the rectory's front room, while one of their four daughters
amused herself by painting saucy murals above the staircase. The vicar's vagueness was notorious. (On one occasion, the absent-minded
Alwynne actually allowed his spouse to fall out of their car, while driving inattentively on.) But it was the Reverend Woodard's goodness of
heart that Roy Stettiford and Ken Sanford both singled out to me for
praise: "He were always kind, a very kind gentleman indeed."[5]

Woodard's first recorded encounter with the Hamers was unfortunate. A few months after the couple's arrival, Rhys had been enraged by
the erection of a barbed wire sheep-fence close to the bedroom window
of their new home. A neighbour, alarmed by the wildness Rhys displayed when her blood was up, summoned the vicar to arbitrate; Rhys,
on this occasion, was both drunk and furious. Nevertheless, while trying to soothe her, Woodard felt an unanticipated sense of rapport.

It was shortly after this incident in the spring of 1961 that the vicar
started to make occasional afternoon visits to the intriguing Hamers.
Sometimes, to the consternation of a watchful village, he took along

a bottle of whisky and shared its contents with a woman whose mind had struck him from the first as being out of the ordinary. Keeping clear of the topic of difficult neighbours, they talked about books. It seemed that Cheriton's odd new resident was trying to complete a novel. The vicar loaned her *Tom Jones*, which she didn't much care for; his response remains unknown to the copy which Rhys despatched to him of Orwell's *Animal Farm*.

Woodard's appreciation of Rhys as a writer began on an autumn evening in 1961 when, informed by his sobbing friend that she had destroyed her novel, he decided to gather up the scrawled sheets of paper that lay in heaps around the room. Back at the rectory, Woodard persuaded one of his daughters to help assemble the semi-legible handwritten pages into some kind of an order. Helen Woodard eventually retired to bed; the vicar, having spent most of the night patiently collating pages, managed to decipher enough of Parts One and Two of *Wide Sargasso Sea* to recognise that the work in progress was exceptional. From then on, Woodard paid regular and sometimes daily visits to the Hamers' home. He "cheered me up when I was at my last gasp," Jean would tell Diana Athill in August 1963, marvelling at Woodard's kindness to a non-churchgoing member of a community by whom "I've been given up as a bad job I fear."[6]

TODAY, JEAN RHYS's home is the last still standing of a small row of undistinguished one-storey properties: the rest have been destroyed. Across the lane, a hillside field has already disappeared under a new, larger hamlet of residential homes.

The cottage (a word suggestive of a quaint charm that Rhys's home lacks) is now and always was screened from the curious eyes of passers-by, protected by a dense green hedge. To the back of the bungalow, beyond a muddy plot from which Rhys struggled to create a flower garden, she could glimpse cattle and sheep as they roamed the hillside fields. This was Rhys's favourite outlook. Writing to Francis Wyndham in the summer of 1967, at the time of her proposed departure for the less remote Essex flat that had been selected for her future home by Diana Athill, she lovingly recorded all that she could see from her small sitting-room's window: two successively flowering lilacs, a honeysuckle, two apple trees, peonies, Michaelmas daisies, "and so on." That careful inventory spelled out what Rhys could not quite bring herself to admit to her London friends. Despite Miss Athill's kind endeavours to improve her lot, she really did not want to leave Devon.[7]

Rhys was not a skilled plantswoman, but there's no doubt that she loved her Landboat plot. Writing to her daughter in July 1961, Rhys tried to explain the restorative effect on her spirits of digging in the garden: "I like the smell of earth and grass . . ." Two days later, she told Maryvonne of the pleasure she had derived from bringing into the house a single unidentified crimson flower: "not to be believed it is so beautiful."[8] In later years, chatting with her celebrated Devon neighbour, William Trevor, Rhys only ever wanted to talk about one subject: gardening. Encountering the elderly lady out walking in her long coat and neatly knotted headscarf, the younger writer always supposed that the wicker basket on Rhys's arm was for the purpose of gathering flowers. Villagers knew better: Jean's basket was used to carry her bottles home from the local pub.[9]

I revisited Cheriton in 2021 and met Sam Moss, the proud owner since 2004 of Rhys's former home. Like Rhys, Sam often hears scrabblings from the cottage's attic and doesn't relish making an investigation.[10] In their early days at Landboat, one of her sons used to see an old lady sitting by his bed: photographs identified her as Jean Rhys. Today, Sam is good-humouredly used to being approached by Rhys's fans. The most regular visitors to Cheriton are Dutch. We agree that it's time the cottage had a plaque to honour Rhys's nineteen years of residence.

Despite improvements having been made during the last years that Rhys lived here—and many more since Samantha Moss moved in—everything within Landboat Cottage (as it is named today) feels cramped and undersized. Back in 1960, the year of the Hamers' arrival, a tiny bathroom stood just beyond the door: "a delightful thing to have

one," Rhys crowed to Maryvonne: "a luxe."[11] To the right, an equally
small kitchen became her workroom. Here, an open oven door kept
Rhys warm while she wrote at a table covered—Caribbean style—with
a bright square of chequered oilcloth. Overhead, a naked orange light
bulb provided a luridly inadequate substitute for the dazzling sunlight
of a Caribbean childhood.

Space was always limited. Behind the bathroom, a minute spare
room became a store for the battered suitcases in which Rhys kept
old manuscripts and drafts. Beyond the kitchen, the Hamers' bedroom
was dominated by the old-fashioned dressing table at which, throughout her life in Devon, daily court was held by Jean with her reflected
image, reddening pursed lips, blueing lowered eyelids, blotting out the
evidence of many a sleepless night. From the sitting-room to the rear
of the cottage, little windows stared across the garden plot to where a
distant line of scrubby trees stood beyond the first hillside field. Rhys
evoked this view in one of the many poems that she despatched at
irregular intervals to Francis Wyndham. She called it: "A field where
sheep are feeding"—and acknowledged an evident debt to Longfellow's
The Song of Hiawatha.

> The silent field powdered with moonlight,
> And the low hills
> The low, meek unaspiring hills.
> And the tall trees
> The tall proud dark trees
> Leaning down to shallow water
> Looking into shallow water.[12]

Rhys's enduring grievances were not with the smallness and inconve-
nience of a house in which water from burst pipes frequently dripped or
cascaded through the low ceilings, but with a ramshackle iron-roofed
shed. Large enough to house Edward's car when he drove over either
to deliver a Christmas capon, or to make peace with an irate Landboat neighbour, the empty shed also offered a perfect nesting place

for mice. Rhys's attitude to animals could be capricious: a dog lover in earlier years, she was terrified by the pale-eyed mongrel sheepdogs that sometimes roamed the lanes in Cheriton. Cows might be endured ("*They know* who to shy at," Rhys joked to the resolutely urban Francis Wyndham[13]). Mice were another matter. Rats were worse.

During the nineteen years she spent at Landboat, Rhys's correspondence makes it almost possible to predict the onset of a mental health crisis by the increase in her allusions to the unwelcome presence of largely imaginary rodents. In September 1963, writing to Selma Vaz Dias, Rhys claimed that an invasion of mice had caused her—not for the first time—to tear up a chapter of the ongoing novel. ("But that's no excuse.") Writing to Francis Wyndham in October, she darkly noted her growing terror of "my mouse-haunted kitchen" and her creation of a barrier of wood and stones to keep vermin at bay: "quite

This may be the second-hand caravan Rhys bought with Jo Batterham in the last years of her life. Its grim appearance nicely conveys the imagined horror of the sinister shed which forms such a feature of her letters from Devon. *(McFarlin)*

useless of course. Also there are alarming sounds from above where the hot water pipes are. (Things larger than mice?)."[14] Edward Rees Williams became sufficiently worried about his sister's state of mind to pay an inspection visit that same autumn; what he saw in her did not reassure him.

———

WHEN CORRESPONDING WITH an increasing number of friends and admirers in London, Rhys seldom missed an opportunity to voice her dislike for Cheriton Fitzpaine. In December 1960, while writing about the "marooned" Cosways in her novel, she described herself to an anxious Maryvonne as "simply marooned." Like the unhappy young priest at Ambricourt in Georges Bernanos' celebrated novel—*Diary of a Country Priest* was a book that seldom left Rhys's side—she felt that the village was watching her, cat-like, with suspicious eyes. Reaching a particularly low ebb in the early autumn of 1963, when Max was away in hospital, Rhys wailed to Selma Vaz Dias that the villagers hated her "because I try to write . . . More than half the population think I am a *witch*! And that I do harm!!"[15] A follow-up letter identified the vicar's wife—no fan of Rhys—as having relayed the village's suspicions of witchcraft. Mrs. Woodard had added that her husband was praying for Mrs. Hamer's redemption.

"This is not a place to be alone in," Rhys wrote to Selma in that troubled autumn of 1963. The words were heavily underlined; the letter described her home of three years as "stupid," "ugly," "beastly" and even "evil."[16] In some part of her mind, Rhys believed it all. "Sleep It Off Lady," the unnerving title story of her last collection, represented Rhys herself in the guise of "Miss Verney," an overimaginative and often intoxicated old lady who—having been perused and told to "sleep it off lady" by Deena, the cold-eyed child of a disapproving neighbour—is left helplessly lying on open ground in the chilly air of approaching night.*

---

* Rhys's description of the malevolent child is often assumed to have been an unkind

Bad things did happen in the village during Rhys's time there. In 1966, Diana Athill brought back to London an unnerving tale of having been robbed as she lay awake in Rhys's newly built annex by a night visitor who used his long-handled hook to reach through the window and snatch her purse.[17] Athill's tale was true: the thief, a local boy, was subsequently arrested. Miss Verney's miserable death of overnight exposure was the product of Rhys's imagination. So, to a certain degree, was Rhys's much proclaimed loneliness. Evidence abounds, both in the villagers' memories and in Rhys's own letters, of endless acts of kindness towards an eccentric outsider who had settled for good in a village that was neither ugly nor evil. Miss Verney's occasional and gently outspoken visitor, "Mr Slade," is a thinly disguised portrait of Rhys's friend Alan Greenslade, her regular taxi driver and—through his always available telephone—her principal contact with the outside world. Mrs. Greenslade and Roy Stettiford's mother often cooked meals when Rhys wasn't eating, and helped to care for Max. Women like Joy Haslehurst, who never featured in Jean Rhys's plaintive letters to London, were always around to join Mrs. Hamer for a drink at the pub and to see her safely home. Kind Devon friends took Rhys on day outings to local landmarks and beauty spots. Alwynne Woodard watched over her and would summon Edward whenever further help was required. Joan Butler, the prototype for cliché-prone "Letty Baker" in Rhys's story of Miss Verney, paid regular visits. Rhys habitually misrepresented her situation at Cheriton when sharing her thoughts with the outside world. Loneliness was always more a state of mind than a fact of her existence.

Jean Rhys did not love Cheriton Fitzpaine, but it was the place to which she always chose to return. In 1964, on the brink of making her first visit to London in seven years, Rhys admitted to Eliot Bliss that she was already plotting her escape back to Devon: "I've been down

representation of the daughter of one of her Landboat neighbours. She was also drawing on Georges Bernanos' troubled Seraphita, the farm child who, in his *Diary of a Country Priest*, identifies the priest's drinking habit and tells malicious stories about him.

here too long and have almost taken root," she confided before adding with typical bravado: "– though not quite!"[18]

––––––––––––

CHOOSING HER WORDS with care for a modest 2017 leaflet that records Jean Rhys's nineteen-year residence in Cheriton Fitzpaine, Diana Athill concluded it by saying that "here it was that by her own choice, Rhys came to the end of her days."

The words sound a little grudging (Athill would certainly not have chosen Cheriton for her own final years), but they are accurate. For Rhys, a recluse who believed that she must "earn" her death by her writing, a quiet retreat in the tedious, secluded depths of Devon was ideal. Robert Herrick, a poet and priest who elected to return to Dean Prior after being ousted from his Devon parish during the English Civil War, would have agreed:

> Yet, justly too, I must confess
> I ne'er invented such
> Ennobled numbers for the press
> Than where I loathed so much.[19]

17

The Madness of Perfection
(1960–63)

"The difficult thing is the only worthwhile thing."
—Jean Rhys to Selma Vaz Dias, September 1963[1]

HOW LONG HAD *Wide Sargasso Sea* been gestating within Jean Rhys? The truest answer might be all of her life. A more specific answer would be that Rhys's first references to the Sargasso Sea and its depths, beneath a rank cargo of floating, brownish weed, date back to 1936, the year she returned to her homeland, Dominica. At Bude, memories may have been triggered by a similar brownish weed that still floats on dark water above what Rhys described as a "weir" separating Rocket House from the little resort's tidal beach.

In the autumn of 1960, just after the Hamers' move to Cheriton Fitzpaine, when gently pressed about the progress of her novel, Rhys sounded a note of cautious optimism. "It may go better here," she wrote to Francis Wyndham (who had by then left André Deutsch to work for *Queen* magazine).[2]

Wide Sargasso Sea's rebirth at Bude in 1957 had coincided with Max's deterioration in health. Having suffered what seems to have been a first stroke in 1958, he grew much worse in 1959, during the couple's final months at Rocket House. The subsequent move to Landboat Bunga-lows had brought no improvement; it wasn't long before Max was having to spend weeks—and sometimes months—at the nearby hospital in Tiverton (formerly the town workhouse) and in its recovery wing for convalescents, the Belmont. National Health Service care for the elderly was far from perfect in 1960s Britain. Inevitably, Max's growing unhappiness affected a wife who still loved him. Slapping down a well-meaning but occasionally tactless Diana Athill with less than her usual courtesy, Rhys once snapped back that—whatever Miss Athill might suppose—Max was "not a bundle of old rags to me—he is Max. (Nice. Was. A stoic.)"[3]

In December 1960, contemplating what would become a typical Devon winter—with a sick husband, a view across vacant and water-logged fields and icicles hanging by the bathroom wall—Rhys valiantly joked to Maryvonne about being perceived as a comic old eccentric, one who might scandalise her daughter by suddenly showing up in Rotterdam in a bright red wig and purple dress.*

To Selma, whose career by then had begun to ebb, Rhys argued that sadness ("the shadow of light as it were, this black melancholy") was the necessary price of life and experience. "I know it so well, my God, it goes everywhere with me—but almost despair my dear," she added. "Though never quite."[4]

Although disheartened by the lack of easy access in Cheriton either to books or whisky ("Woe. Woe."), Rhys's spirits were lifted by Francis Wyndham's good news in the new year of 1961: the *Sunday Times* and the *TLS*, when reviewing *Winter's Tales*, the annual anthology in which Francis had managed to place one of a clutch of stories Rhys had sent him, had both praised "Outside the Machine" as an exceptional work. Reassured, she sent Francis her revision of "Let Them Call It Jazz." The story was still in her handwriting: the experiences of a mixed-race woman in Holloway prison hadn't seemed prudent material to

---

* Rhys just beat Jenny Joseph to it with her comic image: Joseph's celebrated poem, "Warning," with the now famous opening about an older woman wearing purple and a red hat, was published the following year, in 1961 (Jenny Joseph, *Selected Poems*, Bloodaxe, 1992).

share with any local typist, even back in Perranporth (where Rhys had tried to recruit Maryvonne as an overseas secretary), and certainly not in conservative Cheriton. Understanding her concern, Francis—who rarely performed such a service for a friend, however gifted—typed it out himself.

Rhys's fierce dispute with the local farmer about his obstructive fence had opened the way for a new friendship when Alwynne Woodard stepped in to make peace. The vicar's calming visits had helped Rhys to resume her writing. By the beginning of the autumn of 1961, she had grown confident enough to show—and even read aloud—the opening of her work-in-progress to her brother-in-law. The orderly Alec Hamer, while shocked by the chaos in which Rhys habitually wrote—"it's the way I work—always," she explained to Francis on 11 October—had liked what he heard. Nevertheless, as Rhys admitted, the novel remained a long way from completion. Each week, so Francis gathered, she formed the intention of despatching a chapter to London. "But. Well, but—"[5]

Wyndham, while pleased by the evidence that progress was being made, was disturbed by the news that Rhys was in low spirits. "I've been seeing a lot of the collective face that killed a thousand thoughts lately," she admitted in this same October letter, "and sometimes there is blue murder in my wicked heart."[6]

Rhys chose not to tell Francis Wyndham that she had again been drinking heavily. Within a day or so of writing to him, she had ripped up a chapter of the novel. Alarmed by one of her lightning outbursts of rage—when angered, the ageing Rhys could still spit, bite or scratch a perceived opponent—Gladys Raymond (a postmistress who lived in one of the Landboat bungalows) summoned the vicar.

It was this visit which had led to Alwynne Woodard's decision, after reading some of Rhys's handwritten pages, to help their author in any way he could. By 17 October, Rhys was cheerfully telling Wyndham about her renewed determination to "fix the book up, write it legibly and sooner than you'd believe."[7] The cause was some "wonderful" pep pills that a sympathetic doctor—presumably the helpful vicar's own physician son-in-law—had recommended.

Mandatory drug regulation was still in its infancy during the early 1960s. Jean Rhys was not the only creative person who became innocently addicted to prescribed anti-depressants and amphetamines: Selma Vaz Dias suffered noticeable and adverse effects after being given "Marplan" (an anti-depressant) by the controversial psychiatrist William Sargant.[8] From the first, Rhys spoke gratefully of the "bright red pills" and the immediate surge of energy—she compared the sensation to flying—that they produced. In December 1961, she relied on them as she struggled to cope with a double blow. It was while Rhys was facing her husband's first protracted absence (Max was referred to Tiverton Hospital for examination and rest by the same kindly doctor who had prescribed her medication) that sad news reached her from Holland. Jean Lenglet, the father of her only child, the fascinating, brave and literary-minded man whom she had loved most enduringly, the loyal supporter of her work long after their marriage had ended, was dead. Although long anticipated, the shock of his loss was deeply felt by Rhys at a time of actual and emotional isolation. Pills helped; in need of more, she had only to ask for a repeat. When Max was released from hospital at the end of December—a concerned Edward Rees Williams had been paying regular visits to his sister during her weeks alone at Landboat—Rhys welcomed him wearing a bright red dress to match her uplifting scarlet pills.

It's impossible to know how much the improvement in Rhys's spirits resulted from her new medication, but by the spring of 1962, despite bad flu and a harsh winter that had frozen all the pipes and flooded the streets of nearby Tiverton, she was back at work on the novel. Doubtless, she had also been cheered by the knowledge that some of her finest stories were at last appearing in print. Alan Ross was now editing the *London Magazine*, subsidised by his rich and cultured wife, Jennifer Fry. "Let Them Call It Jazz" had appeared there in February, while later in the year—following its long disappearance within the magazine's office files—the rediscovered story "Tigers are Better-Looking" was finally due for publication.

Alan Ross unwittingly provided Rhys with a fresh source of stimulation for the novel she was at last identifying regularly as "Wide Sargasso Sea." As part of a collection of commissioned essays about how various writers had found their vocation, Ross encouraged Rhys to contribute a brief article on her early years in England. Provisionally titled "Leaving School," the piece would evolve into one of Rhys's most directly autobiographical stories, "Overture and Beginners Please," while laying the ground for her long-planned memoir. Ross had promised a generous fee. More importantly, the subject matter had the unanticipated effect of forcing Rhys to confront her own first response to *Jane Eyre.*

Charlotte Brontë's novel had been a set book at the Perse School in Cambridge—half a century ago—when Rhys first read it. Even in her seventies, Rhys still remembered with pain how she herself had been nicknamed "West Indies" and treated by her fellow pupils as "a Savage from the Cannibal Islands."[9] A hurtful parallel was easily established by thoughtlessly cruel schoolgirls between an easily riled young "Savage" from Dominica and Bertha Antoinette Mason, bred in Jamaica and crudely portrayed by Brontë as a red-eyed and bestial creature who "snatched and growled like some wild animal."[10]

Mining her memories of the Perse for "Leaving School," Rhys thought often and hard about the crass injustice of Brontë's representation of Bertha Mason. Rhys did not, as she explained in several long letters to Francis Wyndham, deny that calculated alliances were historically made between English fortune-hunters and Creole heiresses, or that some of those unfortunate young brides had proved to be emotionally unstable. Her own identification was with Bertha's role as an outsider. "Creole of pure English descent she may be," Rochester remarks of Antoinette, "but they are not English or European either."[11]

Unstated but implicit in Rhys's letters to Francis Wyndham and Diana Athill in 1962–63 was the growing evidence that the writer's own delicately calibrated mental stability increased her empathy with

Antoinette (or "Bertha," as Antoinette's husband in Rhys's novel inexplicably insists upon renaming her). A hint of the depths and complexity of Rhys's feelings emerges from the fact that her own private title for *Wide Sargasso Sea* for a long time was "Before I Was Set Free." Freedom, for the twenty-year-old Antoinette, is to be gained only when she dreams of leaping from her husband's blazing roof into the waiting arms of Tia, her dark twin and nemesis: " . . . I saw the pool at Coulibri. Tia was there. She beckoned to me. And when I hesitated, she laughed. I heard her say, You frightened?"[12]

"Bravo!" wrote Rhys in a letter, after describing her heroine's dream of a self-willed death. "You must earn death," Jean had instructed herself in her diary at the Ropemakers' Arms. Here, in the final pages of her novel, as she transforms Bertha Mason's gothic death-plunge into an act of courage, Rhys and her character appear to merge into a single being. "Now at last I know why I was brought here and what I have to do," Antoinette asserts in the book's last lines as she wakes from a dream of setting Thornfield on fire. The words she uses offer an unmistakeable echo of those in which Rhys would regularly pledge her own solemn purpose and vocation: to write and—like Bernanos—to write with unflinching honesty about the only truth she knew. Her self.

———

WRITING HER NOVEL still felt "like pulling a cart up a very steep hill," Rhys sighed to Maryvonne in March 1962. By now, however, she had at last secured access to a typist who was prepared to take dictation—a new experience for Rhys—while helping to transcribe her shambolic pages of manuscript.

Alwynne Woodard had been the negotiator of this new arrangement. While taking bottles of whisky to Rhys's cottage to add cheer to their long and often daily chats, the vicar had realised how much of his new friend's time was taken up by the difficulty of revising almost indecipherable handwritten drafts of her own work. During the autumn of 1961, Woodard thought he had discovered a solution. Morris Brown, an aspiring television playwright, had rented Pond Cottage, a stone-walled farmhouse at nearby Witheridge, as a quiet occasional retreat for himself and his wife while he worked on a life of Jesus for the BBC. Katherine Brown, marooned on an isolated Devon hilltop, had time on her hands. Intrigued by Woodard's accounts of a local author who was at work on a remarkable novel, she offered to act as Miss Rhys's unpaid typist.

All began well. In December 1961, Woodard conducted Rhys to the Browns' farmhouse. The couple were warm and welcoming; Jean, gloved, hatted and smiling, was at her courteous best. An arrangement was set up for day-long visits, during which Rhys read aloud from her handwritten draft. A patient and efficient typist, Katherine Brown admired what she heard enough to suggest introducing Rhys to their Yorkshire-born friend Olwyn Hughes, should she ever need an agent (a recommendation which Olwyn herself would follow up some four years later). Less wisely, she and her husband began contributing ideas to the novel-in-progress. This was unacceptable. In September 1962, Rhys sheepishly admitted to Francis Wyndham that her latest handwritten submissions were the result of a row after the well-meaning Browns had started "suggesting this and that—I just ran away (*as usual!*)."[13]

The winter of 1962/63 proved to be one of the coldest on record; trapped in a small, cold house with thin walls, the Hamers quarrelled furiously. Early in April, Max's doctor despatched his patient to a quiet clinic on the south Devon coast. "Whatever you call me I love you and only you and always shall," a forlorn Max wrote in the only note to his wife which she chose to preserve.[14]

Jean Rhys, throughout that harsh winter and bitter spring, continued recklessly popping red pills, washed down with whisky while she tried to combine work on her novel with a long first draft of the autobiographical "Leaving School" for the *London Magazine*. Writing belatedly to thank Eliot Bliss for her welcome Christmas gift of cash, Rhys admitted that she had come "damn near a complete crack up for the first time in my life."[15] One unfortunate outcome of that "crack up" seems to have been that Rhys—having renewed the connection—finally lost the services of her friendly typist.

No clear account exists of what went wrong with the convenient arrangement that Alwynne Woodard had set up with Katherine Brown. Writing to Diana Athill in May 1963, Rhys began by suggesting that Morris Brown had been shocked by overhearing her dictate Mr. Rochester's seduction of his wife's maid (described to Athill as "that very tame affair with the coloured girl.") Less disingenuously, she admitted that Katherine Brown's husband had annoyed *her* by his habit of walking in and interrupting her attempts to dictate. Angry words were apparently exchanged. Brown nobly agreed to banish both Christ and himself to a remote garden shed, but the initial warmth had gone. When Rhys attempted to renew the arrangement with Pond Cottage towards the end of May, she was fobbed off by the Browns with weak excuses.[16]

Given the circumstances, Francis Wyndham must have been astonished to receive at last and without warning what he described to Diana Athill on 4 May 1963 as "the makings of an extraordinary book."[17] The "makings": Athill, while sharing her former colleague's delight in the exceptional quality of the novel's opening section (Mrs. Brown had typed out the chapters leading up to Antoinette's marriage), agreed with Francis that the rest (the long honeymoon section set on an unnamed Dominica had not yet been written) remained unresolved. Publication, despite André Deutsch's own unconcealed impatience—following six years of Rhys's unfulfilled promises—would have to wait.

Max, sent home in May, suffered another stroke. Back once more at the Tiverton Hospital that June, her husband grew so thin and forlorn that Rhys, making one of her weekly visits, burst into tears. "How could the nurses be so inhuman?" she stormed to Selma Vaz Dias on 24 June; why wouldn't they let the poor man smoke in bed? It comforted her to learn that life-enhancing, exuberant Selma and Alec Hamer—anxious to see his brother again after Rhys's alarming reports about Max's failing health—aimed to visit Cheriton together at the start of July. Diana Athill had meanwhile contrived a temporary typing solution: her younger colleague, Esther Whitby, had volunteered to go to Cheriton in late July, in order to work with Rhys on her latest revi-

sions. Conscious of her author's drinking habits, Diana Athill thoughtfully supplied Esther with an escape from unwelcome pressure; Mrs.
Whitby, Athill imaginatively explained in advance, was suffering from
a temporary allergy to alcohol.

Selma and Alec suffered from no such constraint; to Rhys, their
visit from 3–5 July 1963 was an unqualified delight. Her guests—they
stayed at the Ring of Bells, the prettier of Cheriton's two inns—seemed
to enjoy each other's company as much as they took pleasure in hers,
although Alec, finally visiting the hospital in Tiverton, was appalled
by his brother's decline. Rather than discussing progress on her current novel, as Rhys had dreaded, Selma wanted only to talk about her
persistent hope of adapting, for a multi-voiced broadcast on the BBC,
*Voyage in the Dark.**

Intent upon making *Voyage* sound authentic, Selma had brought
along Clifton Parker, a suave and well-regarded composer for whom
she wanted Rhys to sing the old Kwéyòl songs that flicker through
Anna Morgan's memory in the novel.

Mr. Parker put his considerable charm to good use during his visit to
Rhys's home. The tape recording that he made at Cheriton survives in
the Rhys collection held at the McFarlin Library in Tulsa. Eerily and
sweetly, a light and lilting voice quavers out into the dusty air, hesitates,
then starts again. "It's not quite right," Rhys says. Her voice sounds
plaintive; evidently, she's on the verge of tears. Parker's voice speaks
gently, reassuring the singer about how well she's doing. "You got every
word absolutely right, except *bon dieu*," Selma's richer voice chimes in.
"I know," says Jean. "I know." Comforted, she begins to sing: "*My belle
ka di* . . . no, that's not right." Silence falls. The tape whirrs, crackling.
Unexpectedly, the tremulous voice gathers new strength, before Rhys
changes her tone and bursts into a rollicking ditty; the words tell the
story of a bad, greedy woman from Grenada who's being told to take
her gold earrings, pack her bags and go home. "*Doggee doggee go bone*"

---

* It's possible that Selma had been influenced by hearing the multi-voiced performance of *Good Morning, Midnight* on Radio Bremen in 1958.

runs the chorus and, halfway through it, Rhys bursts into giggles. "I don't know . . . something like that . . ." She pauses with a question in her voice, hesitating, waiting for the approval that will surely come, like a child.

But she's *performing*, I suddenly realise; she's an actress, performing for an actress. And, sitting quite alone in the University of Tulsa's dimly lit McFarlin Library, in the late afternoon, listening to the soft and charming voice of a seventy-two-year-old woman who is also— very definitely—conscious of a flattering masculine presence in the room, I find myself smiling in delighted recognition. "A siren" was how Francis Wyndham once described Jean Rhys; just for a moment, I understand exactly what he meant.[18]

―――――――――――――

THE SUCCESS OF Selma Vaz Dias's visit to a friend she hadn't seen for six years had much to do with the fact that—following three years of a shrinking stage career, illness and a period of depression treated by therapy and heavy medication—the actress appeared to be restored to her impulsive and charming best. Giddy with relief that she was not to be persecuted about her unfinished novel and well plied with whisky, Rhys thought nothing of signing a scrap of handwritten paper which assigned to her friend 50 per cent of any future payments for the use of Rhys's work, together with the right to exert complete artistic control.

The financial division was unusual only in extending beyond Selma's personal involvement;* far rarer was the case of a writer handing over artistic control to a single person. At the time, in a blur of drink and euphoria, it all seemed to make perfect sense. In 1963, Rhys's own name was still only known to an elite group of admirers; armed with her hastily scrawled signature, and still at ease in a world to which

―――――――――――――

* In 1957, for example, Peggy Ramsay drew up what was then regarded as a standard contract, dividing 50 per cent of the rights to Tito Strozzi's *Play for Two* between Strozzi's translator, Smylka Perovic, and the adapter, Selma Vaz Dias, who became one of Peggy's first clients (private collection).

Rhys's own connections were limited, Selma promised to become a zealous promotor of her less celebrated friend's work.

And so—for a short time—Vaz Dias proved to be. Immediately after her return from Devon, an elated Selma began talks with the BBC about her ongoing adaptation of *Voyage*, while warning a naive Rhys not to go signing agreements with anyone until a suitable literary agent had been located by her truest friend. Finding one didn't take long; within a fortnight of her Devon visit, Selma had persuaded John Smith of the well-regarded Christy & Moore agency—their clients included Georgette Heyer and George Orwell—to visit Rhys at Cheriton. A letter written by Smith on his return to London advised Selma to expect a percentage from the forthcoming publication in a Hungarian magazine of "Let Them Call It Jazz"; Rhys's new agent evidently foresaw no difficulties with the financial division that had been—however informally—agreed between a pair of friendly ladies.

Shortly after Selma's visit, her blithely announced decision to mould together two of *Voyage*'s most dissimilar characters caused Rhys to regret that impulsive relinquishing of her own right to artistic control. If Selma failed to distinguish between "Laurie"—a tough call girl whom Rhys, in 1963, compared to Mandy Rice-Davies, a star witness in the trial of Stephen Ward—and "Maudie," a soft-hearted chorus girl aspiring to a quietly respectable marriage, what might she not do to destroy poor, half-formed Antoinette? Rhys's pleas on behalf of Laurie and Maudie were ignored; so were the comparisons of herself to an anxious mother cat trying to protect her kittens with which Rhys resisted sending any part of the unfinished novel to her persistent friend. Rhys underrated Selma's determination. "Mrs Rochester" was *their* baby, in Selma's view, and Vaz Dias was determined to have her share in that precious infant's future.

Selma had already left Devon when—following Rhys's insistence—a greatly weakened Max Hamer arrived home from the Tiverton clinic on 11 July. "I do not forsake people," Rhys wrote the following day to the daughter she had so often abandoned in orphanages. To Diana Athill she wrote that it was impossible to leave Max in a place where he was so unhappy: "Besides I miss him."[19] Nevertheless, and not only for her own sake, Rhys returned Max to the Belmont clinic for a few days at the beginning of August. She was about to be visited by Esther Whitby, an unknown editor from André Deutsch. Max, a proud man, would hate to be identified by a stranger as a mere bedridden invalid.

The morning after Mrs. Whitby's arrival—the Woodards had offered to lodge Esther at the rectory—the vicar drove his guest up the narrow lane to Landboat Farm.

Almost sixty years later, Esther remembers her sense of shock that such a frail old lady could endure such a home: "the wretched little back-to-front bungalow was entirely charmless." The visitor's first day was spent in creating a working copy out of the litter of unnumbered pages that lay in scattered heaps around and about Jean Rhys's chair. The second and third days were given over entirely to taking dictation as Rhys read in a tiny voice from the illegibly scrawled (and overscrawled) pages of manuscript. The intensity of Rhys's quest for the perfect phrase was no less remarkable, in Esther's view, than the obstinacy with which the author refused to relinquish a single page.[20]

Back in London, Mrs. Whitby was eagerly interrogated. Selma Vaz Dias, invited to lunch with Diana Athill and Francis Wyndham shortly before her own summer visit to Cheriton, had represented Jean Rhys as a tall, thin, gothic-looking woman. (Selma's bizarre account was almost unchanged from the one she had written for the *Radio Times* back in 1957.) Their faith in Selma's veracity waned after Esther described a small, pale, white-haired and neatly dressed lady who cried often and lunched—if at all—on chocolates. Pressed further by Diana about Rhys's eating habits, Mrs. Whitby thought she remembered having seen an unwashed egg cup by the sink. Their intriguing author apparently drank very little; she had not at any time—as Esther took care to stress—been drunk.[21]

Esther Whitby's industry paid off; a month after her visit, a provisionally complete version of Part One of the tripartite "Wide Sargasso Sea" reached London. Rhys herself, however, was entering a period of acute paranoia.

The summer of 1963 was the first time that Rhys had been exposed to long periods of isolation while living within a watchful village since her unhappy wartime months at West Beckham. Writing to Selma on 6 September, she expressed her fervent longing for Max to return from hospital and help stave off "this terrible anxiety and loneliness." As at West Beckham, it seemed that everything and everyone was against her: she felt convinced that she was "hated."[22] Maryvònne, urgently summoned from Holland, found her mother tearing up pages of manuscript and constructing barriers against invisible rodents (a detail put to good use later in Rhys's portrait of lonely Miss Verney in "Sleep It Off Lady"). Edward, seeking a medical opinion, was advised that his sister was not insane, but in need of a rest-cure. Rhys agreed. "*Je suis cassé*" [*sic*] (I'm worn out) she informed Francis. A rest was all that was required.[23]

Francis Wyndham did his best to help stave off the encroaching darkness. Accompanying his generous personal gift of a cheque for £100 (£2,100 today), intended to pay for a fortnight at a rest home, he produced what should have been a delightful piece of news. *Art and Literature*, a new international cultural magazine, was funded by Anne Dunn, the wealthy friend who had first introduced Wyndham to Rhys's work. Now, Dunn and her editorial colleagues (John Ashbery, Rodrigo Moynihan and Sonia Orwell) were requesting something by Rhys for their first issue (March 1964). Francis's suggestion that they should publish the opening section of "Wide Sargasso Sea," together with an introduction written by himself to Rhys's work, was received by the magazine's board with delight.[24]

Rhys's reaction was disappointing. Ignoring the purpose of Wyndham's cheque, she set it aside as a future gift for her hard-up and overworked daughter, out in Holland. The idea of a magazine's publishing what she herself considered to be unfinished work goaded Rhys to a whole new level of hysteria. Innumerable revisions must immediately be made—but how? Should she attempt to continue working amidst the scandal and hatred that she firmly believed now surrounded her in Cheriton? Should she abandon Max (still in hospital) and accept Selma's tempting offer of a quiet workroom at her comfortable Hampstead home? How (crescendo) should she find the *time*!

Haunted by worries about invading vermin, scandal-spreading neighbours, extensive revisions and the need to be on hand for poor Max, Rhys dithered. "We long to receive you into the bosom of our family," Selma cooed soothingly from her London home on 21 November; five days later, however, she rashly instructed Rhys to bring with her the long-awaited extract from "Mrs Rochester." Alarmed, Rhys backed off, pleading that she could only work at home; besides: "*I am ill.*"[25]

A well-meant invitation soon developed into a battle royal; in the early spring of 1964, the projected visit to Hampstead was still being discussed when Selma abruptly accused her friend of betrayed promises, while an aggrieved Jean pointed out that her suitcase had been packed for the journey to London since before Christmas. The fault was not of her making, Rhys concluded in a tone that brooked no dispute: "the only definite dates *were cancelled. By you. By wire.*"[26] The sense of injustice was angry and mutual; silence descended between the two women for the next nine months.

Always meticulous, Rhys was still frantically correcting Part One of her novel and firing off entreaties for more time when John Ashbery wrote to explain that her latest list of changes had missed the new magazine's deadline. The extract (edited by Sonia Orwell) was published in the March edition of *Art & Literature*; while it is close to the final version of *Wide Sargasso Sea*, Rhys had yet to introduce several key episodes, including the visit subsequently paid by Antoinette to her imprisoned and deranged mother. Wyndham's accompanying introduction made mention of Ford Madox Ford's admiration for Rhys's style, while Francis himself drew attention to the fact that "the elegant surface and the paranoid content, the brutal honesty of the feminine psychology and the muted nostalgia for lost beauty, all create an effect which is peculiarly modern."[27]

The ground had been prepared: all that was necessary now was for

Rhys to complete her novel. Jean's valiant effort to meet that challenge
was impeded by a despair that neither pills nor whisky could assuage.
Max had spent the Christmas of 1963 in hospital; alone once more, his
wife's sense of being trapped within a hostile and judgemental community escalated into hysteria. Off in London, both Francis and Diana
were besieged by wild, voluminous letters, a bombardment that they
struggled to answer and did not always even bother to keep.

Once again, the understanding Alwynne Woodard came to the rescue. Early in March 1964, a distraught Rhys was carried off to the
rectory and encouraged—to the considerable irritation of Woodard's wife—to treat it as she would a hotel. As at the kindly Willis
Feast's Norfolk rectory, meals were left outside a cherished guest's
door; Rhys's time was all her own. After dinner, escorted to Woodard's
study and snugly installed beside a crackling fire, Rhys talked about
her novel. She had been missing male company; warmed by the vicar's
understanding manner and encouraged by his intelligent interest in
her progress, she blossomed.

Diana Athill had already made the suggestion that Rhys should
create a period of happiness for Rochester and Antoinette before an
estrangement which, in the novel's original version, had struck both
Wyndham and Athill as too abrupt to carry conviction. Talking the
novel through with Woodard, Rhys came to appreciate the shrewd-
ness of Athill's observation. Part Two, rewritten in Rochester's voice
and showing that he was initially consumed with passion—but never
love—for his beautiful young bride, was first worked out during these
pleasant evenings at the rectory. By the end of March, Rhys felt cheerful enough to satirise her slow progress to an anxious Francis by borrowing an apt line from Oscar Wilde's best-known play. "I never knew
anybody take so long to dress," Algy twits his friend Ernest, "and with
so little result." (Rhys was by then aware that Francis's grandmother,
Ada Leverson, had been the playwright's beloved "Sphinx.")[28]

That April, back at the bungalow, Rhys sat up all night, every
night, either at the kitchen table or huddled in bed, navigating her
way through the "wild sea of wrecks" that had floated into her mind

in the form of the latest and most powerful of her spontaneous poems. Writing "Obeah Night"—so Rhys disclosed to Francis Wyndham on 14 April 1964, in a letter containing that long, remarkable work in full—had finally enabled her to look through the eyes of Rochester at his bride, the young woman whose mind forever flutters, like Rhys's own, on the dark brink of madness.

Narrated by the man Rhys still called both "Rochester" and "Raworth," "Obeah Night" is the self-aware poem in which Antoinette's husband justifies his own cruel plan to lock his white Creole bride away, after her suspected transformation into a zombie. ("*Did* you come back I wonder," Rochester asks himself after his anxious young wife visits her old nurse, Christophine, in order to obtain a love potion: "Did I ever see you again?")[29]

Later, Rhys would shift the cause of Rochester's altered view of his wife onto the stories he is told by Antoinette's malevolent older cousin. It's from the embittered Daniel Cosway that he first hears tales of rumoured madness in Antoinette's family;* tales, even, of her affair with an islander: "a *terrible* thing for a white girl to do" in those times, as Rhys explained to Francis Wyndham in that same impassioned letter of 14 April. "Not to be forgiven."[30]

By April, Rhys was living entirely within the world of her novel; the present-day world entered her letters rarely, when she grumbled at hearing dustbins being emptied outside. Weeds grew up over the windowsills. A kitchen chair was propped under the inside handle to the front door to keep well-meaning neighbours out. Max Hamer lay mute and unvisited inside the hospital that he would never again leave. His wife couldn't bear even to take time off to buy herself food. She simply could not stop.

All the signs of another approaching crack-up are apparent in Rhys's letters, as both Wyndham and Athill must surely have seen with dismay. "Yes I need a holiday," she admitted to Francis in her long, wild

---

* Rhys never forgot having heard such tales in her own family. It was said that one of her mother's aunts had been "insane."

letter of 14 April; "all this *write write write all night* and food such a bore," she told Athill two weeks later. "Not so-o good."[31]

Even under pressure, Rhys could prove surprisingly efficient where work was concerned. When Diana announced that she had found a competent typist in London, Rhys laid down the law, insisting that Mrs. Kloegman must always submit three copies, ready to be marked up with her own ongoing (and seemingly, never-ending) revisions. Advised that Deutsch intended to republish two of her novels, she somehow managed to complete a light edit of both *Voyage in the Dark* and *Good Morning, Midnight* within a single week.[*]

Such moments of clarity were becoming rare and Rhys knew it. On 15 July 1964, she told Francis about having been "in a very blue mood lately," with "awful pits of despair."[32] A few days later, she attacked one of her Landboat neighbours. Difficult though it is to imagine a small woman in her mid-seventies endangering anyone's life, Rhys's behaviour seemed crazy enough to raise the alarm. Edward was summoned for an urgent discussion by a concerned Alwynne Woodard. By the middle of July, acting on professional medical advice, Edward had reluctantly consigned his sister to the Belvedere clinic (formerly Ward 12) at the Exminster branch of the Exe Vale Hospital, still better known by its old name as the Devon County Lunatic Asylum. The decision had been "sad but inevitable," Edward wrote to a dismayed Diana Athill. At this dark stage, he could not predict whether his sister would ever resume work on her novel. "But let's hope . . . "[33]

---

[*] Deutsch's sudden interest in republishing the earlier novels before the appearance of *Wide Sargasso Sea* was prompted by Alan Ross's interest in doing just that himself (possibly at the suggestion of Francis Wyndham, who was eager to build awareness of Rhys). When Ross dropped the project, so—until the publication of *Wide Sargasso Sea* had secured a market for their client's work—did André Deutsch.

18

An End and a Beginning
(1964–66)

"Disaster seems to be so much her element."

—Diana Athill to Alec Hamer, 3 March 1966[1]

RHYS'S CAPACITY TO endure hardship, ill health and mental breakdowns was remarkable and would remain so until the end of her life. On 28 July 1964, the same day that her brother wrote despairingly to Diana Athill about the remote chances of the novel ever being completed, Rhys wrote to her daughter from the Exe Vale Hospital to announce that, despite having felt "rather rotten for some time," she was now on the mend.

Gruesome stories about Britain's recently nationalised asylums in the 1960s aren't hard to find, but Rhys was not insane and—as earlier at Holloway prison's psychiatric wing—she was treated reasonably well. By 2 September, defying medical advice to convalesce, Rhys was back at her bungalow and hatching plans to travel to London. No mention was made of staying with Selma Vaz Dias after their falling-out; instead, a Kensington hotel was booked by Diana Athill, who also made plans for a celebratory lunch with her author. Determined to keep the visit short, Rhys left Cheriton accompanied only by a small suitcase and her latest revisions to the efficient Mrs. Kloegman's typescript.

The day after Rhys's arrival in London, she had a heart attack. Giving Diana the bad news, the hotel in Kensington reported that Rhys had almost died. She spent the next month in a west London hospital; visitors included her cousin Lily Lockhart, a worried Maryvonne, and Esther Whitby, who had not forgotten the stubborn old lady she'd met in Devon. Selma, anxious to make legal her informal agreement with Rhys, gained only a whispered apology from a patient who felt "too rotten" for a business discussion.[2] Visiting the hospital on that same day, Diana Athill later claimed that she heard Vaz Dias describe their mutual friend as a former prostitute. While it's reasonable to suppose that Rhys had occasionally accepted cash for favours when she was hard-up, would a singularly broad-minded woman really have described her stricken friend in such a way? Might Selma merely have suggested a link between Rhys and vulnerable, desperate Anna Morgan at a time when she herself was adapting *Voyage* for radio? Whatever was actually said, it gave Rhys's forceful editor a reason to turn against Vaz Dias for good.[3]

Rhys's condition was serious—she would require heart medication for the rest of her life—and the process of recovery was slow. Writing to Diana Athill from a pleasant nursing home at Caterham in Surrey towards the end of the year, Rhys mentioned a bundle of corrected pages for Part Two (the honeymoon section which is set on Dominica) that had been left behind at the bungalow. Fearing that the long-awaited novel might never reach completion, Athill asked Edward Rees Williams to collect whatever he could find and bring it to London for her to edit. Presented by him with a jumbled bagful of indecipherable pages (Rhys took an almost wilful pride in the fact that nobody but herself could read her drafts), Miss Athill conceded defeat. The bag of papers was silently returned to Cheriton after Edward's visit to his sister's sickbed. Rhys was never told.[4]

By the end of January 1965, Rhys was installed at the Caroline Nursing Home in Exmouth, a seaside town within easy reach of her brother's home at Budleigh Salterton. Complaining to Maryvonne on 25 February about Edward's thoughtlessness at expecting her to share a room with two strangers (economy had played its part), Rhys sounded what would become a wearyingly familiar note. How much she would have preferred to pay a loyal daughter to become her mother's nurse! Surely Job Moerman could spare his wife in a time of such maternal need?

Rhys had not lost her wits, but her health remained precarious. John Smith, the agent found for her by Vaz Dias, felt uneasy when a commanding Selma instructed him to prepare a formal written contract between herself and his elderly, ailing client. Cautioned by Smith against signing anything she did not entirely understand, Rhys nevertheless readily put her signature to what now became a legal agreement. Rhys was no businesswoman; she never saw anything wrong with rewarding her friend's endeavours. Only on the subject of "Wide Sargasso Sea," as the novel was now known to all but a stubborn Selma (still clinging to the abandoned title "Mrs Rochester"), did she remain inflexible. Nothing—not a page, not a word—was to be sent to Miss Vaz Dias until the work was complete, and until she herself had authorised the action.

By March 1965, Rhys had returned to Cheriton. Her neighbours were kind. Forthright Mrs. Raymond carried her letters to the post; Mrs. Stettiford and Mrs. Greenslade took turns to cook Rhys's lunches; bunches of spring flowers were left by well-wishers at the bungalow door. If she felt strong enough, Alan Greenslade was always ready with his taxi to drive her over to Tiverton, where Max still lay, unspeaking, scarcely conscious of his grim surroundings. His wife's dutiful visits to the hospital became increasingly rare.

Low in spirits and struggling to continue work on the novel, Rhys received news from an unexpectedly ebullient Selma. While it did not surprise her to learn that the actress's adaptation of *Voyage* had been rejected by the BBC (Rhys herself had never been able to see the novel as a radio play), Jean was delighted to hear that her friend's waning stage career had received an unexpected boost. A controversial new tragi-comedy called *The Killing of Sister George* was due to go on an extensive try-out tour before opening in London. Beryl Reid and

Eileen Atkins were to play the leads as a bizarrely dissimilar same-sex couple: Selma Vaz Dias was cast as their neighbour Madame Xenia, a comic clairvoyant. The role was just what she wanted; life was on the up!

In the summer of 1965, the two old friends were independently pulled into terrible downward spirals. While Selma was enduring the considerable humiliation of appearing, night after night, in what felt to *Sister George*'s beleaguered cast like a doomed production (Frank Marcus's treatment of butch lesbianism, however entertaining, did not go down well in the provinces), Rhys's spirits also plunged, and for reasons she could not explain. Terrified of being returned to the asylum, she retreated into silence. It would take almost a year for her to feel able to refer to "the perfectly awful time between March and October last year." It had been an experience, she would confide in 1966 to a sympathetic Olwyn Hughes, which "I wouldn't live again for millions."[5]

Almost no evidence survives of that long, black summer in Devon. Edward, himself nursing a dying wife, was possibly unaware; concerned letters to Rhys from Diana and Francis were left unanswered. A hint of the depth of Rhys's unhappiness finally emerged in a frantic August appeal to Maryvonne ("*please* if you can come") from a mother who admitted that she had become too sad even to write. That in itself, Rhys wrote, was perhaps the worst part of what had befallen her.[6]

Maryvonne became her mother's sole confidante during an interval of darkness which Rhys described to her daughter on 15 September as like living in a nightmare. By October, somebody had persuaded Rhys to visit a doctor. Armed with new medication (no more scarlet pills), the seventy-five-year-old author struggled to pull herself together with a new regime of early nights and a pre-dawn start, fuelled by strong tea and a nourishing pack of cigarettes.

It helped. Gradually, Rhys became cheerful enough to start weaving fantasies about an entrepreneurial new career for her deft-fingered daughter: why should Maryvonne not make the fortune she lacked (the unfortunate Moermans had remained penniless ever since their return from Indonesia) by opening her own Quant-style boutique! Rhys was only half joking when she put in an early request to be made her own special dress, a very last one, pretty as the ones in Vienna that she had once so adored. Rhys had always believed that beautiful clothes brought her good luck: might the solace of a new outfit restore her will to write? Inspired, she summoned the obliging Alan Greenslade to take her on a clothes shopping visit to Exeter, where she invested in a smartly fashionable trouser suit.[7]

Superstition; a new outfit; different pills: whatever achieved it, the spell had been broken. By 15 November, a relieved Diana Athill was in receipt of a fresh batch of revisions and inserts. Responding, she complimented Rhys on being a "perfect" writer. Athill's admiration had grown all the more heartfelt for witnessing the struggle Jean Rhys had

Diana Athill at her last home in Highgate, two years before her death. The smile and bright clothes marked the point at which she had decided I was worth her time. *(Author picture)*

endured to complete a novel that would ultimately contain no more evidence of effort than the glitter of light on dark water:

> "Do you think that too," she said, "that I have slept too long in the moonlight"?
>
> Her mouth was set in a fixed smile but her eyes were so withdrawn and lonely that I put my arms round her, rocked her like a child and sang to her. An old song I thought I had forgotten:

> *Hail to the queen of the silent night,*
> *Shine, shine bright Robin as you die.*

> She listened, then sang with me:

> *Shine, shine bright Robin as you die.*[8]

"I SPY A STRANGER," one of Rhys's most troubling and brilliant stories about madness, was published for the first time by *Art & Literature* in January 1966: its warm reception heralded what promised to become a remarkable year. Writing to Francis Wyndham for the first time in several months, Rhys (still unaware of her friend's role as a literary adviser to the magazine's board) proudly passed along the joyful news that the magazine had purchased three more of her stories from the 1940s: "The Sound of the River," "The Lotus" and "Temps Perdi." Rhys's happiness was increased by the fact that *Art & Literature* paid unusually generous fees.[9]

Signs were emerging that the hard work put in by both Francis Wyndham and Diana Athill to raise awareness of Rhys's writing was paying off. Back in the 1960s, the publishing world remained small and clubbable; while Francis plotted with the kind and well-connected Sonia Orwell at *Art & Literature*, Athill made use of the same social network to ensure that Rhys would be in line for prizes and awards. It was she who approached the widely loved publisher Jamie Hamilton, an influential figure who had known Rhys ever since the publication of *Quartet*. Horrified to learn of the financial difficulties amidst which the elderly writer was apparently producing a masterpiece, Hamilton immediately agreed to act as her sponsor. The result, as Diana happily announced to Rhys on 15 February 1966, was that she could now rely upon receiving an annual payment of £300 (worth only a little under £5,000 today) from the Royal Literary Fund.

Grateful though she was (Jean wrote an appreciative note to Hamilton, following an affectionate letter from Leslie Tilden Smith's former employer), Rhys was too engaged in the last stages of revision to pay much attention to events outside the novel. Diana, like Francis, would often be consulted about the best way to tell Antoinette's unhappy story. Rhys herself took the decision, at this late stage, to rip up a scene describing the Thornfield house party. In Brontë's novel, the house party takes place while Bertha Mason is locked away in the attic; for Rhys, writing from Antoinette's perspective, it was not only a distraction, but unsuited to her own and discrete version of Mr. Rochester. Out it must go, reduced to Antoinette's incurious awareness of "strange people in the house . . . laughing and talking in the distance, like birds . . ."[10] The novel was almost done; just a few more days were needed . . .

However deeply immersed in her work Rhys was, she must have been growing aware that the literary world had started to wake up to her existence. Olwyn Hughes, without mentioning that she was the sister of the reclusive widowed poet who lived near Rhys in Devon, had driven down to Cheriton towards the close of 1965, in order to present herself as an agent with excellent connections at the BBC. Selma Vaz Dias had achieved nothing in this particular line since her own visit to Devon in 1963; Rhys, blithely disregarding her previous agreement with Selma, instantly offered Hughes the right to represent both her short stories and her first two novels. Meanwhile, Arthur Mizener, the future biographer of Ford Madox Ford, declared his willingness to help get Rhys's early novels republished in America. Gathering that an elated Jean now seemed to have acquired no fewer than four agents

(Selma Vaz Dias, John Smith, Olwyn Hughes and now Mizener), Francis Wyndham prudently forbore to comment. Rhys, as he had learned, never listened when her spirits were high.

Trouble emerged, not from mild-mannered John Smith, but from the intervention of an unexpectedly furious Selma at what she perceived as an encroachment by Olwyn Hughes on her own legitimate right to represent Rhys to the BBC. True, there had been a signed agreement, but it had led to nothing, Rhys reassured a puzzled Miss Hughes on 25 February; a little guiltily, she added that poor Selma wasn't well. What about a compromise arrangement, one by which Selma could be given first reading rights of any stories that Olwyn could place with the BBC? And, of course, she must have a share of any payments. "I will write to Selma tomorrow," Rhys promised, confident that she could dispel her old friend's rage.

The anger with which Vaz Dias greeted Rhys's proposed defection to Olwyn resulted in part from her own misfortunes. Resoundingly booed from Bristol to Hull and beyond in *The Killing of Sister George*, Eileen Atkins and Beryl Reid gamely stuck by Marcus's play until—during its early London run-up—a carefully selected gay audience finally got the joke. A deadly provincial flop was transformed into one of the hottest tickets in town (and, eventually, a long-running hit). But Selma had been unable to cope with the strain of being jeered at, night after night. By the time the play crawled into London, another actress was playing Madame Xenia. *Sister George* would become a milestone in the ascent of Reid and Atkins; for Selma Vaz Dias, it marked a bitter ending to a prestigious stage career. Apart from a new interest in painting, leading to several well-received exhibitions in Paris and London, Selma now had little left to boast about, other than her starring role as the first discoverer and proud representative of Jean Rhys.

Answering Rhys's hopeful request that Selma should cede her agent's role to the younger and more experienced Olwyn Hughes, Vaz Dias coldly reminded her friend of the legal status of their own agreement. A second pleading letter from Devon went unanswered. In Selma's view, the matter was closed. She was not to be replaced.

Selma's silence coincided with ominous news of Max. On 3 March, a distraught Rhys wrote once more, begging Selma to make peace with Olwyn and relating the Tiverton hospital's warning that Mr. Hamer could die at any moment. "I keep a tight hold of myself," she added pleadingly, "or I'd crack [up] completely—again."[11]

Alec Hamer and Maryvonne reached Cheriton in time to be with Rhys on 7 March, the date on which Max Hamer, a shrivelled ghost of his former sturdy self, died. The cremation—a large number of bouquets testified to Max's popularity in the village—took place at Exeter two days later. The east wind felt sharp as a knife. Back at her kitchen table later that same day, Rhys wrote to Diana Athill. The novel was finished. A dream had revealed it to her as a baby, puny, but safely delivered and lying in its cradle. Rhys's work was done: now, "I don't dream about it any more."[12]

Athill, visiting the bungalow at the end of March to make note of any final revisions before she herself carried the pages back to London, was astonished by Rhys's calmness. Later, back at her cousin Barbara Smith's home in Primrose Hill, where Diana shared a top-floor free flat with the Jamaican playwright Barry Reckord, Athill read "Wide Sargasso Sea" once again. Later still on that same night, she wrote to praise its author as "a rare and splendid creator." She meant it. Talking to me in the last year of her life, Athill emphatically described Jean Rhys as the only "genius" she had ever known. I asked about V. S. Naipaul, another author she felt proud to have helped. Athill paused to consider before granting that "Vidya" was indeed "a bit of a genius. But not the *real* thing. Not like Jean."[13]

And what was Jean's reaction to Max's death? Did his widow grieve? Writing to Diana shortly after the funeral, Rhys admitted only that she was finding it hard to believe that he was gone. She mourned him in her own way and on her own terms. It was during the bleak early spring of 1966 that, according to the Cheriton gossip tree, a few small boys gathered to laugh and throw stones at the little old lady whom they saw standing in the road outside Landboat Bungalows with a row of medals pinned across her chest. "Wings up! Wings up!" she shouted at the sky, before she shuffled out of view behind the high green hedge that screened her home from public view.

Fact or myth? It's a strange story. Why would Rhys shout "Wings up," when Max had served in the navy? Leslie had been a pilot in his youth. Jean Lenglet had helped the fliers of wartime planes to escape the Nazis. Had she conflated three lost husbands in a confused moment? Was she troubled by the giggling children, or even by the handful of stones they flung at her? Possibly. Possibly not. What mattered, seemingly, was the offering of a personal homage to Max Hamer, a man who, for all his faults, had never ceased passionately to love his wife.*

---

* Rhys herself related this curious incident several years later to her friend David Plante, who included it in the account of his own relationship with the elderly writer which he published in *Difficult Women* (Gollancz, 1983).

VII

UNWELCOME FAME

19

No Orchids for Miss Rhys*
(1966–69)

"I've always hated personal publicity (Why necessary?). Only
the writing matters."

—Jean Rhys to Francis Wyndham, 21 July 1960[1]

"BLOODY BUT UNBOWED," was how Alec Hamer described his sister-
in-law to Diana Athill shortly after Max's death in March 1966.[2] Nevertheless, the shock had hit Max's seventy-five-year-old widow hard.
Only a miracle could save her now, Rhys informed a still irate Selma
Vaz Dias on 18 March; to Maryvonne, who returned to Holland
shortly after the funeral, she made a more direct appeal. "I am very
lonely . . . perhaps you will be the miracle that will bring me to life."[3]

Valiantly, given her economic circumstances, Maryvonne made
three separate visits to England that year. Unable to commit herself
to becoming her mother's carer, as Rhys wished, Maryvonne thought

---

* The McFarlin archive contains an undated draft letter Rhys wrote in response
to an essay George Orwell published in *Horizon*, October 1944. "The Ethics of the
Detective Story from Raffles to Miss Blandish" praised James Hadley Chase's grue-
somely brilliant novel of 1939, *No Orchids for Miss Blandish*, while describing the
extreme violence of its imagined world as the "distillation" of a fascist society in
which monstrous deeds, if boldly executed, become the norm. (Jean Rhys to George
Orwell, McFarlin, 1.1.f3.)

that books might help to assuage sadness, especially since the travelling
library van had stopped visiting Cheriton.

Maryvonne's initial choice, *A Moveable Feast*, failed to please a reader
who deplored the self-serving nature of Hemingway's recollections of
Paris; V. S. Naipaul's exquisite *A House for Mr Biswas*, sent along by
Francis, was greeted with more enthusiasm. Mary McCarthy's *Memories
of a Catholic Girlhood* (Athill's choice, after second thoughts about the
suitability of Truman Capote's *In Cold Blood*) was pushed aside as Rhys
gave thanks for the more welcome arrival of a £50 (£950 today) advance
for *Wide Sargasso Sea*, with a further £200 to be paid on publication.

Athill had prudently reserved herself a room at the Ring of Bells
inn when she visited Cheriton to gather up the completed "Sargasso"
in March 1966. Entering Rhys's bungalow for the first time during
that brief descent on Devon, she was shocked. Brought up at Ditch-
ingham Hall in Norfolk—a secure world of nannies, ponies and family
prayers—Athill found it impossible to imagine that a recently widowed
woman in her early seventies (Jean had long since lopped several years
off her true age) would wish to continue living alone in such circumstances. Rhys, always ready to condemn Cheriton to critical outsiders,
initially welcomed well-organised Miss Athill's offer to find her a more
congenial abode. No time was wasted; by May, Diana was negotiating
with the administrators of a new housing development at Chingford, a
quiet community on the fringes of Walthamstow in north-east London.
Sonia Orwell and Francis Wyndham both approved the scheme, while
Edward Rees Williams generously volunteered to cover the required
£1,000 deposit (£18,750 today). It occurred to none of them, even though
Rhys clearly dreaded the move, that she actually liked being a hermit.
"I was never very fond of a mob," Jean admitted to her new confidante
Sonia Orwell, in November 1966, adding that of late her attitude had
grown more extreme: "I'm really afraid of most people."[4]

Conscious that the Royal Literary Fund's newly agreed annual
payment of £300 would not go far in keeping Rhys from penury, the
efficient Diana also managed to secure for her pet author the modest pension due to a naval serviceman's widow. Sixty pounds a year

wasn't princely, but every penny mattered to a woman who was regularly going without meals in order to fund her weekly purchases from the village pubs. ("Whisky is now a must for me," Rhys informed her disapproving daughter on 4 July, and she meant it.)

Wide Sargasso Sea was to be published in October. From April onwards, Rhys's loyal support team united with Deutsch's ebullient new publicist, the Viennese-born Ilsa Yardley, to plot a campaign that would ensure maximum exposure both for the book and its reticent author. Francis Wyndham, from his influential perch as a commissioning editor of contemporary culture for the new colour supplement at the *Sunday Times*, arranged for Rhys to have her first post-publication interview with Hunter Davies, author of the newspaper's popular *Atticus* column. Sonia Orwell undertook to obtain coverage on "The Critics," the best-known radio review programme of its day. Advance copies were personally delivered by Sonia and Francis into the hands of all the literary opinion-makers whom they knew, together with duplicates of the prescient appraisal of Rhys's significance that Francis had published back in 1950 in *Tribune*. Recipients included Anthony Powell, Cyril Connolly, John Lehmann, Raymond Mortimer and Beatrix Miller, editor of English *Vogue* (and Francis's friend since his days at *Queen*). The word was spread that a remarkable author had seemingly returned from the dead, bringing with her a masterpiece; a work of genius; everything, in fact, was done to ensure that Rhys's name would reach every corner of London's intimate literary world well before the day of *Sargasso*'s publication. Small wonder, then, that Diana Athill told Sonia Orwell on 10 October that *Wide Sargasso Sea* would go "splendidly," or that Sonia shared Diana's optimism about their "well-laid plans."[5]

Selma Vaz Dias, as long promised, received an early proof copy from the publisher; on 30 July, John Smith independently sent an early copy to the formidable Peggy Ramsay, with news that the novel's author was due to become the centre of "a little cult."[6] It's unclear whether Smith was aware that Ramsay already represented Vaz Dias, who meanwhile hastened to send her own copy to the BBC, accompanied by her vision for "Mrs Rochester" as a radio play, starring Selma herself.

The BBC wasted no time in rejecting Selma's proposal. Salt was rubbed into her wounds by a report from Rhys that Olwyn Hughes's approach to *Woman's Hour* had proved more rewarding. A radio abridgement was to be commissioned, but not from Selma; the central role of Antoinette Cosway was to be played by Nicolette Bernard, a talented actress who had recently starred in an award-winning television production, *One Free Man*, with Oliver Reed. For Selma, the final straw was the news that Elizabeth Hart, a young film producer, wanted to option *After Leaving Mr Mackenzie*. Hart did not wish Selma either to write the screenplay or to play Julia Martin.

Pleading to Selma on 16 September that she needed "all the cash I can lay my hands on," while reminding her friend of the half-share in any profits that she would receive, Rhys's tone became nervously conciliatory.[7] Uselessly so; two months later, without consulting Rhys, Selma wrote to inform the disconcerted producer of *Woman's Hour* that she alone controlled all Rhys's dramatic rights. Nicolette Bernard was declared unworthy of the central role; enclosed with Selma's letter was her own taped reading for the part of "Bertha," the name that Vaz Dias still persisted in giving to Antoinette. An equally aggressive letter about the planned filming of *Mackenzie* was seemingly despatched to Elizabeth Hart.

Selma did not achieve her aim, but she did destroy Rhys's moment of opportunity. *Woman's Hour* hastily abandoned their project, while Elizabeth Hart withdrew her offer; John Smith, exhausted by the difficulty of dealing with an emotional Selma's demands, threatened to resign as Rhys's primary agent. Smith relented (Christy & Moore would still be representing Rhys well into the 1970s), but the future for Rhys's work, in any form other than print, did not appear bright.

Solace was on hand. *Wide Sargasso Sea* was to be launched with a conspiracy afoot to ensure that Rhys should enjoy her first taste of public success. Edward offered to pay first-class train fares to London for Rhys and Maryvonne, while Diana booked, for the duration of Rhys's London visit, a smart service flat in Belgravia. Twenty, Chesham Place (now the Hari Hotel) provided access to a pleasant restaurant and—

crucially—an excellent bar. Maryvonne, back in England for the third time since Max's death, passed along reassuring news of the lightened atmosphere at Rhys's bungalow. It was all quite marvellous, she relayed to Diana. Rhys was *so* happy, and Maryvonne herself was willing to do whatever was required of her in order to ensure that everything went smoothly, from running errands to—in rueful acknowledgment of Rhys's volatility—acting as her scapegoat.[8]

Rhys meanwhile busied herself with drawing up a list of the loyal friends whom she wished to receive finished copies of her novel. Gladys Raymond, the robust but goodhearted postmistress whom Rhys had attacked and whose boisterous young family were an ongoing source of complaint, ranked high on the list. Perhaps a proud novelist wanted a sceptical neighbour to know that she wasn't only drinking when she sat up late at night. It's more likely that Rhys's complaints about Mrs. Raymond to urban friends masked a grudging respect for one of the few women able to match Rhys—expletive for expletive—in bandying insults.

No record survives of what form the book launch took or what Rhys decided to wear—pink, lilac and pale blue were the colours she now felt suited her best—but it's certain that she prepared herself with fastidious care: clothes, like make-up and wigs, were increasingly deployed by Rhys as a protective uniform. The occasion was sufficiently crowded for Diana Athill to succeed in keeping a frustrated Selma at bay. Five days later, however, Vaz Dias made a lengthy journey from her new home in Golders Green for the express purpose of visiting Jean Rhys at Chesham Place. Rhys, holding court from her bed, struck her visitor as looking both "decorative and demure"; describing her impressions to Diana Athill, Selma added an ungrudging tribute to her old friend's astonishingly girlish complexion: "What a skin!"[9]

WIDE SARGASSO SEA has become the best known of Rhys's works. An immediate success is easy to assume, especially since an award led to its swift republication as a Book Club choice (adorned with the same crudely lush depiction of a bridal Antoinette imprisoned in a green jungle that André Deutsch had finally chosen—against Rhys's wishes—for the cover of their first edition*). Nevertheless, despite all the careful preparations, reviewers did not rush to embrace *Wide Sargasso Sea*. In the *Guardian*, Shusha Guppy's sensitive praises for "a mirror in which women can see their own inner selves" were undercut by her odd misreading of Antoinette's eventual fate as a consequence of her "predatory temperament." In the *Sunday Times*, Kay Dick dismissed the book as an awkward annotation of Brontë's novel: "only Jean Rhys's grip on tragedy saves *Wide Sargasso Sea* from melodrama." Alan Ross, accustomed to the harsher voice of Rhys's wartime stories, condescended to the book in *The London Magazine* as mere "romantic evocation." Nobody picked Rhys's novel for their Christmas Book of the Year. Instead, Margaret Drabble chose Maureen Duffy's *The Microcosm* (ahead of its day in its portrayal of life in a lesbian club), while Rebecca West opted for *The Journal of Beatrix Potter*. All perfectly nice, as Rhys ruefully reported to Eliot Bliss, but it seemed a shame that only one reviewer of the pack—Rhys didn't say which—had appeared to grasp what her novel was about. Whisky, meanwhile, provided more reliable good cheer than sniping critics—"and what the hell! It isn't what the doctor ordered."[10]

What was it that an evidently disappointed author thought the reviewers had missed?

Rhys's frequently declared intention had been to redress the injury done by Charlotte Brontë to the white Creole class of which Rhys herself was a member. But a prequel novel necessarily set in the years that followed the abolition of slavery had also forced Rhys to confront the question of her own family's complicity in that act of human enslave-

---

*   Deutsch never returned the four cherished paintings of Geneva by Brenda Lockhart (Rhys's aunt), which Rhys had sent to Diana Athill for possible use on her novel's front cover. Rhys's frequent claims that the paintings had been stolen from her were dismissed by her friends as histrionics, but her aunt's watercolours were Rhys's very last family link to Dominica. The paintings formed part of Tom Rosenthal's sale of the André Deutsch archive to Tulsa between 1988 and 1994.

ment. Many of the stories upon which Rhys drew derived from her great-aunt Jane Woodcock's unreliable family memories, but the book's deep connection between Antoinette, a slave-owner's daughter brought up in Jamaica, and Rhys herself, whose Lockhart forebears had owned and trafficked slaves on Dominica, is never stated. The critics of 1966, unconscious of Rhys's family history and only vaguely aware of the small, remote island on which she was born, read her novel without subtlety. They saw it as a romantic and deeply felt reworking of an aspect of Brontë's greater work. Today, the richer underlying themes of *Wide Sargasso Sea* are more readily perceived when firmly anchored within the book's colonial context.

The novel's best secret lies in its use of historical names as almost soundless evocations of a hidden past. Rhys's quiet braiding into her narrative of the name of the dispossessed Bertrand family, first owners of Geneva and of Hampstead, seems to weave an imaginative union between "Bertrand" (the gentle "nameless boy" despised by Rochester) and Hampstead's carefully identified "Bertrand Bay" as the settlement from which the novel's Jamaican freed slaves emerge to punish their former owners. Grandbois, Rhys's name for Antoinette's honeymoon retreat on another island which is still patently Dominica, clearly references the old Kwéyòl name, "Gwan Bwa," for the inaccessible refuges of the maroons or escaped slaves, deep within Dominica's interior of mountains and rainforest. Locked away by a husband who scorns and seeks to banish her ("She was only a ghost. A ghost in the grey daylight"), Antoinette refuses to become another in that anonymous throng of nameless sufferers, that nearly inaudible incantation from the depths of the Great Forest.

Rhys devised subtle ways to suggest her family's complicity in slavery and colonial persecutions. "Now we are marooned," Antoinette's mother says, after her horse is poisoned, it would seem, by "the black people [who] stood about in groups to jeer at her, especially after her riding clothes grew shabby (they notice clothes, they know about money)."[11] The use of that word, "marooned," deliberately connects the Cosways to the slave community of maroons who, in Jamaica as in Dominica, fled for refuge to the island's interior. Maillotte Boyd's name—or so Rhys had implied in *Voyage in the Dark*—was picked from an authentic list of the house-slaves who had once worked for Rhys's promiscuous forebear. We learn from Antoinette that her malevolent cousin, Daniel Boyd, has adopted the name Cosway in order to goad the planter who became his mother's white lover;[12] the possibility lurks that Antoinette's closest childhood friend, Maillotte's daughter Tia, may be her own darker-skinned half-sister. When Tia tearfully throws a stone at Antoinette's face after the torching of Coulibri, the Cosways' home, she evokes the crime—the throwing of a stone that merely grazed the cheek of a plantation owner—for which a slave had been hanged in 1844. Alighting at Massacre for his island honeymoon, Rochester—his obtuseness is stressed throughout Rhys's novel—never bothers to discover that the little harbour's name records the slaughter by British and French troops of a hundred indigenous islanders in 1674. It's not by chance that Rhys bestows the name of her father's favourite small estate near Massacre on the "little half-caste servant" Amélie, whom Rochester casually beds in the thinly partitioned room next to that of his wife.[13] Significantly, only the English outsider, Rochester, refers to the girl as a "half-caste." His rape is not only of a vulnerable young girl, but of one of Rhys's favourite homes.

Antoinette herself appears to be less a portrait of the young Jean Rhys than a distilled incarnation of Rhys's intense memories of the fiercely beautiful island to which, in her imaginings, she forever sought to return. That should come as no surprise when we remember that Rhys, throughout the painful decade that she spent labouring over her final novel, was simultaneously writing and revising the handful of Dominica-related stories that would eventually be grouped together in *Sleep It Off Lady* (1976). "Heat"; "Pioneers, Oh, Pioneers"; "Fishy Waters"; "The Bishop's Feast"; "Goodbye Marcus, Goodbye Rose" and the haunting little ghost story, "I Used to Live Here Once": these were the fictional tales which helped Jean Rhys to confront and tame the enduring ghosts of her own past on an island in the East Caribbean.

HUNTER DAVIES, INTERVIEWING Rhys at Chesham Place for the *Sunday Times* in late October 1966, had been forewarned by Francis Wyndham that Jean Rhys was unusually reticent. Even so, ushered into the presence of a smartly dressed old lady (Rhys was now seventy-six), Davies was startled both by the hesitancy of her responses and the extreme quietness of her voice. Miss Rhys was "strange, shy, very dignified," Davies wrote in the *Atticus* column published two weeks after the launch of Rhys's novel; her book struck him—like herself—as interesting but odd. Rhys was better pleased by the accompanying photograph of herself in her heyday, dressed up for a day out in Vienna, than by the article's jaunty heading: "Rip van Rhys."[14]

Widely read at the time, that chatty profile by Davies enabled Joan Butler, a briskly practical widow who lived in Cheriton Fitzpaine, to connect his description to the pale old lady she had often seen tottering alone through the village, shading her face from the sun (or perhaps from inquisitive strangers) with a broad-brimmed hat. Calling at the bungalow for the first time early in 1967, Butler received a cautious welcome. Over time, however, a pattern of fortnightly visits enabled Joan Butler to help supervise Rhys's welfare, while acting as a useful source of information on their friend's well-being to Diana Athill and Sonia Orwell. Intellectually and politically far apart (Butler's views were closer to those of the left-wing Max Hamer's than his widow's), Joan nevertheless established with Rhys an undemanding friendship on which the age-weakened writer would increasingly come to rely.

More welcome to Rhys than Joan Butler's extended hand in the aftermath of her novel's London launch was a typically generous letter from Sonia Orwell asking what sort of an all-paid winter holiday would suit her best. The invitation was thoughtfully accompanied by a bottle of whisky and followed up, to Rhys's delight, by an elegant, tissue-wrapped dress in her favourite shade of pink. Rhys's gratitude was profuse.

Until the launch, Rhys had known George Orwell's widow only as an occasional and kind-hearted correspondent who had proof-read the section of *Wide Sargasso Sea* published in *Art and Literature*, along with several of her best short stories. Meeting Sonia in London in the autumn of 1966, Rhys felt instantly at ease with a generous, intelligent and opinionated woman with blue, slightly bloodshot eyes, a blazing smile and a love of Paris that equalled Rhys's own. Their rapport was immediate; Rhys was never exposed to the more hurtful side of Sonia Orwell's personality, or to that of the occasionally capricious and petulant Francis Wyndham. Francis and Sonia: here were two friendly allies who liked one other and understood Rhys well enough to be outraged when Athill suggested that pretty clothes were wasted on an old woman. A degree of frivolity—as they understood and Diana did not—was essential to Rhys's happiness, and even to her work.[15]

Where Diana Athill excelled was as a wily and intelligent editor who fought Rhys's battles with the skill of a fencing champion. All her considerable adroitness was required to negotiate a way past Rhys's ill-considered—and, by now, greatly regretted—agreement with Selma

Sonia Orwell, whom Rhys regarded as the kindest of all her literary friends.

Vaz Dias. Selma's interference with *Woman's Hour* had proven disastrous; on 1 December, an apprehensive Rhys confided to Athill that Selma, without consulting her, had approached the BBC with a revised adaptation of *Voyage in the Dark*. Remembering Selma's casual attitude towards two of the novel's characters—Maudie and Laurie—Rhys feared sabotage. "I know how easily my books could be utterly spoiled," Jean wrote, forgetting that she had once remarked that she didn't care what became of work that had already been published. She added that she no longer trusted Selma "very far. Not at all!!!" The following day, Rhys expressed bitter regret at having signed away artistic control over her own work; not for the first time, and certainly not for the last, she claimed that the agreement made with Selma was no more than a joke.[16]

To Selma, the agreement was solid and legitimate; the worry for Rhys's publisher was that Vaz Dias's interventions could easily destroy any chance of Rhys's novels ever being staged or filmed. Action had to be taken. While Rhys's thoughts were focused on a post-Christmas holiday at Brighton—Sonia promised her a hotel room stocked with new books (carefully pre-selected by Jennifer Ross), champagne and fresh flowers and (this came "tops" in Jean's opinion) freedom to spend all day in bed—Diana made her move.[17]

It remained a source of pride to Selma that she was still represented by her old friend Peggy Ramsay, then London's best-known theatrical agent. Conscious that no agent likes to relinquish their cut of a deal, Athill cannily opened negotiations by reassuring Ramsay on 2 February 1967 that the financial division agreed between Rhys and her client was not in dispute. Only in the tricky area of artistic control, Athill explained, did Selma need to be kept "right out of the matter."[18]

Diana's masterstroke was simultaneously to sidetrack Selma by deferentially seeking her professional advice on the possible future for Rhys's works on stage and screen. "It seemed to me," the flattered actress wrote to Ramsay on 5 February, while making plans to visit Peggy for further discussions about her own role in Rhys's future, "that you were the most suitable and reliable person to deal with the situation."[19]

Selma's letter arrived too late; by 3 February, alarmed by Diana's account of Selma's reckless interventions, Peggy Ramsay had changed sides. Evidence of her abrupt shift of allegiances survives in an extraordinary letter fired off by Peggy on that same day. Writing to Bryan Forbes, she urged the film director to beware of "a madwoman" called Selma Vaz Dias, lest she should wreck his proposed production of *Wide Sargasso Sea* with her preposterous demands. A baffled Forbes wrote back to explain that he had neither read the novel nor considered filming it. He had no wish, having read her warnings about the alarming Selma, to make an offer.[20]

Uninformed of these crafty intrigues, Rhys herself learned only from Diana that her worries were over; Selma had agreed to renounce authorial control. What Rhys did not yet know was that Diana had won her a powerful new ally. The impressive bulk of the British Library's Ramsay files concerning Jean Rhys bears witness to the birth of an improbable but enduring friendship.

IT'S SURPRISING TO find that Diana Athill chose Jean Rhys for her confidante in 1967 about her ongoing and increasingly unsatisfactory love affair with Waguih Ghali, a volatile young Egyptian exile whose wittily original novel about life in Cairo, *Beer in the Snooker Club*, she had edited for André Deutsch. Grateful for Diana's help over Selma, Rhys offered her lovelorn editor the consolation—Diana enjoyed literary social events as much as Rhys detested them—of accepting on her behalf the Heinemann Foundation Award, bestowed by the Royal Society of Literature, of which Rhys now became a belated fellow. The ceremony took place in July 1967. Reporting on the august occasion to Rhys, Diana mischievously passed along the news that she and Sonia had listened to Rebecca West going into raptures over a writer she had recently ranked below Beatrix Potter. When an old and celebrated poet got drunk and fell flat on the floor, nobody at this distinguished and mildly eccentric gathering had turned a hair.[21]

While stoical about the lame reviews of *Wide Sargasso Sea*, and professedly indifferent to the warmer critical reception of two older novels (Deutsch had cautiously waited until 1967 to publish Rhys's revised editions of *Voyage* and *Midnight*), Rhys confessed to Sonia Orwell that she felt discouraged by the "tepid" response to the new collection of stories that were published during that same summer.[22] Rhys's disappointment was understandable; *Tigers are Better-Looking* contained some of her finest wartime writing, but critical interest in Rhys's work was already—and to her frustration would remain—focused upon the connection between the author herself and the less literate, more victimised women about whom she wrote in her novels. The idea of "the Rhys woman" had begun to take root.

Overshadowing the summer of 1967 was the alarming prospect of leaving Devon for Chingford. Hints were dropped by Rhys of her growing unease. Maryvonne had repainted the inside of the bungalow, making it appear delightfully bright and cottage-like, her mother told Sonia, while sighing to Francis at the prospect of leaving her garden and view of the fields beyond.[23] To Diana, the vigorous organiser of her proposed new life (Diana had even begun to buy suitable pieces of furniture), Rhys meekly apologised for causing trouble. All would be worth it to see Rhys living nearer to London, her efficient editor smiled.

Rhys was unexpectedly rescued from her predicament by eighty-four-year-old Edward Rees Williams. On 7 October 1967, transparently relieved, Jean passed the news along to her mortified editor. Anxious about the fate of his own promised investment, Edward ("kind man," his sibling cooed) had undertaken a five-hour journey from Devon to Essex in order to view the Chingford flat. He was guided around a show apartment before learning that no other had yet been built and that only Diana and he himself had expressed any interest in making an advance purchase. Rhys's flat did not, as yet, exist.[24]

Writing to Sonia in late October, Rhys openly rejoiced. The cancellation of her dreaded move was all she could have wished for: "my best plan now is to stay down here and *take holidays*."[25] The hint was hardly subtle; Sonia promptly invited Rhys to bring her family along for a pre-Christmas holiday at her own agreeable house in west London. The offer was gladly accepted.

THE BIGGEST SURPRISE of 1967 was the news, announced early in the summer, that Raymond Mortimer and Margaret Lane had chosen *Wide Sargasso Sea* for the year's top book award. Winning the £1,000 (£18,270 today) [W. H.] Smith Award guaranteed a prominent week-long display of the chosen novel in every branch of what was then Britain's leading book chain. Telling Diana Athill on 7 October that the Smith award had really "got to" Maryvonne, Rhys wondered whether her daughter might be allowed to accept the prize on her mother's behalf at the customary celebration dinner? The answer—to the disappointment of both Rhys and Maryvonne—was no. Rhys's timid request for Selma Vaz Dias to be invited to the prize-giving dinner was similarly squelched when her publisher (André couldn't stand Selma) instructed her to choose between Miss Vaz Dias or himself.

Back in the 1960s, the [W. H.] Smith Literary Award was as big an event as the Booker or a Pulitzer. Rhys was becoming quite famous. The experience was not one that gave her a superabundance of pleasure: "not fair!" she protested to Francis after being chased into her favourite hairdressing salon by an especially determined photographer.[26] Any happiness that she did feel was blighted by her awareness of the growing resentment of Selma Vaz Dias.

An autumn spent witnessing her friend's success had hardened Selma's determination to have what she regarded as her fair share of the spoils. *She* had rediscovered Jean Rhys; jealously, she scanned the papers for any article about Rhys that failed to mention the role that she herself had played in bringing Rhys into the public eye. In mid-December, while Rhys and her family (even Job came over from Holland for a few days) became the appreciative guests of Sonia Orwell at her house on Gloucester Road, Selma accused Francis Wyndham of exploiting Rhys's name for personal gain, while neglecting ever to mention herself. It must have given Francis a moment's quiet satisfaction to inform Miss Vaz Dias that he was not responsible for editorial cuts in newspapers, and that every penny he earned from praising an author he so much admired went straight to Rhys herself.[27] For the moment, Selma was silenced.

Maryvonne's relationship with Selma was more delicate. Initially, Rhys's daughter had been pleased to learn of Selma's Dutch origins and grateful for the offers of cost-free hospitality which Vaz Dias generously continued to extend to her. But Maryvonne shared Francis's distaste for Selma's assumptions about the vast wealth that Rhys had supposedly accrued. Responding to a barrage of accusations in early December, Maryvonne explained that, while money concerns were actually making her mother "incredibly" anxious and tense, what Rhys most lacked now was peace and quiet: " . . . But I expect you have already had a row."[28]

Staying at Sonia Orwell's home in December 1967 proved to be neither peaceful nor quiet. Rhys's granddaughter still recalls her own nervousness at the smartly chattering guests who trooped through Sonia's home or hosted parties for Rhys at their own splendid residences. She points out that Sonia's unstinting kindness had included social coaching for a shy girl of nineteen.[29] It had included a chance to see Tom Stoppard's arrestingly witty play, *Rosencrantz and Guildenstern Are Dead*. Did Sonia want clever Ellen to discover a connection between Rhys's brilliant reinterpretation of an aspect of *Jane Eyre* with Stoppard's artful reworking of *Hamlet*?

The chance for Rhys to spend most of the day at 153 Gloucester Road, resting and reading in a pleasant back bedroom overlooking a garden (while seeing her family splendidly entertained), was restorative and comforting; writing to thank Sonia later, a grateful Rhys said that the room's tranquil outlook had lulled her back into the security of childhood. By February 1968, however, Rhys's overdue receipt of a

£1,200 bursary from the Arts Council[*] had resulted in her once again being targeted by Selma, declaring that everybody was getting rich "(except me)" from a talent which she, Selma Vaz Dias, had personally "nursed and nurtured and coddled for years."[30]

Admirably, Rhys refused to lose her temper, allowing herself only the secret satisfaction of recommending to her friend a new book about that ultimate drama queen, Sarah Bernhardt. Instructed in return—the tone was almost a command—to buy two paintings by Selma of *her* "Mrs Rochester" (at forty-five guineas apiece), Rhys made her reluctance clear by asking instead for a flower painting, while adding with patent hopefulness: "(You don't do flowers do you?)." A painting of flowers was immediately despatched; the requested £25 payment was as promptly made. But Selma remained displeased; a full year later, Peggy Ramsay gathered that Rhys had wretchedly underpaid Vaz Dias for the tremendous effort required to produce "my one and only flowerpiece."[31]

Selma's steady drip of complaints had no significant impact on her former friend's spirits. Writing to Francis Wyndham in the spring of 1968 within hours of dealing with one of Vaz Dias's challenging letters, Rhys prattled happily about her current interest in biography—she was reading Henri Troyat's life of Tolstoy (in French) alongside Lytton Strachey's older life of Queen Victoria (in English). To Francis, her favourite literary confidant, Rhys also admitted her worry that her finally completed story "Overture and Beginners Please" had greatly exceeded the *London Magazine*'s request for a lively little reminiscence of her schooldays. Once embarked, she had found the pull of the past impossible to resist.

Autobiography was clearly the direction in which Rhys was now heading. While her market-conscious publishers would have welcomed

---

[*]   Under pressure from Sonia Orwell, this long-promised bursary had been personally signed off in January 1968 by Charles Osborne for the Arts Council. On this occasion, Osborne was quietly making up for the fact that he had mislaid one of Rhys's finest stories, "Tigers are Better-Looking," in the files of the *London Magazine*, when he was working for the Rosses as an office junior.

another novel, nostalgic short stories and the beginnings of a memoir were all that they seemed likely to cajole from a writer who was nearing eighty. The need to capture and set down her early memories had frequently distracted Rhys from working on *Wide Sargasso Sea*; now, the moment had come to sharpen and perfect those alluring fragments of recollection. Diligently and patiently, Sonia, Francis and Diana united to encourage the ageing author, often typing out her work themselves and always praising what they were shown. At times, perhaps because Rhys's progress was so slow, they were a little too uncritical where her last stories were concerned.

Self-absorption, always essential to Rhys's work, increased as she grew older. Maryvonne, writing to Leslie Tilden Smith's remarried daughter in the spring of 1968, confided that her mother had "a supreme egocentric view of life"; Rhys's daughter nevertheless knew her mother well enough to understand that passionate self-engrossment was "a must for her kind of writing."[32]

An unforgiving solipsism was indeed central to Rhys's work, but it could make her a difficult friend. In May, while affectionately reassuring Rhys about the existence of an eager audience for her planned collection of tales of long-ago Dominica, Francis Wyndham arranged for "Pioneers, Oh, Pioneers" (Rhys's story about the settler Mr. Ramage's retreat into eccentric seclusion) to be typed by himself. Rhys wanted more. Recalling the distant days when little Gwen Williams had used a special "swizzle stick"* to mix evening cocktails for her father and Ramage, she demanded just such a stick for her evening drink. Patiently, Francis tracked down and despatched an expensive glass cocktail stirrer, from Harrods to Cheriton; all wrong! Rhys groused. This was not in the *least* what she wanted! For a start, the stick must be wooden . . .

There were times when even the fondest of Jean Rhys's London

---

* A Caribbean "swizzle," as drunk by Jean Rhys's father and his friends, is made by mixing gin and chartreuse with squeezed lime, sugar, a dash of Angostura bitters—and lots of crushed ice.

friends felt relieved that she preferred to live in distant Devon. Absence made it possible for them to retain real tenderness for a stubborn old woman whose child-like need for sympathy and attention could—and increasingly often, did—become relentless. What almost certainly would have killed off such unstinting affection was the greater trial of daily proximity.

20

Rhys in Retreat (1967–74)

"It's a great effort to chat & I don't do it well."
—Jean Rhys to Oliver Stonor, 3 August 1968[1]

IF ASKED WHAT else she still wanted from life after the publication of *Wide Sargasso Sea*, Jean Rhys would never have requested celebrity. An invitation to talk with Francis Wyndham on television in December 1968 was firmly rejected: "I'd be nervous and self-conscious. However kind you were—this would happen." The following year, Peggy Ramsay approached her about *Late Night Line-Up*, the well-regarded television culture programme on which even the secretive Marcel Duchamp had consented to appear. Rhys turned the opportunity down without a blink.[2]

Away from London, privacy was easier to maintain. As mistress of her own time and—until 1971—with distractions threatened by neither a telephone nor a television, Rhys continued to rise at dawn, now her favourite time for writing. Later in the day, she dutifully responded to a growing stream of letters from young readers who found themselves reflected in her fiction and wanted to visit—some dreamed of coming to live with and care for—their heroine. Such aspirations were courteously discouraged in letters executed in ball-point on small sheets of paper torn from a block and addressed with the cramped neatness of an aged schoolgirl. Penning them, as Rhys ruefully confided to one of her earliest interviewers, Marcelle Bernstein, imposed a considerable physical strain.[3]

Huddled under a favourite rug, Rhys might spend a wet afternoon in Devon reading a novel recommended by Francis (vainly hoping she would share his admiration for Anna Kavan's *Ice*) or by Sonia (urging Rhys to read the latest work by her close friend, Marguerite Duras). When Maryvonne and her daughter paid visits, they, too, brought books; Rhys's granddaughter remembers almost losing her coursework volumes of stories by Chekhov and Maupassant to her grandmother: "always a sign of approval."[4] An evening sweetened by half a bottle of whisky from the Ring of Bells ("Hells' Bells" to an uncharmed Maryvonne Moerman) was usually followed by an early bed with some less challenging literature. Marcelle Bernstein wasn't the only interviewer to hear of Rhys's fondness for reading herself to sleep on a windy night with Marcel Boulestin's recipes. Appreciative though she was of gourmet food when it came her way, Rhys may never have attempted to cook any of the Parisian chef's delicacies on the two-ring stove in her doll-sized kitchen.

Such, for eleven months of the year, was Jean Rhys's tranquil routine, but her life in the country was less lonely than her letters implied. Oliver Stonor and his plump, sweet-natured wife Mollie, were the hospitable owners of a picturesque stone cottage at Morebath, close to Exmoor, where Rhys often went to lunch to meet a few of the couple's restfully undemanding friends. One guest, an older woman, won Rhys's approval simply by dressing with exceptional elegance; another was just forgiven for declaring that she lacked only the time to become a novelist herself. Preferring more youthful company, Rhys was delighted when the Stonors' friend Christopher Cox, a young Devon book-dealer, offered to help her to recreate an approximation of her lost library of novels and poetry. Alexis Lykiard, a poet and translator who lived close to Cheriton with his model girlfriend, Diane Leigh, was a well-read young Francophile who introduced Rhys to the self-styled "Comte de Lautréamont's" influential prose poem on the nature of evil,

*Les Chants de Maldorer** and some of the more ghostly tales of Sheridan
Le Fanu. Apparently, she loved *Carmilla*, the Irish writer's sumptuously
creepy novel about a female vampire, pre-dating Bram Stoker's *Dracula*
by almost thirty years. Lykiard, noting the way Rhys sometimes rolled
her now slightly watery blue eyes towards heaven, and knowing a little
about her Caribbean background, wondered if the writer he so admired
was of "mixed race."

An unexpected hit at one of the Stonors' lunches for Rhys was Herbert Ronson, a chivalrous travel journalist from Cheshire. Calling at
Rhys's bungalow in the summer of 1969, Ronson found his hostess
clinging to the side of her open front door with the wistful grace—in
his own words—of a tiny deposed queen. Was it by chance that Rhys
allowed the belt of her dress to slip to the ground as—while showing the
visitor around her garden—she softly wondered whether Herbert might
like to arrange a joint trip to Portugal? (This project replaced Rhys's
recent plan to visit a new literary admirer, Gerald Brenan, at his home
in Andalucía, cancelled in 1968 after Brenan's wife, Gamel, became
terminally ill.†) Relating his story twenty years later in the pages of
the *London Magazine*, Ronson recalled himself as having behaved like a
man under a spell; he had been "entirely captivated . . . robbed of volition." There had been many such travel requests; at the last minute,
Rhys always changed her mind, but Ronson never lost his desire to
grant pleasure to a charming and capricious old lady.[5]

At Cheriton, despite the watchful kindness of neighbours like the
Greenslades and friends like the Stonors, Rhys had to look after herself for most of the time. Visiting London each winter, she relied upon

---

* Isidore Lucien Ducasse's celebrated phrase in *Maldorer* about the improbable con-
junction of a sewing machine and an umbrella on an operating table was later seized
upon by André Breton and the surrealists during the 1920s, when Rhys lived in Paris
and took an interest in their writings.

† Generously quoted in Jonathan Gathorne Hardy's biography, *The Interior Castle* (Sinclair-Stevenson, 1992), Gerald Brenan's correspondence with and about Rhys
included an especially shrewd observation (to David Garnett) that her writing "keeps
one all the time at the central point of feeling."

Sonia Orwell to organise every aspect of her life and to ensure that it was filled with treats. Sonia did not disappoint. Visits to beauty salons and excitingly modern shops like Biba and Miss Selfridge vied with afternoons at the ballet, where Rhys preferred *Swan Lake* and *Giselle* to more challenging fare. ("I know it's escapist," she wrote to a new young novelist friend, Rachel Ingalls, "but why not? There's such a lot to escape from.")[6]

Less enjoyable, always, were the carefully prepared parties which played a key part in Sonia Orwell's life. Not even the hair-styling and beautiful clothes provided by her thoughtful hostess succeeded in banishing Rhys's nervousness of the strangers who crowded around her and asked clever questions about her work. "It's really a great effort to chat," as she sadly confessed to Oliver Stonor, "& I don't do it well. Never mind. I think a lot."[7]

SONIA'S UNSTINTING GENEROSITY to Rhys's close family helped compensate for her friend's own conscious—and considerable—failings as a parent. A major reason for Rhys's growing unhappiness about the continued division of her income with Selma Vaz Dias was the knowledge that she had deprived her good-humoured, middle-aged daughter of a precious potential source of financial security.

Much of the trouble with the arrangement Rhys had originally made with Selma stemmed from Rhys's complete unworldliness about money. In 1963, she had signed her name to Selma's proposed financial division without a thought; in 1967, following a delightful lunch at the Savoy Grill with a well-spoken American academic, she promised to send Howard Gotlieb the only draft pages that survived of her work on *Wide Sargasso Sea*. On this occasion, Oliver Stonor came to her rescue by instructing Gotlieb either to send back Miss Rhys's chapter or pay £300 (£5,250) for it; the manuscript was swiftly returned. From this point on, Rhys's awareness of the error she had made in signing Selma's document was heightened by the evidence of growing interest in the staging and filming of her work. In 1968, Patrick Garland began planning to stage *Quartet* (Garland was about to make his name directing Alan Bennett's *Forty Years On*); in 1969, Peggy Ramsay was approached for a film option on *Wide Sargasso Sea*. Negotiating with the producer, Ramsay began to have second thoughts about the fact that Selma Vaz Dias, who remained on Peggy's client list, was still legally entitled to receive 50 per cent of everything—stage, film, radio, translations—relating to the work of Jean Rhys.

Normally, Ramsay might have contacted Diana Athill about rene-gotiating Selma's portion. Since Athill was grieving over the suicide in her north London flat of her young Egyptian lover, Peggy decided to deal with the matter herself. On 10 June 1969, Selma was insis-tent about receiving her legal half share; three days later, she agreed to a compromise.[8] By 1 August, the new agreement had been finalised. While far from ideal, Ramsay's renegotiation reduced Selma's share to one third.* Writing to thank Peggy on 18 August, Rhys claimed that the good news had released her from a long period of creative sterility.[9]

The behaviour of Rhys was startlingly similar to that of her old friend in regard to their disputed agreement. Like Selma, Rhys both denied the past and rewrote it, insisting that she had never intended her signature to be binding, while angrily underlining sections of old letters in which Selma had expressed gratitude. A month after thank-ing Peggy for her intervention, she almost lost a powerful supporter by instructing a Devon solicitor to inform Mrs. Ramsay that he could obtain a far better deal from Selma: "We will of course bow out," a livid Peggy informed Rhys, who hastily backed down.

The friendship between Selma and Rhys did not survive Ramsay's efficient negotiations. Rhys grumbled to Francis Wyndham in October 1969 that Selma's deception had been worse than a burglary. Until her own death in 1977, Selma believed that Wyndham and Diana Athill

---

* Selma's husband, Hans Egli, continued to receive her renegotiated third share until 1985, when the Rhys estate unilaterally withdrew from the arrangement. Three of Selma's five grandchildren received a single payment of £100 (£270) apiece in 1988 through a trust created by Selma. No further payments were made to Selma's family, either from the Rhys estate or a Rhys-related trust (Tara Fraser to author, July 2020).

had conspired to efface her role in Rhys's rediscovery—and that an insufficiently grateful Rhys had betrayed her trust.[10]

RHYS DID NOT miss Selma much at a time when she was surrounded by admiring and far less challenging young women. Among these was Marcelle Bernstein, a staff writer whose lengthy article on Rhys for the *Observer Magazine* was published on 1 June 1969.

Opening up during her interview with Bernstein, a perceptive journalist in whom she had already placed her trust, Rhys used a question about early love affairs to distance herself from the women about whom she wrote in her novels. While agreeing that they often underwent similar experiences to their author, and bore an acknowledged resemblance to aspects of her personality, Rhys pointed to a crucial difference. They were victims. She herself was not. "I wasn't always the abandoned one, you know," Rhys told Bernstein, somehow forgetting her unhappy romance with Lancey or all the times in Beckenham that she lay alone at night. And why, if she was the quitter, did she end relationships so impulsively? A shrug. She grew tired of the person, or the place; the spell broke: who could say? Pressed by her sympathetic interviewer for more detail—lovers in Paris? boyfriends during her dancing days?—Rhys retreated behind an inscrutable wall of reserve.[11]

Rhys's correspondence with Bernstein dated back to October 1968, eight months before this major interview was published. Unusually, Rhys liked what Bernstein wrote about her; she also liked Marcelle herself. A perceptive reader of the novels, Bernstein still has fond memories of their long and congenial lunches out (always at Marcelle's expense), and the teas for which the abstemious Bernstein soon learned to bring along a bottle of whisky. In 1973, Rhys suddenly ended the relationship. Letters went unanswered; no explanation was ever provided. Today, recalling what Rhys had said in the interview about her role as the leaver, never the abandoned one, Bernstein still sounds wistful and uncomprehending.[12]

Bernstein was not alone. The photographer Barbara Ker-Seymer earned her spurs as a new friend in 1969 by making a habit of despatching well-reviewed new novels from London to Cheriton Fitzpaine. Rhys seemed delighted. Two years later, Ker-Seymer was ghosted, and again, no explanation was given. Once Rhys had cut the lines of communication, there was no going back.[13]

Barbara Ker-Seymer had first made contact with Rhys through an introduction by Francis Wyndham. It was the well-connected Francis who also introduced Rhys to Antonia Fraser, after much gentle beseeching on Lady Antonia's part. A grand title appealed less to Rhys than the unexpected gaiety of Antonia's spirit; it was hard to resist a beautifully buxom young woman who made jokes about her attempts to slim with "Miss Trim"—plastic leggings that inflated the sweating wearer into an approximation of a poolside lilo.[14] In London, Antonia good-naturedly indulged her heroine's taste for undemanding entertainment. If the future wife of Harold Pinter was disappointed by Rhys's request for a matinee visit to *The Mousetrap*, compensation was on hand. Unusually, while visiting London, Rhys consented to join the younger woman and her family for regular Sunday lunches at their home in Campden Hill Square. Unaware of Rhys's scorn for the concept of reincarnation (Rhys once mischievously remarked that she'd only care to return as a mouse or a crocodile), the Fraser family still remembers the alacrity with which, asked by one of Antonia's daughters whom she might previously have been, their usually reticent guest opted for a doomed princess from the court of Marie Antoinette. ("No hesitation at all," Lady Antonia recalls. "She was absolutely clear."[15])

Is there a connection here to André Breton's *Nadja* (always a firm favourite with Rhys), in which the novel's tragic heroine also dreams of having been a princess at Marie Antoinette's court? Perhaps. Less open to conjecture is the evidence that a part of Rhys's mind still inhabited the Paris through which Nadja—like Rhys herself—had wandered in the blue twilight of the Twenties.

Rhys's novels and short stories entered the French consciousness in 1969. Sympathetically translated by some of the finest practitioners of their craft, Rhys's fictions read almost as if they had emerged from their own language. So, in a significant sense, they had. Chatting with a French interviewer at the beginning of 1970, Rhys explained her mental trick of translating a difficult passage into French before attempting to rewrite her English version. Learned from Ford, along with an enduring respect for the technical skills of Flaubert and Maupassant, the exercise had served Rhys well. Her habit of thinking in French was never entirely dropped. Maryvonne, visiting her eighty-year-old mother in 1970, was an astonished witness to the ease and fluency with which Rhys participated in an interview for a French culture programme.

Among the respectful and admiring letters which reached Devon via Rhys's French publishers, Denoël, the most unexpected came in April 1970 from a prison in Lyon. Having admired Jacqueline Bernard's fine translation of *Good Morning, Midnight*, Rhys's correspondent hoped that the writer who had created such an empathetic victim as Sasha Jansen might sympathise with the situation of a jailed businessman who had been falsely accused of murder. Perhaps Marc Verney's eloquent appeal reminded Rhys of the sentences served by two of her husbands; she wrote at once to her favourite and greatly respected French translator, Pierre Leyris, asking him to find a lawyer willing to look into the case. Verney's eventual fate remains unknown, but in July 1971, he despatched to Devon a tiny pair of sabots that he had carved from wood during his imprisonment. Given Rhys's love of such trinkets, they probably joined the "awfully corny" china cherub candlesticks which held an honoured place on a Landboat mantelpiece.[16]

On 21 May 1970, Sonia Orwell, en route to France to nurse the novelist Marguerite Duras, received an equally startling letter.[17] Here, and in an equally ebullient missive to Maryvonne, Rhys gleefully described how Jan van Houts, a middle-aged Dutch poet and teacher, had tempted her out of the village for a five-day vagabond tour around Devon. Eleven years later, publishing his recollection of their joint escapade, Houts would stress that no romance took place between himself and the elderly writer he admired. He did, nevertheless, emphasise the delightful transformation that he had witnessed during their jaunt, as a quiet, reserved old woman disclosed the skittishly vain and happy siren who had at times in the past—very rarely—revealed herself to Francis Wyndham. Houts made a point in his memoir of describing the Parisian poster of a skilfully twirling girl-skater that he had noticed hanging in Rhys's tiny entrance hall. For him, the image evoked Rhys's own combination of a rigorous discipline with flirtatious charm.[18]

Rhys's fantasy of pursuing a new love affair was abruptly terminated by the death that autumn of her beloved elder brother, Edward. Knottsfield, the house at Budleigh Salterton, had already been sold after the death of Edward's wife, and the ageing widower had moved into a couple of rented rooms, where he was visited at least twice by his favourite sister. On one of these occasions, or during his own last visit to Cheriton at the end of 1969, the childless Edward disclosed his intention of making Maryvonne the principal beneficiary of his modest estate. To Rhys herself, her brother left both the income from a third of his investments and lifetime ownership of the bungalow that he had leased her at a peppercorn rent for the past decade. Chauffeured to Edward's funeral in the faithful Alan Greenslade's new Vauxhall, an inconsolable Rhys dissolved into predictable tears. According to Owen Rees Williams' perennially unsympathetic widow, Rhys's howls drowned out the vicar's words of divine consolation.

Writing to Maryvonne, Rhys admitted that, knowing nobody and overwhelmed by grief, she had asked Mr Greenslade to take her home early, "& he did."[19] Rhys's discomfort, perceived by Owen's hard-up and hostile relict as the typically bad behaviour of overdressed, hysterical "Gwennie" (showing up in a posh chauffeur-driven car), is not hard to understand.[20] Brenda Powell, whose mind was moving slowly towards dementia, could not safely be left alone by her long-suffering husband; the couple's sole representative at the funeral was an adopted son, a nephew whom Rhys had never met. She had encountered Owen's widow just once; she had not seen Owen's English son, John, now forty years old, since his childhood. If Rhys dressed smartly for the funeral, she did so not to outshine unrecognised relations, but to honour a brother who had always been kind.

UNRECORDED IN EARLIER biographies of Rhys is her late and significant friendship with the novelist Rachel Ingalls. Fifty years younger
than Rhys, Ingalls was the formidably bright daughter of a Harvard
professor of Sanskrit. She was just twenty-five when she arrived in
London from New England in 1965. A writer whose stories combine
bizarre situations (an unhappy wife is seduced by a towering and sexually insatiable sea creature in "Mrs Caliban") with adversarial dialogue
and a ruthlessly economic style, Ingalls was praised by Charles Monte-
ith, her editor at Faber, as "a genius, not a word I use lightly."[21]

Rhys first met Ingalls in the spring of 1970. A self-sufficient young
woman, Rachel avoided literary society as zealously as her compatriot
and good friend David Plante sought it out. Plante remembers arranging the introduction because he knew how much Ingalls admired
Rhys's work; what he did not anticipate was that an immediate bond
of recognition would develop into a warm correspondence which was
maintained until 1973, when osteoporosis would make writing by hand
too difficult a challenge for Rhys to maintain. This problem may also
have played a part in a proud woman's abrupt severance of her relationships with Ker-Seymer and Bernstein: we can't be sure.

While the physical process of writing became increasingly arduous
as Rhys aged, her imagination remained unrelenting. "I've been having
such strong dreams that I must really be feeling guilty," Rhys confided
to Ingalls in July 1970 when she was working on one of the two late
and disturbing stories to which she gave a Devon setting, "Sleep It Off
Lady" and "Who Knows What's Up in the Attic?" A month later, Rhys
admitted to her new friend that she was finding it hard to settle down:
"as for working, it's grinding out line after line or else lying awake with
words rushing through one's head too quickly to catch."[22] Writing the
chilling fate of Miss Verney in "Sleep It Off Lady" had, as she admitted to Ingalls, frightened her so much that she had to take a short spell
away from her desk.

Holding this unexpected collection of letters in my hands has brought me a little closer to Jean Rhys. As always, she can be relentless, pressing Ingalls to get David Plante to plead with his Rome-based friend Jerry Bauer for a set of author photographs that Rhys is desperate to obtain. (Deutsch—somewhat unusually for a publisher—did nothing to help their authors in this respect.[23]) For the most part, however, the letters are almost maternal, begging Ingalls not to cut her luxuriant, shoulder-length hair ("Dear Rachel your hair is so pretty as it is . . . I've spoilt mine") and saying fondly that Ingalls's cosy gift of a large red shawl is worn in part because it always keeps the "dear" giver in her thoughts. While Rhys took a close and persistent interest in Ingalls's work, she was especially struck by *Theft*, an early novella set in a Southern jail during a riot. Did Rhys look upon Ingalls as her literary heir? The possibility is strengthened by the evidence of her steady reassurances, her regularly expressed hopes for the younger woman of "a prize or two, and all the luck there is," and the tender prediction: "Surely all sorts of nice things—all sorts—are waiting for you."[24])

Unusually in Rhys's long life, she seems to have found in Ingalls— hailed in a recent appraisal for her "hallucinatory realism"—a woman writer whose own disciplined habits she was willing to respect.[25] David Plante—as he himself readily admits—never minded running errands for Rhys (mainly as a service to Sonia Orwell, at whose house he was rewarded by meeting the cream of London's intelligentsia); Ingalls was at nobody's command. She would send Rhys thoughtful gifts (her present of a catalogue from the great Tutankhamun exhibition was better received than Diana Athill's offer to push the supremely self-conscious Rhys round the crowded show in a wheelchair). She would take her elderly friend off to the cinema (a Chaplin film proved more successful than *The French Connection*). Like Rhys herself, she refused to be bullied.

Rhys would have agreed with the tributes that were to be paid, decades later, to an exceptional writer, at the very end of Rachel's life (Ingalls died in 2019). Today, David Plante concedes the justice of Ingalls's anger when she read the portrait of Rhys with which he opened *Difficult Women*, a brilliant but treacherous work published in 1983. From that day on, Ingalls never spoke to him again.[26]

———————

THE YEAR 1971, another unproductive one for Rhys's writing, ended with an unexpected and delightful tribute to the power of her imagination: *Memories of Morning: Night*, a hauntingly evocative monodrama which the widely admired young composer Gordon Crosse based upon *Wide Sargasso Sea*, was given a warm welcome at its premiere at the Royal Festival Hall, with the mezzo-soprano Meriel Dickinson singing the role of Antoinette. Regarded today as one of this sensitive musician's finest works, Crosse's tribute may have seemed to Rhys to be an augury. While 1972 would be darkened by the deaths of her valiantly independent young cousin, Lily Lockhart, and of Max Hamer's brother, Alec (well described by himself, so a grieving Rhys felt, as "a simple soldier"), the year also ushered in a new phase in Rhys's growing fame.

Rhys herself entered 1972 in valedictory mode, paying Sonia Orwell to host what she wistfully described to Rachel Ingalls as her "farewell party" at Gloucester Road. Adieux seemed in order; Patrick Garland had abandoned his attempt to stage *Quartet*, while Rhys's final collection of stories for Deutsch was refusing to come together. A fall, resulting in a cracked rib, was an unkind reminder to Rhys that she was about to turn eighty-two.

Change was in the air. A warm appreciation of *After Leaving Mr Mackenzie* in the *New York Times* was pleasing; the news from Peggy Ramsay that Susan Sontag was chasing an option to film *Good Morning, Midnight* and *Wide Sargasso Sea* sounded intriguing. Neither event prepared Rhys for the glowingly intelligent and sensitive appreciation of her novels which appeared on 18 May 1972 in the *New York Review of Books*.

V. S. Naipaul was a prolific contributor of substantial essays to the *NYRB* in the early Seventies: another from 1972 was an evaluation of the work of Borges. His tribute to Rhys showed the Trinidad-born British novelist at his generous best. "What a stoic thing she makes the act of writing appear," he exclaimed in an appreciation which moved Rhys to tears by what she described to Francis Wyndham as its "marvellous, and a nearly complete understanding of my life." Naipaul also performed the valuable service of distinguishing the writer from her subjects. For the first time, an eminent critic was prepared to consider the women about whom Rhys wrote, not as self-portraits or alter egos, but as independent creations whom Naipaul intuited to be far "cruder, and less gifted than herself." Naipaul identified Rhys's vagabond women as "bohemian, in the toughest sense"; he saw their self-elected rootlessness as part of the author's prescribed journey for her protagonists as they travelled "from one void to another." He understood how important it was to Rhys that they should remain watchful outsiders, "schooled by their society in the arts of survival."[27] The influence of Francis Wyndham, who had stayed close to Naipaul since first persuading André Deutsch to publish the young novelist's work, hovered behind a number of the essay's penetrating observations about Rhys herself.

The effect was immediate, and not entirely welcome. While visits that summer from both Francis and Sonia to Cheriton were rapturously received, Rhys resisted a growing interest in her personal life. A disappointed Peggy Ramsay learned from Diana Athill in August that Michael Lindsay Hogg's proposal for a television documentary interweaving Rhys's life with her novels must be turned down; Rhys would not permit such an invasion.

Rhys completed her two new stories with a Devon setting by the end of the summer of 1972, before she allowed herself the challenge of reading Arthur Mizener's year-old biography of Ford Madox Ford. Her claim to have come across a new and expensive literary biography by accident while visiting Cheriton's poorly stocked mobile library van is unconvincing; more likely, she ordered or asked for it. The book infuriated her. Mizener had not only broadcast the knowledge that Rhys had received an allowance from Ford and Stella for several months, but had included a footnote which suggested that Rhys had given birth to a "love child."

An extant document titled *"L'affaire Ford"* presents Rhys's rambling rebuttal of Mizener's claims.[28] Publicly, Rhys had always praised Ford as a mentor while denying—to all but a chosen few—the existence of their love affair. Now, too upset to continue working on the story collection she had promised to Deutsch, Rhys ranted to close friends about Mizener's allegation with a passion that gave it credence. An intrigued David Plante was not alone in wondering whether Mizener's claim might be true, and why it was that Ford and Stella had been so anxious to pay Rhys off at the end of the affair.[29]

British interest in the reclusive novelist and her sharply contemporary novels was growing almost by the month. Peggy Ramsay's announcement that John Mortimer was to adapt *Voyage in the Dark* for the stage was followed by news that a television version, starring Jacqueline Tong as Anna Morgan and George Baker as Walter Jeffries, was in production. (Watching it on her new television set, Rhys was disappointed; Tong seemed too hard and knowing for her own vulnerable Anna.) Meanwhile, in June 1972, Rhys learned that Glenda Jackson was keen to acquire *Good Morning, Midnight.*[30] No evidence survives of which role was being considered for the twenty-year-old actress who had most recently partnered forty-eight-year-old Marlon Brando in *Last Tango in Paris*, but Francis Wyndham heard in October from a dazzled Rhys that Maria Schneider had proved to be so ravishingly lovely in person—we don't know where they met—that she herself lost her wits and could only mutter "banal things in French."[31] More thrilling still for a recent convert to television, and described by Rhys to Francis as almost the nicest surprise of an astonishing year, was the gift from a friend of the autograph of her favourite television performer, Ronnie Corbett.

For Francis, as for an anxious Diana Athill, the best news from Rhys in the late autumn of 1972 was that she had resumed work on her stories. Encouragement was always required, however, and Francis demonstrated once again that his patience and perseverance were unending when it came to Jean Rhys. It was Wyndham who arranged for "The Insect World" and "Pioneers, Oh, Pioneers," stories which had been obsessively revised and rewritten over decades, to be published in, respectively, the *Sunday Times* and *The Times* as tasters of what was to come. Meanwhile, Francis persuaded Rhys to return to "Night Out," one of her best early tales about Paris, by offering to work over it with her himself. When Francis advised, Rhys listened: she obeyed when he insisted that Rhys's meticulous reworking of an old Lenglet story, "The Chevalier of the Place Blanche," must carry an acknowledgement to its first author.

Other, more recent stories guided Rhys gently forward towards the memoir of her early life that she had been wistfully contemplating for forty years. All she had lacked until now was the voice in which to tell it. And now—miraculously—that voice came into her mind.

"I can still shut my eyes and see Victoria grinding coffee on the pantry steps." These are the simple, declarative words that Jean Rhys used to open an artfully structured reminiscence of her childhood in Dominica that she named: "On Not Shooting Sitting Birds." The slow evolution of "Overture and Beginners Please" from a *London Magazine* request for a short piece on her experiences at school had first focused Rhys's thoughts on a memoir. But it was the little group of Dominica-based stories that found their final shape in the early 1970s which gave Rhys the voice in which to tell it. The voice was clear, strong and strikingly youthful. Her memory and her imaginative power remained intact. The question was whether an octogenarian whose gnarled hands now struggled to clasp a pen retained the physical energy required for such a daunting task.

21

"Mrs Methuselah" (1973−76)

"I rode a swing—swing high, swing low. That's been my life."

—Jean Rhys to Mary Cantwell, *Mademoiselle*, October 1974

THE PERSONAL HIGHLIGHT of Rhys's eighty-third year was the transformation of a barely habitable bungalow in Devon into a cosy cottage. The miracle was worked by freckled, red-haired, outspoken Jo
Batterham—a favourite niece of Francis Wyndham's friend, the landscape and portrait painter Derek Hill—with the help of an attractive
and well-read young woman called Virginia Stevens.

During the colder months of each year, from 1972 onwards, Rhys's
regular perch in London, chosen and paid for by Sonia, became the Portobello Hotel in Stanley Gardens, Notting Hill. First taken there by
Francis to meet a writer whom she and "Gini" Stevens revered (the couple had already—unsuccessfully—attempted to doorstep Rhys during
a visit to Devon), Jo was thrilled to see the painting of a rose hanging
above the writer's bed. The artist, as Batterham explained to her hostess,
was Jo's own father, a notable interior decorator; Rhys had purchased
the picture on impulse a week earlier while visiting John Hill's recently
acquired showroom with the ballet critic, Richard Buckle.* Jo Batterham

---

* John Hill had taken over Abbott & Green, a Wigmore Street shop famous for its
William Morris–style wallpapers.

had inherited her father's talent; before leaving the Portobello that evening, she volunteered her services as an unpaid advisor on the transformation of Rhys's Devon home.

Rhys's initial aspirations were touchingly modest. She wanted bright
colours on the walls, to remind her of the Caribbean; she needed a
comfortable spare bed for the use of her visiting daughter. Above all,
she wanted to see an end put to the gaunt, ramshackle shed which had
once served as an occasional garage for Edward's car. Rhys's wish was
granted; by the summer of 1974, the hated shed had been demolished
and replaced by a sweet-smelling cedarwood sleeping annex that could
double as a writing room. A creature of habit, Rhys always preferred to
use her kitchen table as a desk.

Rhys could joke about herself to close friends as "Mrs Methuse-
lah," but age was taking its toll. Towards the end of 1973, the year in
which she brusquely terminated several handwritten correspondences,
rheumatism defeated her ability to operate a pen for longer than a few
minutes at a time. This, for a woman who had always written her work
by hand, presented a serious problem; Jo's partner Gini Stevens volunteered to do what she could to help solve it. While Jo Batterham,
caring for a young son at her Putney home, directed the bungalow's
improvements from afar (the village builder, Mr. Martin, carried out
her instructions), Gini began driving down to Devon for ten days of
each month to work as Rhys's unpaid amanuensis. The task wasn't easy;
recalling her role for a magazine article in 1974, Stevens conjured up
the relentless commitment of Rhys at work, "dictating version after
version to me, sometimes continuing for a five or six hour stretch, ruthlessly paring everything that is not essential."[1] A grant was eventually
obtained by Diana Athill to cover Gini's time and travel costs, but it
wasn't surprising that the young woman sometimes skipped a visit.

Rhys became extremely fond of Gini. By the summer of 1974, she
had found a way to keep Stevens close to her by appointing an enthusiastic amateur to replace the experienced Olwyn Hughes as the agent
for her early works and short stories. (John Smith of Christy & Moore
continued to represent the later books.) Gini took her new role seri-

ously; within weeks, she had proudly reported to Diana Athill her successful advance sale of the world rights to Rhys's still uncompleted final stories. Untutored in the ways that publishers operate, Gini had no idea that Deutsch themselves expected to sell the tales abroad and take a commission. Scolded by Diana, Gini found an unexpected supporter in Francis. Mistrustful of "stingy publishers," Francis told an apprehensive Rhys that Gini and she should stick to their guns.[2]

Clear evidence of the warmth of Rhys's feelings for her two new friends emerges from the fact that—anxious to escape from chilly Devon in the bitter autumn of 1973, when a rash of strikes and a steep rise in oil prices led to national restrictions on energy use—Rhys invited herself to spend a month at Jo Batterham's spacious home in Putney.[3] Much admired (and still fondly remembered) by Jo's small son, Luke, for her purple hat, her pinkly powdered cheeks and her handsome gift of a £1 note for every drawing that an artistic little boy became unsurprisingly eager to present, Rhys made a charming guest. Away from the usual London pressure to put on a performance, she relaxed. According to Jo Batterham, she drank with enjoyment, but never to excess. Back at the Portobello Hotel for a more challenging post-Christmas sojourn in the city, Rhys relied on alcohol to help her face the ordeal of interviews, photoshoots and—least appealing of all—the literary gatherings her publishers required her to attend. It was—as she well understood—the price to be paid for Sonia's generosity in paying her bills.

Listening to people who remember Rhys's mid-winter residences at the Portobello Hotel during the early 1970s, it's clear that, in England at least, Rhys was becoming a literary cult. Expected to amuse in return for being feted by social networkers, authors and grandees, she often drank too much. Quieter events were always preferable. Rhys loved to dress up for an early-evening hotel visit from Francis or Sonia. She enjoyed going out to a cheerful bistro lunch in Chelsea with David Plante and Rachel Ingalls. She never rejected a chance to be swept around the West End shops and salons by a new young friend, Diana

Melly, owner of a vividly hippified camper van often driven by Diana's boyfriend, Jeremy d'Agapayef.

In a small group, Rhys could always hold her own. Introduced to an admiring Glenda Jackson at an Italian restaurant lunch that was hosted by the actor Peter Eyre, she delighted the actress by unexpectedly praising her consummate comic timing, having become a keen follower of Jackson's appearances on the *Morecambe & Wise Show*. It's likely that Rhys relished a threesome lunch with Edna O'Brien, for which Mrs. Melly's handsome young lover was bidden to stay, while Diana—Rhys's kind chauffeur that day—was blithely dismissed.

Rhys's bookshelves, sharply observed by Alexis Lykiard on his visits to Cheriton Fitzpaine, now included copies of several novels by O'Brien, standing alongside the Liverpool Poets. Did she even notice the absence of poor Diana from the lunch table of O'Brien, a writer who was then being considered as an adapter of one of Rhys's novels for the screen? Self-absorption remained one of Rhys's most striking characteristics. Peter Eyre, the mellifluous-voiced young actor who had arranged the lunch with Glenda Jackson, never forgot the strangeness of carefully painting Rhys's ageing face with theatrical make-up in order that—or so Eyre assumed from her serene farewell when his nerve-racking task was completed—Rhys, seated at her hotel dressing table, drink in hand, might commune alone with the ghostly reflection of a younger stage self. On more sociable occasions, Eyre was permitted to escort Rhys to a ballet matinee or to squire her to Don Luigi, her favourite Chelsea restaurant. The rules for these intimate suppers never changed: Eyre must arrange a corner table, dimly lit, from which an unapologetically inattentive Rhys could weave a romance about herself and one of the other restaurant guests, preferably a distinguished older man, dining alone. She ate, Eyre recalls, with the gusto of a woman of half her age.[4]

One of the most disappointing experiences of Rhys's two visits to London during that chilly winter of fuel rationing in 1973/74 was to be told—after the prolonged but exquisite pleasure of being robed in

couture for a *Vogue* profile—that the silk dresses and jackets were mere
borrowed plumage, not gifts. Back in Devon at the end of February
and grumpily perusing the words for "My Day" that she had written to
accompany the profile, Rhys's spirits were lifted by news from Francis
Wyndham. A major appreciation of her work was about to be published
in the *New York Times Book Review*; an elated Francis was ready to predict the result: "One of those fantastic American successes which mean
lots and lots of money."[5]

Al Alvarez was an influential and regular writer for the American
literary pages. Published as the *Book Review*'s lead piece on 17 March
1974, his critical assessment of Rhys's work described both *Good Morning, Midnight* and *Wide Sargasso Sea* as masterpieces, before declaring
their author to be, quite simply, "the best living English novelist."
Wyndham was right; Alvarez's impressive tribute changed his old
friend's fortunes in America almost overnight. A fresh flurry of film
and interview interest gratified Rhys less than the news of immediate
bulk reprints of *Good Morning, Midnight*, *After Leaving Mr Mackenzie*
and *Wide Sargasso Sea*. *Quartet*, out of print in the US since 1957, was
snapped up and reissued; 100,000 copies were hastily printed of *Voyage
in the Dark*.

One of my own favourite pictures among the many taken of Rhys in her
later years, this accompanied Julie Kavanagh's interview. *(Willie Christie)*

Alvarez had beaten Wyndham to it. Having cannily despatched
an advance proof of his appraisal to Rhys in early February, he had
received her pleased response four days later. Eager to interview her
for Ian Hamilton's magazine *The New Review* (in which "Sleep It Off
Lady" was due to make its debut that October), Alvarez paid his first
visit to Cheriton Fitzpaine at the end of March. Stockily handsome,
with a razor-thin strip of moustache, Alvarez was a man whom Rhys
found both empathetic and physically attractive. Rhys had read the
poetry of her equally reclusive neighbour, Ted Hughes. She was a
greater admirer of the self-laceratingly honest work of his first wife,
Sylvia Plath. It's possible that Alvarez and she discussed *The Savage
God*, Alvarez's recent book about suicide—notably that of Sylvia Plath;
it's more certain that they discovered a shared love of poetry. (Alvarez
was one of the few people to whom, during five years of confiding and
affectionate friendship, Rhys would regularly send copies of her own
poems.) A more personal interest—as Alvarez loved to tell the story—
was apparent in the way that Rhys had gazed into his eyes during their
first meeting, while insouciantly caressing a slender stockinged calf.
His description of glimpsed layers of frothy white petticoats (as Rhys
saucily crossed her still elegant legs) was more imaginative. Frilly petticoats were never Rhys's style, but Alvarez's own embroidery nicely
captures the hint of flirtation in the air.

––––––––––

THE YEAR 1974 marked the climax of Rhys's success, bringing with it a
rush of new requests for interviews. A handful of the supplicants made
it through; few of them managed to pierce the armour of their subject's
reserve. "I was having rather a troublesome time," was all Rhys would
admit to Julie Kavanagh, a bright young journalist interviewing her for
the influential US paper, *Women's Wear Daily*, when Kavanagh asked
about the years in postwar England during which Rhys had vanished
from public view.[6]

Rhys's reticence with Kavanagh may have been due in part to a
serious bout of summer flu. Just a month earlier, Mary Cantwell was

granted one of the most revealing interviews Rhys ever gave, for *Mademoiselle*, an American magazine that was aimed at a target audience of educated young women who read as avidly as they pursued the latest fashions. (Joan Didion guest-edited one issue; Sylvia Plath drew on her time working as a *Mademoiselle* intern for her boldly autobiographical novel, *The Bell Jar*.)

Cantwell's interview with Rhys in the summer of 1974 coincided with one of Maryvonne's visits to the Devon cottage; Rhys was communicating, however indirectly, with her daughter when she told Mary Cantwell about the "awful misery" she had felt over the loss of her first-born child; her baby son. Cantwell herself was more struck by Rhys's image of herself as a woman who dreaded social gatherings: "I'm a person at a masked ball without a mask" was how she described it. Sipping sweet vermouth and soda while her fingers restlessly flicked the on–off switch of a tiny electric heater, Rhys struggled to explain to an attentive Cantwell how the troubled leading characters in her novels always evaded the net of any conscious plans that she herself had made for them, seeming to act and speak of their own volition. How, then, could Julia Martin, Sasha Jansen or Anna Morgan be seen by readers as mere versions of herself? Perhaps Maryvonne scolded her mother for drinking alcohol outside mealtimes; unexpectedly, Rhys suddenly confessed to her visitor that—having once had what she considered "a good head"—she could no longer drink without consequences.[7]

If none of Rhys's friends picked up on that hint in Cantwell's illuminating interview—it's hard to imagine either Francis Wyndham or Diana Athill as readers of *Mademoiselle*—it may simply have been that they knew better. Rhys had spoken of her characters as moving beyond her control; she herself could not bear to be placed under restraint. Covertly watching the octogenarian writer methodically swilling down a lethal two-handed combination of whisky and champagne, glass after glass, as she sat on a sofa alone, apart from a cluster of chattering party guests, the young writer James Fox (he was one of Wyndham's literary protégés) once caught Rhys's eye. What he saw there disturbed him; it was a "hell-bent, give me more pain and just watch me" stare of black defiance. And up to her lips went yet another glass.[8]

Since 1967, Rhys had resisted all pleas for television interviews; in the early autumn of 1974, she relented. Setting the crown on a remarkable year was Tristram Powell's documentary tribute for *Omnibus*. Shown in late November, with a pensive, slender Eileen Atkins playing an amalgam of the women of the novels, the programme concluded with an interview granted by a visibly nervous Rhys. Powell, who places Rhys alongside Lucian Freud and Beryl Bainbridge as a genuinely reluctant performer, regards that reticence as evidence of a rare artistic integrity.[9]

Rhys's nervousness with such a practised interviewer as Tristram Powell may once again, in an autumn when she was struggling with the aftermath of her summer flu, have owed something to ill health. Shortly after thanking Sonia Orwell, on 15 November 1974, for all her help over the past years ("you are the most generous woman in the world," Rhys would exclaim as Sonia offered to finance the purchase of a west London flat for her young granddaughter), she was rushed into St. Vincent's, a London nursing home where she would spend the next two months. Rhys was still at St. Vincent's when Selma Vaz Dias started threatening a lawsuit over the absence of any reference to herself in Tristram Powell's documentary. Had Francis Wyndham objected to being left out of the programme, an impatient Peggy Ramsay demanded? Wasn't there enough reward for Selma in knowing that she, too, had contributed to the revival of her old friend's career? Perceptively, but with an excess of candour, Peggy commented: "It's as if you want to become Jean Rhys."[10]

Nineteen seventy-four had been a glorious year in terms of recognition, but the occupational hazards of success took Rhys away from her writing. Diana Athill remained anxious about the slow progress of the story collection that her pet author had contracted to supply to Deutsch by the following spring—and to which Gini Stevens had already sold the world rights from under Diana's affronted nose. Athill caused a lengthy delay of her own when she decided at the last moment, in the spring of 1975, that one of Rhys's personal favourites must be excluded. The tale in question was "Imperial Road," Rhys's barely fictionalised account of her quixotic endeavour, back in 1936, to demonstrate the completion of a road that had, in truth, foundered after seventeen treacherous miles.

Rhys had been labouring over various versions of "Imperial Road" for thirty years, but times had changed dramatically in the Caribbean during the 1970s. A house boldly rebuilt upon the scorched foundations of the Lockharts' home at Geneva had recently been burned down; "Black man time is come! White man had his fun!" ran the opening line of a calypso song for Roseau's carnival in 1974.[11] Fired up by the accounts from Dominica that arrived in news clippings sent by Phyllis Shand Allfrey, living out on the island, Rhys nobly urged Francis Wyndham to publicise the environmental threat posed by unscrupulous British timber firms to Dominica's magnificent rainforest;[*] it was not, however, the time to start celebrating Britain's past presence on the island. To Diana, Rhys's clearly autobiographical story read like an endorsement of colonialism. She ruled it out. Rhys, outraged and miserable, ceased to work.

As so often in Rhys's later years, a tricky moment was quietly resolved by Francis Wyndham. While reluctant to get involved in Rhys's championing of her beloved island's rainforest, he promised to get "The Imperial Road" published as an independent story in the *Sunday Times*, for which he worked.[†] Wyndham then offered the services of Sonia and himself as first readers of the stories that Rhys had been

---

[*] Phyllis Shand Allfrey had resumed contact with Rhys in 1973, when a film crew arrived in Dominica to scout locations for *Wide Sargasso Sea*. It would be another twenty years before a film was made, using Jamaican locations. A BBC version followed in 2006.

[†] Although "The Imperial Road" was never published in the *Sunday Times*, it survives in multiple drafts. Rhys intended it to form part of her memoir. Diana Athill, who finished editing *Smile Please* shortly before Rhys's death, decided, once again, to exclude an unfinished work for which her enthusiasm had always been scant.

intermittently dictating over the past two years to Gini Stevens. He chose shrewdly: Sonia Orwell had earned her editorial spurs on Cyril Connolly's *Horizon*—and Jean trusted her.[12]

Soothed by Wyndham's assurance that all would be well, Rhys returned to work on one of her finest late stories in the summer of 1975. Writing to Phyllis Shand Allfrey back on 16 May 1973 about her longing to "lay my bones" in Dominica, Rhys had told her Caribbean-born friend of a poem called "Return," written and then lost during her first lonely months of living at Maidstone. Rhys described "Return" to Phyllis as a poem about going back to Dominica and only realising that she was already dead "when no one recognises or sees me." As always with Rhys, no sign of the long gestation ("I've tried over and over again to rewrite it," she told Shand Allfrey) was visible in "I Used to Live Here Once," the exquisitely simple ghost story of just such a return that she finally dictated to Gini Stevens in the summer of 1975.[13]

The stories for *Sleep It Off Lady* (Rhys's first collection since *Tigers are Better-Looking*, back in 1968) were delivered to an anxious Athill in the autumn of 1975. Alone in Devon, and increasingly prone to anxiety, Rhys started to worry about the large sums of money that her new—and her first—financial advisor, Michael Henshaw, was now handling on her behalf. Henshaw was a charming man who represented a dazzling list of writers and actors, but his methods were often highly unorthodox. Weaving dreadful scenarios in which the cottage was to be confiscated and she herself sent to prison (shades of Jean Lenglet and Max Hamer), Rhys blamed the shock of a dawn raid on the cottage by a sinister—evidently imaginary—official for a fall which cracked one of her ribs. "I was NOT drunk!" she joked to Francis in October, while gallantly declining to add that she was in considerable pain.[14]

Reading on through this same surprisingly cheerful letter, Francis discovered the source of Rhys's good humour. An unnamed literary admirer from New York was courting her. Should she boldly cross the Atlantic? Visiting her with champagne and flowers at the grim West Kensington care home where Sonia had lodged her temporarily incapacitated old friend, a frisky Al Alvarez encouraged Rhys to dream.

Why should a still beautiful woman not set herself up in a comfortable apartment in Manhattan for a while and allow herself to be adored? Alvarez himself would take charge of her social life; her unnamed beau would see to all of the glorious rest. But who *was* he? Rhys wouldn't say.

The identity of Rhys's American suitor remained unrevealed. Conceivably, she misread the courtly manner of Frank Hallman, an American Southerner who was in the process of publishing her *Vogue* piece ("My Day"), together with two autobiographical fragments, in a special edition of 750 copies. To Rhys, Frank's generous flood of gifts (stockings, French scent, silk scarves) may have looked like courtship; it's entirely possible that a grateful Hallman—Rhys had personally managed to sign most of the insert sheets during his brief visit to Devon earlier that year—did encourage the idea of a trip to New York. What Rhys failed to grasp—she perhaps was never told—was that her swain was happily partnered by Richard Schaubeck, his devoted companion until Hallman's tragically premature death in the spring of 1976.

Rhys's plans for New York were pure fantasy; an eighty-five-year-old with a cracked rib was not fit to go travelling anywhere, except in her dreams. In dreary times, however, confined to a hotel for ailing senior citizens, the thought of a solicitous admirer offered consolation. Tongue-in-cheek, Rhys often referred to the unnamed East Coast "suitor" as her last lover.

———————

ONE OF THE oddest items tucked away in the stiff rows of boxes of Rhys-related papers and manuscripts held in the McFarlin Library at Tulsa dates from Rhys's autumn at the Kensington care home. Written in scrawled red biro on lined foolscap paper, it is defiantly titled "Shades of Pink." Closer inspection reveals an unexpected first collaboration between Jean Rhys and David Plante.

Rhys had first encountered Plante's name when they both contributed stories to a Penguin anthology published in 1969. In 1970, when they were introduced to each other by Sonia Orwell, the personable young writer from Provincetown quickly became a friend. *Diffi-*

cult Women, Plante's controversial 1983 character study of himself in his relationship with three extraordinary and forceful women (Sonia Orwell, Germaine Greer and Jean Rhys), opened with the startling episode which took place five years after that first meeting, in December 1975, when he paid his first visit to the dreary west London hotel at which Rhys remained confined. Oddly, Plante had received no warning that Rhys, well prepared for the occasion by Sonia, was expecting a professional meeting at which she would dictate material for her memoir to an obliging friend.

Plante's far-from-artless memoir presented Rhys at the hotel as a recent acquaintance, an ancient mariner who was drinking hard while relating interminable tales of her childhood in the Caribbean. Rhys rambled on; Plante, matching her drink for drink, listened. Eventually, the physically diminished and still disabled Rhys hobbled into the bathroom. The next thing Plante heard was a pitiful wail; Rhys's skinny posterior had been trapped in the well of her own bathroom lavatory. The fault lay with Plante, as he realised too late: having previously made use of the old lady's loo, he had neglected to re-lower the seat.

Eight years later, working up that disastrously mismanaged encounter for public consumption, Plante omitted to mention that his hostess was expecting him to take dictation for her memoir. Instead, he offered a brutally candid portrait of a snorting, spitting, dishevelled Rhys in decline. "Shades of Pink," the unpublished and never completed work on which Rhys invited Plante to collaborate, was her own more generous attempt to wrest a comic story from a mortifying incident, one which had been replete with misunderstandings. Plante himself was transformed into urbane "Maurice Denis," visiting a youthful "Lucy Nicholson" at the recognisably odious hotel. Plante's version dwelt on a puddle of piss on the bathroom floor; the knickers hanging around Rhys's ankles; the "battered" hat perched askew on her lolling head. Rhys's version presents a moment of sheer comic delight as Lucy rises up into her saviour's arms from her porcelain well with buoyant exhilaration: "like a cork out of a bottle."[15] The surviving fragment of "Shades of Pink" offers a late example of Rhys's unique capacity in her fiction both to mock and to transcend herself in portraits that are only ever partially autobiographical. Plante was charmed and a little shamed by Rhys's generous interpretation;[16] Diana Athill was not amused. The project was dropped.

Early in 1976, when Rhys was happily restored to her beloved suite at the Portobello, Plante paid his forgiving old friend a further visit. It was on this occasion that a chastened David (Sonia Orwell had given him a stern dressing-down for his inept handling of Jean at the West London hotel) first volunteered to transcribe Rhys's memoir. Some progress was made until—anxious to establish a logical sequence for the random episodes which Rhys provided—Plante requested an oral chronology. To a sensitive author, it seemed as if a pushy young man was attempting to take control of her most personal project. Rhys lost her temper. All talk of a collaboration was dropped.

Rhys's black mood had lifted when she wrote on 15 February to tell Francis Wyndham that she had been enjoying Antonia Fraser's adaptation of *Rebecca* for radio. Antonia's version of elegant, suave Max de Winter was declared to be Rhys's ideal: "a dream of a man."[17] Romance was on Rhys's mind once more; just as she began researching the possibility of a jaunt to New York and her mystery lover, a second and far more serious fall landed her, first, in hospital and then—to her dismay—back in a London nursing home. The medical report was grave: in addition to four cracked ribs, two dating back to the previous autumn, the X-rays revealed an enlarged heart. Rhys's days of independence were over. From 1976 on, age-friendly accommodation would be required whenever she visited London; down in Devon, discreet feelers were put out for a suitable nurse-companion.

Joan Butler, Jean's country neighbour, produced a solution that would not impinge too much on Rhys's enduring desire for privacy. Janet Bridger was a forthright young Canadian district nurse who, after five years of working for an Inuit community, had settled in Devon. Janet was willing to spend four hours a day at the cottage doing whatever was required, including discreet supervision of Rhys's intake of alcohol. Several visitors to the cottage were startled by Bridger's gauchely truculent manner (Jo Batterham detested her), but there was no doubting Janet's commitment. Her first year with Rhys went quite well.

The problem of where to find West Country help with transcribing the dictated memoir was solved by the discovery in a nearby village of Michael Schwab. Helpful, efficient and handsome to boot, Michael was willing to double as Rhys's driver—Mr. Greenslade had decided to retire after his wife's death—and typist. By July 1976, Rhys was feeling strong enough to dictate the entire section of the memoir that deals with "Meta"—the violent nurse who had so terrified little Gwen Rees Williams—in a single, exhausting session. Like Gini Stevens, Michael Schwab was astonished by the contrast between Rhys's fragile appearance and her capacity to dictate and revise aloud for hours on end.

Every ounce of Rhys's waning creative energy was now devoted to completing the memoir. Diana Athill, having efficiently secured grants to cover Michael Schwab's driving expenses and time, advised the *New Yorker* that the four stories they were planning to publish ahead of *Sleep It Off Lady* would be the very last that they would receive from the weakened author. For Deutsch, to whom Jean Rhys had become a lucrative investment, it was crucial that she should stay alive long enough to finish the memoir; for Sonia, expressing her thoughts discreetly to Diana Athill in March, the time had come to hope for a merciful ending. Aged almost eighty-six, Rhys surely deserved a peaceful death?[18]

A little wishful thinking was involved on Sonia Orwell's part. While Francis Wyndham was increasingly preoccupied by the need to care for his ageing mother, Sonia herself had fallen victim to an unscrupulous accountant. The hospitable house on Gloucester Road was put up for sale; the days of bankrolling Rhys's holidays in London were over. Vaguely conscious that something was amiss, Rhys took good care—as indeed she always had, year after year—to thank her "darling Sonia" for "ALL you've done for me."[19]

Happily, Jean Rhys's own improved financial position meant that she no longer depended on the generosity of friends like Sonia Orwell.

Everything she produced now carried a perceived value and was received accordingly. *Sleep It Off Lady*, published in October 1976 by Deutsch, and in November by Harper & Row in the US, was the first work she had produced since the outstanding collection titled *Tigers are Better-Looking* in 1968. Francis and Sonia had both gone over it, as had Diana Athill; none of them had been able to get around the fact that a collection which included several stories on which Rhys had been working, on and off, for three decades, together with a handful which had been written on various topics over the past five years, did not make for a well-integrated whole. The title story was widely praised, while both William Trevor and the *New York Times Book Review*'s Robie Macauley thought "I Used to Live Here Once" was among the finest, and certainly the most concise, ghost stories they had ever read. (It's a little over 400 words.) *Kirkus Reviews* described the collection as "sketches" and, rather crushingly, a "*force mineure*," while praising the "desolate allure" which their reviewer identified as Rhys's trademark.[20]

Rhys's plans for a memoir had been at the forefront of her mind when she wrote "Overture and Beginners Please" and "Before the Deluge"; these highly personal stories were the only two to describe her first years in England at school and then on tour. Writing, dictating and revising a group of stories that drew upon her Dominica childhood, while feeling her way towards the best voice in which to narrate her memoir, Rhys seems also to have worried about which remembered episodes were suited to which genre. The best answer, as with the almost purely autobiographical "On Not Shooting Sitting Birds"— clearly more appropriate to a memoir than a story collection—was not always found.

Rhys's discretion meant that little was yet known about her early life. Nobody reading the new collection could have been expected to guess that "Good-bye Marcus, Good-bye Rose," Rhys's troubling story of a little girl being molested by a distinguished older gentleman, was based upon fact. Neither were her readers to know how much personal detail had been worked into "Pioneers, Oh, Pioneers," the story of Mr. Ramage on which Rhys had been working on and off ever since her return to Dominica in 1936, when she first heard about the English settler's mysterious death at his isolated home.

A fierce perfectionist, Rhys herself was dissatisfied by the collection. Her comment to an admiring Oliver Stonor about one widely praised late story, "Rapunzel, Rapunzel," was that "I missed it somehow." It reflected her feeling about them all. Writing to Francis (Wyndham shared Stonor's liking for Rhys's odd little tale about the shearing of a plain woman's proudly displayed golden locks) she disparaged the collection as "the 'So-So Stories'" (for which Wyndham scolded her).

Rhys's growing readership disagreed. In America, especially, sales of her novels continued to soar. While Peggy Ramsay's telephone clamoured with requests from Hollywood, American universities had also begun to show a keen interest in Rhys's manuscripts.

Oliver Stonor had been acting on Rhys's behalf for some time as the middleman in sales of her hotchpotch of literary papers to Bertram Rota, the London antiquarian bookseller and dealer. Rota's own book expert, John Byrne, now stepped in to facilitate a more substantial purchase for the McFarlin Library in Tulsa, where an ambitious young academic named Thomas Staley was in the process of creating a centre for women's studies. In the autumn of 1976, while Diana Athill replaced Rhys's trio of agents with one of her own choosing (the erudite and raffishly charming Anthony Shiel), Tom Staley visited London and offered a thousand guineas to acquire the bulk of Rhys's work. Staley was an attractive man. Rhys's granddaughter, who was shooed away from paying a visit of her own when Staley arrived to discuss the details of the deal, suspects that her still flirtatious grandmother feared competition for the attention of a new admirer. Rhys may also have wished to conceal from her hard-up family just how much money was passing into her hands.

Rhys had spent most of her summer in Devon dictating episodes from her memoir to Michael Schwab. Back in London at the end of 1976, and staying in a service flat near Sloane Square, she summoned David Plante back for a second attempt at collaboration. Some progress was made; it seems to have been during this brief interlude that Rhys humbly described herself to Plante (when compared to her beloved Russian authors) as a mere trickle feeding into the great lake of fiction. Once, apparently, she broke into a perfectly conceived evocation of the lost *mornes* (mountains) of her beloved Dominica. To an enthralled Plante, her description sounded improvised; Rhys's habit of careful mental preparation suggests that she already knew every word that she narrated by heart.

The problem for Rhys of working with David Plante was that he, too, was a writer. His first attempt to extract a chronology had appalled her; now, seeking to impose a structure on the flood of episodes with which Rhys inundated him, Plante asked permission to reshape them. Having painstakingly snipped Rhys's sentences apart and reconnected them into a more logical narrative, Plante read her the result aloud. Hearing what he took for a whisper of approval, he carried his revised manuscript home to type it up.

Both Diana Athill and David Plante were good storytellers. Both of them dined out on the drama of their friend's response. Diana, arriving at Rhys's flat later that same evening to see Jean safely into her bed, encountered a wild creature, untameable in her fury, swearing, drunk and sobbing that her book had been stolen from out of her hands. Never again would she work with David Plante![21]

Rhys's attitude to her work was protective; her anguish at the sense that the memoir had been tampered with is not in doubt. No longer impoverished, she was even willing to fork out £500 to pay David off for his forfeited effort. But she did not want to lose Plante's friendship; Diana was specifically instructed to make the payment through Deutsch, as if the decision had been all their own.

Rhys had always been volatile. It was only a matter of weeks before a nervous David was recalled and forgiven. Work resumed; for the time being, there were no more outbursts. Towards the end of February 1977, the partly completed memoir was sealed by Plante within two sturdy envelopes on the outside of which he wrote, under Rhys's directions, that the contents were to be destroyed if anything should happen to their owner. Authorising the statement, Rhys carefully inscribed her name twice over, once as Jean Rhys and then as "E[lla] G[wendoline] Hamer."

Why such an anxious precaution? In 1977, after over thirty years of living entirely in England, Rhys was making preparations to leave the country. Her health was poor; her bones were increasingly brittle; she was in her eighty-seventh year: anything might happen. If disaster struck, an unfinished, orphaned memoir that presented her younger self to the world without the mask of fiction was in need of the best protection that a mother could provide for a work to which Rhys by now felt as tenderly close as a pregnant mother to her unborn child.

VIII

AND YET I FEAR[*]

* Written when Rhys was in her mid-eighties, "And Yet I Fear" is her finest unpublished poem. Clearly influenced by one of her favourite poets, Emily Dickinson, Rhys salutes death as a massive hidden power; a welcome force that will sweep her up into the universe, to become one with the wind and the stars and "sweet" eternity. Closing on a Shakespearean image of death at sea, this remarkable fifteen-line poem (it would be interesting to know who typed it out for her) suggests that incapacitating old age, rather than death, was what Rhys feared.

22

"The Old Punk Upstairs"*
(1977–79)

"The more I realise the precariousness of Jean's hold on calm, the more valiant she seems to me."

—Diana Athill to Francis Wyndham, 1 January 1980[1]

JEAN RHYS WAS a woman who compartmentalised her friends. So did Sonia Orwell. This helps to explain why Jo Batterham and Diana Melly only met each other late in 1976, a year during which Sonia, working out a plan with Melly for Rhys's future, organised a rota of volunteers to ensure that Rhys, however physically incapacitated, could continue to enjoy her annual visits to London. Several illustrious artists, poets and writers joined the list, although few of them offered more than lip service.

What Batterham and Melly importantly shared was an understanding of the crucial importance to their old friend of details that less sensitive acquaintances might have overlooked. Jo took endless trouble to see that the latest cottage furnishings were in just the right colour to satisfy the changeable wishes of a peculiarly demanding client; inter-

---

* Borrowed from the title of a 1990 newspaper tribute by jazz musician and memoirist George Melly to his friend Jean Rhys ("The Old Punk Upstairs," *Independent on Sunday*, 28 October 1990).

minable discussions took place over the precise shade of yellow velvet for a chaise longue on which a lame octogenarian author might regally recline (Rhys was a great admirer of Sarah Bernhardt's receiving mode) when being viewed by inquisitive journalists. Diana Melly, whose major test of her friendship with Rhys was yet to come, was already putting herself out to hunt down the perfect dress, the exact shade of pink lipstick and even the facial masseur whose calming hands could best restore an illusion of youth to match Rhys's indomitable spirit. More than any other of Rhys's friends, Melly understood how anxiously an outwardly successful old woman continued to fret about her appearance.

Work on Rhys's memoir had progressed well enough in the early part of 1977 for David Plante to tell Sonia that Rhys was worrying about having mislaid an incomplete account of her early years in Paris ("*L'affaire Ford*") which she was evidently planning to revise for inclusion in *Smile Please*. The published memoir ends just before Rhys's first encounter with Ford; the absent section would have let us know—as perceptive readers might already have guessed from the early novels, in which Ford's identity was apparent—that there had been a love affair.

The reward that Rhys had chosen for her own hard work was to be a winter fortnight in Venice, with Diana Melly and Jo Batterham as her appointed chaperones. Rhys's only prior knowledge of Italy derived from a few blissful days spent in Florence with Jean Lenglet, when the couple had visited the Uffizi and gazed at *The Birth of Venus*, the painting that became Rhys's favourite work of art, along with the *Winged Victory* in the Louvre. Had Lenglet pointed out the younger Rhys's resemblance to Botticelli's young goddess, skimming the rippling waves aboard her scallop-shell as detachedly as the pale palaces of Venice's Grand Canal float above their supportive reflections? Maryvonne, who had visited Italy with her husband, Job, described Venice as the most enchanting of European cities. Venice, then, it must be.

Shepherded on board for her first—and first-class—aeroplane flight, a terrified but excited Rhys sipped courage from a mini-bottle of complimentary champagne. Landing, she was conducted to a hotel which had been specially chosen for its romantic associations. Confirmation of Rhys's unquenchably romantic taste comes from Peter Eyre's recollection of being asked, when he visited Cheriton Fitzpaine in 1974, to bring with him recordings of Wagner's *Liebestod* and highlights from *Der Rosenkavalier*. Where, then, in Venice should Jean Rhys stay but at the hotel that had been home to Alfred de Musset, to Marcel Proust and even to Wagner himself?

Passers-by can still glimpse the ornate corner bedroom on the first floor of the old Danieli (not the modern extension) which Rhys occupied during the last week of February and first ten days of March 1977, while Jo and Diana made do with a humbler room next door. Diana's faded travel snaps confirm the state of general enjoyment that glows out of the long, chatty letters despatched by Jo to Sonia in Paris. Here, we see slender, dark-haired Diana and stockier, beaming Jo pushing a crumpled Rhys along in a wheelchair (she was too lame to cross the stepped bridges on foot). There, a careful Diana arranges Rhys's battalions of pills (a task which Diana enjoyed as much as lovingly tidying the five little purses of cosmetics without which the elderly Rhys still never left home). In one image, Rhys waves from the balcony of her high chamber to a throng of tourists, obliviously passing by; in another, a cushioned bolster enables a smiling Jean to gaze at the ravishing city from the back of a gondola.

Life followed an orderly pattern. Rhys's mornings (a leisurely breakfast in bed followed by a lengthy tryst with the hotel's hairdresser) released Diana and Jo from their duties until the stately lunch in the hotel dining room which was Jean's favourite treat of the day. Back at the Danieli after a brisk post-prandial hour of being pushed around the city's chilly *calle* and *campi*, Rhys drowsily read Hemingway's novel of Venice, *Across the River and into the Trees* (renamed "Across the Street and into the Grill" by a mischievous E. B. White). Next door, Jo tapped away, clattering out a daily journal of events for Sonia while Diana, when not busy knitting as she enjoyed a tranquillising joint, studied the

(*Above*) Diana Melly arranges Jean's battalion of medications, a task that pleased her orderly mind. (*Below*) Jo Batterham, pushing a rather depleted Rhys across San Marco in her wheelchair. (*Used with permission of Diana Melly*)

hefty hotel bills. A substantial reduction in their meal and bar charges followed her divulgence to the Danieli's impressed manager that their elderly guest was a writer of international renown.

Evenings began with Negroni cocktails in the hotel bar, where the handsome pianist was always ready to serenade Rhys with one of her favourite old French songs by Piaf or Charles Trenet. Later, after the light snack, glass of cold milk and early bedtime on which Rhys always insisted, Jo and Diana sauntered companionably out, in search of a more vibrant Venice.

Bad moments were rare. "We seem to laugh the whole time, it's in the air," Jo wrote to Sonia—and Jean agreed.[2] Back in Devon and writing to congratulate Melly on the good reviews for her own first novel, *The Girl in the Picture*, a grateful Rhys—she had spent a cheerful week with the Mellys after her return to London—thanked her and Jo again for contributing to her happiness: "You were both so good to me."[3]

Venice gave Rhys a sustained feeling of joy that she had rarely found before, except in an enchanted moment of epiphany. Asked by Tristram Powell, at the end of his television interview with her, whether—had she her life to live over again—she would choose to write, or to be happy, there's no forgetting the pathos with which a yearning Rhys cries out: "Oh, *happiness!*"

FOUR MONTHS AFTER the trip to Venice, Diana Melly received a summons to Devon. The University of Kent, a leader in the rapidly expanding field of Commonwealth literature since 1964, ran a course on African and Caribbean-related studies. Rhys's own recent contribution to Caribbean literature was to be acknowledged by the university with an honorary doctorate.[*] The invitation had come from Professor Louis James, who had been visiting Jean since 1975. Since Rhys

---

[*] The influence on Rhys's postwar writing of the distinguished Caribbean authors living in London during the 1950s remains underexplored. It wasn't by chance that Rhys chose to recast her own experiences as those of Selina Davis ("Let Them Call It Jazz"), a light-skinned newcomer to London from the Caribbean.

Rhys returns to her room at the Danieli after waving to the crowds. *(Used with permission of Diana Melly)*

was understandably reluctant to attend the long, formal ceremony at Canterbury, three representatives of the university, including Professor James and Mark Kinkead-Weekes, had decided to visit Cheriton, bringing with them a black gown, a diploma—and a tape recorder.

Rhys's first official sign of academic recognition, while eased by the arrival on the previous night of a tanned Diana Melly (with a sulky-faced boyfriend in tow), proved a less happy experience than her visitors had anticipated. A glass of champagne failed to calm Rhys's nerves, while the discovery that the imposing gown—as with *Vogue*'s dresses—was simply offered on loan lowered her spirits considerably. The real ordeal was yet to come, when Rhys listened to the oration that had been pre-recorded for her imagined pleasure.

On the following morning, 21 July 1977, Rhys wrote to Louis James, author of the recorded oration, to berate him for having dared to suggest that, while her father had always been considerate towards his black patients, he had been any less attentive than to his patients who were white. All were equal in his eyes: this was the point which Rhys wished to stress. She was mollified by the news, resulting from James's own researches, that "all of Roseau" had followed Dr. Rees Williams's coffin through the town.[4]

Diana Melly spent a peaceful night in Rhys's new cedarwood annex before her return to London; Jo Batterham, visiting Rhys a few weeks later to discuss some further improvements to the cottage's decoration, alarmed both Sonia Orwell and Diana Athill by reporting that Janet Bridger was neglecting her duties and showed no concern for poor Jean's appearance. Janet's cooking was denounced as atrocious; worse, Bridger ordered Rhys about. How lucky for their old friend it was (Jo remarked) that she still possessed kind neighbours like the Stettifords and Mrs. Raymond—the Greenslades had both died—to bring in meals and to lock the door each night (a precaution taken after Athill's frightening experience when a boy burglar stole her purse from a bedside table in the new annex).

Jo's mention of the reported death of Brenda Powell, the last survivor of Rhys's immediate family, was added almost as an afterthought to her long letter. Brenda had suffered nearly a decade of slow mental decline and the siblings had not spoken for many years; nevertheless, according to Janet, Rhys had burst into tears when she heard the news. Brenda had belonged to the old Caribbean world in which, endlessly rehearsing the scenes and sentences of her memoir, Rhys now—and perhaps, always—dwelled more intensely than in the present. ("*Swing swing,*" Rhys wrote over and again in her notes, seeming to remind herself of the perpetual shift between past and present experience that had formed a key element in the time-shifting structure of *Voyage in the Dark*: "*Swing swing.*")

Dictating her episode-driven recollections to Michael Schwab in the summer of 1977 (David Plante had decamped for a long holiday in Italy), Rhys slipped effortlessly back into the mind of a little girl, the doctor's favourite daughter, growing up in Roseau at the end of the nineteenth century. Titled "The Yellow Flag," and eventually placed in

the opening section of *Smile Please*, a fragment of an early draft which
survives in the British Library's Rhys Papers describes the abandoned
Victorian quarantine station around which Rhys had once played with
her friends. The published version quotes a few lines from an old military ditty which the children sang as they rocked to and fro on the
"broad and comfortable" seats of their chosen playground's swings.

Rhys's original draft of the song had included the response given
to a young maid's naive plea for a husband. "How can I marry such a
pretty little girl, / When I haven't got a shirt to put on," the married
soldier teases the girl, as she innocently hastens to provide the elegant
clothes her dashing suitor claims to lack. "Swing swing," Rhys added
at the end (as well as the start) of her draft—and she marked out that
second "Swing" with a long, low and suppliant "S," one that looks as if
she intended it to represent a small, submissive body. The station was "a
safe, bland, self-satisfied place," Rhys wrote in her final version, before
adding: "and yet something lurked in the sunlight." As with the childhood memory related in *After Leaving Mr Mackenzie* of a frightened
little girl running home from a silent, sunlit place, and never revealing
what has scared her, it feels as if Rhys has deliberately placed on view
a sinister recollection from the past, as sharply evoked as the unspoken scent of terror that haunts some of Henry James's most troubling
works. The connection is not irrelevant; Rhys's letters show that she
had read *The Turn of the Screw* at least six times.

Dark thoughts ran deep within Rhys, and never more so than when
she was alone in Devon. The Canadian-born Janet Bridger took it
calmly when a stone was flung at her one day in Cheriton, a village
where outsiders were often viewed with suspicion. Bridger was a good
deal more frightened when, following an altercation with Rhys, she
found herself locked inside the cottage with its owner, who, elfishly
taunting and triumphant, flourished aloft what Rhys imagined to be
the only key to the door. Janet's thankful recollection of a spare key,
kept in a dresser drawer, flattens the climax of her dramatic tale with
her escape into the Devon night, but it also adds plausibility to a disturbing episode.

BY THE LATE summer of 1977, it was becoming apparent to Rhys that she could no longer rely upon friends to take care of her whenever she left Devon. Francis's spare time was occupied by the needs of his dying mother, while Sonia Orwell was frequently absent in Paris. In August, Rhys looked into the possibility of spending time at a Catholic retreat in London, vaguely referred to as "The Blue Nuns." Informing Sonia of the failure of another tentative plan, Rhys confessed a modest dread of imposing her weakened body and its daily needs on the kindness of well-meaning acquaintances. "Between you and Di [Melly] you are really Jean's only hope," Sonia wrote a little desperately from Paris to Jo Batter-ham on 16 August; three weeks later, Rhys herself echoed that sentiment. "I haven't got many friends in London now," Jean told Jo, "in fact, Diana Melly and yourself are the only ones I'm sure of."[5]

Sonia was acting with the best of intentions when she arranged for Rhys and Janet Bridger to spend the autumn of 1977 together at Oatlands Hotel, an expensive nursing home in Surrey. Grand surroundings—the hotel stood proudly on the site of a royal Tudor palace—failed to disguise the ubiquity of wheelchairs and medical trol-leys. Janet fled back to Devon after three dispiriting days; visited by a sympathetic Athill, Rhys glumly joked that one ancient resident's enthusiasm for killing off new germs must be directed at herself, the unwelcome new pest. Of course (as Rhys acknowledged with a giggle), she was being paranoid, but please, couldn't Athill find her a way to escape? Diana did her best, placing a carefully worded advertisement for rooms in a private London home that might suit a "distinguished elderly woman" with independent means and "outside sources of care." An unknown Mrs. Hatch offered an upstairs bedroom with narrow stairs up which her daughters could carry an elderly tenant, when required. If they were around. If they chose: it's hardly surprising that Rhys turned the offer down.[6]

The obvious solution was for Rhys to be taken in either by Jo Bat-terham or by the Mellys. But taking Jean in also meant gratifying her expectations, which were often unreasonably high. "I know [clothes] shopping is tiring," the eighty-seven-year old Rhys hopefully advised Jo on 27 October, "but I find it so exciting and it would please me so much." The fact that a distraught Jo felt unable to face the ordeal of conducting a frail old woman around London's finest dress shops had much to do with the fact that her beloved Gini Stevens had just left her to marry an American.[7]

Rhys was unaware that the kind-hearted Mellys were already on her case. George was sympathetic to needy women, especially when they were as interesting as Jean Rhys; Diana relished the idea of rearranging their family home in Gospel Oak—only the first-floor rooms housing George's magnificent collection of surrealist paintings were ruled out of bounds—in order to ensure the happiness of a cherished guest.

The preparations, outlined in an entertaining and moving article which George Melly would publish some thirteen years later, were tremendous. George relinquished his beloved box mattress, the lowest and least dangerous form of bed the Mellys could produce for an unsteady old lady with brittle bones; Diana, moving out of her own airy bedroom on the second storey of a three-floor maisonette at 102 Savernake Road with views of Hampstead Heath, redecorated the entire ensuite in what she knew were Rhys's favourite shades of pink: rosy pink lampshades; sunrise pink curtains; marshmallow pink for the freshly painted wooden floors. The result, so an admiring George recalled with the sad hindsight of 1990, was "incredibly pretty . . . as warm, cosy and mildly exotic as a gypsy caravan." Here, surely, even such a perennially wistful writer as Jean Rhys might allow herself to feel happy? "She would have no practical worries, proper meals, lots of treats and outings, friends when she wanted company, help with her make-up, an important chore . . ." (George had already persuaded the Mellys' friend Mary Quant to send Rhys a bag of her daisy-themed cosmetics during the summer) " . . . and any amount of love and goodwill. We were longing for her arrival."[8]

Of the three months that the octogenarian Rhys would spend under George and Diana's roof, the first two were an almost unqualified success. A document of proof survives in the form of a daily journal kept by the Mellys' lodger. Fresh from reading Oriental Studies at Cambridge, young Sarah Papineau found their guest captivating, demanding, and capricious.[9]

It took a week, so an intrigued Papineau recorded in her diary, for a haphazardly coiffured Miss Rhys (increasingly blind and averse to wearing glasses, Jean often put her pink or white wigs on back to front) to venture down the stairs. A few days later, Sarah attended a kitchen lunch at which a radiant Rhys—Diana had spent the morning shopping on her behalf at *Chic*, an expensive Hampstead boutique—regaled the two of them with memories of her early years in Paris. Publicly, Rhys had always been resolutely discreet; feeling herself to be among friends on this occasion, she opened up. It seemed that she hadn't warmed to the Fitzgeralds, but the dashingly handsome Hemingway, praised for

At home with the Mellys at Savernake Road. *(Used with permission of Diana Melly)*

his matchless skill with dialogue in fiction, was approvingly described as having been "shy and unassuming" in person.[*] She mentioned an early experiment with opium as a disappointment (it had produced no effect at all), before expressing a shy curiosity about the musky joints that Diana Melly was pleasurably inhaling with her coffee. (A shared spliff would often prove useful when Rhys became emotional.) Still tucking into her toffee pudding, Rhys begged for her appointment with an unknown new doctor to be deferred; she didn't want to be seen looking "awful" by a stranger. "She looked beautiful!" an admiring Sarah added to her journal of a memorable day.[10]

Sarah Papineau swiftly became Diana Melly's dependable supporter in the house, taking Rhys breakfast in bed, helping her to clamber into the bath and sometimes rushing back early from her evening waitressing duties at Ronnie Scott's, just to make sure that their celebrated visitor was safe and snug in her room. On 27 November, in a typical diary entry, Sarah noted that she had carried up the stairs a three-course lunch prepared by herself for their guest. A happy afternoon chatting to Rhys about punk rock had prefaced a warm invitation to Devon. Later that day, after the novelist Bernice Rubens had popped in for a quick visit (Rubens had her own house key to the Mellys' easy-going home), Sarah took Jean's glass of milk upstairs and settled the honoured guest safely into her bed.

The combination of circumstances was extraordinary. Here was a reclusive and frail old lady residing as the acknowledged queen of a household where jazz music, modern art, recreational drug-taking, theatre chat and the Mellys' own complicated love life, created a heady brew. Athill, after dropping in from her nearby home in Primrose Hill, reported to an anxious Sonia that, while "pink and lame," Rhys looked "ravishing" and "happy as a bee."[11]

Events that had been painstakingly arranged for Rhys's enjoyment

---

[*] Rhys's account adds a little credence to Jean Lenglet's claim in a Dutch publication that she had introduced him to Hemingway, whom he allegedly interviewed for his former employer, the *New York Herald Tribune*.

didn't always go well. George recalled the uncomfortable lunchtime occasion when Jean mischievously informed a disconsolate Penelope Mortimer, the respected author of *The Pumpkin Eater*, that Caroline Blackwood was the only woman writer in England who wasn't actually murdering the language. (Rhys had been devouring *Great Granny Webster*, Blackwood's disturbing and award-winning story of a loveless old grandmother, obtained by Sarah Papineau at Jean's urgent request.) The actor Peter Eyre, arriving for lunch at Savernake Road on a chilly day wrapped in a long, high-collared coat, had to be asked to leave because his appearance reminded a weeping Jean of the doomed aristocrats in the Russian Revolution. Contretemps often proved entertaining: George Melly's mother visibly sulked when Rhys hogged the limelight at a Christmas family lunch, while Al Alvarez was told off after giving a giggling Jean so much champagne that she fell on the floor: "all her recent accidents have been due to that," Sonia Orwell reproachfully reminded Diana Melly from Paris.[12]

Some of the disasters had comic overtones: Rhys once pulled so hard on the lavatory chain that the whole cistern crashed down; on another occasion, Diana Melly crossly compared herself, the forceful Athill and Jo Batterham to limp tea towels as they debated whether to answer angry thumps on the floor above, reminding them that a trapped Rhys wanted a top-up to her drink. Requests were not always so graceful. A polite manner had long concealed the formidable power of Rhys's will. As age stripped away the niceties of courtesy, she grew ever more ruthless about exerting that remarkable faculty to get her way.

By and large, Rhys threw tantrums only in the company of those she knew could be subdued. George, who allowed nobody to subdue him, could spend a tranquil evening watching an old Hitchcock film with their guest, or chatting about books. (A well-read Francophile, George shared Jean's affection for Breton's *Nadja*.) His wife, meanwhile, resigned herself to a volley of screams and curses whenever—which was increasingly often—she failed to please. "The thing is that you never know whether to talk to an old woman or to Jean," Diana Melly sighed to a distant Sonia, while wishing she could do more to make their guest happy. Sometimes, caressingly patted and told that she possessed the Caribbean islanders' gift for creating "magics" (a form of bewitchment) as she perched on the edge of Jean's bed to share a puff of her own late-evening joint, Diana believed for a fleeting moment that she had succeeded.[13]

There were many good times. Rhys loved being taken to Ronnie Scott's to hear George singing with John Chilton's band, the Feet-warmers, for whom she wrote the ruefully ironic lyrics to "Life Without You." But her patient hostess was not alone in feeling the strain. *Take a Girl Like Me*, the admirably candid memoir which Diana Melly published in 2005, recalls the occasions on which a grey-faced David Plante crept down their stairs from a tough two hours of labouring over the smallest details of Rhys's memoir. "I had now heard Jean's stories many times," he would write in *Difficult Women*. Rhys's title—*Smile Please*—was a given; the content now consisted of endless tiny refinements, the same ones being made over and again to the text that he was perpetually being instructed to read aloud. "Shit!" Rhys would shout if David spoke too quickly, or if some unbidden memory caused her pain. And then, out of the blue, just as when she assured Diana Melly that she possessed the power of "magics," there would come a murmured observation that caused all the humiliation and despair to slide away. Today, Plante still remembers how much it meant whenever Jean Rhys spoke to him as a valued colleague, explaining, on one fondly recalled occasion, the difficulty she always had with creating a sense of space around each word. "Yes," he remembers her saying in her soft little voice. "I tried to get that. I thought very hard of each word in itself."[14]

On 7 February 1978, Rhys was chauffeured to Buckingham Palace to receive a CBE from the queen. Diana Athill had persuaded one of the academic world's most adept fixers, Noel Annan, to arrange the honour; it was an award which appeared a perfect way to crown Rhys's achievements. A small celebration lunch was held afterwards in the Mellys' home at which Jean presided, smiling, sober and impeccably dressed. Her conversation with the queen was reported to have been pleasant but brief; it seems unlikely that Her Majesty was one of Rhys's keenest readers.

By February 1978, the dark side of Rhys's volatile personality had begun to emerge once more. Al Alvarez arrived at Savernake Road just in time to dissuade a distraught Jean from tearing up a latest—and last—short story: thanks to Alvarez's intervention, a delicate homage to Dominica and to Rhys's best-liked cousin, Lily Lockhart, "The Whistling Bird," would be published in the *New Yorker* in September that year. Diana Melly reached a point at which, so she recalls, she often felt like physically spitting into the bowl of soup being carried upstairs to their screaming guest. George Melly jokingly suggested that the two unhappy ladies might perhaps like to go in search of the local canal and drown themselves after supper. Plante, shocked by the violence of one of Rhys's rages, took an unkept vow never to visit her again.

What was going on? In part, the problem derived from the fact that Rhys felt both beholden and insecure. Kind though the Mellys had been, they were not her family and, however thoughtful their behaviour, she could imagine herself as their prisoner, shut away in her pretty pink suite. Rhys was also unsettled by the news that had reached her of a biography that Thomas Staley was determined to write. Confiding in his English friend John Byrne on 28 December 1977, Staley admitted that Rhys was reported to be unhappy and even alarmed, but added that he intended to go ahead with a critical work in which only a single chapter would be addressed to her personal life.[15] A chapter was still enough to cause dismay, however; having been distraught by Arthur Mizener's revelations in his biography of Ford, Rhys feared the very worst for herself at the hands of another American academic.

Equally terrifying to an old lady living in a house that was not her own was the prospect of being abandoned. Planning a winter weekend at her Welsh retreat during George's absence on a road trip, Diana Melly persuaded Sarah Papineau to return to act as Rhys's companion at Savernake Road. It was already well known that Jean liked Sarah. All, surely, would go well.

Returning from Wales three days later, Diana was greeted by an exhausted and ashen-faced Sarah. She described Jean as having passed completely beyond reason; entering Rhys's bedroom, Diana was met with such fury that its force seemed to hurl her back against the door. Melly remembers it having been on the following day that Maryvonne Moerman was informed by a wild, knife-wielding Rhys that she would slash George's treasured surrealist paintings to ribbons if her daughter dared to leave the house. According to Diana, the usually stoical Maryvonne passed out from sheer fright.[16]

The change in Rhys at this point was absolute and devastating. Her loving hosts had become the enemy. Everything they did was wrong. Nicknaming her "Johnny Rotten"—after the punk prince of bad behaviour—was George's way of trying to dispel a darkness in which no glimmer of light appeared. All their good times had been blotted out. Rhys ranted to everybody who dared to come near her that she was a helpless victim, deserted for weeks on end by a woman who—the unkindest cut of all—produced hideous clothes which her imprisoned guest was then *compelled* to buy. Even now, Diana was trying to prevent her from going home. Of course, as George wrote in his ruefully honest account of the debacle, the converse was true: "Di could hardly wait."[17]

Sonia, advising the Mellys from Paris, knew Jean Rhys well enough to take her new mood seriously. Writing to Diana, she warned her that "you must, must must protect yourself." Conscious that Diana herself had a fragile psyche and that she was heroically determined to escort Rhys down to Devon, Sonia warned her not to go unaccompanied: "You must not be alone with her at Cheriton Fitz."[18]

Diana did as she was told. A workman joined her for the long journey when, towards the end of February 1978, she escorted a glowering Rhys back home. Reports of heavy snow ahead almost forced their car to turn back; Jean's face conveyed her scepticism. Only the presence of large drifts beside the narrow lanes leading down into Cheriton finally convinced her that "bad weather" was not part of a cunning plan to drag her back to Savernake Road. Flowers sent by Jo Batterham and a warm welcome from her Landboat neighbours were received in silence. Not a word was forthcoming, not even when Diana and her companion thankfully took their leave.

It was difficult for Diana Melly to acknowledge such abject failure, when she herself had tried so hard. The persona she would self-mockingly name "Mrs Perfect" (and even crown with a cartoon halo in her 2005 memoir) had imagined that she possessed the ability to make Jean Rhys feel happy. Writing to Sonia in Paris, Diana sadly admitted that "I can't do that, I can't even make her feel all right."[19]

NORMALLY, A CHANGE of scene could lift Rhys's spirits, but not this time. Visiting Cheriton in May to record Rhys's latest minute revisions to her memoir, David Plante grew so disheartened that he took Joan Butler's advice and left after two days. When Jo Batterham tentatively reminded Rhys that she herself was still owed the cost both for an elegant chaise longue and its expensive upholstery, Rhys rebuked her for preying upon a helpless pauper. And yet, as Batterham sadly recalls, nobody could have been kinder after Gini Stevens's defection than Rhys, who took her out to lunch and—offering a pretty flower across the table—gently reassured her unhappy friend that life would brighten with the coming of spring.[20]

Dictating an essay, commissioned by *Harper's*, to a flattered Janet Bridger (Janet wrote it neatly out by hand on sheets of pink paper, all ready for the typist), Rhys could still rally her powerful gift for sardonic self-scrutiny, even in the last year of her life. "Making Bricks without Straw" offered a darkly comic self-portrait of the author in interview mode, wondering how much eyeshadow to apply and where to place the chaise longue in order to expose her face to the most flattering light. But, once again, the peevish voice of complaint pushed its way to the fore. Why must these well-meaning interviewers always assume that Rhys's own life had been as miserable as the wretched women whom she described? Why must they keep trying to pigeonhole her as a white Creole, or as a feminist?[*] And why must they regard every careless word she uttered—after the couple of stiff drinks required for the ordeal of being interrogated—as gospel truth?[21]

The essay was written for public consumption. Privately, Rhys recognised that she was fast losing the war between a frail body and her ferocious will. "Well, you are a fighter," remarked one of the nurses who now regularly came in to bathe her, when Rhys refused to make use of her cane to stump back into the bedroom. Maybe so, Rhys pondered in one of her last, painfully executed handwritten notes, but, "What exactly am I fighting for?"[22]

By the end of the summer, professional interviews had become too taxing for Rhys to undertake. Nevertheless, when Olwyn Hughes and Diana Athill mentioned a young book rep who was visiting Exeter and eager to meet her, Rhys managed a handwritten note to welcome Madeline Slade for a visit to the cottage in what would be the last autumn of her life. Feigning surprise when her guest arrived, Rhys was nevertheless beautifully dressed and—as it was mid-afternoon—eager to be poured a gin and vermouth. Dismayed by the cottage's exterior, Slade complimented her hostess on the transformation that had been worked within. ("She told me how hard she had tried to make it look nice.") Once Slade had put away a typed list of questions, Rhys relaxed, asking whether Madeline was a writer, too. ("She got very serious when I said I'd stopped. 'It doesn't do to stop,' she said. 'You need to keep practicing.'") But what remained with Slade most strongly was Rhys's response when a woman neighbour called in. ("They chatted about the woman's young daughter, and Jean was so interested; she wanted to know how the little girl was; everything about her. Just then, when she forgot I was there, I thought that she seemed really happy.")[23]

---

[*] Rhys steadfastly declined to be a poster girl for feminism. At Holloway, she had expressed her solidarity with the suffragettes who were imprisoned there. But when asked for her thoughts about the brave suffragette who had died after throwing herself in front of a galloping horse on Derby Day in 1913, Rhys, who adored horses, expressed her sympathy for the colt.

ONE OF THE free-standing sections of Rhys's memoir (dictated almost without hesitation to Michael Schwab during the post-Venice summer of 1977) had described "Meta," the abusive nurse whose harsh behaviour and suggestive name (so close to the Latin *mater*) seem to connect her to Rhys's mother. *Smile Please* makes no pretence of a happy relationship between the author and Minna Lockhart. But it was to Minna that Rhys touchingly dedicated the completed pages which reached Diana Athill in November 1978. "This is such a cold, grey country," Julia Martin had imagined her mother sadly saying of England, shortly before her death at Acton in *After Leaving Mr Mackenzie*. "This bouquet I hand to you, my silent mother, who died so unhappily in a cold country," was what Rhys wished her final and most personal work to say, perhaps as a token of apology for her own past lack of sympathy for Minna's loss of her husband, her home, her health and—even—of her difficult daughter. It's always startling to realise the number of years during which a literary perfectionist like Rhys could continue to meditate upon the best way to use a particular phrase, once it had taken root in her mind.

The memoir was already overdue for publication; given Rhys's age and increasing frailty, the risk of waiting for a revised second portion covering the author's life after her arrival in England was deemed too great. Athill decided that the book should be edited immediately and published within six months. Privately, Diana admitted to Anthony Shiel her disappointment at the meagre "Brownie snaps" Rhys had supplied as illustrations; writing to Jean, Athill combined enthusiasm with some practical observations. Two submitted episodes from Rhys's later years didn't sit comfortably, in Athill's view, with the remarkable evocation of her childhood in Dominica. The story of the completed Imperial Road—Rhys's last attempt to smuggle that deeply felt false memory into print—would also have to go. And so—but Athill did not tell Jean this, or offer any explanation—would the words she had specifically chosen as a dedication to her mother. Later, when Diana offered David

Plante the chance to become Rhys's posthumous dedicatee, he refused. David, in his own odd but passionate way, did love Jean Rhys. He knew what Jean herself had wanted.

Unaware of the fate of her carefully worded dedication, an always meticulous Rhys worried that Athill appeared to be less concerned with checking the text than with reshaping the book. (Loosely linked episodes were skilfully rearranged by Athill and assigned titles: "Geneva"; "The Doll"; "Carnival"; "Paris," and so forth.) On 12 December, an apprehensive Rhys wrote to ask Oliver Stonor what she could do about it all. Nothing, was the dispiriting answer. Esther Whitby, who had returned to work part-time at Deutsch, confirms that it was customary practice, when Athill was busy, for any proofreading tasks to be passed along to a colleague. In this case, although Athill was indeed distracted, since her mother was dying, *Smile Please* never left her own possessive hands.

The result of what seems to have been Athill's combination of necessary haste and an uncharacteristic inattentiveness amounted to a flurry of careless errors and misprints in the published text of Rhys's last work. Courteously pointed out to Athill by Oliver Stonor in 1979—his handwritten list survives in the McFarlin archive—they have never been corrected. In her preface to *Smile Please*, Diana poked fun at Rhys for (so Athill claimed) having objected to the absence of a mere "then" and a "quite" from the published text of *Wide Sargasso Sea*. Such a prodigiously careful reviser of her own work would assuredly have been dismayed to see "Brokenhurst (for Brockenhurst), "No Theatre" (for Noh Theatre) and a celebrated Italian play quaintly retitled *Paula and Francesca*, appearing alongside a playwright called Richard Brindsley Sheridan and a piece of sheet music titled "Flora Dora" (a misnaming of the charming Edwardian musical, *Florodora*, which Rhys had artfully slipped into her childhood memories as a foreshadowing of her life on stage). It's a shame. *Smile Please* seems to have been the work that Rhys herself valued more than any other she wrote, perhaps because it was so personal and achieved in such difficult circumstances.

AT THE END of 1978, and still concealing from friends and editors alike her actual age of eighty-eight, Rhys felt vigorous enough to plan a spring trip to London. In February 1979, a "crack-up," Rhys's habitually terse code for a breakdown, took her instead into a nursing home near Exeter. Her appetite had become bird-like. Always conscious of her weight—she had hated it when, during the 1960s, she briefly became a little plump—Rhys boasted to Oliver Stonor of having shrunk to a mere six stone. Addressing a new admirer, Elaine Campbell, she gallantly promised to write the foreword to a planned reissue of Phyllis Shand Allfrey's Caribbean novel, *The Orchid House*.

"Onward and upward," Rhys chirruped to Stonor from hospital. Sure enough, by 11 March, she was home again and feeling strong enough to ask Diana Melly to book her into Blake's (London's most luxurious boutique hotel was a firm favourite with Princess Margaret) for a month of final revisions. Evidently, she intended to regain control of her precious text.

The details have never been entirely clear about the fall which took Rhys into a West Country city hospital rather than to Blake's Hotel in the late spring of 1979. Diana Athill, no fan of Janet Bridger's, wondered whether an obstreperous Rhys might have been given a rough shove before Janet remorsefully settled the dazed old lady into a chair and hastened home. Janet herself claimed that an intoxicated Rhys had been alone when she fell. Urgently recalled to the cottage by one of Rhys's alarmed neighbours, Bridger had summoned the doctor, who diagnosed a fractured hip bone. Immediate attention was required. Rhys was rushed by ambulance to the main hospital in Exeter.[24]

Rhys's ancient body failed the trial of anaesthesia and surgical invasion. For six weeks, disabled and silent, she lay in the Creedy Ward of the Royal Devon and Exeter Hospital. Plans for the spring publication of *Smile Please* were resumed after Athill had paid a brief, unsatisfactory visit to Rhys's bedside. A few days later, George Melly, popping into the

hospital on his way to keep a jazz date in Exeter, had trouble in recognising the shrunken features of a patient identified on the information
card above her bed as: "Joan."

On 14 May, a sudden impulse caused Jo Batterham, who had taken
her son out for lunch from Bryanston School that day, to drive west on
a seventy-five-mile detour to Exeter. Having found her way to Creedy
Ward, Jo shared George Melly's difficulty in recognising the pale,
wigless little figure whom she found clawing at the bedclothes, open-
eyed and staring, but unable to speak. The doctor in charge, when
questioned, breezily opined that "Joan" might survive another month.
Appalled, Batterham left the hospital and drove down to the coast.
Walking beside the sea, so Jo says today, she "just willed" her ancient
friend to die. Back in the ward, she clasped one of Rhys's restless hands
and softly sang the Piaf song that seemed to fit the moment best: "*Non,
je ne regrette rien*." ("And do you think she did regret anything?" I ask.
"I doubt it," answered Jo.)[25]

Back in London that same evening, Jo heard the news that Rhys had
died and rang Diana Melly. Diana told her that she was looking out of
the window, watching a pink cloud sail away, high above the rooftops
of north London. "And there goes Jean," Diana said.[26]

The Stonors, who were holidaying in France in the spring of 1979,
learned from their young friends, Olive and Christopher Cox, that
Rhys's funeral in Exeter had been a muted affair. Maryvonne and her
daughter, Ellen, represented the family; friends included Francis Wyndham and the two Dianas (Athill and Melly). Peggy Ramsay sent lavish flowers; Al Alvarez, although absent, wrote an obituary in which
he reaffirmed his view of Rhys as one of the most important British
writers of the twentieth century, while praising Francis Wyndham
(appointed by Rhys as her literary executor) for his unstinting perseverance and enthusiasm. Selma Vaz Dias, two years dead, went unmentioned in the tributes.

Some years after Rhys's cremation, Diana Athill arranged for the
placing of the modest memorial—for which Maryvonne chose the
wording—which stands in the graveyard of St. Michael's at Cheriton

When the clearance of Rhys's cottage began, this pink mohair shawl, a gift from Sonia Orwell, was still hanging, neatly folded, on the back of her writing chair. *(Used with permission of Carmela Marner)*

Fitzpaine. At present, no stone or plaque commemorates Jean Rhys on the green Caribbean island where she was born and where—speaking to us through Antoinette Cosway in *Wide Sargasso Sea*—she hoped to die. "If you are buried under a flamboyant tree," I said, "your soul is lifted up when it flowers. Everyone wants that."[27]

Following the overnight demolition of her family's Roseau home in 2020, nothing physical survives to connect Rhys to Dominica, the island where she had—more directly than through Antoinette—told Phyllis Shand Allfrey that she wished her bones might be buried. "I Used to Live Here Once," the title of a story completed four years before her death, suggests that Jean Rhys already knew the truth. There would be no return. There was no need. The island that had cast its haunting spell over Rhys's imagination would live on, enduringly, within her work.

Afterlife

JEAN RHYS'S DREAD of publicity, combined with the mass of correspondence that she evidently destroyed, testifies to her fear of being
subjected to a biography. Nevertheless, Tom Staley's short critical
study of her novels, which appeared in the year of Rhys's death, contained nothing that would have distressed her. As indicated in his 1977
letter to John Byrne, Staley's book contained only a brief prefatory
chapter about the author herself, in which a bare outline of the skimpy
known facts of Jean Rhys's life was provided. Admirers curious to know
more about Rhys turned with interest to *Smile Please*, published in May
1979, the month of her death. Reviews of the memoir were perfunc-
tory; readers felt deprived by the absence of a narrative shape, and disappointed that so little space had been found for a famously reticent
author's experiences after leaving Dominica.

Initially governed by Jean Rhys's strong desire for privacy, Francis
Wyndham would eventually comply with Diana Athill's wish to permit
a young Canadian-born academic, Carole Angier, to deploy her skills
as a tenacious researcher to uncover the story of Rhys's life, combin-
ing her independent sleuthing with use of the growing archive now
held at Tulsa. Angier's generous-spirited and invaluably detailed book
was published in 1985, alongside a brief, perceptive study of the novels
which Angier contributed to the *Lives of Modern Women* series, edited
by Francis Wyndham's friend Emma Tennant.

First, however, came David Plante. Intimations of what was afoot emerged at a PEN event in January 1980, at which both Jo Batterham and David Plante took the stage before an audience of Rhys's admirers. Recalling the evening for me in the summer of 2018, Diana Athill was as dismissive of Batterham's romantic eulogy as of Plante's shrilly disloyal put-down of his old friend as "a silly, bigoted woman." Like Athill, Plante recalls the fury with which a protective Harold Pinter verbally attacked him from his seat beside Lady Antonia Fraser in the front row; Batterham, writing to Plante in March, did not hold back. Defending himself, Plante responded that he was only being honest: "Jean would have understood what a writer must do."[1]

I'm inclined to agree with Plante. The controversial portrait which he provided in *Difficult Women*, published in 1983, was no crueller about Rhys than about Plante himself. Today, his book reads as a carefully stylised presentation of partial or imaginative truths shot through with moments of wit, compassion and considerable insight. To Rhys's supporters, however, the act of betrayal was unforgivable. Rachel Ingalls was not the only former friend who never spoke to David Plante again.

Diana Melly and Francis Wyndham meanwhile embarked upon a selected edition of Rhys's letters which was published in 1984. Frustratingly truncated because of an absence of almost any correspondence from the first forty years of Rhys's life, it spans the years 1931 to 1966, ending on the verge of the publication of *Wide Sargasso Sea*. Equipped with sensitive linking passages and notes contributed by Wyndham, the edited *Letters* provided many readers with their first introduction to Rhys's wilful, witty and laceratingly self-aware personality. Reading the letters that she wrote to Wyndham himself—I only wish that we could also read his to her—it's easy to understand why Francis found Jean Rhys so irresistible.

Wyndham himself approved and admired *The Blue Hour* (2010), an intuitive and often illuminating short biography of Rhys which was written with passion and empathy by Lilian Pizzichini. Invited to single out the book which she believes best captures her grandmother in the context of her work, Ellen Moerman recommends *Genèses d'une folie créole: Jean Rhys et Jane Eyre* by Catherine Rovera (Hermann, 2015).

A meticulously researched examination of the sources of Rhys's best-known novel, Rovera's eloquent study also illuminates the author's creative processes.

For newcomers to Rhys who want to look beyond the novels, there exists no better introduction than *Smile Please*. Much of what you have read here is grounded in Rhys's own artfully circumspect account of her life, starting out when she first faced a camera on her sixth birthday, and ending as her work was about to be seen and judged by Ford Madox Ford. For a biographer, part of the fascination of *Smile Please* lies in the memoir's conspicuous absences: within its pages, there's no mention of Jean Lenglet's imprisonment; no name for the gentlemanly lover who got Rhys pregnant and broke her heart; no hint that her childhood beau, identified only as "a little boy called Willie," was the son of Roseau's leading doctor, Sir Henry Alford Nicholls (an admission which would implicitly have acknowledged the subordinate role of Rhys's own beloved father).

Against the absences, we can set a quiet store of revelations. *Smile Please* tells us just how young Rhys was when she first started to write for herself; she was still a child in Dominica when she began keeping "my secret poems exercise book" and wrote plays for home performance. Glancing at her subtle reference to "the Sensitive Plant" that grew wild—as it still does—on the hillside at Geneva, we might almost miss the hint of just who that sensitive plant might represent. There's even an alluring suggestion of just how closely the memoir and the story "Sleep It Off Lady" became entwined in the ageing Rhys's thoughts, when she remembers in the memoir that one of the chorus girls in *Our Miss Gibbs* addressed her as "Verney": Miss Verney is also the name of the unfortunate "Lady" of the story. "There were supposed to be rats in the dressing-room," Rhys comments a few lines later in the memoir, "but I never saw one." Miss Verney, in the story Rhys had plotted out alongside the gestating memoir, suffers from a fixation about an imaginary rat.

Is the intertextual echo simply a slip or one of the author's literary tricks? Is it an accident that Antoinette Cosway and young Rhys ride a horse that bears the same name: Preston? We can't be sure. It's seldom useful or enlightening to attempt to overanalyse Rhys's fiction. Neither does it help us to compare Rhys to the writers whom she admired and sometimes challenged. Influences abound in her work, but—like Emily Dickinson, in whose wittily broken lines and ghostly shafts of light Rhys may have found the clearest mirror for a mind that looked always into itself—Rhys demands, and deserves, to stand alone. Writing from pitiless self-knowledge, Jean Rhys addresses the watchful and lonely outsider who lurks within us all. And here, I believe, lies the answer to the enduring power of a novelist whose softly insistent, knowing and *sui generis* voice speaks with more power to our times even than to her own.

Acknowledgements

My thanks for help with Dominica-related material to: Pearle Christian, Peter Harrington, Lennox Honychurch, Sonia Magloire Akba, Gregor Nassief, Polly Pattulo, Marina Warner, and also to the *Observer* for commissioning a travel essay on Jean Rhys's Dominica, which enabled me to visit that unforgettable island before writing a book to which it has contributed so much.

My thanks for help about Rhys's relationship with Lancelot Hugh Smith to: Charles Abel Smith, Dorothy Abel Smith, Andrew Lycett, Elizabeth Macdonald Buchanan, Andrew Martin Smith, Julian Martin Smith, Faith Raven and Victoria Wakefield. Also to Zachary Leader and to Gilly King, both for enabling me to visit Mount Clare at Roehampton and for access to an unpublished memoir by Lady Hugh Smith; and to Jennifer Zulfigar for arranging access to Lancey's former Mayfair home (now part of the Royal Embassy of Saudi Arabia).

My thanks for help in researching Rhys's life and homes in the West Country to: Ellie Babbedge, Frieda Hughes, Alice May, Samantha Moss, David Thorn, Roy Stettiford, Frances Wood.

My thanks for help about Willis Feast's family (Rhys's hosts in Norfolk): to John Bolland.

My thanks to Tara and Nigel Fraser, Gerry Harrison; Judith Landry, Kika Markham and Susannah Stack for their especially generous help about Selma Vaz Dias, and to Hugh Fleetwood and to Kate Pocock, for leading me to Rhys's important friendship with Rachel Ingalls; to Selina Hastings, regarding Rhys's significant connection to Rosamund and John Lehmann; to Richard Schaubeck, regarding her friendship with Frank Hallman; and to Sophie Oliver, especially for sharing images of Rhys's one surviving dress from her first years in London.

My thanks for help with interviews, correspondence, hospitality and—above all—their time: Carole Angier; the late Diana Athill; Gaia Banks; Jo Batterham, Marcelle Bernstein; a mother-daughter contribution from Gwen Burnyeat and Ruth Padel; John Byrne; Helen Carr; Susannah Clapp, Gordon Crosse, Polly Devlin, Meriel (Dickson) Gardner; Anne Dunn; Peter Eyre; Ruth Fainlight; James Fox; Antonia Fraser; Valerie Grove; Glenda Jackson; Alan Judd; Julie Kavanagh; Alexis Lykiard; Diana Melly; Paul Mendez; Sarah Papineau; David Plante; Tristram Powell; Diana Quick; Catherine Rovera; Madeline Slade; Barbara Smith; Hilary Spurling; Tom Staley; David Tobin (Walden Books); Esther Whitby; Rachel Wyndham.

Thanks for translation help to Martine Orsmond (Dutch) and to Stephen Romer (French).

Thanks for access to manuscripts and books are due to the British Library; the London Library; Megan Barnard, Elizabeth Garver, Jim Kuhn and Rick Watson at the Harry Ransom Center in Austin, Texas; and Frank Bowles, Cambridge University Archive, for the papers of Sir Henry Hesketh Bell.

Particular thanks are due to Marc Carlson and his team for all their help at the McFarlin Library, Tulsa, to Sean Latham for arranging for me to give a talk at the library, and to Joli Jenson for arranging everything to make my stay in Tulsa so memorably agreeable.

I am particularly indebted to Helen Carr, Lennox Honychurch, Peter Hulme, Polly Pattulo and Catherine Rovera for undertaking to read parts (and in Peter's case, most kindly, all) of the work in progress and to make useful comments.

I'm grateful to Victoria Dickie for inviting me to a book club discussion of *Wide Sargasso Sea* which enabled me to air a few ideas at an early stage, and to rethink some important points.

More particular and considerable thanks are due to Francis Wyndham's literary executor, Alan Hollinghurst, for a meticulously observed, thoughtful and so generously expressed reading of an almost final version of the book.

My special thanks and love, always, to my dearest Ted: my wise first reader, editor and loving supporter on what has proved to be an unsurprisingly emotional voyage into the often dark corners of an extraordinary woman's mind.

As always, Anthony Goff and George Lucas have been magnificent—and inspiring—agents. My gratitude and unquantifiable thanks are also due to John Glusman and Helen Thomaides at Norton; to Arabella Pike, Kate Johnson and Jo Thompson at HarperCollins, and to Katy Archer, whose project editing has been a model of its kind. My heartfelt thanks to Emma Pidsley, at HarperCollins, and Ingsu Liu and Matt Dorfman, at Norton, for their gorgeous covers; Mark Wells for indexing; and Martin Brown for the map of Dominica. It's been wonderful to be buoyed up by such commitment and enthusiasm for a book that means so much to me.

I am especially grateful to Jean Rhys's granddaughter, Dr. Ellen Moerman, and to Catherine Rovera, separately, for their generous and discrete contributions.

Last, but far from least, my thanks to Anthony Griffiths for the good-humoured and patient tech support and expertise that I could always rely upon to rescue me from disaster.

All mistakes are, of course, my own.

Notes

The following abbreviations are used in the Notes:

AA—Al Alvarez
BL—British Library
DA—Diana Athill
DP—David Plante
EB—Eliot Bliss
EM—Ellen Moerman
ERW—Edward Rees Williams
ES—Evelyn Scott
FW—Francis Wyndham
GR—Germaine Richelot
JL—Jean Lenglet
JR—Jean Rhys
LHS—Lancelot Hugh Smith
LTS—Leslie Tilden Smith
McFarlin—McFarlin Library (Special Collections), University of Tulsa, Oklahoma
MH—Max Hamer
MM—Maryvonne Moerman
OH—Olwyn Hughes
OS—Oliver Stonor
PAS—Phyllis Antoinette Smyser
PK—Peggy Kirkaldy
SO—Sonia Orwell
SVD—Selma Vaz Dias

Foreword

1   Jean Rhys, *Smile Please: an Unfinished Autobiography*, "From a Diary: at the Rope-makers' Arms," André Deutsch, 1979, p. 163.

PART ONE: A WORLD APART

Chapter 1—Wellspring (1890–1907)

1   Jean Rhys, *Wide Sargasso Sea*, Part 2, Penguin, 1966, p. 85.
2   Lizabeth Paravisini-Gebert, *Phyllis Shand Allfrey: A Caribbean Life*, Rutgers University Press, 1996, p. 15. Willie's wildness was further confirmed when he was sentenced to six months' hard labour in an English prison in 1927, after stealing a fellow lodger's suit and defrauding three constables.
3   JR to FW in her poem, "Obeah Night," 14 April 1964, in Francis Wyndham and Diana Melly (eds.), *The Letters of Jean Rhys, 1931–1966*, André Deutsch, 1984, p. 265.
4   Jean Rhys, "The Sound of the River," *Tigers are Better-Looking*, André Deutsch, 1968.
5   Jean Rhys, *After Leaving Mr Mackenzie*, Jonathan Cape, 1931, Part 2, Chapter 12, "Childhood."
6   Catherine Rovera discusses Rhys's reworking of these events in her notebooks, in relation to *Good Morning, Midnight* and the first stirrings of *Wide Sargasso Sea* in: "Jean Rhys's Phantom MSS: 'December 4th 1938. Mr Howard's House. CREOLE'," in *Women: A Cultural Review*, 31:2, pp. 187–98, 18 August 2020; online, DOI:10.1080/0957042.2020.17/67836.
7   Rhys, *Wide Sargasso Sea*, Part 2, André Deutsch, 1966, p. 147.
8   Rhys, "Geneva," *Smile Please*, André Deutsch, 1979.
9   Rhys, *Wide Sargasso Sea*, Part 3, André Deutsch, 1966, p. 173.
10 House of Commons reports, 1 July 1844, p. 247.
11 Rhys, *Wide Sargasso Sea*, Part 2, André Deutsch, 1966, p. 155.
12 JR to DP, nd, McFarlin, Plante Papers, 007.15.f2.

Chapter 2—Floggings, School and Sex (1896–1906)

1   Jean Rhys, "My Day: 3 Pieces," in *Invitation to the Dance*, edited by Frank Hallman (New York, 1975).
2   JR to DP, nd, McFarlin, Plante Papers, 007.15.f1.
3   Rhys, "Meta," *Smile Please*.
4   JR, McFarlin 1.6.f11.
5   JR, McFarlin 1.3.f8.
6   JR, McFarlin 1.1.f6.
7   JR, McFarlin 1.1.f16.
8   JR, McFarlin 1.6.f11.

9   JR, McFarlin 1.1.f1.

10 Henry Hesketh Bell, *Glimpses of a Governor's Life from Diaries and Memoranda*, Sampson Low, 1946.

11 GBR/0115/Y3011C-N, Sir Henry Hesketh Bell Collection, Royal Commonwealth Library, Cambridge University Archive.

12 Rhys, "The Zouaves," *Smile Please*.

13 JR to EM, 11 January 1960, Wyndham and Melly (eds.), *Letters*.

14 Jean Rhys, "Mixing Cocktails," *Jean Rhys: The Collected Short Stories*, Penguin, 1987, p. 36.

15 Rhys, "Goodbye Marcus, Goodbye Rose," *Collected Short Stories*, p. 278.

16 Rhys, "Goodbye Marcus, Goodbye Rose," *Collected Short Stories*, p. 277.

17 See Chapter 1, n. 6.

18 JR, "Triple Sec," unpublished manuscript, McFarlin 1.5.11-12.

19 JR, Black Exercise Book, McFarlin 1.3.f5 and 1.3.f11.

20 Rhys, "Leaving Dominica," *Smile Please*.

21 Rhys, "First Steps," *Smile Please*.

PART TWO: ENGLAND: A COLD COUNTRY

Chapter 3—Stage-struck (1907–13)

1   Rhys, *Wide Sargasso Sea*, Part 2, Penguin, p. 65.

2   Rhys, *Wide Sargasso Sea*, Part 2, Penguin, p. 70.

3   Rhys, "From a Diary: at the Ropemakers' Arms," published as an appendix to *Smile Please*.

4   Rhys, "First Steps," *Smile Please*.

5   Rhys, "Overture and Beginners," *Collected Short Stories*, p. 307.

6   Rhys, "First Steps," *Smile Please*.

7   Peter Eyre interviews with author, July 2018.

8   Rhys, "Chorus Girls," *Smile Please*.

9   JR to MM, 19 November 1959.

10 JR to FW, 26 October 1961, McFarlin 2.15.f1.

11 Rhys, "Chorus Girls," *Smile Please*.

Chapter 4—Fact and Fiction: A London Life (1911–13)

1   Extract from unpublished memoirs of Constance, Lady Hugh Smith (1900), Roehampton University Archive, pp. 88–91.

2   Rhys, "The Interval," *Smile Please*.

3   Rhys, "The Interval," *Smile Please*.

4   Jean Rhys, *Voyage in the Dark*, Constable, 1934, Part 1, p. 7.

5   Rhys, "First Steps," "Christmas Day," *Smile Please*.

6   Rhys, "First Steps," "Christmas Day," *Smile Please*.

7   JR to PK, May 1950, Wyndham and Melly (eds.), *Letters*.

8 JR to MM, November 1965, Wyndham and Melly (eds.), *Letters*.

9 Carole Angier, *Jean Rhys, Life and Work*, André Deutsch, 1990, p. 87.

10 JR, McFarlin 1.1.5.f9.

11 Rhys, "World's End and a Beginning," *Smile Please*.

12 Stella Bowen, *Drawn from Life, Reminiscences*, Collins, 1941, p. 37.

13 Nina Hamnett, *Laughing Torso*, Constable, 1932, p. 36.

Chapter 5—London in Wartime (1913–19)

1 Adrian Allinson, "A Painter's Pilgrimage," unpublished memoir in typescript, McFarlin.

2 Bowen, *Drawn from Life*, p. 36.

3 Hamnett, *Laughing Torso*, p. 86.

4 Janie Lomas, "War Widows in British Society 1914–1940," unpublished PhD thesis, appendix A, Table 1, Stafford University.

5 Rhys, "Leaving England," *Smile Please*.

6 Rhys, "Leaving England," *Smile Please*.

PART THREE: A EUROPEAN LIFE
Chapter 6—A Paris Marriage (1919–25)

1 In what seems to have been forgetful old age, Rhys annotated this group of photographs as: "Austria."

2 JR, Green Exercise Book, McFarlin 1.1.2; Jean Rhys, *Good Morning, Midnight*, Constable, 1939, p. 100.

3 Fonds Louis Gustave Richelot (1858–1956), Repertoire numerique detaille, d/AB/XIX/4224-AB/XIX/4227, Archives Nationale de France, 1015.

4 JR, unpublished poem, "Prayer to the Sun," McFarlin 1.2.f10.

5 JR, McFarlin 011.1.f10, from the scattered pages of a typescript titled "And Paris Sinister," later incorporated into Jean Rhys, *The Left Bank: Sketches and Studies of Present-Day Bohemian Paris*, Jonathan Cape, 1927.

6 JR, "Prayer to the Sun," McFarlin 1.2.f10.

7 JR, McFarlin, Plante Papers, 007.15.f5.

8 Jean Rhys, *After Leaving Mr Mackenzie*, Part 2, Chapter 5, "Acton."

9 Rhys, "Vienne," *Collected Short Stories*, p. 110.

10 Rhys, "Vienne," *Collected Short Stories*, p. 118.

11 Rhys, "Paris Again," *Smile Please*.

Chapter 7—"L'affaire Ford" (1924–26)

1 JR, McFarlin 1.5.f9.

2 Paul Nash to Anthony Bertram, 2 March 1925, quoted in Max Saunders, *Ford Madox Ford: A Dual Life: the After World*, Vol. II, OUP, 1996, p. 282.

3   Saunders, *Ford Madox Ford*, p. 284.

4   JR to FW, 16 July 1967, McFarlin 2.14.f1.

5   All details concerning Rhys's departure from Paris and stay in Cros de Cagnes come from the unpublished memoir of Margaret Odeh Nash, and from Paul Nash's subsequent letter to Anthony Bertram, 2 March 1925. Nash papers, quoted in Saunders, *Ford Madox Ford*, p. 282.

6   Rhys, "La Grosse Fifi," *Collected Short Stories*, p. 78.

7   Saunders, *Ford Madox Ford*, pp. 284, 603.

8   Bowen, *Drawn from Life*, p. 167.

9   JR, "L'affaire Ford," McFarlin, Plante Papers, 1981–007 f5.

10 JR, "The Forlorn Hope" (unpublished) was drafted in two versions and related to David Plante in 1977, McFarlin 1.1.f17.

11 JR, "L'affaire Ford," McFarlin, Plante Papers, 1991–007 f5.

12 JR, first page of Black Exercise Book, McFarlin 1.1.f3, later incorporated into the story "Tigers are Better-Looking."

13 JR to JL, nd, McFarlin 2.15.f4.

14 Here, I have followed Max Saunders, since his is the most convincing explanation of a complicated sequence of events, *Ford Madox Ford*, pp. 295–7.

15 Bowen, *Drawn from Life*, pp. 166–7.

Chapter 8—Hunger, and Hope (1926–28)

1   Patrick Hamilton to his brother Bruce Hamilton, May 1927, quoted in Sean French, *Patrick Hamilton: A Life*, Faber, 1993, p. 86.

2   Valentine Williams to GR, 19 January 1927, McFarlin 2.9.f6.

3   Saunders, *Ford Madox Ford*, p. 608.

4   Saunders, *Ford Madox Ford*, p. 608.

5   Pearl Adam to JR, 13 December 1926, McFarlin 2.1.f1.

6   Rhys, *After Leaving Mr Mackenzie*, Part 2, Chapter 5. "Acton," Chapter 9, "Golders Green."

7   LHS to JR, 5 May 1927, McFarlin 2.5.f11. The folded paper is apparent from the fact that the upper part of the words "dear kitten" is missing.

8   LHS to JR, 27 May 1927, McFarlin 2.5.f11.

9   Rhys, *After Leaving Mr Mackenzie*, Part 2, Chapter 6, "Mr James."

10 GR to JR, 18 November 1929, McFarlin 2.9.f11.

11 JR, nd, Green Exercise Book, McFarlin 1.1.f3.

12 BL, Rhys Archive, ad. ms 57859.

13 GR to JR, September 1927, McFarlin 2.9.f6.

14 Jean Rhys, *Quartet*, Chapter 1; GR to JR, September 1927, McFarlin 2.9.f6.

15 Rhys, *Quartet*, Chapter 23.

16 Rhys, *Quartet*, Chapters 18, 21.

17 Rhys, *Quartet*, Chapter 18.

18   GR to JR, 15 November 1928, McFarlin 2.9.f6.

19   Rhys, *Quartet*, Chapter 12.

20   *Manchester Guardian*, 26 October 1928.

21   Rhys, *Quartet*, Chapter 12.

22   JL to JR, 21 February 1929, BL, Rhys Archive, ad. ms 8819.

23   A report from "the inner sanctum of Simon & Schuster, US, by 'M.L.S.'," in the
     substantial collection of documents copied from the McFarlin Library originals,
     BL, Rhys Papers, ad. ms 8819.

PART FOUR: THE RHYS WOMAN

Chapter 9—Two Tunes: Past and Present (1929–36)

1   Rhys, *After Leaving Mr Mackenzie*, Part 1, Chapter 3, "Mr Horsfield."

2   Rhys, *After Leaving Mr Mackenzie*, Part 3, Chapter 3, "Last."

3   Rhys, *After Leaving Mr Mackenzie*, Part 1, Chapter 1, "The Hotel on the Quay."

4   Rhys, *After Leaving Mr Mackenzie*, Part 1, Chapter 1, "The Hotel on the Quay."

5   Rhys, *After Leaving Mr Mackenzie*, Part 1, Chapter 2, "Mr Mackenzie."

6   Rhys, *After Leaving Mr Mackenzie*, Part 2, Chapter 3, "Uncle Griffiths."

7   Rhys, *After Leaving Mr Mackenzie*, Part 2, Chapter 6, "Mr James."

8   Rhys, *After Leaving Mr Mackenzie*, Part 2, Chapter 6, "Mr James."

9   Rhys, *After Leaving Mr Mackenzie*, Part 3, Chapter 1, "Île de la Cité."

10   *Observer*, 8 February 1931; *Daily Telegraph*, 30 January 1931; *Saturday Review of
     Literature*, US, 25 July 1931.

11   *The Times* and *Times Literary Supplement*, 5 March 1931.

12   Rebecca West, *Daily Telegraph*, 30 January 1931.

13   PAS to DA, 27 January 1967, McFarlin 2.4.f7.

14   JR, Black Exercise Book, McFarlin 1.1.1, pp. 12, 98–9.

15   André Breton, *Nadja*, Librairie Gallimard, 1928, p. 142. Rhys's fellow admirer was
     the francophile musician, George Melly.

16   JR to PK, 4 May 1931, Wyndham and Melly (eds.), *Letters*.

17   ES to JR, 9 June 1931, Wyndham and Melly (eds.), *Letters*.

18   MM to PAS, 30 April 1968, McFarlin 10.2.f1.

19   JR to FW, 19 June 1964, Wyndham and Melly (eds.), *Letters*.

20   Rhys, *Voyage in the Dark*, Part 1, ch. 1.

21   Rhys, *Voyage in the Dark*, Part 1, ch. 6.

22   Rhys, *Voyage in the Dark*, Part 1, ch. 7.

23   Rhys, *Voyage in the Dark*, Part 4, ch. 1.

24   Charlotte Brontë, writing her Introduction to Emily's *Wuthering Heights* as "Cur-
     rer Bell."

25   JR to ES, 1933, nd, Wyndham and Melly (eds.), *Letters*.

26   JR to ES, 1933, nd, Wyndham and Melly (eds.), *Letters*.

27   JR to AA, 7 September 1974, BL, Alvarez Papers, ad. mss. 88595.

28 JR to AA, 7 September 1974, BL, Alvarez Papers, ad. mss. 88595.

29 PAS to FW, 5 June 1982, McFarlin 10.3.f1.

30 LTS to JR, nd, private collection.

31 Rhys, manuscript of *Voyage in the Dark*, McFarlin 1.5.13.

32 Rhys, *Voyage in the Dark*, Part 4, Chapter 1.

33 Angier, *Jean Rhys*, p. 293, quoting from a personal interview with Dorothy Rees Williams.

34 Transcript of Paul Bailey BBC radio interview, 15 April 1981, McFarlin 1.2.f11.

35 MM to DA, nd, McFarlin 2.2.f10.

36 JR to ES on her drinking habits, 18 February 1934, Wyndham and Melly (eds.), *Letters*.

37 Angier, *Jean Rhys*, p. 338, quoting from her interview with Rosamond Lehmann, 1986, p. 701.

38 JR to ES, 16 February 1936, McFarlin 2.9.f11.

Chapter 10—A la recherche, or Temps Perdi (1936)

1   JR to ES, December 1935, Wyndham and Melly (eds.), *Letters*.

2   JR to ES, nd, Wyndham and Melly (eds.), *Letters*.

3   LTS to PAS, 19 March 1936, McFarlin 2.10.f1.

4   The term "white zombi" appears in "Pioneers, Oh, Pioneers," a story about Mr. Ramage which Rhys worked on for many years and which was published in her final collection "Sleep It Off Lady." *Collected Short Stories*, pp. 264–73.

5   Rhys, "Geneva," *Smile Please*.

6   Phyllis Shand Allfrey, *The Orchid House*, Rutgers University Press, 1996. Introduction by Lizabeth Paravisini-Gebert, p. xxiv.

7   Rhys, "Geneva," *Smile Please*.

8   JR to ES, nd., "Hampstead," Wyndham and Melly (eds.), *Letters*.

9   Elma Napier to Alec Waugh, 30 January 1949, Waugh Papers, Boston University 20th Century Archive.

10 LR to PAS, 29 February and 18 March 1936, McFarlin 2.10.f1.

11 Rhys, "*Temps Perdi*," *Collected Short Stories*, p. 262.

12 Rhys, "*Temps Perdi*," *Collected Short Stories*, p. 263.

13 Jean Rhys, "The Imperial Road," version 4, *Jean Rhys Review*, 11, 2, Spring 2000.

14 LTS, map, McFarlin 2.10.f1.

15 LTS to PAS, 19 March 1936, McFarlin 2.10.f1.

16 JR to ES, 10 August 1936, Wyndham and Melly (eds.), *Letters*.

17 JR to ES, 1936, nd, Wyndham and Melly (eds.), *Letters*.

18 ES to Emma Goldman, 25 May 1937, quoted in Wyndham and Melly (eds.), *Letters*, p. 34.

Chapter 11—Good Morning, Midnight (1936–39)

1   JR, Green Exercise Book, McFarlin 1.1.2.

2   JR to DA, 29 May 1966, McFarlin 2.3.f5.

3   JR to ES, 10 August 1936, Wyndham and Melly (eds.), *Letters*.

4   JR to ES, 10 August 1936, Wyndham and Melly (eds.), *Letters*.

5   JR, "The Martyr," Orange Exercise Book, McFarlin 1.1.f4.

6   JR to PK, 9 March 1949, Wyndham and Melly (eds.), *Letters*.

7   Paravisini-Gebert, *Phyllis Shand Allfrey: A Caribbean Life*, p. 48.

8   JR, Orange Exercise Book, McFarlin 1.1.f4.

9   Angier, *Jean Rhys*, pp. 361–2.

10 Rhys, *Good Morning, Midnight*, p. 128.

11 Rhys, *Good Morning, Midnight*, Penguin, 2019, p. 3.

12 Rhys, *Good Morning, Midnight*, Penguin, p. 4.

13 Rhys, *Good Morning, Midnight*, Penguin, p. 4.

14 Rhys, *Good Morning, Midnight*, Penguin, p. 17.

15 Rhys, *Good Morning, Midnight*, Penguin, p. 11.

16 Rhys, *Good Morning, Midnight*, Penguin, p. 40.

17 Judith Thurman, "The Mistress and the Mask: Jean Rhys's Fiction," *Ms*, 4, No. 7, January 1976, pp. 51–2.

18 Judy Froshaug, "The Book-Makers," *Nova*, September 1967, p. 45.

19 Rhys, *Good Morning, Midnight*, Penguin, p. 6.

20 Rhys, *Good Morning, Midnight*, Penguin, p. 6.

21 Rhys, *Good Morning, Midnight*, Penguin, p. 15. Stephen Romer points out that Rhys has altered the original line in a poem by Desnos, reading: "Belle, comme une fleur de verre, Belle, comme une fleur de chair" (flesh) to read: "Beautiful, she's beautiful as a flower in glass, Beautiful as a flower in earth."

22 Jean Rhys used these words to describe the tone employed by George Moore in *Esther Waters* in a letter to OS, 5 March 1953, Wyndham and Melly (eds.), *Letters*.

23 Rhys, *Good Morning, Midnight*, Penguin, p. 190.

24 Rhys, *Good Morning, Midnight*, Penguin, p. 27.

25 Rhys, *Good Morning, Midnight*, Penguin, p. 130.

26 Rhys, *Good Morning, Midnight*, Penguin, p. 169.

27 Simon Segal to JR, nd, Wyndham and Melly (eds.), *Letters*, pp. 138–9. With thanks to Stephen Romer for this translation.

28 Rhys, *Good Morning, Midnight*, Penguin, p. 43. With thanks to Stephen Romer for this translation.

29 JR to SVD, 4 November 1956, Wyndham and Melly (eds.), *Letters*.

30 Rhys, *Good Morning, Midnight*, Penguin, pp. 7, 25.

31 JR to FW, 14 May 1964, Wyndham and Melly (eds.), *Letters*.

32 Violet Hammersley to JR, McFarlin 2.5.f8.

33 JR, "Creole," McFarlin 1.3.f5.

34 Rhys, *Good Morning, Midnight*, Penguin, pp. 145–6.

35 JR to PK, [October] 1945, Wyndham and Melly (eds.), *Letters*.

36 Author interviews with Carole Angier (12 September 2019) and David Plante (28 November 2019), to whom Rhys would eventually give her single-sheet plan for "Wedding in the Carib Quarter." I'm also indebted to Catherine Rovera for drawing my attention to her fine essay, "Jean Rhys's Phantom Manuscript: 4 December 1938. Mr Howard's House. CREOLE," *Women: a Cultural Review*, 18 August 2020, 31:2, pp. 187–99.

PART FIVE: DARKNESS AT NOON

1 Peggy Kirkaldy, "Portrait of a Lost Friend," McFarlin 2.7.f1.

Chapter 12—At War with the World (1940–45)

1 Rhys, "A Solid House," *Collected Short Stories*, p. 212.

2 JL to JR, 17.1.1940, McFarlin; Edouard de Néve, "Jean Rhys, romancière inconnu," *Les Nouvelles Litteraires*, August 1939.

3 Rhys, "Temps Perdi," *Collected Short Stories*, p. 249.

4 Rhys, BL, Rhys Archives, ad. mss. 57858.

5 *Norwich Mercury and People's Weekly Journal*, 1 August 1940.

6 Rhys, "From a Diary: at the Ropemakers' Arms," *Smile Please*.

7 Angier, *Jean Rhys*, pp. 442, 707, based upon letters to Carole Angier from Willis Feast's daughter and Eric Griffiths.

8 Angier, *Jean Rhys*, pp. 442, 707; John Bolland to author, 28 June 2021.

9 Angier, *Jean Rhys*, pp. 442, 707; John Bolland to author, 28 June 2021.

10 Rhys, "A Solid House," *Collected Short Stories*, p. 218.

11 Angier, *Jean Rhys* (p. 219) identifies Louis Rose but provides no confirmation that he treated Rhys; John Bolland to author, 28 June 2021, provided further details on Rose.

12 JR, "Cowslips," McFarlin 1.1.f13.

13 Rhys, "The Insect World," *Collected Short Stories*, p. 343.

14 Rhys, "Outside the Machine," *Collected Short Stories*, p. 196.

15 Rhys, "I Spy A Stranger," *Collected Short Stories*, p. 144.

16 Dr. Ellen Moerman kindly supplied or confirmed the information about her mother given in this paragraph.

17 Rhys, "The Sound of the River," *Collected Short Stories*, p. 230.

18 JR to PAS, 10 October 1945, Wyndham and Melly (eds.), *Letters*.

19 Rhys, "The Sound of the River," *Collected Short Stories*, p. 228.

20 JR to PK, [October] 1945, Wyndham and Melly (eds.), *Letters*.

21 Angier, *Jean Rhys*, p. 431, from interviews with DRW.

Chapter 13—Beckenham Blues (1946–50)

1   JR, Orange Exercise Book, McFarlin 1.1.4.
2   JR to PK, 11 February 1946 and 3 July 1946, Wyndham and Melly (eds.), *Letters*.
3   Information about Job kindly supplied by Dr. Ellen Moerman.
4   JR to PK, 21 April 1950, Wyndham and Melly (eds.), *Letters*.
5   JR to PK, 1950, Wyndham and Melly (eds.), *Letters*.
6   *Bromley & West Kent Mercury*, 1 April 1948.
7   JR to MM, 11 January 1949, Wyndham and Melly (eds.), *Letters*.
8   JR to PK, nd, 1950, Wyndham and Melly (eds.), *Letters*.
9   Dr. Ellen Moerman in conversation with author and Gaia Banks (Sheil Land Agency), December 2019.
10 JR to PK, 9 March and [October] 1949, Wyndham and Melly (eds.), *Letters*.
11 JR to PK, nd, 1950, Wyndham and Melly (eds.), *Letters*.
12 *Beckenham Journal*, 27 May 1949.
13 JR to PK, nd., 1950, Wyndham and Melly (eds.), *Letters*, "Let Them Call It Jazz," *Collected Short Stories*, p. 161.
14 JR to PK, 4 October 1949, Wyndham and Melly (eds.), *Letters*.
15 JR to MM, 10 July 1949, Wyndham and Melly (eds.), *Letters*.
16 JR to MM, 24 October 1949, Wyndham and Melly (eds.), *Letters*.
17 Tara Fraser (granddaughter of SVD) to author, 13 July 2018.

Chapter 14—The Lady Vanishes (1950–56)

1   JR to OS, 5 March 1953, Wyndham and Melly (eds.), *Letters*.
2   JR to PK, 10 March 1950, Wyndham and Melly (eds.), *Letters*.
3   JR to PK, 21 April 1950, Wyndham and Melly (eds.), *Letters*.
4   JR to PK, 21 April 1950, Wyndham and Melly (eds.), *Letters*.
5   JR to PK, May 1950, Wyndham and Melly (eds.), *Letters*.
6   JR to PK, 21 April 1950, Wyndham and Melly (eds.), *Letters*.
7   JR to DP, McFarlin 14.2.f1.
8   Rhys, "Ropemakers' Arms," *Smile Please*.
9   Rhys, "Ropemakers' Arms," *Smile Please*.
10 Rhys, "Ropemakers' Arms," *Smile Please*.
11 JR to MM, 22 June and 31 August 1952, Wyndham and Melly (eds.), *Letters*.
12 MH to OS ("Morchard Bishop"), 29 December 1952, Wyndham and Melly (eds.), *Letters*.
13 JR to OS, 27 January 1953, Wyndham and Melly (eds.), *Letters*.
14 JR to OS, 5 March 1953, Wyndham and Melly (eds.), *Letters*.
15 JR to OS, 7 April 1953, Wyndham and Melly (eds.), *Letters*.
16 JR to SVD, 27 March 1953, Wyndham and Melly (eds.), *Letters*.
17 JR to SVD, 8 June 1953, Wyndham and Melly (eds.), *Letters*.

18   JR to MM, 8 June 1953, Wyndham and Melly (eds.), *Letters*.
19   JR to MM, 29 August and 16 September 1953, Wyndham and Melly (eds.), *Letters*.
20   JR to MM, 31 January and 4 April 1954, Wyndham and Melly (eds.), *Letters*.
21   JR to MM, 5 July and 16 October 1956, Wyndham and Melly (eds.), *Letters*.
22   JR to MM, 22 October 1956, Wyndham and Melly (eds.), *Letters*.
23   SVD to JR, 19 October 1956, Wyndham and Melly (eds.), *Letters*.
24   JR to SVD, 12 November 1956, Wyndham and Melly (eds.), *Letters*.
25   JR to SVD, 18 March 1957, Wyndham and Melly (eds.), *Letters*.

PART SIX: THE PHOENIX RISES

1   JR, Green Exercise Book, McFarlin 1.1.2.

Chapter 15—A House by the Sea (1957–60)

1   JR to MM, 14 January 1958, quoting from her own unpublished fragment of a
     children's story for Maryvonne—and then her granddaughter—about "Mitsou
     San," Wyndham and Melly (eds.), *Letters*.
2   PK to JR, no date but evidently 1957, McFarlin 2.7.f1. The cache of letters from
     Rhys to Peggy Kirkaldy published in Wyndham and Melly (eds.), *Letters* was
     found in a doctor's surgery in Colchester and provided to Rhys's letter-editors
     in the 1980s.
3   JR to SVD, 6 November 1957, Wyndham and Melly (eds.), *Letters*.
4   Anne Dunn to author, 30 May 2020.
5   JR to FW, 29 March 1958, Wyndham and Melly (eds.), *Letters*.
6   Francis Wyndham's funeral tribute (copy provided by Alan Hollinghurst to author).
7   Margaret (Peggy) Ramsay to SVD, 2 October 1958 (private collection).
8   I'm again indebted here to Dr. Ellen Moerman for details about the Moermans'
     difficult life in the Netherlands.
9   JR to SVD, 21 December 1957.
10   JR to MM, 4 May 1959; 28 December 1960, Wyndham and Melly (eds.), *Letters*.
11   JR to MM, 4 June 1959, Wyndham and Melly (eds.), *Letters*.
12   JR to MM, 19 November 1959, Wyndham and Melly (eds.), *Letters*.
13   JR to MM, April 1958, Wyndham and Melly (eds.), *Letters*.
14   JR to SVD, 9 April 1958, Wyndham and Melly (eds.), *Letters*.
15   JR to SVD, 10 January 1959, Wyndham and Melly (eds.), *Letters*.
16   JR to SVD, 27 May 1959, Wyndham and Melly (eds.), *Letters*.
17   JR to SVD, 14 June 1959, Wyndham and Melly (eds.), *Letters*.
18   Alec Hamer to JR, 31 January 1959, McFarlin 2.2.f8.
19   JR to FW, 14 September 1959, Wyndham and Melly (eds.), *Letters*. Wyndham had
     taken the reference to Rhys's Scottish blood—she had distant Scottish forebears
     on her Lockhart side—from Selma's 1957 article for the *Radio Times*.

20 JR to EB, 2 February 1960, McFarlin 2.1.f4.

21 JR to SVD, 24 February 1960; to FW, 12 April 1960; to MM, 22 June 1960, Wyndham and Melly (eds.), *Letters*.

22 JR to MM, 6 October 1960, Wyndham and Melly (eds.), *Letters*.

23 JR to FW, 31 May 1960, Wyndham and Melly (eds.), *Letters*.

24 JR to FW, 14 July 1960, Wyndham and Melly (eds.), *Letters*.

Chapter 16—Cheriton Fitzpaine

1 Robert Herrick, "Discontents in Devon," in *The Poetical Works of Robert Herrick*, edited by F. W. Moorman, Clarendon Press, Oxford, 1915, p. 19.

2 Author interview with Roy Stettiford, 26 April 2019.

3 JR to SVD, 17 September and 27 November 1963, Wyndham and Melly (eds.), *Letters*.

4 JR to DA, 3 August 1963, McFarlin 2.3.f3.

5 Author visit to Cheriton Fitzpaine, 20 June 2019.

6 JR to DA, 3 August 1963, McFarlin 2.3.f3.

7 JR to FW, 23 July 1967, McFarlin 2.14.f1.

8 JR to MM, 15 and 17 July 1961, Wyndham and Melly (eds.), *Letters*.

9 Frances Wood to author, 27 March 2020. Wood learned about William Trevor's friendship with Rhys when talking to him during a Booker shortlist photoshoot at Hatchards in 2002.

10 Author interview with Samantha Moss, 7 July 2021.

11 JR to MM, 6 October 1960, Wyndham and Melly (eds.), *Letters*.

12 JR to FW, 6 June 1961, Wyndham and Melly (eds.), *Letters*.

13 JR to FW, 23 May 1961, Wyndham and Melly (eds.), *Letters*.

14 JR to SVD, 25 September 1963 and to FW, 16 October 1963, Wyndham and Melly (eds.), *Letters*.

15 JR to SVD, 17 September 1963, Wyndham and Melly (eds.), *Letters*.

16 JR to SVD, 30 September 1963.

17 DA to author, 24 September 2018.

18 JR to EB, 2 October 1964, McFarlin 2.1.f4.

19 Robert Herrick, "Discontents in Devon," *Hesperides* (1647).

Chapter 17—The Madness of Perfection (1960–63)

1 JR to SVD, September 1963, Wyndham and Melly (eds.), *Letters*.

2 JR to FW, 6 October 1960, Wyndham and Melly (eds.), *Letters*.

3 JR to DA, 28 April 1964, Wyndham and Melly (eds.), *Letters*.

4 JR to SVD, 9 January 1961, Wyndham and Melly (eds.), *Letters*.

5 JR to FW, 11 October 1961, Wyndham and Melly (eds.), *Letters*.

6 JR to FW, 11 October 1961, Wyndham and Melly (eds.), *Letters*.

7 JR to FW, 17 October 1961, Wyndham and Melly (eds.), *Letters*.

8   Author interview with Tara Fraser, 8 July 2021.

9   JR to SVD, 9 January 1961, Wyndham and Melly (eds.), *Letters*.

10   Charlotte Brontë, *Jane Eyre, an Autobiography*, Smith, Elder & Co., 1847, Chapter 26.

11   Rhys, *Wide Sargasso Sea*, Part 2, Penguin, p. 40.

12   Rhys, *Wide Sargasso Sea*, Part 3, Penguin, p. 123.

13   JR to FW, 12 September 1962, Wyndham and Melly (eds.), *Letters*.

14   MH to JR, April–May 1963, Angier, *Jean Rhys*, p. 498.

15   JR to EB, 18 April 1963, McFarlin 2.1.f4.

16   JR to DA, 5 June 1963, Wyndham and Melly (eds.), *Letters*.

17   FW to DA, 4 May 1963, McFarlin 2.4.f10.

18   Francis Wyndham, Introduction to Wyndham and Melly (eds.), *Letters*, p. 12.

19   JR to DA, 7 July 1963, Wyndham and Melly (eds.), *Letters*.

20   EW to author, 20 May 2020; Esther Menell, *Loose Connections*, West Hill, 2014, pp. 144–5.

21   EW to author, 20 May 2020.

22   JR to SVD, 6 September 1963, Wyndham and Melly (eds.), *Letters*.

23   JR to FW, 11 October 1963, Wyndham and Melly (eds.), *Letters*.

24   Anne Dunn to author, 30 May 2020.

25   SVD to JR, 21 and 26 November 1963, McFarlin 2.12.f1; JR to SVD, 27 November 1963, Wyndham and Melly (eds.), *Letters*.

26   JR to SVD, March 1964, Wyndham and Melly (eds.), *Letters*.

27   Francis Wyndham, Introduction to *Wide Sargasso Sea*, first published in *Art and Literature*, March 1964.

28   JR to FW, 25 March 1964, Wyndham and Melly (eds.), *Letters*.

29   "Obeah Night," in JR to FW, 14 April 1964, Wyndham and Melly (eds.), *Letters*.

30   JR to FW, 14 April 1964, Wyndham and Melly (eds.), *Letters*.

31   JR to FW, 14 April 1964, Wyndham and Melly (eds.), *Letters*.

32   JR to FW, 15 July 1964, Wyndham and Melly (eds.), *Letters*.

33   ERW to DA, 28 July 1964, Wyndham and Melly (eds.), *Letters*.

Chapter 18—An End and a Beginning (1964–66)

1   DA to Alec Hamer, 3 March 1966, McFarlin 2.2.f8.

2   JR to OH, recalling Selma's 1965 hospital visit, 25 February 1966, Wyndham and Melly (eds.), *Letters*.

3   DA interview with author, 20 July 2018. Tara Fraser to author, 20 September 2021.

4   DA told me this well-honed story in June 2018, but also DA to ERW, 8 January 1965, and ERW to DA 14 January 1964, McFarlin 2.4.f10.

5   JR to OH, 25 February 1966, Wyndham and Melly (eds.), *Letters*.

6   JR to MM, 4 August 1965, Wyndham and Melly (eds.), *Letters*.

7   JR to MM, 9 November 1965, and (nd) November 1965, Wyndham and Melly (eds.), *Letters*.

8   Rhys, *Wide Sargasso Sea*, Part 2, Penguin, p. 70.
9   Anne Dunn telephone interview with author, 30 May 2020.
10   Rhys, *Wide Sargasso Sea*, Part 2, Penguin, p. 149.
11   JR to SVD, 3 March 1966, Wyndham and Melly (eds.), *Letters*.
12   JR to DA, 9 March 1966, Wyndham and Melly (eds.), *Letters*.
13   DA to JR, 28 March 1966; DA to author, 23 July 2018.

PART SEVEN: UNWELCOME FAME

Chapter 19—No Orchids for Miss Rhys (1966–69)

1   JR to FW, 21 July 1960, McFarlin 2.3.f5.
2   Alec Hamer to DA, March 1966, McFarlin 2.2.5.
3   JR to MM, 18 March 1966, Angier, p. 571.
4   JR to SO, 17 November 1966, McFarlin 2.7.f8.
5   DA to SO, 2 October 1966; SO to DA, 13 October 1966, McFarlin 2.5.f9.
6   JS to Margaret (Peggy) Ramsay, 30 July 1966, BL, Ramsay Archive, ad. mss. 88915
       1/182/7.
7   JR to SVD, 16 September 1966, McFarlin 2.12.f2.
8   MM to DA, 15 October 1966, McFarlin 2.5.f10.
9   SVD to DA, 1 November 1966, McFarlin 2.4.f9.
10   JR to EB, nd, 1966, McFarlin 2.1.f1.
11   Rhys, *Wide Sargasso Sea*, Part 1, Penguin, p. 16.
12   Rhys, *Wide Sargasso Sea*, Part 2, Penguin, p. 106.
13   Rhys, *Wide Sargasso Sea*, Part 2, Penguin, p. 55.
14   Hunter Davies to author, 21 June 2020. Davies's interview appeared in the *Sunday
       Times*, 6 November 1966.
15   SO to FW, 11 April 1967, BL, FW archive (not yet catalogued).
16   JR to DA, 1 and 2 December 1966, McFarlin 2.3.f8.
17   JR to SO, 7 January 1967, McFarlin 2.3.f9.
18   DA to Margaret (Peggy) Ramsay, 2 February 1967, BL, Ramsay Archive, ad. mss.
       88915 1/182/7.
19   Selma Vaz Dias, 5 February 1967, BL, Ramsay Archive, ad. mss. 88915 15/1/206.
20   MR to Bryan Forbes, 3 February 1967; BF to MR, 6 February 1967, BL, Ramsay
       Archive, ad. mss. 88915 1/182/7.
21   DA to JR, nd, July 1967, McFarlin 2.3.f10.
22   JR to SO, mid-July, nd, 1967, McFarlin 2.7.f8.
23   JR to FW, 23 July 1967, McFarlin 2.1.f4.
24   JR to DA, 7 October 1967, McFarlin 2.3.f10.
25   JR to SO, 20 October 1967, McFarlin 2.7.f8.
26   JR to FW, 13 December 1967, McFarlin 2.14.f2.
27   FW to SVD, 19 December 1967, McFarlin 2.12.f8.
28   SVD to MM, 6 December 1967; MM to SVD, 8 December 1967, McFarlin 2.12.f8.

29 EM to author, 15 December 2020.

30 SVD to JR, 6 February 1968, McFarlin 2.12.f3.

31 JR to SVD, 6 February and 3 April 1968, McFarlin 2.12.f3; SVD to MR, 10 June 1969, BL, Ramsay Archive, ad. mss. 88915 15/1/206.

32 MM to PAS, 30 April 1968, McFarlin 10.2.f1.

Chapter 20—Rhys in Retreat (1967–74)

1   JR to OS, 3 August 1968, McFarlin 10.2.f5.

2   JR to FW, 2 December 1968, McFarlin 2.14.f2; JR to MR, 9 August 1969, BL 88915/1/182.

3   Marcelle Bernstein: "The Inscrutable Jean Rhys," *Observer Magazine*, 1 June 1969, and to author, 13 July 2020, and 18 March 2021.

4   EM to author, 12 December 2020.

5   Herbert Ronson, "Meeting Jean," *London Magazine*, July 1988, pp. 75–8.

6   JR to Rachel Ingalls, 20 June 1971, private collection.

7   JR to OS, 3 August 1968, McFarlin 10.2.f5.

8   SVD to MR, 10 June, BL, Ramsay Archive, 88915, 15.1.206.

9   JR to MR, 18 October 1969, McFarlin 2.4.f5.

10 MR to JR, 11 September 1969, BL, Ramsay Archive, 88915/1/182; JR to FW, 22 October 1969, McFarlin 2.14.f5.

11 Marcelle Bernstein, "The Inscrutable Jean Rhys," *Observer Magazine*, 1 June 1969.

12 Marcelle Bernstein to author, 20 June 2020.

13 Barbara Ker-Seymer to JR, 15 January 1969, McFarlin 2.6.f10. A correspondence of fifteen letters between Rhys and Ker-Seymer (1969–70) is in the Tate Archives at Millbank.

14 JR to Antonia Fraser, 26 October 1969, McFarlin 2.5.f7.

15 Antonia Fraser to author, 12 May 2018; 5 September 2018.

16 JR to Rachel Ingalls, 25 July 1971, private collection.

17 JR to SO, 21 May 1970, McFarlin 2.8.f4.

18 Jan van Houts, "The Hole in the Curtain," in Pierrette M. Frickey, *Critical Perspectives on Jean Rhys*, Three Continents, 1990.

19 JR to MM, 26 November 1970, Angier, p. 603.

20 This was how Dorothy Rees Williams described the funeral scene to Carole Angier, *Jean Rhys*, pp. 602–3.

21 David Plante, in an unpublished article about Rachel Ingalls, 2019, and to author, 20 June 2020; Ingalls, *Times* obituary, March 2019.

22 JR to Rachel Ingalls, 25 July and 24 August 1970.

23 Author interview with DA, 23 May 2018.

24 All quotations are from Rhys's privately owned letters to Rachel Ingalls, July 1970 to August 1974.

25 Lidija Haas, "The Hallucinatory Realism of Rachel Ingalls," *New Yorker*, 4 March 2019.

26   Author interview with DP, 9 July 2020.

27   V. S. Naipaul, "Without a Dog's Chance," *New York Review of Books*, 18 May 1972, pp. 29–31.

28   "L'affaire Ford" was drafted out in JR's Green Exercise Book, McFarlin 1.1.1.

29   DP to author, 9 July 2020.

30   FW to JR, 30 June 1972, McFarlin 2.14.f10.

31   JR to FW, 20 October 1972, McFarlin 2.14.f10.

Chapter 21 — "Mrs Methuselah" (1973–76)

1   Virginia Stevens, *Radio Times*, 21 November 1974.

2   FW to JR, 17 August 1974, McFarlin 2.15.f1.

3   JR to Jo Batterham, 27 October 1973, private collection.

4   I'm indebted for these details to Glenda Jackson, Alexis Lykiard, Peter Eyre, Diana Melly and Edna O'Brien, in conversations and correspondence during September 2020.

5   FW to JR, 26 February 1974, McFarlin 2.15.f1.

6   Julie Kavanagh to author, 22 and 26 July 2020.

7   Mary Cantwell, "I'm a Person Without a Mask," *Mademoiselle*, October 1974.

8   James Fox to author, 18 January 2019.

9   Tristam Powell to author, 14 January 2019.

10   MR to SVD, 10 December 1974, BL, Ramsay Archive, ad. mss. 88915 15/1/206.

11   Paravisini-Gebert, *Phyllis Shand Allfrey*, p. 243.

12   FW to JR, 25 July 1975, McFarlin 2.15.f2.

13   Paravisini-Gebert, *Phyllis Shand Allfrey*, p. 245.

14   JR to FW, 9 October 1975, McFarlin 2.15.f2.

15   JR, "Shades of Pink," McFarlin, Plante Papers 14.f4.

16   DP to author, 20 April 2020.

17   JR to FW, 15 February 1976, McFarlin 2.15.f2.

18   SO to DA, 2 March 1976, McFarlin 2.2.f12.

19   JR to SO, nd, McFarlin 2.9.f4.

20   *Kirkus Reviews*, review of *Sleep It Off Lady*, 1 November 1976.

21   DP and DA to author 18 and 20 July 2018.

PART EIGHT: AND YET I FEAR

1   Rhys, "And Yet I Fear," BL, Rhys Archives, ad. mss. 57858.

Chapter 22 — "The Old Punk Upstairs" (1977–79)

1   DA to FW, 1 January 1980, Wyndham Papers, BL (uncatalogued).

2   JB to SO, 10 March 1977; the rest of the details are from Diana Melly to author, January 2019–January 2020.

3   JR to DA, 29 March 1977, McFarlin 2.3.f8.

4   Louis James, "The Lady is Not a Photograph," *Journal of Caribbean Literatures*, 3 (2003), pp. 175–84.

5   SO to JB, 16 August 1977; JR to JB, 7 September 1977 (private collection).

6   Jo Batterham paraphrased the advertisement to SO, 3 October 1977 (private collection); DA to SO, 1 November 1977, McFarlin 2.2.f13.

7   JR to JB, 27 October 1977 (private collection). JB to author, 1 August 2020.

8   George Melly, "The Old Punk Upstairs," *Independent on Sunday*, 28 October 1990.

9   Sarah Papineau to author, 9 July 2020, with comments and excerpts from her diary for 1977–8 (private collection).

10 From the private collection of Sarah Papineau.

11 DA to SO, 1977, McFarlin 2.2.f9.

12 SO to DM, 22 December 1977, McFarlin 2.7.f1.

13 DM to SO, 6 January 1978, and to author, 15 January 2020.

14 Plante, *Difficult Women: A Memoir of Three*, Gollancz, 1983, pp. 17, 46, 51.

15 Thomas Staley to John Byrne, 28 December 1977 (private collection).

16 DM to author, 15 January 2020.

17 Melly, "The Old Punk Upstairs."

18 SO to DM, February 1978, McFarlin 2.7.f1.

19 Diana Melly, *Take a Girl Like Me: Life with George*, Chatto, 2005, p. 125.

20 JB to author, 18 July 2020.

21 Rhys's "Making Bricks without Straw" was first published in *Harpers*, July 1978. Reprinted in *Vogue* in 1979, it is included in Frickey (ed.), *Critical Perspectives of Jean Rhys*.

22 JR, June 1978, nd, McFarlin 1.3.f7.

23 Madeline Slade interview with author, 8 December 2021.

24 DA to author, 17 June 2018 and also DA to SO, nd, McFarlin 2.2.f9.

25 JB to author, 12 September 2018.

26 JB to author, 12 September 2018.

27 Rhys, *Wide Sargasso Sea*, Part 3, Penguin.

Afterlife

1   DA to author, 20 June 2018; DP to JB, 21 March 1980 (private collection).

Sources and Bibliography

The main collection of Jean Rhys's papers—it includes photographs, official documents, correspondence, poems, four exercise books, manuscript and typed drafts and personal papers—is held in twenty-three boxes at the McFarlin Library (Special Collections) at Tulsa, where Tom Staley, during the 1970s, initiated the library's role as a special collection for women writers. The library also holds the archives of André Deutsch, and the section of David Plante's papers which relates to Jean Rhys in particular.

The British Library also possesses numerous manuscript notes and drafts, together with a substantial collection of copy documents from McFarlin. The Alvarez Papers—including a large number of the reviews of Rhys's work and interviews with her—are also held at the British Library.

WORKS BY JEAN RHYS

The Left Bank: Sketches and Studies of Present-Day Bohemian Paris, Jonathan Cape, 1927; US: Harpers, 1927

Perversity (with the translator's name given as Ford Madox Ford), translated by Jean Rhys from the novel by Francis Carco, US only, Pascal Covici, 1928

Postures, Chatto & Windus, 1928; US: *Quartet*, Simon & Schuster, 1929

"The Christmas Presents of Mynheer van Rooz," *Time and Tide*, 12, November 1931, pp. 1360–1

After Leaving Mr Mackenzie, Jonathan Cape, 1931; US: Knopf, 1931

Barred, translated by Jean Rhys from Jean Lenglet's work as Edouard de Néve, Desmond Harmsworth, 1932

Voyage in the Dark, Constable, 1934; US: William Morrow, 1935

Good Morning, Midnight, Constable, 1939; US: Harpers, 1970

Wide Sargasso Sea, André Deutsch, 1966; US: Norton, 1967

Tigers are Better-Looking, with a Selection from "The Left Bank," André Deutsch, 1968; US: Harpers, 1974

My Day, US: Frank Hallman, 1975

Sleep It Off Lady, André Deutsch, 1976; US: Harpers, 1976

Smile Please: An Unfinished Autobiography, André Deutsch, 1979; US: Harpers, 1980

Jean Rhys: The Collected Short Stories, Penguin, 1987; US: Norton, 1987. Several of Rhys's stories, including "I Spy a Stranger," had not been included in the earlier collections, but were first published during her lifetime in magazines (notably the *London Magazine*, the *New Yorker* and *Art and Literature*) and, less frequently, newspapers.

A SELECTION OF BOOKS AND ARTICLES RELEVANT TO JEAN RHYS

Angier, Carole, *Jean Rhys, Lives of Modern Women*, Penguin, 1985
——. *Jean Rhys, Life and Work*, André Deutsch, 1990
Athill, Diana, *Stet*, Granta, 2000
Atwood, Thomas, *The History of the Island of Dominica*, Joseph Johnson, 1791
Bell, Henry Hesketh, *Obeah, Witchcraft in the West Indies*, Sampson Low, 1889
——. *Glimpses of a Governor's Life*, Sampson Low, 1946
Benstock, Shari, *Women of the Left Bank, 1900–1940*, University of Texas, 1986
Bernabé, Jean, Patrick Chamoiseau and Raphael Confiant, *Eloge de la Creolité*, Gallimard, 1993
Bhaba, Homi K., *The Location of Culture*, Routledge, 1994
Bliss, Eliot, *Luminous Isle*, Cobden-Sanderson, 1934
Bowen, Stella, *Drawn from Life: Reminiscences*, Collins, 1941
Brathwaite, Edward Kamau, *The Development of Creole Society in Jamaica 1770–1820*, Clarendon Press, Oxford, 1971
——. *Contradictory Omens: Cultural Diversity and Integration in the Caribbean*, Mona, Savacou Publications, 1974
Callard, D. A., *Pretty Good for a Woman: The Enigmas of Evelyn Scott*, Norton, 1986
Carr, Helen, *Jean Rhys*, Northcote, 1996
Chambers, Colin (ed.), *Peggy to her Playwrights: The Letters of Margaret Ramsay, Play Agent*, Oberon Books, 2018
Clyde, David, *Two Centuries of Health Care in Dominica*, Pre Printing Press, India, 1981
Curtin, Philip D., *The Rise and Fall of the Plantation Complex: Essays in Atlantic History*, Cambridge University Press, 1992
Devlin, Polly, *Writing Home*, Pimpernel Press, 2019
Elkin, Lauren, *Flaneuse: Women Walk the Streets in London, Paris, New York, Tokyo and Venice*, Chatto & Windus, 2016
Emery, Mary Lou, *Jean Rhys at "World's End": Novels of Colonial and Sexual Exile*, University of Texas, 1990
Frickey, Pierrette M. (ed.), *Critical Perspectives on Jean Rhys*, Three Continents, 1990
Froude, J. M., *The English in the West Indies; or, The Bow of Ulysses*, Cambridge University Press, 1888
Le Gallez, Paula, *The Rhys Woman*, Macmillan, 1990
Gates, Henry Louis, *Writing and Difference*, University of Chicago Press, 1986
Gikandi, Simon, *Writing in Limbo: Modernism and Caribbean Literature*, Cornell University Press, 1992
Gilbert, Sandra M., and Susan Gubar, *The Madwoman in the Attic: The Woman Writer and the Nineteenth-Century Imagination*, Yale University Press, 1980

Glissant, Edouard, *Le Discours Antillais*, Seuil, 1981

Gregg, Veronica Marie, *Jean Rhys's Historical Imagination: Reading and Writing the Creole*, University of North Carolina Press, 1995

Grieve, Symington, *Notes Upon the Island of Dominica*, AC & Black, 1906

Hardwick, Elizabeth, *Seduction and Betrayal* (1974), Faber, 2019

Hearn, Lafcadio, *Two Years in the French West Indies*, Harpers, 1890

Hughes, Richard, *A High Wind in Jamaica*, Penguin, 1947

Hulme, Peter, "The Locked Heart: The Creole Family Romance of *Wide Sargasso Sea*," in F. Barker, P. Hulme and M. Iverson (eds.), *Colonial Discourse/Postcolonial Theory*, Manchester University Press, 1994, pp. 72–88

Hulme, Peter and Neil L. Whitbread (eds.), *Wild Majesty: Encounters with Caribs from Columbus to the Present Day*, Clarendon Press, 1992

James, Louis, *Jean Rhys*, Longman, 1978

Jordis, Christine, *Jean Rhys*, La Manufacture, 1990

———. *Jean Rhys, La Prisonnière*, Stock, 1996

Judd, Alan, *Ford Madox Ford*, Collins, 1990

King, Bruce, *West Indian Literature*, Macmillan, 1979

Kloepfer, Deborah Kelly, *The Unspeakable Mother: Forbidden Discourse in Jean Rhys and H.D.*, Cornell University Press, 1989

Leigh Fermor, Patrick, *The Traveller's Tree*, John Murray, 1950

Lisser, Herbert G. de, *The White Witch of Rosehall* (1958), Macmillan Caribbean, 2007

Ludwig, Ralph (ed.), *Ecrire la "parole de nuit": La nouvelle literature antillaise*, Gallimard, 1994

Lykiard, Alexis, *Jean Rhys Revisited*, Stride, 2000

———. *Jean Rhys: Afterwords*, Shoestring Press, 2006

Maurel, Sylvie, *Jean Rhys: The West Indian Novels*, New York University Press, 1986

———. *Jean Rhys (Women Writers)*, Palgrave Macmillan, 1999

Maximin, Colette, *La Parole aux masques: Litterature, oralité et culture Populaire dans la Caraibe anglophone au XXe siècle*, Editions caribéennes, 1991

Melly, Diana, *Take a Girl Like Me: Life with George*, Chatto, 2005

Menell (Whitby), Esther, *Loose Connections: from Narva Mantee to Great Russell Street*, West Hill Books, 2014

Michie, Elsie B. (ed.), *Charlotte Brontë's* Jane Eyre: *A Casebook*, Oxford University Press, 2006

Moers, Ellen, *Literary Women*, The Women's Press, 1978

Oates, Joyce Carol, "Romance and Anti-Romance: *Jane Eyre* to Rhys's *Wide Sargasso Sea*," *Virginia Quarterly Review*, No. 61 (1), Winter 1985, pp. 44–58

Oliver, Sophie, "Fashion in Jean Rhys/Jean Rhys in Fashion," *Modernist Cultures*, November 2016; curator of a 2016 Exhibition at the British Library on Making the Reputation of Jean Rhys http://blogs.bl.uk/english-and-drama/2016/10/rhys-cycled-.html

Paravisini-Gebert, Lizabeth, *Phyllis Shand Allfrey: A Caribbean Life*, Rutgers University Press, 1996

Pizzichini, Lillian, *The Blue Hour: A Portrait of Jean Rhys*, Bloomsbury, 2010

Plante, David, *Difficult Women: A Memoir of Three*, Gollancz, 1983

Pope-Hennessy, James, *West Indian Summer: A Retrospect*, Batsford, 1943

————. *The Baths of Absalom: A Footnote to Froude*, Allen Wingate, 1954

Raiskin, Judith L., *Snow on the Cane Fields: Women's Writing and Creole Subjectivity*, University of Minnesota Press, 1996

————. *Wide Sargasso Sea, a Critical Edition*, Norton, 1999

Rovera, Catherine, *Genèses d'une folie créole: Jean Rhys et Jane Eyre*, Paris, Editions Hermann, 2015

————. "(Out)Rage against the Machine: "Parasexuality" and Subversion in Jean Rhys's *Voyage in the Dark*," Etudes Brittanniques Contemporaines, September 2013

Saunders, Max, *Ford Madox Ford, A Dual Portrait*, Oxford University Press, 1996

Savory, Elaine, *Jean Rhys*, Cambridge University Press, 1999

Scott, M. A. *The Perse School for Girls: The First Hundred Years, 1881–1981*, Cambridge, 1981

Scura, Dorothy McInnis and Jones, P. C., *Evelyn Scott: Recovering a Lost Modernist*, University of Tennessee Press, 2001

Shand Allfrey, Phyllis, *The Orchid House*, Constable, 1953

————. *It Falls Into Place: the Stories of Phyllis Shand Allfrey*, Papillotte, 2004

————. *Love for an Island: The Collected Poems of Phyllis Shand Allfrey*, Papillote, 2014

Spurling, Hilary, *The Girl from the Fiction Department: A Portrait of Sonia Orwell*, Penguin, 2002

Staley, Thomas F., *Jean Rhys: A Critical Study*, Macmillan, 1979

Thomas, Sue, *The Worlding of Jean Rhys*, Westport Connecticut, 1999

Vreeland, Elizabeth, "Jean Rhys: The Art of Fiction LXIV," *Paris Review*, 76, Autumn 1979, pp. 218–37

Warner, Marina, *Fantastic Metamorphoses, Other Worlds: Ways of Telling the Self*, Clarendon Press, Oxford, 2002

————. *Signs and Wonders: Essays on Literature and Culture*, Chatto, 2003

Waugh, Alec, *The Sugar Islands*, Cassell, 1958

Wilson, Mary and Kerry L. Johnson, *Rhys Matters: New Critical Perspectives*, New Caribbean Studies, 2013

Wyndham, Francis and Diana Melly (eds.), *The Letters of Jean Rhys, 1931–1966*, André Deutsch, 1984

Credits

Many of the letters quoted from in this book are in private collections, as indicated within the notes. Dr Ellen Moerman, Rhys's granddaughter, also retains a collection pertaining to her grandmother, including books which Rhys still owned at her death. A full list of extracts used with permission of Dr Moerman is below:

Extracts from *Good Morning Midnight* reprinted by permission of Dr Ellen Moerman © 1939 (Jean Rhys)

Extracts from *Smile Please: An Unfinished Autobiography* reprinted by permission of Dr Ellen Moerman © 1979 (Jean Rhys)

Extracts from *Collected Short Stories* reprinted by permission of Dr Ellen Moerman © 1987 (Jean Rhys)

Extracts from *Jean Rhys: Collected Letters* reprinted by permission of Dr Ellen Moerman © 1995 (Jean Rhys)

Extract from "Mixing Cocktails," "Vienne," "La Grosse Fifi" and "In the Rue de l'Arrivée" reprinted by permission of Dr Ellen Moerman © 1927 (Jean Rhys)

Extracts from "A Solid House," "Outside the Machine" and "The Sound of the River" reprinted by permission of Dr Ellen Moerman © 1968 (Jean Rhys)

Extracts from "Temps Perdi" and "I Spy a Stranger" reprinted by permission of Dr Ellen Moerman © 1969 (Jean Rhys)

Extracts from "Goodbye Marcus, Goodbye Rose," "The Insect World" and "Overture and Beginners" reprinted by permission of Dr Ellen Moerman © 1976 (Jean Rhys)

I am particularly indebted to the published selection made by Diana Melly and Francis Wyndham (eds), in *The Letters of Jean Rhys, 1931–1966* (André Deutsch, 1984).

Index